Belize

DISCOVERY CHANNEL

APA PUBLICATIONS
Part of the Langenscheidt Publishing Group

![INSIGHT GUIDE Belize]

Editorial

Project Editor
Huw Hennessy
Editorial Director
Brian Bell

Distribution

United States
Langenscheidt Publishers, Inc.
36–36 33rd Street 4th Floor
Long Island City, NY 11106
Fax: 1 (718) 784 0640

UK & Ireland
GeoCenter International Ltd
Meridian House, Churchill Way
West Basingstoke, Hants RG21 6YR
Fax: (44) 1256 817988

Australia
Universal Publishers
1 Waterloo Road
Macquarie Park, NSW 2113
Fax: (61) 2 9888 9074

New Zealand
Hema Maps New Zealand Ltd (HNZ)
Unit D, 24 Ra ORA Drive
East Tamaki, Auckland
Fax: (64) 9 273 6479

Worldwide
Apa Publications GmbH & Co.
Verlag KG (Singapore branch)
38 Joo Koon Road, Singapore 628990
Tel: (65) 6865 1600. Fax: (65) 6861 6438

Printing

Insight Print Services (Pte) Ltd
38 Joo Koon Road, Singapore 628990
Tel: (65) 6865 1600. Fax: (65) 6861 6438

©2006 Apa Publications GmbH & Co.
Verlag KG (Singapore branch)
All Rights Reserved

First Edition 1995
Second Edition 2004
Reprinted 2006

CONTACTING THE EDITORS
We would appreciate it if readers
would alert us to errors or out-
dated information by writing to:
Insight Guides, P.O. Box 7910,
London SE1 1WE, England.
Fax: (44) 20 7403 0290.
insight@apaguide.co.uk

www.insightguides.com
In North America:
www.insighttravelguides.com

ABOUT THIS BOOK

The first Insight Guide pioneered the use of creative full-color photography in travel guides in 1970. Since then, we have expanded our range to cater for our readers' need not only for reliable information about their chosen destination but also for a real understanding of the culture and workings of that destination.

Now, when the internet can supply inexhaustible (but not always reliable) facts, our books marry text and pictures to provide those much more elusive qualities: knowledge and discernment. To achieve this, they rely heavily on the authority and experience of locally based writers and photographers. This major new edition of *Insight Guide: Belize* is carefully structured to convey an understanding of the country and its culture as well as to guide readers through its sights and activities:

♦ The **Features** section, indicated by a yellow bar at the top of each page, covers Belize's history and culture in a series of essays.

♦ The main **Places** section, indicated by a blue bar, is a complete guide to all the sights and areas worth visiting. Places that will be of special interest are coordinated by number with the maps.

♦ The **Travel Tips** section, with an orange bar, provides data on travel, hotels, shops, restaurants and more. Its index is conveniently located on the back flap.

also a major contributor to the last edition, revised several of this edition's features on the Belizean people, culture and wildlife, as well as updating most of the Places section of the book. She says that she loves Belize, with all its cultural and natural diversity, and wants visitors to love it too – which aptly sums up most Belizeans' positive attitude to their country.

The Dangriga, Placencia and Far South chapters were updated by Huw Hennessy. Several of the history features were revised and updated by **Nick Caistor**, a specialist in Latin American affairs. The *Fishing* feature was revised by **Dr Mike Ladle**, a UK-based fly-fishing enthusiast, drawing attention to the burgeoning status of Belize's fishing grounds among the world's fly-fishermen. The *Birdwatcher's Paradise* feature was updated by **Ellen McRae**, a marine biologist based on Caye Caulker, who also wrote the new picture feature on *Marine National Parks*.

Neil Rogers, an expert Mayanist and hotelier, wrote the picture features on *Unravelling Maya Mysteries* and *Ecotourism in Belize*. The picture feature on *Toledo's Maya Villages* was written by contributing photographer **Lesley Player**. The entire book is kept up-to-date by **Peter Eltringham**.

The *Travel Tips* section of the book was thoroughly overhauled by Karla Heusner and Huw Hennessy, reflecting Belize's growing tourism industry and the country's popularity as one of the world's leading ecotourism destinations.

Thanks also go to **Sylvia Suddes** for proofreading the book and to **Isobel McLean** for indexing it.

The contributors

This redesigned new edition of *Insight Guide: Belize* was supervised by managing editor **Huw Hennessy** at Insight Guides' editorial office in London, building on the contributions of the previous edition's writers, who included **Tony Perrottet**, **Tony Rath**, **Dr Colville Young**, **Carolyn M. Miller**, **Errol Laborde**, **Joshua Starr** and **Lynn Meisch**.

The book has been completely updated with the invaluable help of a number of expert writers. The chief contributor was **Karla Heusner**, a freelance journalist and former teacher who calls herself 50 percent Belizean (with a Belizean father and an American mother), and who is working on the new Museum of Belize, which exhibits some of the country's archeological treasures for the first time. Heusner, who was

Map Legend

— ·· —	International Boundary
– – – –	District Boundary
– · –	National Park/Reserve
– – – –	Ferry Route
✈ ✈	Airport: International/Regional
🚌	Bus Station
❶	Tourist Information
✉	Post Office
† ✝	Church/Ruins
†	Monastery
☾	Mosque
✡	Synagogue
🏰	Castle/Ruins
∴	Archeological Site
∩	Cave
𝟏	Statue/Monument
★	Place of Interest

The main places of interest in the Places section are coordinated by number with a full-color map (e.g. ❶), and a symbol at the top of every right-hand page tells you where to find the map.

INSIGHT GUIDE
Belize

Contents

Maps

Palm leaves
hanging up
to dry

Insight on ...

Information panels

Travel Tips

◆ **Full Travel Tips index
is on page 305**

Places

CAYE ATTRACTIONS

Squeezed in between its larger Central American neighbors, tiny Belize is bursting with cultural and natural wonders

"If the world had any ends", wrote Aldous Huxley in *Beyond the Mexique Bay* (1934), Belize "would certainly be one of them. It is not on the way from anywhere to anywhere else. It has no strategic value. It is all but uninhabited." Huxley's off-hand observation remains the most famous made by a foreign writer about Belize, if only because he was one of the few to ever visit what was at the time the most irrelevant corner of the British Empire.

Indeed, Belize's sheer obscurity had been the country's defining trait for centuries: first settled by English and Scottish pirates in the 17th century, it soon became a secret haven for loggers and their African slaves who operated under the noses of the Spaniards. By the 19th century, British Honduras (the name Belize was only taken upon independence in 1981) had become the ultimate backwater, an English-speaking, largely black Creole outpost in Central America.

In an irony that Huxley might have appreciated, Belize's centuries of under-development have guaranteed the country's greatest resource: nature. Today, Belize is squarely on the map as one of the world's leading "ecotourism" destinations. Contained within its borders are vaste swathes of untouched rainforest, endless savannah and mangrove coasts, all containing the greatest variety of animal habitats north of the Amazon basin. Offshore, Belize's coral reef is the most splendid in the Western hemisphere, second in size and grandeur only to Australia's Great Barrier Reef, with around 200 small islands or cayes (pronounced *keys*) dotted around it. Add to that the 900-plus ancient Maya ruins scattered around the country and you begin to see why Belize has enjoyed a sudden popularity.

Even so, Belize's most beguiling attraction remains its Old World eccentricity. It's a place where villages are named Double Head Cabbage, Go-To-Hell Camp, Pulltrouser Swamp and Bound To Shine. With a population of just over 250,000, Belize remains as relaxed and intimate as a small country town; yet, while everyone seems to know everyone else, it is one of the most cosmopolitan places on earth – a mixture of black Creoles, Spanish-speaking Mestizos, Maya, East Indians, Syrians, Mennonites, Chinese and North Americans, all getting along in a far more amicable fashion than most of its Central American neighbors.   ❏

PRECEDING PAGES: Lazee Man Caye, off Placencia; wreck on Half Moon Caye; shoal of jackfish on the reef; dawn over the Maya Mountains.
LEFT: heading for the cayes off Placencia.

Decisive Dates

THE ANCIENT MAYA

c. **2000 BC** Earliest remains of fixed Maya settlements found in Mexico.

600 BC First major evidence of the Maya in Belize.

500 BC First monumental Maya buildings at sites like Tikal and Dzibilchaltún; style influenced by the Olmec culture of the north.

300 BC Izapa-type pottery and hieroglyphs first appear. Beginning of the Classic Period when the most important ceremonial centers were built.

AD 100 Cities of El Mirador and Cerros founded.

700 Maya civilization at its peak, spreading through southern Mexico, Guatemala, parts of Honduras, and El Salvador and Belize.

900 Decline of the Maya: cultural achievements are reduced to the levels of the Formative Period before AD 250. Other influences begin to be felt.

1000 New civilizations compete for dominance in Central America (still including some Maya).

1250 Mayapan is an important trading center and the center of influence in the Yucatán Peninsula. Trading thought to have taken place between the Maya in Belize and the Yucatán.

1440 Maya in decline again, concentrated only in small pockets of influence.

THE SPANISH CONQUEST

1512 Two Spaniards arrive in the Yucatán following shipwreck. First European contact with the Maya world.

1519 Spanish conquest of Mexico begins. First Mass held in Mexico.

1520 Smallpox, hookworm and malaria brought from Europe by conquerors begins to spread through remaining Maya communities. Spanish influence is felt throughout Central America.

1523 Defeat of the Quiché and other Maya armies in Guatemala by Pedro de Alvarado.

1562 Maya are persecuted by Friar Diego de Landa who orders burning of Maya books and sculptures.

ARRIVAL OF THE BRITISH

1600s Settlement of the first "Baymen" around the mouth of Belize River. Trade in logwood for dyes.

1634 Captain Peter Wallace – after whom Belize, corrupted from Wallace, is believed to be named – sails into Belize Harbour

1638 The territory of Belize is founded by a group of British seamen, who name their settlement St George's Caye.

1670 Treaty between Britain and Spain to end piracy in the Caribbean.

1697 Conquest of the Itzá on an island in Lake Petén Itzá, Guatemala – the last Maya stronghold in Central America.

1700s Start of mahogany trade, which brings the first influx of black slaves from Jamaica to Belize.

THE MAKING OF BRITISH HONDURAS

1765 "Burnaby's Code" drawn up as first constitution for territory to be known as British Honduras.

1779 Spanish force burns down St George's Caye and Belize Town.

1787 First British-appointed administrator arrives in British Honduras.

1789 Garifuna people arrive in Belize after being deported from the island of St Vincent.

1798 Defeat of Spanish fleet in the Battle of St George's Caye establishes British rule more firmly.

1802 Spain acknowledges British sovereignty in Belize at the Treaty of Amiens.

1820s British start extracting large amounts of mahogany from Belizean forests.

1821 Mexico and Central American nations win independence from Spain. El Salvador and Honduras form Central American Federation and try to claim Belize. British settlers occupy three times the amount of land awarded in Treaty of Amiens.

1823 Central American leaders agree to abolish slavery at a time when slaves constitute a large part of the workforce in Belize.

1826–39 War culminating in the break-up of the United Provinces of Central America.

1847 The War of the Castes in Yucatán, a Maya revolt lasting over 50 years. Many Maya flee to Belize.

1859 Convention between United Kingdom and Guatemala recognizes boundaries of British Honduras – something that has been disputed by Guatemalan governments ever since.

THE BRITISH COLONY

1862 British Honduras is officially declared a British colony.

1866–70 Influx of Confederate supporters from southern US found town of New Richmond.

1871 Belize becomes a crown colony of the British Empire, ruled by a governor and legislative council appointed by the British Government.

1893 Mexico renounces its claim to British Honduras and signs a peace treaty. Guatemala still claims sovereignty.

1910 Start of Mexican Revolution which results in the overthrow of dictator Porfirio Díaz.

1919 Riots started by black Belizean soldiers over their bad treatment during World War I. Belize City is looted by 3,000 people including police.

1921 United Negro Improvement Association is set up, marking the rise of black consciousness.

1926 Death of Baron Bliss, benefactor of Belize.

1931 Twin disasters of Great Depression and hurricane, killing 2,500 people, hit Belize.

1931–35 First written account of the colony's history, *Archives of British Honduras*, is compiled.

GROWTH OF PEOPLE'S POLITICS

1939 "Natives First" movement wins seats on Belize Town Board.

1941 Belizean Labour Party is set up.

1950 People's United Party (PUP) is founded.

1952 Radio Belize, the nation's first radio station, begins transmission.

1954 Universal adult suffrage is introduced.

1958 Arrival of first members of Mennonite community from Mexico.

1961 Hurricane Hattie hits Belize's eastern shoreline, destroying most of the buildings in Belize City.

PRECEDING PAGES: restored Maya frieze, Xunantunich.
LEFT: carved stone mask, Lamanai.
RIGHT: although the British army has officially left Belize, troops still come here for training exercises.

1964 Self-government granted to Belize. George Price is First Minister in the new system.

1970 New administrative capital of Belmopan is officially inaugurated.

1980 United Nations passes unanimous resolution, calling for the independence of Belize.

INDEPENDENT BELIZE

1981 British Honduras becomes independent and is officially renamed Belize.

1984 United Democratic Party (UDP) wins general election for the first time.

1991 Guatemala recognizes the self-determination of the people of Belize in return for Caribbean

coastal waters. Belize becomes a full member of the Organization of American States (OAS).

1992 Guatemalan Congess ratifies its decision to recognize Belize.

1993 Final British garrison leaves.

1995 Maya groups protest sale of land in the Southern Columbia Forest Reserve to logging companies.

1998 People's United Party (PUP) return to power in a victory that gives them all but three seats.

1999 Guatemalan Congress restates its claim to Belizean territory.

2002 Proposal to settle border dispute with Guatemala subject to a referendum in both countries.

2003 People's United Party (PUP) win an unprecedented second term. ❑

THE ANCIENT MAYA

Little remained of a highly creative and ritualized Maya society by the time
of the Spanish conquest, but site excavations have gradually yielded its secrets

When the Spaniards arrived in Mesoamerica in the early 16th century, they found the Maya living in scattered groups, with no central organization. They were not unified in any great political or ceremonial centers, and did not seem to the Spaniards to belong to any great civilization, in contrast to the Aztecs, further north in Mexico, or the Incas of Peru. Although in some places, such as Tulum on the Yucatán Peninsula or Lamanai in Belize, the local Maya were still living in some of the ancient centers, they were apparently unable to explain who had built them, and could not read the inscriptions on the monuments.

In their search for riches, the Spaniards rapidly destroyed much of what remained of the ancient Maya culture. As they colonized the lands of the Maya in Mexico and Central America, they brought Christianity with them. The Franciscan friars, who were distributed throughout the Yucatán and Guatemala, were often the people who accumulated most knowledge about the religion and customs of the Maya. And it was one of them, the Spanish friar Diego de Landa, who helped later generations piece together an understanding of the ancient Maya.

Notes of the enemy

De Landa, who was sent to the Yucatán to convert the Maya, committed barbarous attacks against Maya culture in the 16th century, the most famous being the auto-da-fé in 1562 at Mani, where he destroyed the last known hieroglyphic Maya texts (although at least four have been discovered since). Upon his recall to Spain to face legal charges brought against him for his actions, he wrote *Relación de las Cosas de Yucatán*, containing a virtual ethnography of the Yucatán Maya used for his legal defense. The ancient cities of the Maya had been abandoned long before de Landa's arrival, but his detailed accounts of 16th-century Maya life have

LEFT: carved stone Maya figurine.
RIGHT: Spanish Franciscan friars both attacked and defended the Maya, all in the name of the Church.

proved, with archeological confirmation, that it was very similar to that of their more famous ancestors, whose culture reached its apex from around AD 250–900 (the Classic Period).

As the Spaniards consolidated their rule, interest in the lives of the ancient Maya diminished. Occasional explorers stumbled on ruins in

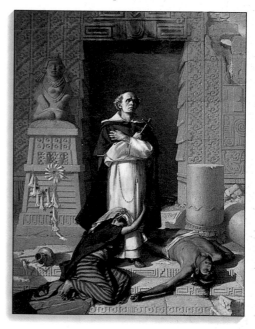

the jungles of Central America, but no real effort was made to uncover or assess them for several centuries. It was only at the end of the 18th century that the Spanish king ordered Captain Antonio del Río to make a thorough investigation into the site at Palenque in southern Mexico.

When del Río's findings were published in Europe in 1822, they immediately aroused great curiosity. But del Río was one of the first of many Europeans who refused to believe that natives of Central America could have been responsible for such splendid architecture and sculptures. Many researchers tried to prove that the Maya must have been influenced by the great Classical civilizations of the Greeks, the

Romans or the Egyptians, rather than having created the riches of the jungles themselves. This kind of explanation has survived to the present day, with some writers still arguing that the Maya must have been visited by "superior beings" from outer space, or that their land was host to the lost civilization of Atlantis. But, as more evidence of the growth and development of Maya centers throughout the region is uncovered, these fanciful theories have gradually given way to more rigorous explanations.

Unlike those of the Aztecs or Incas, the Maya civilization was never unified and controlled by a single ruler. Instead, the region was controlled by competing cities, rather like Greek city states. Yet the whole region was unified through common cultural beliefs, technologies, languages and trade.

The Maya world view

At the core of ancient life was a belief that everything – animate and inanimate – had a place in a cosmic order, and that everything contained some form of spirit or power. This ideology contradicts the Western notion of separation between the natural and the supernatural or unexplainable. The Maya attributed special powers to time, stars, stones, trees and other natural phenomena.

They believed they lived in a Middle World, beneath the 13 levels of the Upper World and above the nine levels of the Lower World, or Xibalba. They believed in an after-life or a paradise, to which ruler, priests and those who die by sacrifice, suicide, in battle or in childbirth gain automatic entrance. And they believed in the destruction of an earlier world by flood.

A string of gods, often with good and evil sides, represented the power held by all objects, but found in various forms: they appeared as different dates, days and colors. Rituals and offerings to the gods insured the continuance of the basic needs of life, health and sustenance. A complex procedure of sacrifices, fasting, feasting and incense-burning was held on annual occasions, including New Year, and also used to induce rain, and for success in hunting, fishing, honey-collecting and war.

The most powerful offering was blood – especially the blood of a king, who was considered a kind of god. The ruler would use an

MAYA CALENDARS

The ancient Maya had a complex system for measuring time. Many sites, such as Chichén Itzá in the Yucatán, are thought to have contained observatories where skilled astronomers checked the path of the stars and calculated dates. Their motivation was their belief in the delicate balance of the universe, and that, unless it was protected, the Maya world could end in death and destruction.

The Maya evolved two separate but interconnected calendar systems. The first was based on a "month" of 20 days that were connected like a wheel with the numbers one to 13, giving a complete cycle of 260 days. This calendar was used for ceremonial life and giving birth dates.

The second system was based on the movement of the sun. This calendar had 18 months of 20 days, making a cycle of 360 days to which were added an extra five days so that the period more or less coincided with the annual solar cycle. The time of greatest uncertainty for the Maya was during these five extra days at the end of the cycle. This was when they sacrificed humans to the sun god.

The two calendars were thought to operate independently of each other, but they coincided every 52 years. This was a time of even greater uncertainty for the Maya, and some experts believe they may have abandoned some of their cities during this crucial period.

obsidian blade made from volcanic rock or a stingray spine to pierce his penis, lip, tongue or earlobe and use the blood to anoint an idol. During the blood-letting, the king would hallucinate and visualize a famous ancestor who would validate his power.

Human sacrifices

The ritual significance of blood was such that the Maya indulged in human sacrifice on a regular basis. Friar Diego de Landa, despite his cultural ignorance, gives a vivid account:

"If [the victim's] heart was to be taken out, they conducted him with great display and concourse of people, painted him blue and wearing his miter, and placed him on the rounded sacrificial stone, after the priest and his officers had anointed the stone with blue and purified the temple to drive away the evil spirit. The *chacs* then seized the poor victim and swiftly laid him on his back across the stone, and the four took hold of his arms and legs, spreading them out. Then the *nacon* executioner came, with a flint knife in his hand, and with great skill made an incision between the ribs on the left side, below the nipple; then he plunged in his hand and like a ravenous tiger tore out the living heart, which he placed on a plate and gave to the priest; he then quickly went and anointed the faces of the idols with that fresh blood..."

In many rituals the Maya would ingest special concoctions like *balche*, a mixture of fermented honey and bark from the balche tree, to enable them to meet with ancestors or other powers. Special tobacco leaves were used to make cigars; some scholars speculate about the use of hallucinogenic mushrooms, peyote, water lilies, morning glory and glands from tropical toads (occasionally a quick ingestion by means of an enema). Incense was another mainstay at ceremonies – usually copal, which would be formed into small cakes.

The Maya timeline

It was during the Middle and Late Preclassic periods (roughly 800 BC to AD 250) that the Maya developed systems of agricultural terraces, raised fields and irrigation channels. The staple food was corn, or maize, which was controlled by its own god, Yum Kaax (also known

as God E). Farmers would also allow wild trees and plants to grow – in cutting arable plots, the Maya were careful to not destroy the ecosystem and exhaust the topsoil.

The apex of Maya culture was the Classic Period (roughly AD 250–900), when trade and the arts flourished. During this period the great cities were rebuilt, and it is the Classic Period remains that survive at the major archeological sites. The men of conquered cities possibly spent one month a year in work tribute to the victor, building *sacbeob*, the raised roads, or public architecture such as pyramids, temples and palaces. Otherwise, the local residents

might have undertaken the construction themselves, for the labor-intensive process of cutting, transporting (without pack animals or wagons) and placing the stones required a mind-boggling number of man-hours.

At some point in Maya history, there was an increase in the number of human sacrifices – possibly as natural resources diminished and the gods demanded extra blood in return for their blessing. Prisoners were sought from neighborhood cities, so confrontations snowballed. During the Early Postclassic Period (AD 900–1200) Maya culture collapsed quickly and mysteriously, and most of the great cities were abandoned. The causes of the apocalypse are

LEFT: jade head of Kinich Ahau, Maya sun god.
RIGHT: pottery figure of the Lord of Lamanai.

still hotly debated, with everything from earth-quakes to famine and disease thrown into the theorizing. However, a few cities – including Lamanai in modern-day Belize – survived until the arrival of the Spanish.

Everyday life

At their cultural apotheosis, the Maya cities would have looked very different from the skele-tons one sees today. Imagine replacing the ocean of green rainforest with wide open areas of farmland, roads and public plazas, with stone

LIVING ON SITE

Contrary to earlier belief, not all Maya cities were solitary ritual centers for peace-loving priests; many were lively centers of art, commerce and political power.

given name, the father's family name, the *naal kaba* or father's and mother's family names combined, and the *coco kaba* or nickname.

At age four or five, a small white bead was fastened to a boy's hair and a girl had a red shell hung around her waist. These remained in place until a puberty ceremony when, before a public audience in a sponsor's house, priests recited prayers and the youths were anointed. After a gift exchange, the children could abandon the beads and shells. Young unmarried men lived together

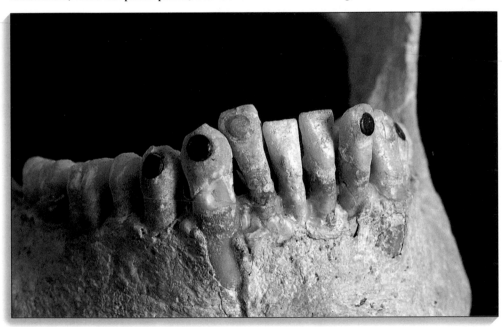

buildings plastered and painted white or in var-ious colors. The average family lived in a thatched hut located on the outskirts of a city and a few miles from the family's maize field.

The Maya life cycle was carefully regulated. Upon a child's birth, the family and perhaps the shaman would look at the 260-day almanac to determine the destiny and character of the baby. The ancient Maya probably conducted something similar to the modern Maya nam-ing or *hetzmek* ceremony in which two god-parents carry the child and circle nine times around a table holding nine symbolic objects the child will use in adult life. The child receives three or four names – a *paal kaba* or

and helped their fathers in farming, while the young women were instructed in cooking, weaving and housekeeping.

Most adult men continued to work in agri-culture, though other occupations were per-mitted – pottery, stone cutting, mining, salt- or shell-collecting and trading. The Maya used cacao beans and other natural items like red shells for money.

Matchmakers negotiated with parents and young couples to arrange marriages. The groom's family would give a dowry of dresses and other articles. The marriage ceremony was brief, followed by a small feast for the families and special guests. The son-in-law lived and worked for six or seven years with his in-laws. Apparently, divorce was simple: the Maya were monogamous, but the men eagerly left their wives for other mates.

In death, relatives would silently mourn by day and wail in sorrow at night. The family often buried the deceased inside or near their home, and unless the family was very large, they would abandon the house soon afterwards. More important people were either cremated or buried in elaborate vaulted tombs – often with food and pieces of carved jadeite as currency, as well as idols and tools, which the deceased would need in the afterlife.

Not all Maya fashions were so dramatic. Common Maya men wore a loincloth, or *ex*, wrapped around the waist and often decorated with feathers, abstract designs and representations of faces. Covering their shoulders was a square cotton *pati*, decorated according to their position in society. Women wore a variation of the *huipil* still worn today in Mesoamerica – often a white dress or blouse with a square cutout for the head and holes for arms – along with a *booch*, a strip of material thrown over the head that acted as a headdress and scarf. Both men and women wore double-thonged leather sandals that were bound to

High fashion, Maya style

The ancient Maya had some unique concepts of beauty. A good-looking Maya aristocrat would have had his or her forehead well flattened (the parents bound their children's heads between a pair of wooden boards). He or she might also have been cross-eyed (parents dangled balls between their baby's eyes). All Maya men had a bald spot burned into their pates. And some men filed their teeth to a point and inlaid them with pyrite or jadeite.

LEFT: ancient dental work with inlaid stones.
ABOVE: a noble's skull, flattened at childhood as a mark of aristocratic bearing and beauty.

their ankles with rope; their black hair was worn long and often braided.

The upper classes wore more colorful costumes with intricate woven designs, animal skins and feathers (including the quetzal). Priests wore jaguar skins. High-ranking Maya wore a dazzling range of jewelry – bracelets, necklaces, earrings, nose rings, lip plugs and pendants made from jade, shell, teeth, claws, wood and stone. Every few days, men and women also anointed themselves with a red, sweet-smelling ointment. The men often painted their bodies: unmarried young men black, warriors black and red, priests in blue (the color associated with sacrifice).

Myth and history

The intimate connection between daily life and the supernatural is shown by the role of a ball game that was played in every Maya city. The game was also played to re-enact parts of the creation myth, the *Popul Vuh*, in which the Ancestral Hero Twins trick and defeat the Lords of Death of *Xibalba* (the Underworld). In Maya legend, the ball court was where the legendary Twins actively challenged and outwitted the gods.

The basic rules were simple enough. Two teams, using only particular body parts (usually hips or knees), tried to send a rubber ball

through a hoop sticking out of a wall or atop a post in a playing field between two parallel buildings. The rules, team size and court size varied by region and changed through time. One famous tradition held that, upon shooting the ball through the hoop, the successful player could claim the jewelry of the spectators unfortunate enough to witness the event. The game often held ritual significance when played by nobles or rulers, or with captives (who, when they lost, were sacrificed and sometimes bound up like a ball and rolled down pyramid steps).

The Maya living in Belize today speak nearly 30 variations of the Mayan language, the most common being Yucatec. In ancient times there were also many varieties, but only one form of written hieroglyphs, a standard used throughout the civilization.

A key source of surviving hieroglyphs are the stelae, tall needles of stone planted to resemble ceiba trees. They were commissioned to commemorate important anniversaries, bloodlettings, conquests and coronations. The messages solidified the power of the ruling lineage over the people, and let visitors know whose land they were entering. It is uncertain how many people could actually read these messages, however. For the illiterate masses, the geometric and free-form designs found on pottery, clothing, stelae and architecture may well have communicated the same propaganda as the hieroglyphs.

New sites found

In recent years, our knowledge about the Maya has increased dramatically. Great strides have been made in interpreting the stelae, other monuments and the written codices. New sites have been found and scientifically explored. In Belize, for example, Maya population centers have been uncovered in the northern lagoons at Chac Balaam. Here it is thought that as many as 10,000 ancient Maya lived, trading in salt and pottery with the inhabitants of other centers further north on the Yucatán coast.

In 1957, one of the most important rediscoveries was made when a bulldozer clearing a track through the jungle north of Belize City crashed into the Maya city of Altun Há *(see page 187)*. Scientific excavation of the site began in 1963, and was rewarded with the discovery of many jade artifacts, including the famous jade head of the sun god Kinich Ahau, now kept under strict security in vaults of the Belize Bank in Belmopan.

Another important center that has yielded its secrets is La Milpa *(see page 203)*, which is thought to have rivaled the famous city of Tikal in northern Guatemala during the Classic Period. And in the 1990s, a number of exciting finds were made in the Maya Mountains in the south of Belize. All of these suggest that the Maya population of the country may once have been much greater than that of today. ❑

LEFT: Maya pottery ocarina.
RIGHT: pyramid at Lamanai, Belize's most picturesque Maya site, on the banks of the New River Lagoon.

THE MONUMENTAL MAYA MYSTERIES

The secrets of 5,000 years of Maya history are being painstakingly unraveled as archeologists explore the remains hidden by the tropical forests

Scientists are piecing together the spiritual and intellectual legacy left by a civilization that was ruled by living gods from more than 50 city-states, such as Tikal, Copán, Palenque, Calakmul, and Caracol. The classic Maya society (200 BC to AD 900) developed through trade, religion and statecraft, and left its imprint in hieroglyphical texts and superb monumental architecture. Fine artwork in jade, stone and clay pottery depicted scenes from mythology, the supernatural, politics, science, and warfare and recorded events from everyday life. Etchings chronicled Maya kings' births, coronations, marriages, conquests and deaths.

ARCHEOLOGISTS VERSUS LOOTERS

Today the texts written on tombs' interior walls help unlock Maya secrets, yet these texts are all too often destroyed by looters foraging for artifacts for the lucrative, illegal pre-Columbian art trade. Regional governments and archeologists are racing against time to find and protect important undiscovered sites. Today, scientists are turning to airborne sensors operated from aircraft and satellites. The Landsat satellite provides data that delineates natural and large, man-made features. This data could help find as yet unknown ancient cities.

▷ **MAYA CERAMICS**
Maya pottery often depicted historical figures and events, providing a great deal of useful archeological data.

△ **EXPERT GUIDES**
Archeologists at work on some sites are ready to answer questions on ancient Maya mysteries.

▷ **UNDERGROUND CAVE**
The huge network of potholes and caves in Belize and the Yucatán have revealed some rich finds of Maya ceramics.

◁ XUNANTUNICH
Excavation work has continued at Xunantunich since the 19th century, focussed on the towering El Castillo pyramid.

△ DETAILED MURAL
Colorful Maya murals on temple walls provided a mass of information about their everyday life – in particular, about work and trade.

ARCHEOLOGICAL EXPEDITIONS

The birth of modern Maya archeology traces its popular origin to the epic expeditions, between 1839 and 1842, of adventurers John L. Stephens and Frederick Catherwood. Their discovery of immense ruined cities among the tropical jungles of Mesoamerica caught the imagination of the academic world.

Catherwood's beautiful lithographs of the ruins of Chichén Itzá, Uxmal, Palenque and Copán were widely published in Europe and North America. The explorers' tales of discovery were hailed as the greatest of the century.

Some 50 years later, archeologists such as Thompson, Morley, Tozzer, Joyce and Maler led expeditions to the jungles of Central America to try and unlock the mystery of the Maya civilization.

But it was only in the 1950s, with the help of modern technology, that archeologists began to decipher more than dates and numerals. Today's research is cracking the "Maya code" to reveal intricate details of Maya history.

△ CATHERWOOD'S ART
The 19th-century drawings of Maya ruins by Frederick Catherwood captured the world's imagination.

▷ JADE FIGURINE
A huge cache of finely worked jade pieces was found at Altun IIá, a major Maya site in northern Belize.

BUCCANEERS AND BAYMEN

*Formative Belize – the Bay Settlement – was a refuge for Maya escaping the
Spanish in Mexico and a hideout for pirates, plundering galleons in the Caribbean*

I n Belize City they sell a T-shirt proclaiming: "Where the Hell is Belize?" It has ever been thus. Well into the 17th century, when Spanish rule had been ruthlessly stamped on the rest of Central America, authorities were only barely conscious of the region that now goes by the name of Belize. Spanish explorers avoided its coral reefs, and few conquistadors or missionaries ventured south of the Yucatán. Those that did reported none of the cities of silver and gold that would excite a conqueror's imagination, only murky swamps and mosquito-filled forests.

Nor were the local Maya inhabitants friendly. Their first encounter with Spaniards set the tone for relations, when a handful of shipwrecked sailors landed in northern Belize in 1511. Five were sacrificed, their still-beating hearts torn from their bodies, and the rest were made slaves. Most Spaniards decided to seek their fortunes elsewhere.

As a result, Belize became the first refugee crossroads of Central America. Thousands of Maya fled the Spanish subjugation of Mexico and Guatemala in the 1500s, which reached ferocious heights of cruelty. During Captain Alonso Pacheco's campaign against the Maya of Chetumal in 1544, for example, conquistadors routinely garotted men and women, tied them to weights and threw them into lakes to watch them drown, chopped off their prisoners' noses, ears or hands, and had others dismembered alive by wild "dogs of war."

Those Maya that survived faced enslavement, the break-up of their families, and re-location. Little wonder that the Franciscan monks who brought the gospel (and demands for Spanish taxes) into the Belizean jungle in the early 1600s provoked open rebellion. The few churches the missionaries managed to build were soon sacked and burned down.

PRECEDING PAGES: a pirate crew with their captive.
LEFT: a triumphant pirate raid in the Caribbean.
RIGHT: walking the plank was more artistic license than actual pirate practice.

Logwood and piracy

The Maya of Belize got on much better with a few motley Britons who turned up along the Bay of Campeche in search of logwood. The British were out simply to remove a few trees and make money, and showed not the slightest interest in taxing or converting anyone. Their

small camps congregated in Belize's most miserable swampland, where the hard-as-stone logwood was to be found – its black, red and gray dyes were essential for the woolen industry in Britain – which fetched £100 a ton, a small fortune in those days.

At first, the Spaniards ignored them. But before long, the barely inhabited coastline of Belize began to attract another kind of British entrepreneur: the buccaneer. It was a perfect hideout for a Caribbean freebooting operation. The buccaneers sailed fast, shallow draft ships that could chase down a heavily laden Spanish merchantman, capture the cargo and out-pace the pursuing warships. Once inside the Belizean reef, with its low water, treacherous coral heads and mud flats, they were safe. From there, the loot could be transported to the Bahamas, Bermuda or, after the British captured it, Port Royal in Jamaica, where the market for plundered goods was insatiable.

One of these "Gentlemen of the Coast" was Captain Peter Wallace, who in 1634 sailed his ship the *Swallow* into the shallow harbor that would eventually become Belize City. A Scotsman who had served under Sir Walter Raleigh, Wallace remains a shadowy figure. Nobody knows if he was strictly speaking a "buccaneer" (captain who preyed on the enemy) or "pirate"

(one who preyed on his own nation's ships); he was reputed to be behind a whole fleet of ships pillaging the Caribbean. Whatever the truth, it is possible that Wallace gave his name, in corrupted form, to Belize. (Others suggest it comes from the Maya word *beliz*, "muddy-watered," which accurately describes the Belize River for much of the year – but the Wallace connection is usually cited as more romantic.)

The pirates' honest trade

Logwood was a valuable enough commodity which many buccaneers logged in their spare time. Some of the most famous names in Caribbean piracy – "Admiral" Benbow, William

Dampier, Bartholomew Sharpe, Edward Low, "Blackbeard" Teach, Nicholas van Horn, William Bannister and John Coxon – were all, at one time or other, involved in the trade. Together, they make up a Who's Who of 17th-century villainy.

The legend of Blackbeard

None was as picturesque, or enduringly remembered, as Edward Teach, better known as Blackbeard – who, according to local legend, spent a good deal of leisure time hiding out on Ambergris Caye. According to records of the day, Teach was such a terrifying sight that crews of enemy ships were known to throw down their arms without a fight. His huge black beard, one writer noted, was "like a frightful meteor," hanging down to his waist and twisted with colored ribbons. In battle he wore a leather holster with three pistols over each shoulder. More oddly, he "struck lighted matches under his hat, which, appearing on each side of his face, his eyes naturally looking fierce and wild, made him altogether such a figure that imagination cannot form an idea of a fury from Hell to look more frightful."

This archetypal pirate was born in Bristol, went into training in Jamaica, and embarked on his pirate career by pillaging the coasts of Virginia and the Carolinas. After capturing a large, 40-gun French ship, which he renamed Queen Anne's Revenge, Teach began to roam the Caribbean, often using the Belizean cayes off the Gulf of Honduras as a rendezvous (Ambergris Caye was one of his favorites, and fanciful tales of buried treasure are sometimes still trotted out in the bars of San Pedro).

A surviving fragment of his log shows a typical day under Blackbeard's command: "Such a day, rum all out – our company somewhat sober – a damn'd confusion amongst us! Rogues a plotting – great talk of separation – so I look'd sharp for a prize – such a day, took one, with a great deal of liquor on board, so kept the company hot ... then all things well again."

As he captured more ships, several crews agreed to join Blackbeard in his depredations, until he commanded a small fleet. Things were going so well that when one English captain informed him of a royal decree pardoning all pirates who ceased activities, he laughed in derision. The only major problem seemed to be venereal disease, which drove Blackbeard to lay siege to Charleston, Carolina until several hundred pounds' worth of medical supplies were provided.

Finally, desperate merchants and shippers appealed for help to the Governor of Virginia, who hired Lieutenant Robert Maynard of the Royal Navy to hunt down Blackbeard in the heavily armed *Pearl*. They caught him off the North Carolina coast on 22 November, 1718, and the following dialogue was recorded:

Blackbeard: "Damn you for villains, who are you? And whence came you?"

Maynard: "You may see by our colors we are no pirates."

Blackbeard demanded that Maynard come closer alongside, but Maynard replied: "I cannot spare my boat, but I will come aboard of you as soon as I can with my sloop."

Blackbeard (swilling a jug of rum and toasting his enemy): "Damnation seize my soul if I give you quarter, or take any from you."

Maynard: "I expect none, and will give none."

After this exchange, the two opened up cannons on one another. Maynard hid a number of his men below decks, tricking Blackbeard into boarding with only 13 men. Realizing his deception, Teach flew into a drunken rage. As the deck ran thick with blood, several guns were fired point-blank into Blackbeard's body, without obvious effect. He knocked down Maynard in a cutlass duel and received 20 sword slashes before suddenly dropping dead from lack of blood. Maynard, wounded but not mortally, lopped off the pirate's head and hung it from his bowsprit.

Although feared for his ferocity, Teach earned the grudging respect of his enemies. He showed great tactical skill, fought to the death and never harmed his prisoners – a true "Gentleman of the Coast."

From larceny to logging

The death-knell for Caribbean freebooting was tolled in 1670, when a treaty between England and Spain pledged to supress piracy on the high seas. Although it took a long time, the assorted captains and crews eventually realized that the hangman awaited, whoever captured them. Many decided to try logging full-time, and settled around the mouth of the Belize River – a

---

LEFT: Edward Teach, alias Blackbeard the pirate.
RIGHT: Blackbeard's fatal last stand in 1718.

humid, swampy delta chosen not for its setting, which was dismal, but because this was where the logwood trunks were floated from the many upriver camps.

The whole was referred to as the Bay Settlement, and its inhabitants, Baymen. By 1700, a rough society of some 300 people was beginning to emerge, commuting to the logging camps, called Banks, upriver. Few English women dared settle here (even the prostitutes preferred the bright lights of Port Royal in Jamaica), although some loggers took Maya women as common-law wives, starting up the famous Belizean melting pot.

One upper-crust ship's captain who was wrecked here in 1720 was horrified by the lawlessness he found among its rowdy citizens: "The Wood-Cutters are generally a rude drunken Crew, some of which have been Pirates; their chief Delight is in Drinking; and when they broach a Quarter Cask or a Hogshead of Wine, they seldom stir while there is a Drop left... keeping at it sometimes a Week together, drinking till they fall asleep; and as soon as they awake, at it again, without stirring off the place. I had but little Comfort living among these Crew of ungovernable wretches, where there was little else to be heard but Blasphemy, Cursing and Swearing."

The arrival of the slaves

This small society of reformed pirates and drunkards was transformed when the world's best quality mahogany began to be pulled from the rainforests. Mahogany was much more valuable than logwood – the rich and powerful demanded it for their furniture in Britain and across the American colonies – and required a larger workforce to extract it. New fortune seekers arrived in Belize, bringing with them boatloads of black slaves from Jamaica.

With names like Congo Will, Guinea Sam or Mundingo Pope reflecting their African homeland, the slaves soon outnumbered white set-

had to be paid. A slave could buy his freedom, and many did, and any black man who turned up in Belize was declared free unless proven otherwise. Any female slave who was taken as a common-law wife or mistress by a settler was freed, and by the late 1700s a substantial portion of the settlement was recorded in the census as people of "Mixed Colour."

Nevertheless, slaves had few legal rights and slavery could be just as brutal in Belize as anywhere else. Several small-scale rebellions occurred in the bush, including one where six white men were murdered and a dozen slaves escaped to freedom in the Yucatán.

tlers by roughly ten to one. Belizean slavery was a much more liberal institution than that in, say, the southern United States. Instead of rigidly controlled plantations, a white slaver might take a handful of slaves up the river to set up a loosely structured logging camp. Every slave had a machete or an ax, and a few were given muskets and pistols for hunting and for defense against attacks by hostile Maya. Each slave had his own tent, wherever he wished to build it, and if the slavemaster had a whip, he probably used it on his mule.

Meanwhile, local slave laws baffled foreign visitors. For example, slaves only worked five days a week. If a slave worked on Saturday, he

Frontier democrats

The free Baymen ruled themselves by voting for magistrates at a public meeting – in much the same way that pirate captains had been freely elected by their crews. All free men could vote, regardless of property or color, to the disgust of visiting aristocrats from England (although women could only look on from the balconies, waving their handkerchiefs).

Meanwhile, Belize Town was growing, filling up the swampland with wood chips, conch shells and empty bottles of Santa Rita rum. The whites and "free coloreds" lived on St George's Caye a few miles offshore, flanked by a small fortress, while on the mainland a warren of backstreets developed for the black population. As in other Caribbean outposts, African religious practices such as *obeah* were rife, despite attempts to control it. (Slave revolts in other islands had made the white settlers nervous, and the night-long playing of gombay drums was banned as they "deprive the Inhabitants therein from their natural rest.")

A dozen or so of the richer, older white families became known as the "Old Baymen" and made up a minuscule locally born elite. They made a half-hearted attempt to maintain their British way of life in this malaria-ridden outpost. A Presbyterian church service on Sunday, said under a canvas canopy with the congregation in stifling black coats, might be followed by an afternoon's fishing from a dory, or wooden dugout, and swimming in a remote river (after first digging about with your "setting pole" to clear out the snakes and crocodiles). In the dry season, families headed upriver to their Banks, living in tents and eating "bush stew" of gibnut, turtle and peccary, spiced up with fried plaintain and Johnny cakes ("No man should crave more toothsome food," wrote a contemporary).

It was back-breaking work, but lucrative: one Scottish family who moved to Belize bought a moderate holding upriver and earned £5,700 in the first season.

Trouble with the Spaniards

Although vast fortunes were to be made in the Belizean forest, the life of the loggers was desperately insecure. Apart from tropical diseases, poisonous snakes and clouds of mosquitoes, there was the Spanish threat. The Spaniards had never recognized the British presence, and the story of the 18th century is one of constant conflict between the settlers, cut off from Britain or any outside aid, and the surrounding enemy. (And since the majority of settlers were of Scottish origin, they saw an English prejudice in the authorities' indifference.)

Not that the Baymen were blameless. Although a treaty was fleshed out in 1765 to limit their activities, loggers continually crossed into Spanish territory, bribing frontier guards and customs officials, and smuggling anything they

could into Mexico. Meanwhile, bandits based in the Yucatán made continuous forays into Belize, often storming the isolated logging banks. One chronicler records how his young fiancée, fresh off the boat from Scotland, was kidnapped by a bandit named Diego Bustamente while she was paddling a canoe near the camp. Friendly Indians led the Baymen to a remote Maya ruin, where Diego had holed up and was preparing to force himself upon his captive. The settlers were able to surprise the bandit and his men, and rescued the distraught woman – who, despite her ordeal, chose to remain in Belize.

Throughout the 1700s, the Spanish kept up raids on the timber camps, but the Baymen could always slip away into the forest. The conflicts with Spain might have remained petty and limited except for the American War of Independence. The Baymen first learned about it when a strange ship, *The George Washington*, pulled into St George's Caye. A few citizens went out in their dories to meet Captain Hezikiah Anthony of the United States Navy, only to be immediately imprisoned as ransom for rum.

Unfortunately for the Baymen, the American struggle prompted Spain to declare war, yet again, on Britain, and use it as an excuse to wipe

LEFT: gun-toting Baymen in the swamps.
RIGHT: dangerous overcrowding was the norm on the sailing ships arriving from Jamaica.

out Belize. A sizeable Spanish force attacked St George's Caye in 1779, burning it and Belize Town to the ground. Most of the Baymen escaped into the forest, but the unfortunates on the Caye were captured and sent on a forced march 300 miles (480 km) into the Yucatán.

One Bayman, Tom Potts, was captured with his wife Charlotte and daughter. The hard-bitten couple survived the forced march, and had a second child in a dungeon while awaiting trial. After several more years in a prison in Cuba, they were released and headed back, by sea and land, to Belize – and Potts eventually became Belize's chief magistrate.

Renewed hostility with Spain

The Bay Settlement was rebuilt, logging recommenced and and new arrivals of British settlers, forced by treaty to leave the Mosquito Shore of Honduras and Nicaragua, boosted the numbers back to over 3,000 souls. Then, in 1796, Britain and Spain started squabbling again in Europe: this time the battle for Belize would be for good.

News of an imminent invasion caused a commotion amongst the Baymen. Public meetings turned into riots over the question of whether to stay and fight. Running away from the Spaniards was an old and honorable tradition in Belize, and many favored it now. After all,

the British authorities offered no protection other than a single gunship from Jamaica.

Others were adamant that they would defend the colony: it had grown too large to abandon, there were too many fine buildings and too much equipment could be lost. Tom Potts, the chief magistrate who had personal experience of Spanish dungeons, wanted out, but Thomas Paslow, a fiery Irishman, thundered that "A man who will not defend his country does not deserve to reap the benefits of it."

In a close vote – 65 to 51 – the majority elected to remain. Many of the deciding votes were cast by a group of free blacks led by Adam Flowers. Despite the acrimony, however, everyone stayed to fight: not a single Bayman left.

The final conflict

The Baymen spent the next couple of years preparing for an attack. Finally, on September 3, 1798, a Spanish force of 32 ships, including 16 heavily armed men o' war and 2,000 troops, bore down on the Baymen. They had managed to dig in on St George's Caye and had armed all the slaves, but their rag-tag naval forces consisted of one Royal Navy battleship, the *HMS Marlin*, five schooners and seven logwood barges fitted out with a single cannon each. But the Baymen had geography on their side: when the Spaniards advanced, four ships were bogged in mud flats and blown out of the water.

Every day, the Spanish advance party was pushed back. Then, on September 10, the Spaniards made a major effort to land on St George's Caye, sending fourteen of their largest ships close to its shore. This time they were caught in a narrow channel and ravaged by the Baymen's fire. The British naval officers attempted to coordinate an attack on the foundering ships, but the boatloads of slaves and free blacks attacked without orders (and with great success – the sight of the huge slaves, with machetes in their teeth and a pistol in each hand, was terrifying). The Spaniards withdrew, this time ending their claims to the territory forever, and the settlement, for the first time, was secure.

A century later, September 10 was declared a national holiday in Belize, and the battle of St George's Caye is still celebrated as National Day throughout the country to this day. ❑

LEFT: surprise attack on the high seas.

The *Chicleros*

There have been many extraordinary figures throughout the colorful history of Belize. Perhaps the oddest were the *chicleros* – the men who went into the jungles of Belize, the Peten region of Guatemala and Mexico's Yucatán Peninsula to gather chicle gum.

The tree that provides the sap that is made into chicle is the chicozapote (Manilkara zapota), also commonly known as the sapodilla, whose rot-resistant wood was used by the Maya for lintels in their temples throughout the region. There is evidence that they also cultivated the tree for its fruit in nearby plantations.

The medicinal uses of the chicozapote have long been known to the peoples of Mexico and Central America, where the tree is native: various parts have been used as treatments against a wide range of ailments, from dysentery to coughs and colds, diarrhea, kidney stones, snake bites and poisonous insect stings; the latex was even used as a temporary filling for tooth cavities.

The first commercial use of the chicle gum as chewing gum, however, dates back to the late 19th century. In 1866, New York dentist Thomas Adams was given a kilogram (2.2 lbs) of chicle gum, by the Mexican general, Antonio Lopez de Santa Ana. A year later, after a series of tests, Adams produced the first commercial chicle-based gum, and – so the story goes – the chewing gum industry appeared on the scene.

The role of the *chicleros*, however, remained pivotal to the commercial success of chewing gum. Many of these men were Maya or Waika indigenous people, who had come to Belize from the Mosquito coast, in present-day Honduras. They obtained the chicle by making diagonal slashes in the trunks of the chicozapote tree during the rainy season. The latex sap would drip down the slashes and collect in containers left at the foot of the tree, which the *chicleros* picked up the following day. They would then heat up the liquid latex until it had reduced, and form it into solid blocks weighing some 4 kg (10 lbs), which were then shipped to factories in the United States. At its peak productivity in 1930, over 6.3 million kg (14 million lbs) of chicle was exported from Belize and other Central American countries.

RIGHT: the *chiclero's* work is a manual task, unchanged in over a hundred years.

As a result of their expeditions into little-known territory, the *chicleros* also acquired intimate knowledge of the trails through the dense jungle where the Maya sites had been hidden for centuries. It was thanks to the chicle-hunters that the Austrian explorer Teobert Maler was able to find and photograph such important sites as Tikal, Yaxchilan, Piedras Negras and El Naranjo.

As the industry boomed, many methods were employed to replace the costly collection techniques of the *chicleros*, who were running into problems such as over-tapped trees and deforestation. Plantations were started, but these did not prove to be a practical alternative and were abandoned.

After World War II, however, business slumped, with cheaper synthetic substitutes for chicle being introduced, and increased competition from other parts of the world, particularly Asia.

The demand for natural chicle never totally disappeared, however, and today a few *chicleros* in Belize continue to gather the white sap in much the same way as their forefathers did in the 19th century. The largest market for the gum is Japan, and the rising interest in natural, organic products in Europe and the US is also keeping the latex business bouncing. Maya gatherers and others are again being employed in this strange trade, and stumbling on yet more ancient sites in the jungle not seen for hundreds of years. ❏

BRITISH HONDURAS

After its historic defeat of the Spanish, the new British colony
then lapsed into two hundred years of lassitude

As the smoke cleared after their victory at St George's Caye, the Baymen jubilantly looked forward to the 19th century as a new era of peace and prosperity. With the Spanish threat broken, it seemed that they could carry on making fortunes from logging and bathe in a glow of patriotic pride. "Many colonies have been won for England by her brave soldiers and sailors," crowed one Bayman in his memoirs, "but British Honduras is, I believe, the only one in which a mere handful of settlers, without help from home, wrested the lands from a powerful foe and added them to the British Empire."

Things were not, of course, that simple. News of the great victory barely reached the halls of power in London, where the Napoleonic Wars were of far more immediate interest. As far as the British government was concerned, Belize was more of an irritation than a valued aquisition. It was not officially a part of the Empire at all. The Baymen were not even British subjects – they were just an unruly bunch of loggers, working in a godforsaken backwater, entirely on Spanish suffrance.

It was not until 1862 that Westminster officially recognized Belize as the Colony of British Honduras, sending out a proper governor and ordering a colonial parliament. But Central America remained all but unknown to the outside world, and played next to no part in the great strategic struggles of the day. In short, British Honduras may have become a part of the Empire, but to the politicians and traders who orchestrated it, the acquisition seemed almost an irrelevance.

An American in Belize Town

One of the few who took an interest in Belize in this period was the American John L. Stephens, an amateur archeologist whose memoirs form the basis of modern research on the Maya world (they are still in print and widely read to this day). The account provides the classic view of Belizean society in the making.

Arriving in 1839, Stephens found Belize Town firmly established as the settlement's capital (during the battle with the Spanish, the Bay-

men had burned every building on St George's Caye, so they wouldn't fall into enemy hands). Indeed, when seen from a distance, the town was almost picturesque. Seeing several boats in dock and dozens of canoes plying the river, Stephens was moved to compare it to Venice or Alexandria. Equally impressive were the canoes that came out to his ship, made of single, huge mahogany trees that would have been worth a fortune in New York City.

A fine wooden Government House had been built by the shore, lined with groves of coconut trees, and a bridge was erected over the river. Settlers imported bricks from London – the same used to build mansions on Regent Street,

---

PRECEDING PAGES: 19th-century Belize City.
LEFT: mahogany cutters, the source of continual conflict with Maya farmers and Mexican bandits.
RIGHT: a river log-jam.

they noted with some pride – to build St John's Cathedral. It was Belize's first brick building, its first permanent church, and the perfect place for the British to crown the Indian "Mosquito Kings" of the neighboring Mosquito Coast (present-day Honduras), ensuring their allegiance throughout the 19th century.

Once on shore, however, Stephens's favorable impression evaporated when he found that the "town seemed in the entire possession of blacks." A pre-Civil War American used to a strictly segregated society, Stephens confessed that he "hardly knew whether to be shocked or amused" by the hubbub of African vendors,

polite. They talked of their mahogany works, of England, hunting, horses, ladies and wine..." In Belize, Stephens mused, "color was considered mere matter of taste."

Just as baffling to Stephens was the operation of Belize's "Grand Court," where no lawyers argued cases because none of the judges had legal training. Two were merchants, one a mahogany cutter, and one, a mulatto, was a doctor. The eminent American left the settlement soon after to seek out the Maya ruins in Honduras (Belize's as yet being hardly discovered), with the soldiers from Jamaica providing a 13-gun salute.

black soldiers from Jamaica in red uniforms and women in white frocks with ("I could not help remarking") nothing on underneath.

Slavery had been abolished in Belize in the early 1830s, although the position of the average logging worker was hardly much improved. Even so, Belize's racial melting pot was already well advanced, as Stephens discovered to his horror when invited to lunch one day, only to find British officers dining with mulattoes: "By chance a place was made for me between the two colored gentlemen," writes Stephens bravely. "Some of my countrymen, perhaps, would have hesitated about taking it, but I did not; both were well dressed, well educated, and

Bandits and warlords

Even as Belize was being drawn into the fold of British colonial rule, the surrounding Spanish Empire in Central America was breaking into independent republics – creating waves of civil war, frontier disputes and domestic chaos that spilled over into Belize. Just as the Baymen had had to defend themselves from the Spaniards, so the colonial Belizeans spent the entire 19th century fending off their new neighbors.

Raids by Mexican bandits made life out on the logging camps a constant peril. Worse came after 1847, when the Maya of the Yucatán rebelled against the ruling Mexican *ladinos* (mestizos) in the great Caste Wars. The conflict would continue until 1900, and spill over the borders into Belize.

At first, the British traders happily sold arms and supplies to the largest Mayan state, Santa Cruz (so named because they worshipped a miraculous speaking cross). But this brought them into conflict with another Maya group, the Icaiche. What's more, British loggers were steadily intruding onto Mayan *milpa* or slash-and-burn lands (the Crown in Belize Town distributed permits to the countryside with little interest as to who was actually living there). Traditional good relations between British and Maya soured, and when the Icaiche rebel, General Marcus Canul, attacked Belize, most of the local Maya villages willingly supported him.

In 1866, Canul captured a British mahogany camp on the Río Bravo and held its members for $3,000 ransom. Next year, he attacked the sugar plantation of Indian Church near Lamanai, forcing local settlers to retreat to Belize Town. Matters were grave enough for the governor to order evacuation ships readied in the harbor, although the expected attack never came. In 1870, the Icaiche occupied the town of Corozal, and in 1872 besieged Orange Walk Town. Luckily for the inhabitants, a troop of US Confederate soldiers had settled nearby; fresh from the Civil War, their modern rifles devastated the Maya ranks. Canul himself was shot from his saddle, and later died, taking the wind out of the Icaiche rebellion.

The lost Confederates

How did the American soldiers happen to be there in the first place? When Lee surrendered to Grant at the Appomattox Court House, ending the American Civil War in 1865, many Southerners decided to escape Yankee rule forever and head for Latin America. Some 7,000 Confederates abandoned the United States for isolated colonies where they hoped to recreate the Old South – complete with plantation houses, belles in hoop skirts, gentlemen drinking iced tea and droves of black workers out in the fields. Most of these voluntary exiles went to Brazil, where slavery was still legal. But around 1,500 decided to try their luck in the wilds of British Honduras.

Southern curiosity in this obscure Central American republic had been piqued long before the Civil War, and when reconstruction began, the interest became intense. Emigration agents sprang up in every Southern city, and a fortnightly steamship service began from New

LEFT: banana boat in Punta Gorda.
ABOVE: prayer group in Belize City.

Orleans to Belize in 1866. First reports from settlers were positive, and the British government encouraging: import duties were waved for Confederate families, and London even promised that the young colony would soon be independent (broadly hinting that the Southerners could take the reins). The British governor even entertained new arrivals at state dinners, when the halls echoed with patriotic renditions of *Bonnie Blue Flag*, *My Maryland* and *God Save the King*.

From 1867 to 1869, the *Trade Winds* and *General Sherman* were bringing 100 settlers per trip. The majority were Confederate sol-

diers and their families, including many of high rank. The American consul in Belize noted with astonishment that "generals and colonels meet one at every turn."

Most of the new arrivals were appalled by Belize Town with its largely black population, and pressed on into the countryside. Some 300 followed the Reverend B.R. Duval of Virginia south to a spot near present-day San Pedro, setting up a town they named New Richmond (the whole colony was envisaged as "Confederate County"). Another group from Louisiana – including Captain Beauregard, brother of the the famed general, and a certain Colonel Benjamin, brother of the Confederate secretary of

war – bought sugar plantations on the New River, south of Orange Walk Town. Other smaller groups of settlers scattered in remote pockets through the Belizean countryside.

The Confederates' stated aim was to withdraw from the rest of the world to recreate an antebellum fantasy. But the realities of Belizean frontier life caught up with them quickly. Conditions were much harsher than many had expected: apart from the constant heat, the rain and mosquitoes, settlers faced rampant diseases, problems with food supplies and incessant Indian raids in the north. Even more galling, black employees could simply walk away if pressed too far. Most Confederate exiles packed up and left Belize within a few years, returning to the United States poorer but wiser. But others stayed on, using their skills and wealth to establish themselves in Belizean society, usually in the professions.

Although many Belizeans today can trace their lineage to former Confederate soldiers, the Southern community soon lost any social cohesiveness. Children were sent back to the United States to be educated and find white spouses; many did not return. The families that remained in Belize were drawn into the more relaxed local attitude towards race, soon intermarrying with members of the black and Hispanic communities.

Territorial claims

During the last quarter of the 19th century, the British were able to relocate demoralized Maya groups in towns, mixing their numbers with refugees from Guatemala. Even so, the frontiers were not fully secure after the end of the Caste Wars until the late 1890s. In 1897, the Mexican and British governments signed a treaty, as a result of which Mexico formally renounced its claims on Belize.

Diplomatic problems with the neighboring Guatemalans were not so easily resolved. When it achieved independence in the 1820s, Guatemala picked up Spain's centuries-old claim to Belize, and pressed it enthusiastically. A treaty was signed between Britain and Guatemala in 1859 to settle the dispute, but Britain reneged on a key clause that entailed building a road between Guatemala City and the Atlantic coast (various routes were surveyed, but the price tag of £100,000 seemed a little steep just to secure Belize). Guatemala's threatened invasion and diplomatic pressure over the issue have recurred regularly throughout Belize's history right up to the present day.

Haggis in the tropics

As the 19th century drifted into the 20th, the racial amalgamation of Belizean society was proceeding apace. The Old Baymen families of landowners and merchants, with names like Hyde, Haylock, Usher and Fairweather, had largely been "creolized" through intermarriage. Although they lost their monopoly on land and trade, they went into the professions, training as barristers and doctors, as well as setting up the colony's first newspapers.

Meanwhile a steady flow of British expatriates formed a parallel high society, which ran local business. The majority of new arrivals were Scots, forming a clique with its own social clubs and considerable political clout. When a Scottish governor, Sir David Wilson, arrived in 1897, he was met by the local St Andrew's Club, who presented him with a haggis, sang *Land o' Cakes* and performed the highland fling. Every year, a Burns' Night was celebrated, reducing the congregation to tears.

For the bulk of the population, more humble celebrations were the norm. Anglican missionaries had managed to convert almost the entire black population and replace many African rituals. But Christmas was the time when old traditions reasserted themselves in the slums of Belize Town's South Side: work was suspended for over a week, rifles and pistols were shot off into the air and the drinking and dancing went on around the clock. Members of each African nation joined together to revive their homeland's dances and music. The excess of local energy was also channeled into an annual river regatta through Belize Town, in dories (dugouts) or larger pitpans, with crews of a dozen or so. Prizes and betting ran high, and the races had the advantage of improving crews' skills at bringing logs down-river.

Democrats and rioters

Although the remote society of British Honduras seemed to wallow in a heat-induced somnolence broken only by epidemics of yellow fever and cholera, social upheavals were brewing. The country was rapidly becoming the most backward in Central America. The alliance of white expatriates and old Creole families controlled political power in the form of a five-seat, appointed Legislative Council, often even out-voting the governor. There was no income or land tax in Belize, so no railways were built. Roads were no better than mule trails: it would take weeks to get from San Ignacio to Belize Town by land, so most commuters went by canoe. Agriculture, meanwhile, was in disarray or non-existent. Creoles traditionally disdained farming, and even the most basic foodstuffs needed to be imported from abroad.

A half-hearted attempt was made to include the masses in politics by electing a Belize Town Board in 1910. Unfortunately, thanks to a property qualification, only 282 of the 15,118 Belizeans were able to vote.

World War I brought matters to a head. In 1915 and 1916, some 600 loyal British Hondurans signed up to fight in Europe. But, instead of being sent to cover themselves in glory on the Western Front, this predominantly black contingent was packed off to dig ditches in the Middle East. Protests were met with the news that "it is against British tradition to employ aboriginal troops against a European enemy." Worse, when they arrived in Cairo and

---

Left: Belizean troops marching off to World War I.
Right: Charles Lindbergh's historic landing.

marched in to camp whistling *Rule Britannia*, they were stopped by British officers. One black soldier reports being asked: "Who gave you niggers authority to sing that? Clear out of this building – only British troops admitted here."

Troops returning to Belize in 1919 brought back the weight of these insults and an awareness of the connections between race, class and Empire. They could not help notice that no black soldiers were invited to tea at the golf club after a sports event held by the governor in their honor. Tensions finally broke out in a riot two weeks later. Soldiers marched down

Regent Street in Belize City (as the town was then known), smashing shop windows. Unpopular employers were beaten up. News spread, and the whole population joined in, police included. Some 3,000 people looted the town until dawn the next day, when a gunboat was called in to quell the disturbance.

Between the wars

The riots led directly to the foundation in Belize City of a branch of the United Negro Improvement Association, and a visit in 1921 by its Jamaican-born founder Marcus Mosiah Garvey. A passionate orator and skilled mass organizer, Garvey traveled around the Caribbean raising black political consciousness. At meetings he was careful to have *God Save the King* sung so as not to terrify the authorities unduly, but his speeches were sharp and damning. Black soldiers had fought to protect the Empire, he said, and received in return "a kick and a smile."

But Belizeans were unable to sustain the emotion for very long, and, when Garvey visited again in 1929, he was easily outshone by a visit from the US aviator Charles Lindbergh, fresh from his solo crossing of the Atlantic.

Meanwhile, Belize was about to be hit by the twin disasters of the Great Depression, which put the fragile economy into a tailspin, and a devastating hurricane. For generations, the citizens of Belize City had thought that any approaching hurricane or tidal wave would be spent on the Barrier Reef. Nothing terribly damaging had been done since 1787, so when a fully fledged hurricane finally arrived on the morning of Settlement Day, September 10, 1931, nobody took it seriously. Most of the population, including the governor, was involved in a commemorative parade, which was cut short by a deluge. Retiring to St John's College for patriotic songs, the Imperial Band was soon drowned out by the wind: velocity rose from 40 miles (70 km) an hour at noon to a peak of 132 mph (210 km/h) at 3pm.

Within minutes the sky had cleared and grateful citizens went to check the wreckage of their homes. Tragically, few realized that this was only the eye of the storm, and many were caught when the hurricane returned with even greater force. Whole houses were picked up and smashed by the wind; the Poor House with 41 inmates inside was washed out to sea; the city was flooded and the air was thick with flying sheets of corrugated iron, decapitating passers-by. Some 1,000 people were killed in the disaster, made worse by years of bungled relief work.

A depressed New World

The hurricane only added to Belize's growing economic mire. The chicle trade, which depended on a demand for chewing gum in the United States, was suffering; but, much more seriously, the mahogany trade had collapsed.

During his 1936 visit to Belize, the writer Aldous Huxley observed that a minor fluctuation in British middle-class taste had profoundly affected the lives of woodcutters in the remote forests. "When I was a boy there was hardly a single reputable family which did not eat off mahogany, sit on mahogany, sleep in mahogany," Huxley wrote in the slightly dotty book *Beyond the Mexique Bay*. "Mahogany was a symbol of economic solidity and moral worth. Alas, how quickly such sacred symbols can lose their significance! [Today] my friends eat off glass and metal, sit on metal and leather, sleep on beds that are almost innocent of enclosing bedsteads. Mahogany, in a word, is now hopelessly out of fashion." There, of course, Huxley's interest ended. He was no

Social and economic conditions were so bad that Belize's first labor union was formed, although the leader, Antonio Soberanis, was promptly jailed by the British authorities.

Other political organizations followed, usually starting off as motley public rallies in the sandy Central Park (dubbed "the Battlefield"). For the first time the possibility of independence from Britain was seriously discussed. A "Natives First" movement managed to gain seats on the Belize Town Board in 1939, and in 1941 a firebrand named Joseph Blisset formed a Belizean Labour Party. Amongst its more bizarre proposals was the expulsion of all

more interested in Belize than Stephens had been a century before, and headed straight for the Maya ruins in Guatemala.

The rise of union activism

Belizeans were starting to take a hand in improving their own affairs. The hurricane had left Belize City with a swamp-like appearance, its dirt streets looking like rivers, with sewers overflowing and water supplies regularly drying up. Dysentery, malaria and yellow fever returned as the colony's major causes of death.

Early views of Belize City's river front (**LEFT**); and the Swing Bridge (**ABOVE**).

whites, and Belize becoming the next state of the USA. This led to an all-out brawl on the Battlefield between Blisset's men and the largely white loyalist group called the Unconquerables. Blisset ended up in jail, as did several other more moderate nationalists.

Anti-colonialism was growing by the end of World War II and Governor Sir John Hunter, embarrassed by constantly having to throw Creole activists in prison, suggested to London that they give Belizeans the vote. The Colonial Office replied that they couldn't "go handing out self-government to all and sundry," and the scene for a long political struggle was set. ❑

MODERN BELIZE

For most of the 20th century, Belize was a disputed territory; but since attaining
independent nationhood, it has begun to reassess its place in the region

On September 21, 1981, the British Union Jack was lowered and the Belizean flag raised in its place. Belize had finally become an independent nation – but many Belizeans who attended the ceremonies or listened to them on the radio that night felt only apprehension at what the future would bring.

Many would have preferred to delay independence – not because they disagreed with the idea but because the 19th-century territorial dispute with Guatemala had not yet been settled. Despite assurances from the British government that they would maintain a garrison in Belize "for an appropriate period," Belizeans were nervous. Some even feared that, as soon as the international delegates and media left, Guatemalan troops would swarm over the nation's border.

Long road to independence

During World War II, many young Belizeans traveled outside their country for the first time. Several thousand fought with the British armed forces, and many more traveled to the United States to help in the war effort. When these young men returned to Belize after the war, they found there were no jobs for them, and that they had no say in running the colony's affairs. Thereafter anti-colonial feeling grew apace, fueled in 1949 when a currency devaluation in Britain resulted in the loss of half the value of the British Honduran dollar. The first serious political movements in favor of complete independence began to take shape. Prominent among them was the General Workers' Union which, under the leadership of George Price, in 1950 became the People's United Party (PUP).

One of the first positive results of this new pressure for change came in 1954, when a new constitution for the colony was brought in. For the first time, this gave all literate adults in

PRECEDING PAGES: the Supreme Court, Belize City.
LEFT: Garifuna Settlement Day.
RIGHT: over 40 percent of Belizeans are under 18, making it one of the region's most youthful nations.

Belize the right to vote. Previously, only some three percent of Belizeans had met the strict property qualifications required to vote; unsurprisingly, many felt that the country was being run like an enormous private plantation for the wealthy elite, many of whom were British or American expatriates.

The new constitution also set up a legislative council in which, for the first time, some of the members were elected by the populace, although the British-appointed governor continued to exercise final control. The PUP won eight of the nine elected seats in the first council. It was plain that the political make-up of the colony was changing fast.

Two events in the early 1960s further accelerated this process of change. The first was the natural disaster of Hurricane Hattie, which almost completely destroyed Belize City in 1961. Many Belizeans felt that the colonial authorities had not done enough either to prevent the disaster, or to assist the subsequent relief work. Plans were laid – and eventually realized – for the building of a new administrative capital in the interior, at Belmopan, on a site less likely to be affected by tropical storms. Nevertheless, the experience of Hurricane Hattie gave new impetus to the struggle for independence.

The second milestone of the decade was the constitutional conference held in London in 1963. George Price led the Belizean delegation to the conference, and by 1 January, 1964 he had negotiated a new constitution which

GUATEMALA'S CLAIM

Guatemala claimed Belizean home rule was "a flagrant violation of the sovereign rights of Guatemala," and threatened to go to war over the territory.

Diplomacy was fruitless; twice in the 1970s, Guatemala moved troops to the border and threatened to invade, only being dissuaded by reinforcements of British troops.

The case for Belizean independence was taken to international forums and the turning point came in 1980 when a United Nations resolution supporting independence finally put the wheels inexorably in motion. But controversy lasted right up to the moment of the transfer of power. The "Heads of Agreement," a document outlining proposed

granted the colony full internal self-government. Price himself became the first minister. He officially renamed the colony Belize, and brought in a new flag and a national anthem.

Guatemala protest overridden

Full independence was delayed by hesitancy on the part of the British government and aggressive noises from Guatemala. The latter had renewed its claims to British Honduras in the 1930s; in 1945, it had officially announced that "Belice" (as it is called in Spanish) was a Guatemalan province. When Belize gained self-government, Guatemala's military government broke off diplomatic relations with Britain.

points of negotiation with Guatemala, had caused rioting in Belize City in early 1981; Guatemala closed its border with Belize in protest against Belizean independence. Even so, the ceremony went ahead in September, and Belize became an independent part of the British Commonwealth.

Post-independence

Yet again, it was George Price and the PUP who were the dominant force in Belizean political life. Price became the newly independent country's first prime minister, and his party had a big majority in the new assembly. During the 1970s, however, opposition groups, supported mostly by the business sector, had joined together to challenge the PUP's dominance, and in 1973 they had formed the United Democratic Party (UDP). In 1984, in the first elections after independence, the UDP won a majority in the national assembly. The party's leader, the former schoolteacher Manuel Esquivel, became Belize's second prime minister.

Meanwhile, the sovereignty issue with Guatemala had still to be settled. In 1986 civilian rule was finally returned to Guatemala, and the succeeding civilian regimes showed much greater flexibility on the Belize issue than their military predecessors. In 1991 President Jorge

British-trained Belize Defence Force. With only around 1,000 soldiers, the BDF cannot hope to resist a serious invasion attempt from its much larger neighbor, but Mexico and Britain continue to act as deterrents to any military adventure of this kind.

The sovereignty dispute flared up again in 1999–2000. The Guatemalan Congress decreed that, although it recognized Belize's right to self-determination, this did not mean it renounced its claim to almost half of Belizean territory. Both sides agreed, however, to continue talking in an attempt to resolve their historic dispute peacefully.

Serrano finally announced that Belize's sovereignty would be recognized. Direct diplomatic relations with Britain were also re-established. Belize responded by passing legislation that limited its maritime claims in the Southern Toledo area; this offered Guatemala access to the Caribbean, which had always been one of its key demands.

In 1993, because of the new atmosphere of co-operation, Britain finally withdrew the last of its troops from the Belize garrison. Defense of the country was left in the hands of the small

---

LEFT: Salvadorean refugees collecting water.
ABOVE: police guarding a busload of young felons.

Party politics

Despite the continuing nervousness about Guatemala and numerous social and economic problems, most Belizeans today feel that life is pretty good. Since independence, the democratic process has proceeded smoothly and voter turnout is generally high. But Belizean politics remains a curious affair to outsiders.

Election campaigns operate at a personal level, with candidates handing out T-shirts and making small talk with their supporters. Politicians happily grant personal favors; many Belizeans think nothing of asking candidates for anything from a piece of land to schoolbooks for their children.

Two-party politics

George Price's PUP, now headed by Said Musa, and the United Democratic Party (UDP) are still the main political parties The latter won the elections held in 1984 and 1993, but conceded power to the PUP in 1998. Since then, party loyalty has continued to determine everything from jobs to building contracts; even minor issues become political in some way, and there is tremendous social pressure to choose sides.

This politicization of the workplace has meant that management of public services has been turned over after every change of government, while many development projects have been scrapped half-way through.

But, following the 1998 election result (*see Shock Election Result, below*), which left a tiny opposition in the House, the immediate concern of political observers was the health of Belize's democracy. (The same problem is simultaneously being faced elsewhere in the Caribbean, with the landslide in Belize preceding a series of other, similar defeats.)

The day after the Belizean election, Manuel Esquivel stepped down as the head of the UDP and his deputy Dean Barrow took over. He vowed to head a small but vocal minority opposition and rebuild the party after mass defections. The UDP has begun its task by attempting to attract women and youth, while protesting against just about everything tabled in the House of Representatives.

Meanwhile, for the ruling PUP their awesome mandate has brought tremendous pressure to live up to expectations. They promised 10,000 homes and 15,000 jobs and the voters keep asking for a tally. Both parties are now all too conscious of the power of the people to vote them in, and sweep them out again, all the while smiling and accepting favors, just as they did in 1998.

Cultural loyalties

Following waves of immigration from other Central American nations in the 1980s and early 1990s, some creoles are deeply concerned about what they call the "hispanicization of Belize." As a result, there has been a fair amount of "alien bashing" in the newspapers and on radio call-in programs. But most

SHOCK ELECTION RESULT

The Belize people have opted for a change of government in every general election since 1984, but the change that swept through in 1998 was completely unexpected and sent a powerful message to both parties: the people are in charge.

In the months leading up to the August 27 election it was anyone's guess who would win. The ruling UDP, led by Prime Minister Manuel Esquivel, appeared confident. He felt that his tightening of the economic belt, while uncomfortable, was for the best, and believed the people were with him and would vote red. His ministers ruled their respective fiefdoms believing they had no serious challengers, and made policies that indicated they planned to be around for a while.

Their complacency was shaken to its foundations on election day, however, when the streets became a sea of blue T- shirts and banners. The results were astounding; out of a possible 29 parliamentary seats, the UDP had only won three, while the PUP, even without the legendary George Price, had swept the polls, taking 26 seats.

Even party leader Said Musa, who knew the PUP had run a well-organized campaign, was astonished. He admitted: "It is an extraordinary mandate from the people of Belize."

Belizeans have adopted a wait-and-see attitude, hoping the recent Central American immigrants will follow the pattern set by previous immigrant groups who have embraced the Belizean way of life. Nevertheless, since it emerged that mestizos now outnumber creoles, the new demographic realities have shaken up Belize's traditional self-image as a Caribbean nation that is only geographically part of Latin America.

In truth, Belize's ties to the islands of the Caribbean have been more a matter of tradition and sentiment than actual substance. It shares a British heritage, including the Westminster model of government and British-style legal system, with other Caribbean islands. Cultural connections are also still strong: Belizean youth look to Jamaica in particular as a source of mystical and musical inspiration, often sporting the "Dred" colors of gold, green and red. Videos of the carnivals in Trinidad and Tobago also provide examples of costumes and music which Belizeans are beginning to adapt for their own September celebrations.

Trading partners

But these connections are all second-hand. With no direct flights to the islands, visiting them is expensive and complicated. Except for a few politicians, media people and students attending the University of the West Indies in Jamaica, it is rare to meet a Belizean who has been to a Caribbean country.

Political and economic ties are also weak. To promote integration, Belize became a member of the Caribbean Community (CARICOM), an alliance of Caribbean nations. But many complain that Belize benefits little: few of the other member nations are interested in Belizean goods – most seem to produce similar products – but Belizeans are still expected to "buy Caribbean."

In recent years, it has been the private sector rather than government that has begun turning to Latin America. Guatemalan manufacturers are eager to trade with Belize, which they see as a stepping stone to the Caribbean, and the need for bilingualism is becoming more apparent in education.

LEFT: a warm welcome, if not always a smooth ride.
RIGHT: Belizeans are learning the skills of giving service to visitors with a smile.

The politics of tourism

One of the most significant developments since Belizean independence has been the dramatic rise in tourism. While Belize hopes not to repeat the mistakes of other small Caribbean countries, which have allowed their landscapes and cultures to be devastated, it still hopes to make an increase in tourism one of its main economic goals.

Belizean tourism is still in its infancy. The Belize Tourism Industry Association is more like a family association of bed-and-breakfast establishments than an alliance of large hotel chains. The Belize Tourist Board, the govern-

ment arm of the industry, has failed to maintain consistent policies and is only now actively promoting the country internationally.

So far, government duty and tax exemptions have been aimed squarely at attracting foreign investors. As a result, a huge number of the country's new hotels and "lodges" are owned by foreigners, especially North Americans, who have been able to set up ventures for far less outlay than is required by their Belizean counterparts. At times it seems as if the remoter parts of the country's coastline have been colonized entirely by foreigners – a situation that has, not surprisingly, caused a certain amount of local resentment.

But, rather than opposing tourism per se, Belizean nationalists now want to ensure that local operators benefit from it. After all, the cat is already out of the bag: the cruise ships are beginning to come and the public is starting to accept that Belize's new role as a tourist destination is an inevitable development – one that may even be profitable for them.

Niche markets sought

Although some tour operators would like to see a huge increase in tourist numbers, others argue that Belize should not try to accommodate mass tourism. There is concern that unlimited amounts of tourist traffic would put too much strain on the environment and the culture: it is arguable that visitors to Belize are attracted by its small-scale feel and absence of mass-market international resorts, so different from other tropical destinations.

In an attempt to lure visitors from flashier destinations like Cancún in Mexico – which can bring in tourists at a fraction of the cost – local operators have begun to promote Belize as an "ecotourism" destination. Whether this is just a convenient buzz-word or represents a long-term commitment to the environment is yet to be determined, but for now, the campaign

CREATING A SERVICE CULTURE

Leading members of the tourism industry in Belize are doing what they can to make visitors comfortable and happy. However, the poor quality of service in Belize has been a real problem and is still not solved. The indifferent attitude shown by hotel and restaurant employees is so pervasive that the hardest part of traveling in Belize can be trying to get the check after you eat. In response, a few establishments have resorted to bringing in staff from abroad, or conducting classes in hospitality management. Training of tour guides and other personnel involved in the industry has helped considerably, but there is still room for improvement.

has put Belize on the international map and generated considerable local appreciation for the environment.

One trend that is worrying environmental groups is the phenomenal growth in the number of visitors arriving by cruise ship – up from virtually zero to 500,000 in the last few years.

Another important initiative is the Mundo Maya project, an attempt by tourism operators to join forces with their counterparts in other Central American republics – Mexico, Guatemala and Honduras – on the basis of a shared Maya heritage. ❑

ABOVE: businessman in Punta Gorda.

Refugees

When Belize became independent in 1981, it was in a much more fortunate position than its Central American neighbors. In Nicaragua, soon after the Sandinistas had taken power in a revolution in 1979, the country was rent by civil war – with the "contra" counter-revolutionary forces, financed by the Reagan administration in Washington, trying to overthrow the Sandinistas. The Nicaraguan war spilled over into Honduras, creating instability there. Meanwhile, in El Salvador, guerrillas tried to repeat the Sandinista victory, but were fiercely resisted by the armed forces. And in Guatemala, where an armed struggle had been going on, with varying intensity, since the 1960s, the army took the war to the countryside. The main victims were the peasants, whose lives and livelihoods were threatened on all sides.

Inevitably, many of these people were attracted to the political and economic stability of Belize, and at first the refugees were given a warm welcome. In the 1980s, the Belizean economy was expanding out of its traditional sectors and there was a need for cheap labor in agro-industry – such as citrus plantations – in which the urban creoles had little experience. Unlike in Mexico, refugees arriving in Belize were not obliged to live in camps; many of them not only worked in agriculture, but managed to buy land or to set up in small businesses. Their children were offered free schooling, often in both English and Spanish, and they were given access to health care.

Many of the immigrants had crossed the border illegally, but there were few concerted attempts to discover who they were or to send them back home. However, when a national census in 1991 revealed that between 30,000 and 40,000 Spanish-speaking immigrants had arrived – almost a fifth of the total population – Belizeans were taken aback. More than three-quarters of the new arrivals were from El Salvador; most of the others were Guatemalans. For the first time in the history of the country, according to the census, Spanish speakers represented more than half of the nation, whereas creole Belizeans made up only a third.

This situation led to something of a backlash. The Belizean authorities made more of an effort to check up on immigrants, and to return those with-

RIGHT: refugees queuing for work outside a plantation in Orange Walk District.

out papers to their own countries. The end of the civil wars in Nicaragua, El Salvador and finally Guatemala also meant that some of the newcomers willingly went back. But employment opportunities and wages remained considerably better in Belize, so they had little incentive to return home.

The influence of these newcomers is immediately obvious, particularly in the south of Belize. The people in the countryside are predominantly hispanic; many shops have signs in Spanish, and most people listen to Mexican or Guatemalan radio. The continued presence of the refugees has led to a wide-ranging debate on the future of the country. As creoles continue to emigrate to the

United States, some politicians have called for Belize to recognize that it is only a small territory which needs to foster links with its immediate land neighbors rather than continue to think of itself as part of a community of Caribbean nations.

Others are still suspicious of Guatemala, which has always laid claim to the territory, and want to discourage any further immigration from there or other Central American countries. They stress that Belize should continue to strengthen its ties with the English-speaking world. But throughout its history, Belize has received and absorbed wave after wave of newcomers – from the Baymen to the Garifunas, from the British to the Mennonites – and it is likely to do so once more. ❑

THE BELIZEANS

In spite of the influence of US culture and the economic lure of emigration to America,
Belizeans of all racial origins remain loyal to their own small country

For most Belizeans, the presence of many different ethnic groups in the country is as much a national treasure as the barrier reef or Maya ruins. Belize is not so much a melting pot of cultures as a salad where each element lends a certain flavor to the mix.

From an early age, Belizeans are encouraged to feel proud of their own racial traditions and appreciate those of others. "Cultural presentations," displaying the music, dance and dress of the elements of Belizean society, are a regular part of primary school activities, community celebrations and political rallies. In the words of Belizean artist Phillip Lewis:
"A tink a si wan new Belize weh di creole man, di mestizo, di Garifuna, an di Maya, no separate as a lis dem but instead all da Belizeans."
"I think I see a new Belize where the creole, the mestizo, the Garifuna and the Maya, are not separated as I have listed them, but united as Belizeans."
Or, as the creole saying goes, *All a we mek Belize* – we all make up Belize.

Generations of racial mixing have made it impossible to describe the "typical" Belizean – only a typical room full of Belizeans, whose physical characteristics range from the very darkest to the lightest skin tones, and every imaginable hair and eye color. Even within a single family there is likely to be considerable variation, since the grandparents usually have ancestors from several continents. But, despite the blurring of racial lines, most Belizeans identify themselves with a particular ethnic group.

The search for identity

Belizeans have long described themselves as "a Caribbean nation in Central America," for they have more in common with the distant islands of the Caribbean than their next-door neighbors. This is because Belize has a British

PRECEDING PAGES: greeting the day in Gales Point; Maya family from San Ignacio; Toledo food stand.
LEFT: creole girl.
RIGHT: one of the old-timers.

rather than Spanish heritage; English is the official language and much of the population is black creole, descended from African slaves and British settlers. There have always been the Maya and mestizos (those of mixed indian and Spanish descent) as in the rest of Central America, but historically the creole culture has been

dominant – making Belize's legal, political and educational systems closer to those of the English-speaking Caribbean, while its music, dance, and folklore share many African elements found dotted around the islands.

Things are changing, however. To the surprise of many, a recent census has shown that the creoles now make up less than 30 percent of the total population and the ethnic balance has shifted in favor of the mestizos, who now represent almost 50 percent of all Belizeans. Large numbers of creole Belizeans have been leaving for the United States, while mestizo refugees and immigrants flooded in from war-ravaged Central America in the 1980s. Although peace was restored in the 1990s, immigration from other parts of Central America continued – with the immigrants seeking jobs and land for *milpa* (small-scale cornfield) farming.

These incomers have been adding to the numbers of Spanish speakers who settled in northern Belize in the 1860s, fleeing the bloody Caste Wars in Mexico. The mestizo families who are longer established in Belize mostly live around Orange Walk Town and Corozal and speak both Spanish and creole, or a Spanish which is heavily creolized. They feel they have little in common with the recent immigrants, referred to by most Belizeans as "aliens." Some

INDIANS FROM THE EAST

East Indians comprise only 3.5 percent of the population of Belize, but like the Garifuna they have enjoyed disproportionate success, becoming prominent in Belizean business. They first arrived in the 1860s as indentured laborers on sugar plantations established by former Confederate Americans; their cultural identities soon dwindled, but East Indian physical traits are visible in almost every ethnic group in Belize. A second wave of East Indians arrived in the 1970s and set up as shop-owners in Belize City; this group still makes every attempt to preserve its customs – even traveling back to India to arrange suitable marriages.

creoles are concerned that the increase in mestizos will mean the erosion of creole culture; others believe the new arrivals will adopt the creole language and traditions just as many other immigrant groups have in the past.

Ancient and new inhabitants

Although they represent only 8 percent of the population, the modern-day Maya trace their lineage back to Belize's original inhabitants. There are three distinct Maya groups, the largest being the Mopan, the Kekchi and the Yucatec. But like indigenous people elsewhere, the Maya are on the lowest rungs of Belize's socio-economic ladder. Most are subsistence farmers who live in remote villages and maintain a traditional lifestyle. Many exist outside the official economy, without access to national health care services or education.

The Garifuna were greeted with prejudice and suspicion when they first arrived in Belize in the early 1800s. A mixture of escaped African slaves and Carib indians, they ended up in Dangriga on the south coast after an epic 200-year persecution by European powers *(see Garifuna Odyssey, page 252)*. They make up only 7 percent of Belize's population, yet they have had a great impact on the country, figuring prominently in the professions and the arts.

Adding to the mix are East Indians, Syrians, Lebanese, Chinese and Taiwanese (the latter the latest wave of immigrants), as well as the distinctive Mennonites from the USA and Canada *(see The Mennonites, pages 77–79)*.

Imperfect harmony

Belize is not free from racial prejudice. A visitor might be told by creoles that the Central American "aliens" are very violent and therefore responsible for Belize's rise in crime; mestizos often dismiss creoles as lazy folk who would rather steal than work for a living. There is also resentment in some quarters of the "Chiney", the Taiwanese and Hong Kong nationals, who some claim are "taking over Belize." But these same people who have bad-mouthed other ethnic groups will, moments later, proudly tell the visitor that, unlike other places in the world, there is no prejudice in Belize and everyone lives together in peace – conveniently forgetting the numerous violent attacks and shootings of East Asian shop-keepers by street thugs.

Nevertheless, most Belizeans value racial harmony. Being creole, Maya, mestizo or even Taiwanese is still second to being Belizean, and everyone has the sense that they are helping to "build the nation." With a national population of less than 250,000, tolerance is not only desirable, it is absolutely necessary.

Belize has the intimate, personal feel of a small town. Even in Belize City, strangers usually ask each other how they are related to friends with the same name, or where they attended school. Such familiarity makes it hard to keep things private and gossiping is a favorite pastime. But for most Belizeans, their small society is an advantage: it guarantees them a warm welcome wherever they go in Belize.

Home and abroad

Even so, many Belizeans have never left their villages, and residents of Belize City rarely go out to the cayes or neighboring districts. Because of this, they tend to be very absorbed in local happenings, and almost everything in Belize has a political significance. Party affiliation is important, since everything from buying land to being hired for a job may depend on which political party you supported in the last election. Domestic news is avidly discussed, but there is almost no interest in what is happening in the outside world unless it has a direct bearing on Belize. Foreign films and television programs that mention Belize are always viewed with excitement, as are travel or wildlife articles on Belize in American or European magazines.

But not everyone sees Belize as the perfect home. An unemployment rate of close to 20 percent, low wages and a high cost of living have prompted many people – mostly creoles – to head north in search of a better life. Over the past two decades, thousands of young Belizeans have emigrated, both legally and illegally, to major cities in the United States. Many of them have left small children behind to be raised by grandmothers or aunts. The majority of emigrants are skilled workers and professionals, including teachers and nurses, whose departure is a "brain drain" from Belize which leaves it the poorer.

LEFT AND RIGHT: faces of Belize – despite the drift to the US, most migrant Belizeans still dream of coming home again, one day.

Almost everyone in Belize has relatives in the United States who send home money, clothing and other goods. Access to American television has made Belizean young people crave not only US fashions and music, but a lifestyle well beyond their means. Many young men seem fascinated by the criminal activity and violence they see in movies and music videos. Street gangs modeled on those in urban America have sprung up all over Belize City, complete with drug trafficking, drug abuse and drive-by shootings – often carried out on bicycles. Many wonder whether the search for a better life has cost too much.

The Bel-Ams

Belizeans living abroad don't always have it easy either. Although there are now more Belizeans living in the US than in Belize, they are still small minorities in the cities where they live. They may have to decide for the first time to which ethnic group they belong. Are they African Americans? Latinos? Are they "Mixed" or "Other"? If they stay in Belizean communities there is pressure to conform; if they strike out on their own they feel cut off from the homeland. And no matter how well Belizean-Americans do financially, or how well they adapt to the North American lifestyle, Belize always calls them home – eventually.

They generally make the pilgrimage for the September Independence celebrations, Christmas or Easter. You'll recognize the "Bel-Ams" immediately in the departure lounge of the airport. Both the women and men have the latest designer clothes, gold jewelry on all exposed body parts, carry-on bags that will never make it through the gate and, of course, an exaggerated "Ameriken" accent. Despite the loud talking and laughing and bragging about their success in the US, they can't wait to touch down in Belize, who put down roots in the United States and live there for decades will admit to a secret dream of returning home, "to retire, maybe start a little business."

> **NO PLACE LIKE HOME**
>
> Local people enjoy making connections with American visitors, who will often be told: "I used to live in the States, but I jus felt locked up, no freedom, I jus like "mi li Belize."

A relaxed lifestyle

Despite the recent influence of American culture, most Belizeans are still proud of their own culture – and by no means enamored of the US work ethic. Belize's work environment is much more relaxed than in industrialized countries, and people think nothing of dropping by

where everyone recognizes their names and will feed them local food and take them for a night on the town. Even teenagers born and raised in the US know there is something special about their parents' homeland; just give them a week and they will be trying to learn creole and asking for hot johnny cakes.

Hundreds of Belizeans announce every year that they are "goin a States". They get visas (or plan how to get there "through the back"), quit their jobs, sell their worldly goods, have farewell parties and go. They generally return six months to a year later, then, when their circumstances in Belize continue to frustrate them, they pack up and go back again. Even those

a friend's workplace to chat for a few minutes or stepping out of the office to run errands or to go to the bank. Offices and schools close for lunch, when many families sit down together for the big meal of the day.

Belizeans value leisure time and there is no shortage of public and bank holidays. Even though many have to work a half-day on Saturday, Friday is the preferred night to go out, and any excuse is enough for a get-together. House parties with lots of food and drinks rave on until early the next morning and usually don't end until the liquor runs out.

Sundays are still sacred in Belize. The dominant religion is Catholic, although other evangelical Christian denominations have established a following in almost every town and village. While some reserve the day for worship, for others Sunday is a time for family or a trip to the cayes. For creoles, no Sunday is complete without the traditional stewed chicken, rice and beans and potato salad, washed down with koolaid or another soft drink.

Verbal culture

Belizeans don't read much, perhaps because only a few local authors and poets have published slim volumes of their works, but this doesn't mean Belizeans don't like words *(see*

can get the order correct even if one of the diners has changed his mind several times.

Belizeans also like to invent names for each other. Some people are so well known by their nicknames that their real names are unknown to their friends. Some reflect the person's appearance ("Big George," "Lagrahead," like the loggerhead turtle, or "Red Boy"). Others, like "January Baboon," seem downright insulting, although they are meant to express affection.

Above all, Belizeans are obsessed with giving ordinary conversations sexual connotations, even in the workplace. What North Americans might denounce as sexual harassment is viewed

Creole as She is Spoken, pages 82–83). It is because Belize creole still has no standardized written form – although the "Bileez Kriol Projek" has produced a glossary and translated some folk tales and books of the Bible – that people tend to rely on their ears rather than their eyes for information. As a result, Belizeans are often capable of memorizing astonishingly large amounts of information. A waitress may be serving 10 people at one table, but she won't write a single thing down – and a good waitress

as great fun by most Belizeans, and women see it as their obligation to put any man making unwanted advances in his place. A man might suggestively comment on how delicious a woman's meal looks, how she never gives him any of her food, or how he has something which could help relieve her headache, and from there the repartee begins.

A world of superstition

Although Belize has squarely entered the modern world, many traditions linger. Belizeans, whether they admit it or not, are a superstitious lot: there are beliefs and omens pertaining to just about every aspect of life. Those who are

LEFT: young bread vendors, St. George's Caye.
ABOVE: girls dressed up in their Sunday best for church, in Punta Gorda.

having a hard time, or who face numerous disappointments, often fear they have been "*obeahed*," (fallen victim to someone's black magic), and people in love often consult tarot card readers or write their beloved's name on candles.

The survival of such Africanisms as black magic *(obeah)* and the folklore of both the Maya and European peoples have given Belize a rich variety of magical explanations for everyday events. Not only are Belizeans wary of ladders and black cats, but they also look out for Tataduhende, the little bearded bushman who has his feet on backwards (so that you'll think he's coming when he's really going) and

Llorona, the weeping woman who lures drunken men to their death.

A wealth of pseudo-scientific beliefs relate to medical conditions, pregnancy and birth, and even the most common household activities have magical overtones. Most housewives, for instance, will never sweep all the dirt out of the house (thereby loosing all their luck) and a dropped spoon or fork means that visitors are coming. A guest who overstays his welcome can be made to leave by turning a broom upside down behind a door. Good fortune is continually being sought and dreams are considered a reliable source for lucky boledo (lottery) numbers.

BELIEFS ABOUT BABIES

A pregnant woman is besieged with superstitious warnings of damage to her unborn child if she eats certain foods (conch or pork is said to cause instant death and eating hot pepper will give the baby "spots"). On the other hand, if the expectant mother does not get a food that she craves, it is said that the child will have a birthmark in the shape of that food. After the baby is born, there is constant vigilance lest a malicious person gives it the "evil eye," and menstruating women are not allowed near the newborn. Tickling a baby is believed to cause it to stammer when it grows up and looking at a child from above will make it cross-eyed.

Traditions of machismo

Other relics of the Belizean past are less picturesque. In many ways, Belize is still a man's country and swaggering macho attitudes and customs go back to the days of logging and piracy. The need for constant excitement makes many men feel incapable of accepting responsibility or forming lasting attachments.

Married men work to support more than one family or numerous "sweethearts." Others hardly work at all, preferring to "catch and kill," or make money only when they really need it. The old tradition of "spreeing," or going on a drinking binge at the end of the logging season, is a regular habit for men, who may spend their entire paycheck in one night on liquor for friends.

Belizean women often feel that they don't have any choice but to accept men's infidelity and carousing. Many accept common-law marriages or spend years being a married man's sweetheart. Fifty percent of all children in Belize are born outside of wedlock and it is not uncommon to find a single mother who has several children by different fathers. A woman with few or no children is pitied: children are seen as an insurance against a lonely old age and a compensation for a hard life. With fathers largely absent from the domestic scene, grand-

A young nation

Belize has one of the youngest populations in the world, with more than 50 percent under the age of 18. There are many absentee parents, so a small number of adults is responsible for the care, education and training of the country's future nation builders. Crime, child abuse and unemployment are certainly cause for great concern, yet it is easier to be optimistic about the future when so many of the nation's citizens are young, energetic and have little or no memory of a more restrictive colonial past.

While foreign aid agencies help provide the money for development, people power is begin-

mothers and aunts help with childcare, and cousins are often raised as closely as siblings.

Women make up a large percentage of the workforce. Although they tend to occupy traditional jobs like teaching, nursing and secretarial work, increasing numbers are obtaining degrees and becoming managers, or entering the legal and medical professions. Others work from their homes, taking in washing or baking pastries. Women's wages tend to be very low and few receive any form of child support.

LEFT: sugar cane workers, descendants of Mexican immigrants, in Corozal District.
ABOVE: Garifuna boy from Stann Creek District.

ning to come from Belize's young professionals. Although far too many stay in the US after graduating because of higher salaries and better opportunities, the old desire to "build Belize" pulls quite a few back. These Belizeans are already making a difference in just about every sector of the economy, and they are helping to change an attitude of "we can't do that in Belize" to "we could do that in Belize."

Unlike the visitor to Belize, who may think the country's biggest potential lies in its natural wonders, those who live here still believe, despite the increase in tourist dollars, that the real treasures of their country are its ethnic diversity and youthful population. ❑

THE MENNONITES

Belize's undeveloped interior has provided an ideal home for this hardworking and intensely private community

They stand out in any Belizean crowd: blond, blue-eyed men in denim overalls and cowboy hats, their skin glowing an almost albino pink; severe women whose outfits – ankle-length, long-sleeved frocks and wide-brimmed hats tied down with black scarves – seem in outright defiance of the tropical heat. Polite and reserved, they hang back from the general hubbub, talking quietly amongst themselves. If you should overhear, the language isn't Spanish, English or creole, but guttural German.

The Mennonite settlers of Belize are part of a resilient religious sect that traces its roots back to 16th-century Netherlands. Starting off as an obscure Anabaptist group during the Reformation, they took their name from a Dutch priest Menno Simons. Like the Amish of Pennsylvania, to whom they are distantly connected, Mennonites seek to exist in isolated farming communities without modern technology (calling themselves, at times, *die Stillen im Lande*, the Unobtrusive Ones). They reject state interference in their lives and are firm pacifists.

From Russia to the tropics

Belize is only the latest stop in the Mennonites' three-century search for a homeland. Their more radical beliefs – particularly a refusal to bear arms or pay certain taxes – led to persecution, driving them from the Netherlands to Prussia in the 1600s, then on to southern Russia. When the Russian government revoked the Mennonites' exemption from military conscription in the 1870s, they packed up again and headed for Canada, setting up their closed, autonomous colonies again in the wildernesses of Alberta and Saskatchewan.

Even here the modern world intruded: after World War I, the Canadian government demanded that only English be taught in Men-

nonite schools and, spurred on by anti-German feeling, reconsidered the conscription exemption. Again many Mennonites moved on, this time to the barren highlands of Mexico – only to find in the mid-1950s that the Mexican government wanted to include them in their social security program.

The Mennonites were running out of far-flung frontiers to settle when they decided to try out Belize (then British Honduras). A delegation soon established that this was virgin territory, and that the British authorities were more than enthusiastic to have them: the Mennonites were renowned for their farming skills and industriousness, and the colony had virtually no agriculture. Local creoles had always held farming in complete contempt, and even eggs were imported from abroad.

In 1958, the first of some 3,500 Mennonites began arriving in Belize. Although the Mennonites had largely been able to maintain their religion through their endless odyssey, there

PRECEDING PAGE AND LEFT: strictly traditional Mennonites shun modern technology and travel by horsepowered transport only.
RIGHT: family life on the farm.

were still many divisions within the ranks – particularly on the matters of language and the use of technology. The most conservative groups spoke German and used only those farming implements available in the early 1900s (when an edict had been passed against the use of the combustion engine and against modern science in general).

More progressive Mennonite groups in Canada, meanwhile, had learned English, and were happy to use tractors and fertilizer on their farms.

No Cameras Please!

Like the Amish in Pennsylvania, strict Mennonites object strenuously to having their photographs taken, as they believe that no memory should be left of a person after they die.

although new arrivals maintained the numbers.

Today the Mennonites have ironed out their initial problems and are the most successful farmers in Belize. In fact, they were the first to produce fresh milk in the country and are still Belize's largest suppliers of eggs and poultry (Mennonites can be spotted running a stall in the central market in Belize City every morning).

The Mennonites are also highly accomplished furniture makers, constructing some splendid carved mahogany

Agricultural success story

The progressives – a group called the Kleine Gemeinde, who bought land around Spanish Walk near San Ignacio – soon became successful in Belize, clearing their land and starting production. A more conservative group, called the Altkolonier, purchased a large area of wilderness at Blue Creek on the corner of Mexico and Guatemala, with a breakaway contingent settling near Orange Walk Town at Shipyard and Richmond Hill (where, coincidentally, US Confederate soldiers had tried to settle a century before). They suffered from language barriers and the difficulty of hand-clearing their land: almost half left within a few years,

chairs and tables for sale and export. Some artisans have even branched off from furniture making to home construction. Mennonite contractors build small wooden bungalows for a few thousand dollars for lower-income Belizeans, and they also use the latest computer software to create plans for more lavish homes for wealthy residents. Not only can they put together a custom design, they will construct the house, build the driveway leading up to it and dredge a canal in the back for the boat.

Prosperity has brought danger to the Mennonite community, however, with some becoming targets for criminals. There have been hold-ups, murders and even kidnappings.

Undeterred, the Mennonites of Spanish Lookout were among the first to take boatloads of supplies and food to victims of Hurricane Mitch in Honduras in 1998. They regularly hold summer camps for deaf children from all over Belize and have recently been asked by the government to open a school for the deaf.

Breaking ranks

Even so, there are still serious divisions within the Mennonite Church and splinter groups regularly form and are absorbed. The progressives have relaxed their traditional dress, use power tools and drive pick-up trucks, while their vil-

the pale for strict Mennonites) in a remote community of a dozen families, linked to the highway only by a rough dirt road. Despite the isolation, Freisen and others are happy to meet and talk with interested visitors ("We want to show what Christian people do," he explains).

Communal society

The straightforward community works rather like a 19th-century version of communist society. "We believe that too much property, like too much beer, is not good for one," says Freisen. Strict Mennonites are accepted from any quarter (one member was brought up in Bolivia),

lages look little different from places in the US Midwest. But hard-liners can still be seen on the highways driving their horse-drawn buggies, the men with close-cropped hair and flowing Santa Claus beards, the women modestly dressed in black to ward off prying eyes.

Typical of these conservative Mennonites is William Freisen, an elder at Barton Creek – a break-away group from Spanish Lookout that became disgusted with progressive ways. Freisen lives with his wife, 10 sons and three daughters (contraception is definitely beyond

LEFT: Mennonites taking a boat ride to Lamanai.
ABOVE: some tasks are still timelessly manual.

and disputes are settled by popular vote.

The family's wooden house, a combination of a European dwelling and a thatched Maya hut, is without electricity or telephone. Angered by the lapses of progressive Mennonites, Freisen says steadfastly: "We *know* that the world moved before machines and electricity." The law is strictly observed: even when one of his family falls sick, Freisen drives them by buggy to the highway – although there a car will be hailed to take the patient to a hospital.

And is this the last stop in the Mennonites' seemingly endless peregrinations? Freisen shrugs philosophically. "Belize has been good to us, but if this changes, we leave." ❑

CREOLE AS SHE IS SPOKEN

Creole is not to be confused with pidgin English – it's a complex spoken language with grammatical rules and a fruity turn of phrase

Belizeans have a proverb to describe a person who is self-important: *Fowl caca white an tink e lay egg* – A chicken shits white and thinks she has laid an egg. This illustrates that the official language of Belize may be English but, as any visitor soon realizes, the language of the street is rather different.

An example from everyday speech: *Da weh da lee bwai mi di nyam?* ("What was that little boy eating?") Here, *Weh da lee bwai* can be traced back to the English "what that little boy," but the rest is unintelligible to English speakers. *Da* means "is." *Nyam* is an African word for "eat," from the vegetable yam, while *mi* and *di* are grammatical words indicating the past imperfect tense.

There was a time when the creole languages of the world (and there are dozens in the Caribbean region alone, as well as the version in Louisiana) were regarded as "uncivilized" or "broken" speech – imperfect, childish copies of the colonial languages from which they were derived, whether English, French, Portuguese or Spanish. Today, with more scholarly and objective scrutiny, creole languages are being recognized for what they are: new linguistic creations with fully-fledged, highly nuanced grammatical systems. The process of standardization in many creole-speaking countries is well under way, with grammars and dictionaries being commissioned and panels of scholarly experts working on linguistic problems.

In Belize, the Bileez Kriol Projek has spent several years developing standard spellings for all the words Belizeans toss into the air and catch again so freely. But, although it has produced a small glossary, translated several books of the Bible and written down a few folk tales, its system is not gaining widespread acceptance. One member of the project writes a "kriol" column in a local newspaper, but sad to say most people give up trying to read it after the first or second paragraph. Belizeans may speak creole, but they read English.

Linguistic hybrid

In Belize, the creole people are the products of centuries of inter-breeding between the British colonizers and their West African slaves. The language, Belize creole, is the linguistic result of this meeting: English (including many English and Scottish regional dialects) blended with the diverse language groups of West Africa.

Belize creole's nearest relative is Jamaican creole, also based on English, although the two are quite different. Adding to the Belizean mixture are words from Spanish (*goma* for a hangover, for example) and others from the language of the Miskito indians of Nicaragua (*konka* for a house fly, amongst others).

Although Belize creole was the creation of the creole people, today it is far from their exclusive property. It is the country's *lingua franca*, spoken by mestizos, East Indians, the Maya and Garifunas. To speak it is part of being Belizean – so much so that the US Peace Corps has decided to teach creole to its volunteers. Many travelers have also taken quick courses.

A good place to start solving the mystery of Belize creole – in which hundreds of English words lurk but meanings of phrases are lost in the different grammar – is a small book called *Creole Proverbs of Belize*. Proverbs are a storehouse of folk wit and wisdom in any language and Belize creole proverbs are an amusing way of getting to understand local cadences, as well as customs. For example, one translates: "The man who has lifted his horse's tail knows that the bottom is red," and

A FUN LANGUAGE

Everyone in Belize understands English but it's fun to learn a bit of creole. After all, saying a person went "bliggity blam boom, boff!" is so much more expressive than "he slipped and fell."

– so that when music-playing boxes began to appear in nightclubs and whorehouses, they were naturally referred to as "jook-boxes" or, as it is usually spelled, "juke-boxes." Another Belize creole word still current in the southern US is *pinda* (spelled "pinder" in American English), an old African word for peanuts.

The future of creole

There has been some debate about teaching Belize creole in schools, but the proponents seem to be losing the battle.

another goes: "The bull knows on what part of the barbed wire to rub its balls."

Some Belize creole words have infiltrated the standard English language. The word *jook*, for example, is used by all Belizeans to mean "stick," although its secondary meaning is "copulate." The term migrated to many southern black communities of the United States, where a brothel was often called a "jook-house"

PRECEDING PAGES: chewing the fat.
LEFT: Creole cool speaks louder than words.
ABOVE: although creole remains the most popular spoken dialect on the streets, most schools prefer to teach written English and Spanish.

Most of the parents surveyed by the Education Department, and even the children themselves, seem to feel their future success will depend on their ability to converse in an internationally recognized language such as standard English. There is also increasing demand for Spanish courses, and Spanish has recently been put on the curricula of all primary schools. This is due, of course, to the increasing Hispanicization of the country.

Yet creole is set to remain the common dialect: from the Mennonite carpenter to the Salvadorean fruit vendor, and even the new Taiwanese immigrant (after around three months), everyone knows how to "wap wa li creole." ❑

HOLIDAYS AND MUSIC

Two national days in September, plus Garifuna and Christian holidays,
are celebrated with music, dancing and costume parades

You'll never find Belizeans sitting politely through a concert or throwing a party without dancing. In Belize, music is an irresistible invitation to move, and any social event without a live band, or at least a disc jockey and his "box," is hardly worth attending.

While some radio stations and nightclubs play a seemingly endless barrage of American pop and country music, there is also a healthy dose of Caribbean reggae, soca and dance hall. Rap and variations on the style are favored by the youth, but adults and most folks in the border areas also enjoy Latin American ballads and salsa beats. But as much as Belizeans enjoy these foreign imports, they love home-grown rhythms too. Belizean musicians can always find a loyal following and creative – if not financial – success.

Punta Rock, based on traditional Garifuna music and lyrics with some contemporary electronic alterations, has won the hearts of every ethnic group in Belize, and some artists are now on CD and perform in US and European cities. Like the older-style Garifuna music, Punta Rock lyrics cover topics from social commentary and humorous jibes at community members to the loss of a loved one. No one seems to mind that they are in a language that only a small part of the population understands – everyone tries to sing along anyway.

Local groups also specialize in reggae and soca, and several bands from Mexican-influenced northern Belize employ a salsa or merengue beat. Traditional music is still popular: creoles can claim *brukdown* and a large number of original folk songs, while the Maya and mestizos occasionally explore their musical roots in the few villages that still have a marimba band.

With so many holidays on the Belizean calendar, it's not hard for visitors to find a musical

PRECEDING PAGES: carnival parade, Belize City.
LEFT: glittering carnival marcher.
RIGHT: marching band at the Garifuna Settlement Day parade, Dangriga.

celebration during their stay – especially if they pass through in September.

Patriotic party time

September is the month when Belizeans are at their most patriotic and spirited, celebrating both St George's Caye Day on the 10th – mark-

ing the victory of the British Baymen and their slaves over Spanish invaders in 1798 – and, on September 21, Independence Day. Weeks on either side of these dates are filled with activities, most taking place in Belize City.

Banners with patriotic slogans, red, blue and white streamers and twinkling lights festoon the streets, which are crowded with the Queen of the Bay beauty pageant, bicycle races, concerts and military displays. Many "Bel-Ams" (Belizeans residing in the US) choose this time to come home for a visit.

Music, both old and new, plays a vital role in the celebrations. Every year an assortment of favorite old "Tenth songs" – some patriotic march tunes, others sentimental ballads – hits the airwaves, while Belize's contemporary musicians try to release at least one new song, or perhaps an entire album, in honor of the season. And the party always features at least one calypso or soca band from the Caribbean to give the Belizean crowds something to help them *wine dey waist* (wind their waists).

The Carnival Road March in Belize City has grown from a small children's parade to a fully fledged Caribbean extravaganza. Bands from the districts also head into town for the event, which usually occurs sometime around September 10. Junior and senior carnival bands

as people swarm the parks or main streets for the "jump up" or street fair.

Ole time Christmas

Many of Belize's Christmas traditions go back to logging days, when slaves and apprentice woodcutters got a break from life in the "bush" to visit the town with family and friends. Everyone would celebrate the temporary reprieve with two solid weeks of drinking, dancing, singing and parading through the streets.

Drinking is still a central part of a Belizean Christmas, especially for men – some of whom pride themselves on staying intoxicated for the

spend weeks, even months, fundraising and making colorful costumes. Whereas the adult bands often have corporate sponsors, in the poorer neighborhoods junior band leaders will even pawn their gold jewelry or spend their office syndicate savings so that no child is without a costume for the big day. When the day comes, spectators get out early to find a spot at the side of the street, whose center becomes a mass of costumed dancers accompanied by music blasted from trucks.

Things are a lot more somber at the flag-raising at the courthouse on Independence Eve and the official ceremonies the next morning, but the party atmosphere is revived later in the day

BRAM AND BRUKDOWN

Until very recently, no Christmas was complete without the *bram*. A group of revelers would travel from house to house, push the furniture against the walls and use any household object that could function as a musical instrument to make *brukdown* music. Anything from a broom handle, wash basin or a metal grater to drums, banjos, guitars, accordions and cowbells could be used. The creole lyrics, invented on the spot, would be about famous people or local village happenings. These days, though *brukdown* has lost its appeal for many young people, there are still several "Boom and Chime" bands and singers who are sought-after for private parties.

entire two weeks. As in the old days, most people still turn their houses inside out for a Christmas cleaning, hang new curtains and make *rum popo* (an egg nog with the emphasis on the rum!) The traditional holiday meal, served on both Christmas and New Year's Day, is ham and turkey, rice and beans, and cranberry sauce.

In Dangriga, the Christmas season is greeted by Joncunu (John Canoe) dancers. Outfitted in a pink wire mask, white tunic with flowing ribbons, an elaborate crown with tall feathers and hundreds of tiny shells attached to their knees, the dancers go from door to door dancing the

Garifuna pride

Garifuna Settlement Day, on the other hand, is anything but quiet. Celebrated on November 19, the day commemorates the 1832 arrival of the largest group of Garifuna to Belize's southern shores, and is a non-stop cultural fête.

The best place to witness this convergence is in Dangriga, the town that accommodates the greatest number of Garifuna in Belize. Don't plan on getting any sleep, however, because the previous night is filled with music and dancing in the streets and at the Roundhouse. As well as performing the *wanaragua*, or Joncunu, on the eve of Settlement Day, the Garifuna get

wanaragua, with their arms outstretched and legs together. Some say the dance is meant to be an imitation of white slaveholders and their behavior, which may be why it was popular at Christmas when normal master and slave relations were traditionally more relaxed.

New Year's Eve in Belize is less distinctive, really just a continuation of Christmas. People "ring in" the coming year with parties and champagne, then New Year's Day is usually spent quietly with family or friends.

Left: Garifuna dancing group with attitude.
Above: afternoon singalong Belizean style – acoustic guitar with ghetto blaster providing the rhythm.

the chance to show off their most popular dance, the Punta. In what is supposed to resemble the courtship ritual, a couple circle each other shaking only their hips and plowing the earth with their toes as they alternately propel themselves towards and away from each other. The *hunguhungu* is also performed for Settlement Day, although it usually has a more ceremonial function as part of the *dugu* ritual. *(see "South to Dangriga", pages 241–253).*

At dawn the next morning there is a re-enactment of the arrival of the early settlers in their dories. As they enter town from the mouth of the river, the travelers are greeted by women singing, drums beating, and the waving of cassava sticks and Garifuna flags of yellow, black and white. Everyone then proceeds to the church for a lengthy Thanksgiving Mass.

Mestizo traditions

The religious celebrations of the Mestizo communities of northern Belize are concentrated around Easter, though costume parades begin the weekend before Lent. In Orange Walk, *los mascaradas* wear scary disguises and drag chains through the streets, while others perform humorous skits or *comparsas* door to door. A dummy made of old clothes with a calabash head is dubbed "Juan Carnival" and burned in

a ritual at sundown. In San Pedro, skits tell the story of the mestizos' arrival in the village in the 19th century or relate other major events. In both towns, children roam the streets carrying raw eggs, flour and paint to ambush each other – and hapless adults – "painting" them from head to toe, a tradition said to have been inspired by the mischievous Maya god, Momo.

Good Friday is often observed with a religious procession through the streets. In many communities no liquor is served on Good Friday and in some towns no one is supposed to play loud music or ball games. Many Belizeans are superstitious about swimming or using boats on this day, while others joke that swim-

mers will turn into fish or mermaids. By contrast, the next day is filled with action as the country's most prestigious bicycle race, "The Holy Saturday Cross Country," captures national attention. On Easter Sunday people attend sunrise services and go on family outings; the American-style Easter Bunny has also begun to make his presence felt in recent years.

Most mestizo and Maya villages also have an annual *fiesta* in honor of the town's patron saint. The most prestigious of these is the Benque Fiesta held in July in Benque Viejo del Carmen near the Guatemalan border.

In memory of Baron Bliss

One of Belize's most popular holidays, held every March 9, celebrates the life of a man who not only wasn't Belizean, he never even set foot on Belizean soil. The English aristocrat Baron Bliss spent two months fishing in Belizean waters from his yacht, the *Sea King*, in 1926; already partly paralyzed by polio, he fell ill and died on board. Even so, he enjoyed his stay so much, and was so impressed by Belizean hospitality during his illness, that he left the bulk of his estate in trust for the country.

This gift made possible many of the public facilities Belizeans enjoy today, and helps finance the annual Baron Bliss Day Regatta in Belize City. Held in the waters off Fort George, near the baron's grave, this spectacle draws Belizean sailors piloting every form of craft. The waters are packed with fancy sailboats, working "sandlighters" (boats that bring sand to shore) and brightly trimmed dugout dories, which need a man to *kindola* over the side (hang by the mast) for balance. Meanwhile, the skies over Belize City are filled with kites.

In recent years, La Ruta Maya River Challenge has begun to eclipse the traditional regatta by shifting attention inland. The canoe race starts at first light at the Hawkesworth Bridge in San Ignacio, and for the next three days the teams paddle down the Macal and Belize rivers until they reach the Haulover Creek that takes them into Belize City. The winners are announced at the Belcan Bridge, but station prizes are offered by local businesses, resorts and homeowners along the way *(see panel on page 218 for more details)*. ❑

(see panel on page 218 for more details)

LEFT: Punta bump-and-grind.
RIGHT: masked Joncunu dancer from Dangriga.

FOOD AND DRINK

"Rice and beans" and fried chicken are the local favorites, washed down with

beer or rum – but Belizean seafood and fruits are tempting tropical treats

For Belizeans, eating is a communal act. There is no such thing as a diet in Belize: denying oneself food means rejecting the good intentions of others and the years of tradition behind every dish. Food is to be shared – if an old woman has only one creole bun she will gladly give you half, and plates of dinner appear from all directions whenever someone is ill or falls on hard times. Waste is considered a sin and so is refusing a stranger a glass of water if he or she asks at your door.

Despite this enthusiasm, Belizean cuisine can be mystifying to visitors. The country has an abundance of fresh fruit, meat and fish, yet there is a peculiar fondness for tinned foods imported from Europe. This may be the legacy of Belize's years as a British colonial outpost, or a taste acquired during the days of famine following last century's two major hurricanes. Whatever the case, many Belizean families would be at a loss without their salad cream, tinned luncheon meat and condensed milk.

Equally baffling is how a country that possesses so many different ethnic dishes embraces one of the world's most monotonous daily diets. With an almost religious devotion, the entire country sits down every day at noon for the main meal – which, nearly always, is either "rice and beans" or "stew beans and rice." The former is red kidney beans cooked together with rice; the latter is beans and rice cooked separately, often with a piece of pigtail thrown in for extra zest. The best versions of both dishes use coconut milk in the rice.

Some Belizeans' love of rice and beans borders on addiction. Many eat it every single day of the week, insisting they just don't feel satisfied by anything else, and late night partygoers in Belize City simply cannot go home unless they stop for "Meegan's," the rice and bean dinners sold from a trailer in front of a bank. The traditional Sunday dinner consists of rice and beans, stewed chicken, potato salad and fried plantain.

Down to the bone

Chicken is certainly the Belizeans' favorite meat, and each bird is stretched to the limit.

Except for the head, every bit of the chicken – including the feet – is stewed and served up. The bony rather than meaty pieces are considered the choicest, especially by those who like to suck out the marrow. Even the former Prime Minister, George Price, is said to always ask for the chicken neck, making him a welcome guest in even the poorest homes.

Many Belizeans complain that they would starve if it weren't for Chinese take-out windows selling fried chicken. You used to get a bag for as little as a dollar ("dolla chicken") and can still get a quarter chicken and french fries for BZ$5 from road side stands. In true creole fashion, the more offensive the nickname of the shop (like

---

PRECEDING PAGES: traditional Garifuna meal.
LEFT: nuts from the versatile cohune palm, used for everything from cooking oil to making pipe bowls.
RIGHT: fresh fish on the barbie.

"kick-down-fence" or "fresh kill") the more delicious the product is reputed to be. When they leave the clubs, many Belize City residents grab an order of chicken with "lotta peppa an' ketup!" and head for "the Fort" – the sea wall near the Baron Bliss Lighthouse. Fund-raising groups set up Saturday barbecues on street corners.

Belizean steaks are rarely worth the money, or the jaw-power they take to chew, but decent pork is plentiful. Almost all meat is generally served stewed and seasoned with red *recado*, a spice ball whose main ingredient is anatto seed. The classic dish "bamboo chicken" is actually a type of iguana known for its tender white flesh. In an effort to conserve the species, the dish is banned during the February and March breeding season. Another game meat is armadillo, known locally as "hamadilly," but the most popular game is gibut. This large rodent is considered so delectable that it was served to Queen Elizabeth on one of her visits. The British press had a field day, with headlines blaring QUEEN EATS RAT IN BELIZE. Conservationists may frown on the custom of eating this wild animal (and visitors are not encouraged to try it), but gibnut remains popular, as does the story of its royal connections, and the animal is now referred to as "royal gibnut."

MAYA SOUL FOOD

Perhaps the greatest contribution the Maya and mestizos have made to Belizean culture emerged from their fire hearths and kitchens. Traditional dishes have become so much part of the Belizean diet that many consider foods like *escabeche* and *panades* to be of creole origin. One creole restaurateur coined the phrase "Maya Soul Food" to describe the Spanish heritage foods that he served.

Tamales can be obtained anywhere, anytime in Belize. They are made from ground corn meal, or *masa*, mixed with shredded chicken or pork, wrapped and steamed in a plantain leaf. *Tamales de chaya* are a spinach variation that may include cheese.

Many Belizeans, being unconcerned about their cholesterol levels, enjoy other corn-based, deep-fried Spanish foods. The nationwide favorites are fish or bean *panades* made from corn *masa*, folded over and fried until crispy, and served with an onion and vinegar sauce spiced up with habanero pepper. These can be quite small, so you may have to fill up on *garnaches* – crispy corn tortillas topped with refried beans, grated cheese and tomato sauce.

Spanish soups are more substantial. *Escabeche* is a clear, tangy onion soup with large pieces of chicken; *chichac* is a clear broth that may be spooned over a whole fried fish or contain fish patties.

Bountiful waters

Seafood is abundant in Belize. The standards include red snapper, mackerel, grouper, shark and barracuda (also called "barro"), and fresh- and salt-water snook – a light-textured fish considered "the steak of the sea."

Besides being baked, barbecued or stewed, fish often appears in soups, the richest of which is "serre." This traditional Garifuna dish requires numerous "ground foods" such as yams, cassava and okra, as well as plantains and lots of coconut milk; it is often served with thin, crispy cassava bread. The thinnest fish soup is called "fish tea," typically made by fish-

nese restaurants, but is still a luxury for most. Shrimp farming is fast becoming a profitable business in Belize, but it is mainly for the export market. Conch (pronounced conk) is the most affordable and widely consumed shellfish, although unavailable from the beginning of July until the end of September. It is often chopped up and cooked in lime juice to make "ceviche," a dish common to many Latin American countries; it is also fried in batter as the "conch fritters" sold on the streets.

The once beloved Belizean delicacy of turtle is losing popularity because conservationists warn that its numbers are rapidly decreasing.

ermen camped at the cayes. It uses only onions, black pepper and live fish – they have to be still jumping when they hit the boiling water.

Shellfish, whose supply seemed limitless only a generation ago, now have strictly regulated harvesting seasons. Lobster, unavailable from mid-February to mid-July, has become a lucrative export and fetches handsome prices locally. Shrimp, whose season is closed from mid-April to mid-August, is a little cheaper, especially the freshwater variety sold in Chi-

Although turtle still appears on restaurant menus the creatures are far more interesting when seen in their natural habitat.

Many seafood dishes are reputed to have special sexual powers. If a woman wants to conceive a child, she and her husband are encouraged to eat *behave bruda* ("behave brother"), a soup made from snapper and ground foods with an entire grouper head thrown in (the eyes are said to be the most potent ingredient). If a man wants to increase his sexual prowess or "strengthen his back," he should drink seaweed shakes or eat thick white conch soup. (Cowfoot Soup, which really is made of cow's feet, is another back-strengthening creation, partic-

LEFT: classic Mexican plate, based on corn tortillas and hot salsa
ABOVE: fish served with a flourish at Maruba Resort.

ularly sought-after following a hard night of drinking – although the uninitiated may be put off by its gummy texture.)

Fruit lover's fantasy

Some say it is because the colonial masters discouraged farming that the closest many creole families get to serving vegetables, even today, is from a can. If you are determined to taste a typical Belizean vegetable, however, try a wrinkled green squash called *cho-cho* (which it's said resembles a granny with her teeth out).

On the other hand, fresh fruit is everywhere in Belize. Street vendors sell everything from

the familiar bananas, watermelon, papaya and pineapples to exotica like *craboo* – small yellow balls that are often made into wine or ice cream – and hard little green plums topped with hot pepper and salt. Bags of pumpkin seeds, called *pepitos*, or macobi seeds are supposed to help keep your mind off a failed romance or absent lover.

Yellow cashew fruit is stewed with brown sugar (delicious!) or made into cashew wine. During April and May, there are several varieties of mango, which can be eaten green (sliced and served with salt and pepper), served as chutney or eaten fresh when ripe and sweet. Plaintains, rich in potassium, are often served

with rice and beans or mashed to make Garifuna dishes like *fufu* or *matilda foot*. Coconut is also a key cooking ingredient, with every part used: the milk, the meat, the oil for frying and the husks for fuel.

Breads and sweets

Breads, buns and other pastries are baked in Belizean kitchens almost daily, to be consumed in the morning with a cup of coffee or ovaltine, or eaten with cheese, beans or "fry fish" for evening "tea." Favorites include the small, flaky biscuits known as "johnny cakes" (the original name for which may have been "journey cakes," because they travel well). These are best eaten hot with melting butter or slices of ham and cheese. "Fry jacks" are also delicious. These are made of flour, lard and baking powder – like a *tortilla*, then split in half and deep fried – good with refried beans and cheese.

You can't leave Belize without trying "creole bread," made in round dense loaves using coconut milk for extra flavor, and sometimes with a dash of cinnamon and a smattering of raisins. This is a favorite with hot tea in the evenings. The commercial version, the "Sunny and Tan bun," is a much larger loaf. These are so popular they are sent to relatives living in the United States.

Belizean men admire full, rounded female figures and pity those who are too slim *(magre)*. As a result, desserts are rich, gooey and filled with calories. The sweetest of all is lemon pie, also known as "merengay pie," which has a rich filling of condensed milk and lime (not lemon) topped by light, fluffy meringue. There are coconut pies, tarts and trifles, as well as coconut "crusts," made of grated coconut and brown sugar sealed in a flour shell and cooked over an open fire. Coconut candies include *cutubrut*, chopped coconut meat crystalized in brown sugar, and its cousin, *tableta*, made with shredded coconut. "Stretch me guts" is a taffy-like confection created from a mixture of coconut water, lime and sugar.

The British heritage emerges in desserts such as bread pudding, rice pudding and "potato pung," a heavy cake made of grated sweet potatoes and sprinkled with brown sugar and ginger. Finally, Christmas is always greeted with rum-preserved fruit cakes and *rumpopo*, a sort of rum eggnog.

Liquid refreshments

Despite Belize's Central American location, Belizeans aren't great coffee drinkers. As you might expect in a former British colony, tea is the preferred hot brew, especially in the evenings. It is drunk with condensed milk and, although no one seems to know why, people traditionally knock the spoon against the side of the cup while stirring, to make a tinkling sound.

Belizeans are noticeably addicted to soft drinks and, along with the standard international brands, a local company, Bradley's Bottling Works, has a loyal clientele. Its drinks are known as "lemonade" regardless of flavor.

> **NOT AN APHRODISIAC!**
>
> Orchards in southern Belize produce abundant citrus fruits – but avoid too much lime juice, said by Belizeans to "cut your nature" (decrease your sex drive).

man a drink because this implies that he hasn't enough money.)

Many villagers pride themselves on their home-made wines – concocted from everything from berries and rice to cashew and sorrel. Wine making is becoming a thriving cottage industry, although locals generally drink wine only at Christmas.

The liquor most widely consumed in Belize, however, is rum. It is mixed with anything from coke to pineapple juice. The latter combination is referred to by the lewd

Drinking liquor is an important part of the Belizean social scene, with men doing all the buying. A woman who refuses to accept a drink from a Belizean male, especially an older one, may cause a severe blow to his pride – the offer is made out of courtesy and usually contains no ulterior motive. (The only bigger insult is for a woman to offer to buy a

nickname of "Panty Ripper" and is generally favored by women. Belizean men almost never drink sweet mixed or frozen drinks as it's considered feminine. There are several local brands of rum, of which *Caribbean, Traveler's* and *Durleys* (which is also called "Parrot rum" because of its company logo) are the top sellers. The latest success story is coconut rum.

The most successful Belizean beer, *Belikin*, with a Maya temple on the label, has withstood several challengers over the years, though it is shunned in public by status-seeking local men who try to impress their dates by buying the more expensive imported brands of beer or whiskey. ❑

LEFT: take-out *tamales*, delicious for breakfast, sold steaming hot at roadside stalls.
ABOVE: medicinal teas, a currently revived tradition.

BENEATH THE WAVES

The Belize Barrier Reef is home to an underwater paradise of
multicolored coral and a kaleidoscope of tropical fish

The seaward rim of Belize's Barrier Reef, referred to as the outer fore-reef, is a favorite locale for scuba divers. It's not hard to understand why.

Imagine floating along an underwater mountain ridge. To the east stretches an abyss of nothing but deep blue. Below lies an 80-degree slope, covered by a quilt of magnificently colored coral plates and swaying fronds. A formation of eagle rays cruises past, their 10-ft (3-meter) wings lazily flapping; groupers lurk in the shadow of coral heads, their skins darkening to blend into the surroundings; tiny damsel fish defend their territories against all intruders (including divers); and parrotfish, the grazers of the sea, browse on algae while fluorescent blue chromis float above coral gardens.

Out of nowhere, panic hits. Clouds of fish explode and dart for cover as the silver streak of a barracuda flashes by and collides with a careless hogfish. Scales and bits of fin erupt from the impact. The tail of the hogfish slowly sinks, undulating through the water like a pendulum; the barracuda crushes its prey in its powerful jaws, while yellowtail snappers and bluehead wrasses converge on the entrails in a frenzy, tearing at pieces of floating tissue. Within a minute everything below the waves is as serene as before, except there is one less hogfish on the reef and one more satiated barracuda.

Understanding the Barrier Reef

Coral reefs, it has been said, are visual poems, filling a diver's sense of sight with form, color and patterns. If so, Belize is a master poet, and the Belize Barrier Reef is an epic of colossal proportions. At 185 miles (300 km) in length, dotted with around 200 cayes, the Belize Barrier Reef is the second largest in the world after Australia's Great Barrier Reef, while the variety of reef types and marine life within its borders is unequaled in the northern hemisphere.

Belizean waters are perfect for coral growth. Corals are surprisingly finicky, requiring warm, clear water, steady sunlight and a shallow, firm foundation to grow on. The vast mass of marine life now following the Belizean coast actually grows on a prehistoric reef. This thrived over a

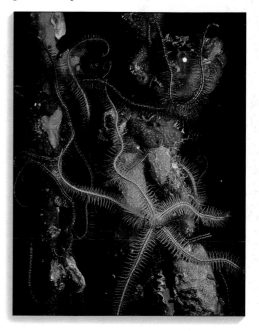

million years ago, when water was imprisoned in gigantic northern glaciers and sea levels were 300 ft (90 meters) lower than they are today. The underlying Pleistocene reef structure contains many of the same coral species divers still see, as scientists found from cores drilled 175 ft (53 meters) below the surface of present-day reefs.

Closer to the surface, at Reef Point on the northern shore of Ambergris Caye, lies further evidence of these ancient reefs. Here, portions of the Pleistocene coral reef intercept the shoreline in an area no larger than a football field. Sharp, skeletal remains of staghorn, elkhorn and brain corals lie exposed, cemented together in a matrix of coral sands. During the winter,

PRECEDING PAGES: breakers on the reef.
LEFT: a diver at Southwater Caye floats over a cluster of Yellow Pencil coral.
RIGHT: delicate sea stars feeding on mangrove roots.

heavy surf pounds this coast, fracturing the ancient reef and tossing limestone fragments upon a 15-ft (4.5-meter) rubble wall, but in calmer weather charter boats slip through a narrow channel from San Pedro. The eroding limestone and fossil corals conjure up images of prehistoric landscapes, but you don't have to go far to see the images come to life.

Diving on the reef

South of Reef Point, the "hard" coral begins to form a true barrier reef, snaking south into the Bay of Honduras. The reef is not one continuous wall of coral, but is splintered into seg-

ments separated by relatively deep channels. The oxygen and plankton carried by the Caribbean Sea flush the Belize coastal zone twice daily through these channels, feeding billions of hungry coral polyps and other reef creatures. Attracting large numbers of fish as a result, they are often excellent for diving and snorkeling (the most popular and accessible is Hol Chan Marine Reserve on Ambergris Caye).

There are over 460 species of fish that a snorkeler or diver is likely to see while swimming over coral reefs. Though some look formidable, most fish are unconcerned by your presence. Barracudas for example, have an

ANATOMY OF THE REEF

The structural framework of a coral reef is limestone; upon this, billions of individual coral polyps form colonies, connected by living tissue. Each coral polyp essentially consists of a set of tentacles, a mouth, and a gut perched atop a limestone skeleton. The polyps have special cells on the outside of their bodies that secrete calcium carbonate.

As the colony grows, polyps build their skeletons from beneath, pushing themselves up or out into a myriad of sizes and shapes. Growth rates vary with different species and different conditions, but coral reefs in warm, tropical waters grow only about 5 inches (13 cm) every century.

A coral reef, then, is actually a thin layer of life on top of ever-growing pieces of limestone. When an inattentive swimmer or errant boat hits or brushes against a piece of coral, the damage may not be immediately apparent but the damaged piece of coral may allow disease or infection to develop. And since the entire colony is connected by living tissue, a small, seemingly inconsequential injury may eventually kill a whole colony that might have taken thousands of years to grow to its present size.

Other coral groups have forsaken a hard shell for a more flexible, internal skeleton. These "soft" corals come in a range of hues – yellows, to reds and purples – and their trunks and branches create colorful underwater forests.

unnerving habit of approaching swimmers and following them about. This is pure curiosity – there has never been a report of an unprovoked attack by a barracuda, and they normally move away when approached. Eels have a nasty reputation, although they are generally non-aggressive. Alarmingly, they open and close their mouths as if preparing to bite, but they are merely pumping water through their gills. But be careful: eels can inflict a nasty bite if annoyed, especially the green moray eel.

DIVE OPERATORS

For more details on diving in the outer reef, see the *Northern Cayes* chapter, on pages 167–80. Recommended diving operators are listed in the Travel Tips section at the back of the book.

mustard color, it grows in two distinct forms, platelike or encrusting. Though it looks like one, fire coral is not a true coral. This hydrozoan has tiny silica needles that break off on contact and can cause intense stinging. Some sponges cause irritation, as do bristle worms.

The best way to avoid any potential problems when exploring the coral reef is never to touch anything – for your own safety and the health of the reef *(see Marine National Parks, page 182–3, for tips)*.

Sharks are not commonly encountered in Belize, with the exception of the docile nurse shark. Chances are that sharks will sense you long before you see them, and move away. However, all sharks should be treated with caution. Even the normally docile nurse shark can become aggressive if molested.

Probably the most serious underwater hazard is the long-spined urchin. Needlelike spines will pierce gloves or wet suits, and the tips easily break off. Fire coral is a danger in shallow water: with a smooth surface and a uniform

LEFT: sponges and sea squirts.
ABOVE: spiny squirrelfish and coral.

Research on the reef

The basic structure of the Barrier Reef is similar all along its 185-mile (300-km) length. At Carrie Bow Caye, a marine lab perched atop the edge of the Barrier Reef, scientists from the Smithsonian Institution's National Museum of Natural History have divided the reef up into the basic zones, or habitats.

A zone is an area where local environmental conditions – temperature, sunlight, water movement – allow certain groups of animals and plants to exist together. Usually one or two species in the group are more abundant than the rest and are used to characterize a habitat. Starting from the shoreward, or western side of the Barrier Reef, four major and 12 minor zones have been established along an east–west line north of Carrie Bow Caye. These zones include grass beds, where conch and striped grunts feed; reef flats, where crabs, small corals and anemones lie concealed among the rubble and sand; and spur and groove formations, where the coral grows in long linear mounds separated by coral sand gullies.

Moored as close as 10 miles (16 km) off the Western Caribbean Barrier Reef lie three of the four coral atolls in the Caribbean: Turneffe Island, Glover's Reef and Lighthouse Reef. The origin of these atolls – shaped like underwater

table-top mountains, with gardens of coral on the summit – is still a matter of speculation. Most geologists agree that the atolls grow over protrusions created by the movement of the tectonic plates of the region. The sequence of uplifting and sinking of the land masses has created magnificent underwater drop-offs, some plunging to depths of 10,000 ft (3,000 meters) to the east of Lighthouse Reef.

The reef systems surrounding these atolls rival the Western Caribbean Barrier Reef in length, with almost 140 miles (225 km) of lush coral growth. Within the coral barrier surrounding the atolls lie thousands of patch reefs; in the case of Turneffe, the largest of Belize's

atolls with an area of over 200 sq miles (520 sq km), there are hundreds of small mangrove-covered islands. Together, these three atolls provide some of the finest wall diving in the world.

The mangrove coastline

Coral reefs do not exist in isolation. Mangroves line much of the Belizean coastline, the cayes and lower reaches of the rivers. Seagrass beds, their blades swaying in the current like prairie meadows, blanket the sea bottom between reef and shore.

Mangrove and seagrass may not look as spectacular as coral reefs but, as giant marine nurseries, they form the foundation of the continuing long-term health of the Belize coastal zone. The quiet, protected water of the mangrove roots and grass blades provides plentiful food and shelter for countless juvenile marine organisms. In fact, most of the shellfish and the fish caught for food or sport off the Belize coast rely on mangroves for at least part of their lives.

Four different species of mangrove thrive in Belize – red, white and black mangrove and buttonwood. As well as stabilizing the coastline against erosion and presenting a natural buffer against destructive hurricanes, mangroves link the rich nutrients on land with the billions of hungry mouths at sea. Every year Belizean rivers transport tons of sediment to the sea from deep within the interior. The nutrients in these loads, deposited along the coast, are often in forms unavailable to marine life. But mangroves thrive on the frequent deposits, producing branches, leaves and seeds.

When a mangrove leaf drops into the waters below, the process of decomposition begins. The leaf slowly releases thousands of minute particles, each coated with millions of voracious micro-organisms. Small invertebrates like worms, shrimp and crabs begin to feed on the microbes; these small invertebrates are in turn eaten by larger creatures, until the nutrients in river silt are passed on through the food chain.

Many of these smaller fish also become prey for flocks of wading birds combing the surf line for food. Belize's coast has an abundance of water birds and nesting colonies, with over 50 mangrove-covered cayes reported to have nesting sites on them. Roseate spoonbills, ibis, herons, and cormorants nest on many of the small mangrove islands in Chetumal Bay to the north. The magnificent frigate bird and brown boobies have established large nesting colonies on many cayes to the south. Man-O-War Caye, east of Dangriga, has one of the largest colonies of frigate birds in the Caribbean. Meanwhile, ospreys locate the highest trees on the cayes, usually black mangroves, to build their nests on top from piles of loose sticks.

A living treasure

The entire coastal zone of Belize is a treasure of sea life, pristine and as yet mostly unexploited. Jewels of evolution are continually being found. For example, scientists from the Smithsonian Institution's marine lab on Carrie Bow

Sponges, anemones and tiny, barrel-shaped sea squirts cling to the prop roots, competing for the limited amount of space.

Smithsonian researchers have identified 43 different sea squirts in this one location, more than was previously known throughout the entire Caribbean. The fish are so abundant that they form layers, with the smaller fry near the surface, the larger ones a level down, and the fat-bodied herrings blanketing the carpet of lettuce coral. The location of this bay will stay a secret until scientists, the government and conservation groups within Belize can agree on the proper management of the area. The risk to any

Caye recently stumbled upon a tiny bay that may be unique in the Caribbean – if not the world. A quirk of nature allows mangrove to grow on the edge of a series of deep sink holes. Healthy colonies of lettuce coral carpet the steep slopes of the depressions. As the slopes rise into shallow water, the scene explodes into activity, with bright oranges and reds, deep purples and blues streaming past; crinoid arms perform silent ballets between 3-ft (1-meter) high loggerhead sponges; star and brain corals flourish among seagrasses and mangrove trunks.

LEFT: a shoal of Caesar gruntfish, Ambergris Caye.
ABOVE: a sailfin blenny, Carrie Bow Caye.

pristine environment can not be overestimated. After all, these marine organisms evolved over millions of years within a stable or gradually changing environment. Any sudden stress – whether from pollution, siltation, overfishing or injuries from a careless diver – can be devastating. For a visitor, kicking a piece of coral is hardly noticed; for the coral it is a matter of life and death; for Belizeans it is slow destruction of a priceless resource.

At present, the bay – and countless others like it – are a gauge of the environmental health of Belize's marine systems. Areas such as these expose Belize as a wilderness country, below the waves no less than in the rainforest. ❑

FISHING

Exciting fishing in Belize can involve wrestling a tarpon, stalking a permit or pitching your tackle against a giant marlin

Before the scuba divers and eco-tourists came to Belize, there were the fishermen. For decades, anglers have been coming to Belize seeking the excitement of jumping a tarpon or seeking out the elusive permit, choosing their locale from the country's mud flats, the rivers, or the deeper waters near the reef.

Whatever type of fish they seek, environmental awareness has rubbed off on fishermen: there is general agreement that Belize's lush, pristine foliage and abundant wildlife add immeasurably to the total fishing experience. It is not uncommon during a river trip to see monkeys, iguanas and crocodiles as well as orchids and bromeliads, and even the cayes are completely different environments from what North Americans and Europeans are used to at home.

The fly fishing craze

Over the years Belize has seen changes in fishing technique. Bait fishing, once the most popular, has to some extent given way to fly fishing – a result of the fever that has taken hold of sport-fishers throughout the world. Fly fishers describe their technique as an art rather than a skill, and consider themselves to be conservationists as well as sportsmen. They are the first to argue in favor of preserving both the fish and their natural habitats in order to ensure healthy populations in the future.

For this reason, most fishing in Belize is now catch-and-release, with very few fish killed, and there's increasing pressure to make this standard practice. The new breed of anglers is more concerned with skillfully landing the fish than with making it a trophy or filling an ice chest to take home; success is not measured by the number of fish brought to the boat, but by achieving a flawless cast or choosing just the right lure.

LEFT: the battle is joined – Belize attracts big game fishermen from around the world, particularly for the famously acrobatic tarpon.
RIGHT: showing off the spoils: a pair of kingfish.

Most fly fishers do not consider themselves to be on vacation in Belize – it's more like they are on a mission. Often they are in the boat before dawn and back at the lodge only at sundown. For these passionate fishermen, Belize offers exotic surroundings and several of the most sought-after saltwater game fish in the world, the most popular of which is undoubtedly the tarpon.

Fly fisherman or not, there is a wealth of sea angling experiences awaiting the visitor to Belize and its numerous offshore islands. Indeed, many species respond better to spinning methods or to natural baits than to artificial flies and it would be a mistake to restrict tackle and tactics in any way. For the angler who enjoys exploring new territory the main excitement is never knowing what may be next to attach itself to the end of the line. A number of the most exciting species to be taken from the shore or boats have ferocious teeth, so it is essential to attach lures or baits by means of a wire trace unless bite-offs are to become a way of life. Perhaps the best and cheapest way to search out the potential is by light tackle spinning. If you arm yourself with a small selection of plugs and spoons, beaches, rocky points, mangroves, flats and reefs can all be investigated.

Polarized sunglasses are an essential item of equipment for spotting fish in clear shallow water. It is unusual to fish for very long without seeing signs of life. Shoals of baitfish spray from the water as huge tarpon strike from below. Groups of bonefish or permit melt away like shadowy wraiths, and table-top sized stingrays glide off from the margins of the flats

at a heavy-footed approach. In contrast, the sword-tipped needlefish race wildly after lures, retrieved at speed just beneath the surface of the water while snapping repeatedly at a fast-moving spoon. Fish will often be present almost in the margin of the sea, particularly at dawn and dusk, and the thrill of hooking a 10-lb (4.5-kg) barracuda, a deep-bodied jack or a gorgeously colored mutton snapper in only inches of water has to be experienced to be believed.

The athletic tarpon

Of course, it is for the recognized big game or sport fish that many visitors come to the Caribbean, and perhaps the prime target in

Belize is the tarpon or silver king, a giant relative of the herring and shad. Known for their spectacular jumps, tarpon in Belize range in size from 5 to 150 lb (2–68 kg), but most commonly weigh between 20 and 60 lbs (9–27 kg). Even the smaller tarpon will twist and turn somersaults, but the real thrill is when a big one takes the bait, fly or plug. A large tarpon will leap into the air shaking its head violently, and for a brief instant will appear to hang in mid-air. This amazing action has led Belizean fishermen to dub the tarpon the "silver Michael Jordan" after the American basketball player. A tarpon is capable of keeping up the fight for two hours, so it is no wonder so many fishermen consider it a real challenge. Guides say most anglers visiting Belize have a good chance of landing a tarpon, although success is measured by how many jumps a fisherman achieves that day or week.

Bonefish are Belize's second most popular game fish. These fish may be small (1–10 lb/ 0.45–4.5 kg) but they have great power for their size. A bonefish can provide a fantastic run once it is hooked, but getting one to take your fly is by no means easy. The bonefish's mirror-like scales also give it almost perfect camouflage as it travels over green sea grass or the gray bottom of the mud and coral flats.

Ghost of the flats

Although a bonefish can be practically invisible in the water, it is the permit that is known as the "ghost of the flats." These powerful, deep-bodied members of the jack family average between 10 and 12 lb (4.5–5.4 kg) and have been described as 10 times more elusive than bonefish. They may also be 10 times more powerful: once hooked, a permit takes off with such explosive force it amazes most anglers the first time they experience it. Fishermen stalk the easily spooked permit by wading through the water, or standing silently in a skiff as their guide poles it. Permit feed almost entirely on crabs and shrimps and, although they will take flies and other artificial baits, it is on live crustaceans that they are most likely to be caught.

Another popular saltwater fish in Belize is the snook. These magnificent fish move up and down river estuaries with the tides and frequent the seaward margins of mangrove forests. They are aggressive, hard-fighting fish and will take plugs, cast close to the mangroves, with seeming abandon. Unlike tarpon, bonefish and permit, which are not considered very tasty, snook are delicious. Dubbed the "steak of the sea," snook used to be standard fare at some fishing lodges, but these days more and more are being released as environmental awareness grows: there has been a marked decrease in the average size of snook from the record of 47 lb (21 kg) over a decade ago to between 6 and 8 lb (2.7–3.6 kg).

FISHING FOR FUN

While those in colder climes are scraping winter ice off their cars, visitors to Belize's fishing lodges are coating themselves with sunscreen before beginning their day in a skiff.

Barracuda and several species of snapper and jack are also plentiful off the Belizean coast, and many tourists charter individual boats from Ambergris Caye to try their luck. Trolling along the outer margins of a reef with shallow running or surface plugs is likely to produce spectacular sport with black grouper or the bright orange-colored cubera snapper. Both species are liable to seek shelter within the reef after being hooked and large specimens will test the knots on the stoutest tackle.

There is some commercial sport fishing for billfish, and the Belize Fishing Association holds yearly ocean tournaments and rodeos for those who want to catch marlin and sailfish. Despite increasing pressure to release these large fish taken in competitions – which can weigh in at up to 450 lbs (200 kg) – most are cut up for their meat. Tuna, wahoo, kingfish and dolphin fish are all likely rewards of trolling for big-game fish in Belize and can each, in their own right, provide the angling event of a lifetime on suitable equipment. Big-game trips are, however, often expensive and it may be preferable to charter a local commercial fisherman informally and troll for these lesser species closer inshore, using plugs or rubber lures.

Fishing lodges and guides

The most reliable way to fish in Belize, however, is through an established lodge or fishing resort that uses qualified guides, rather than simply chartering a boat. There are lodges at Ambergris Caye, the Turneffe atoll, South Water Caye and Glovers Reef, all of which specialize in saltwater fishing, and fishing resorts in Belize City, Punta Gorda and Dangriga, which provide

LEFT: the captor and his catch.
RIGHT: hauling in the big one.

both river and coastal fishing. Individual guide services are also available on Ambergris Caye, Caye Caulker, Placencia and Punta Gorda.

Belize looks set to remain one of the western hemisphere's great fishing venues. The year-round warm weather continues to draw fishermen season after season and, with many years of experience under their belts, Belizean guides are good at what they do. Not only do they know the waters and where the fish are most likely to be, but some can tell great stories about the fish – and they are among the strongest supporters of the increasing establishment of marine reserves, such as at Port Honduras in Toledo, in which catch-and-release must be adhered to.

Most fishermen enjoy being close to nature, and return to their lodges each night full of stories about the orchids and iguanas they have seen during the day. But that doesn't mean tradition is thrown entirely by the wayside: for many, fishing still means competition and exaggerated stories about four-hour battles with a tarpon or the sighting of 30 or more permit. As one angler joked, "A good day for me is when I see more fish than my guide." ❑

IN THE WILD

An abundance of exotic native species lives in Belize's
vast areas of protected natural habitats

For centuries, Belize's small population, limited agriculture and lack of industry doomed it to being a backwater of civilization. Today, Belize has the most accessible tropical wilderness in the Western hemisphere, and wildlife that lures travelers from around the world. Though not as biologically rich as the Amazon or Costa Rica, Belize, for its size, is unique in the number of different habitats and species within its borders.

The reason can be traced back to its climate and geological history. Set in the heart of Central America, Belize is part of a landmass bridging two great continents. This has not always been so. Around 100 million years ago, Belize formed part of an ancient archipelago, isolated from North and South America by primordial oceans. During this time of isolation, many animals evolved that were endemic, or native to the region.

Then, roughly 2 million years ago, giant continental plates began to grind against each other, thrusting up mountains. As water became imprisoned in the colossal ice sheets of the poles, the seas receded, exposing new land. Central America became a land bridge between North and South America, allowing a free flow of migration. The resultant mixture of endemic and immigrant creatures spawned one of the most varied faunas on earth.

Thanks to its complex geological history, Belize's landscape mixes mountains, savannahs, and coastal lagoons, while the tropical climate provides wet and dry seasons, hurricanes and heat. The resulting environmental mix creates an astonishing variety of animal and vegetable habitats: although only the size of New Hampshire in the United States, Belize has over 4,000 species of flowering plants, including 250 orchids and over 700 species of trees. In contrast, the whole of the US and Canada supports only 730 species, giving Belize on average 1,000 times the diversity of trees per square mile.

Scientists have catalogued over 70 kinds of forest in Belize, grouping them into three basic types: 13 percent are open forests of pine and savanna; 19 percent are mangroves and coastal habitats; and by far the largest type, 68 percent,

is covered by broadleaf forests and cohune palms, the rainforests of Belize. This vegetation determines to a large extent what animals will thrive and where.

Into the rainforests

The broadleaf forests (rainforests) support by far the greater diversity of wildlife. They are the result of the most favorable possible conditions for life on land – abundant sunlight, warmth, and moisture. Most of the plants are trees, which grow to form a dense canopy overhead. Lower down are multiple layers of smaller trees and shrubs, tied together by twisting vines. Finally, leaves, fallen branches and

PRECEDING PAGES: dawn in the rainforest.
LEFT: a kinkajou, resident of Belize's inland forests.
RIGHT: a tiny red-eyed tree frog.

fungi litter the forest floor, and are quickly broken down into minerals by soil decomposers and recycled through the forest. Each layer is an animal habitat in itself, allowing space for a multitude of creatures to evolve. The secret of the rainforest is that the majority of the nutrients are stored not in the soil at all, but in the biomass – the roots, trunks, leaves, flowers and fruits, as well as the animals – of the forest.

Despite this, many visitors to the tropics are disappointed with the apparent lack of wildlife. Don't be. The animals are there. Most creatures of the rainforests perceive human intruders long before they themselves are noticed, and the seemingly solid wall of green provides innumerable hiding places. But to the patient, perceptive and informed visitor, the biological wealth of the forest eventually reveals itself.

Midday is a poor time to visit the rainforest. The heat of the overhead sun and the stillness of the air force most creatures into the shade, and humans should probably follow suit: the chainsaw buzz of flies and cicadas, along with the heat and humidity, make walking hard work. For birdwatchers, the best time is sunrise, when the air is cool and filled with the sounds of birds feeding and declaring territories. *(See "A Birdwatcher's Paradise," pages 129–133.)*

VITAL PRECAUTIONS

Though a naturalist's heaven, Belize can become purgatory for those ill-informed about the dangers of tropical wildernesses, so stay safe by following a few simple rules:

● Don't go alone. All forests begin to look alike once you're off the trail, and if you chase a bird or a red-eyed tree frog into the forest, it can be very easy to lose your orientation. It's best to hire a licensed guide; carry a spare flashlight at night.

● Stay on the trails. You are not only less likely to get lost, but also much less likely to stumble over nasties such as the deadly fer-de-lance and coral snakes that live among the litter of the forest floor. (Don't panic: most snakes are non-poisonous, and all will avoid you if they can.)

● Watch where you place you hands and feet. Some palm trees have needle-like thorns sticking out horizontally from their trunks, which will cause a nasty wound. Avoid unexpected meetings with snakes by looking to see what's on the other side before stepping over fallen logs. And check for ants before sitting down.

● Carry sunscreen. You need only leave the protection of the broadleaf canopy for a short time to get burned.

The multitude of insects in Belizean forests is generally more of a nuisance than a serious hazard; but see *Travel Tips, Health*, for the relevant information on how to avoid the more disagreeable species.

On the ground, it's easiest to spot leafcutter ants, also known as "wee wee" ants, carrying a load of leaves along the wide, clean highways they've cleared on the forest floor. The pieces of leaf are carried into huge underground chambers, where they are chewed and processed to grow fungus. The fungus in turn feeds the ants. This incredible relationship is so finely evolved that the fungus can no longer reproduce without the ants. Of the reptiles, the most easily spotted are snakes: of Belize's 54 species, 45 are harmless to man, and even the most poisonous are as eager to avoid you as you are them. Staying on trails is probably the surest way to stay clear of snakes; unless you are sure of identification, do not attempt to handle them.

Rainforest nights

After the sun sets, the rainforests come alive with the creeping, the crawling and the jumping, making it the perfect time to scrutinize vegetation on well-marked trails. Red eyed tree frogs, gaudily colored lizards, and delicate salamanders awake and roam the blackness.

Insects abound in an astonishing array of shapes and sizes. Spiders are one of the most conspicuous creatures encountered at night, the glinting reflections from their multiple eyes visible up to 50 ft (15 meters) away. Delicate crickets, iridescent beetles and mantis prowl the night in search of a meal. Many insects sport antennae two to three times their body lengths, using touch in the inky blackness to catch or avoid becoming prey.

Night is also the best time to view mammals. Bats dart above trails, gathering insects and startling hikers. Armadillos, oppossums and anteaters are nocturnal, foraging along the stream banks and fallen logs of the forest. Most nocturnal animals have large eyes to see by moon or starlight, so pointing a flashlight at rustling in the leaves often produces eyeshine.

The paca, known as gibnut in Belize, is a nocturnal rodent the size of a large rabbit, often heard chewing on cohune nuts and thrashing around the litter of the forest floor at night. It has a large head sprouting from a chestnut-colored body with four distinctive lines of white spots running along its back. This small

animal, with enlarged cheeks, often gives out a hoarse bark or deep grumbling. Gibnut meat is a favorite item in traditional Belizean restaurants – though the eating of wild animals is now widely discouraged by conservationists – and it is also a favorite prey of the five species of Belizean wildcats.

Famous felines

As Central America's largest spotted cat, the jaguar is probably the most celebrated creature of the rainforest, and Belize has created the world's first wildlife sanctuary specifically for the jaguar's protection *(see "Jaguar," page*

123, and the Cockscomb Basin Wildlife Sanctuary chapter, page 257). But roaming beneath the rainforest canopy and along the banks of mountain streams, four other wildcats share the same territory as the jaguar – the jaguarundi, the margay, ocelot, and puma. Though all are endangered throughout their ranges, Belize supports healthy populations of each. That five species of cat, so similar in their ecological needs, can coexist and thrive within the same rainforest is a tribute to the health of the Belizean habitat.

Smallest of the wildcats (and most abundant), the jaguarundi moves like a fleeting shadow. The long, lanky body, slender tail and short legs

LEFT: green iguana, commonly seen basking in trees overhanging Belize's backwater creeks.
RIGHT: the endangered gibnut.

make the jaguarundi unmistakable. No bigger than a house cat, this wildcat feeds mainly during the day on small rodents, birds and insects.

The margay is the most nocturnal of the cats: its large eyes and very bright, reflective eyeshine attest to its highly developed night vision. Superlative balance and great leaping ability – one researcher recorded a vertical leap of 8 ft 2 inches (2.48 meters) – make the margay ideally adapted for life in the forest canopy. Smallest of the spotted cats, the margay prefers primary or old

THE OCELOT'S ORIGINS

The ocelot's name comes from the ancient Aztec word *tlalocelotl*, meaning "field tiger," although it generally prefers secondary growth or recently cut forests.

growth forests and is rarely seen in the wild.

Known locally as the "tiger cat" (a name also used for the margay), the ocelot is about the size of a medium dog. It keeps to the forest floor, feeding occasionally on larger prey such as anteaters and brocket deer. Due to its exceedingly soft and beautiful spotted pelt, the ocelot was hunted nearly to extinction around Central America to produce fur coats.

While the jaguar inhabits lowland forests near streams and swamps, the puma, known as cougar or mountain lion in the US, prefers the highlands and drier ridge areas of the forest. The puma is extremely shy and secretive and probably the least likely to be seen.

The call of the wild

Another celebrated inhabitant of the Belizean rainforest is the black howler monkey, whose guttural cry is often mistaken for the roar of a jaguar. "Baboons," as they are known in Belize, live in troops of four to eight, carving out a territory of between 12 and 15 acres (5–6 hectares). They defend their territories from intruding troops by using their remarkable voices to let other troops know their location. Howlers often begin and end their days by roaring, and the noise can carry for several miles.

The black howler monkey's range is limited to southern Mexico, northern Guatemala and Belize, but the populations are rapidly declining due to increasing deforestation throughout Central America. Belize supports one of the last strongholds of the baboon in the region: at the Community Baboon Sanctuary, a grassroots project where landowners agree to manage their properties to benefit the baboons, there are an estimated 1,200 monkeys. The roaring is deafening at sunrise and sunset around the sanctuary. A project is now underway to transfer howler monkeys from the sanctuary to some of their former homes, including the Cockscomb Basin Wildlife Sanctuary.

Savannah and pine forests

In contrast to the mountainous tumble of rainforests blanketing the interior of Belize are its many areas of flat, relatively dry savannah. With the exception of the pinelands covering the Mountain Pine Ridge in the Cayo District, much of the savannahs, locally referred to as "broken ridge", occur along the level lowlands of the north and the coastal strip east of the Maya Mountains.

The new, unpaved coastal road (also known as the Manatee Road), between Belize City and Dangriga meanders through some of the most beautiful savannahs in Belize, flanked on the coast by mangrove forests, and inland by some of the country's largest citrus fruit plantations. Islands of limestone, surrounded by oceans of wind-blown grasses and knurled trees, attest to the harshness of the habitat.

Savannah flora in Belize evolved to take advantage of the extremes of climate and soil. The plants must deal with alternate water-logging during the rainy season and severe drought during the dry season. The savannah soils are generally acidic and nutrient-poor, allowing only hardy plants like craboo, oaks and palmettos to flourish. (The craboo is a small tree with tiny, yellow flowers that turn red with age. The fruit – cherry-sized and also yellow – is a favorite of Belizeans, used in jams, ice-cream and wine.)

As the name suggests, Caribbean pine is a prominent feature of pine and savannah woodlands. Driving along stretches of the Northern Highway, the new coastal road and much of the Southern Highway, formations of pine align

natural causes. Though the practice is discouraged, hunters will often start fires to flush deer and other game. Fire is not the only threat. In the Mountain Pine Ridge trees have been devastated by the Pine Bark Beetle many have died, while others have been clear-cut to stop the spread of the infestation.

Despite the often scorched, inhospitable appearance of the savannahs, many species of mammal forage there. Most commonly seen is the gray fox, one of the most abundant mammals in Belize, and one that often darts in front of cars or sprints along the side of the road before dodging into roadside vegetation. About

themselves like silent sentries awaiting review. Many of these pines have scorched trunks, blackened by fire – usually lit by lightning strikes in the spring and early summer. The fires start atop dead pines or in the tinder-like grass and may burn and smolder for days. The thick bark of the pines allow many of the trees to survive, while the underground root system of the grasses and shrubs allow them to resprout. In fact, savannah plants are often referred to as pyrophytes, meaning they are adapted to frequent burning. However, not all fires start by

LEFT: howler monkey, known in Belize as a baboon.
ABOVE: the shy tapir, Belize's national animal.

FOREST GIANT

Belize's national animal, Baird's tapir, known locally as the "mountain cow", is the largest creature in the forest. Although weighing up to 650 lbs (300 kg), tapirs can dissolve silently into the forest at the first sign of danger. A distinctive feature of these tapirs is their long prehensile lip, used to forage for leaves.

Tapirs prefer rainforest rivers and swamps, although they can survive in just about any other habitat. Despite their adaptiveness, the tapir is endangered throughout its range (Mexico to Ecuador) by hunting and deforestation. Belize is one of the last remaining strongholds of this magnificent mammal.

the size of a house cat, with a large bushy tail, this member of the dog family feeds on small rodents and birds; it is an excellent climber, spending much of the hot midday in the shade and breeze of the upper branches of the forest. Often seen after a fire is the white-tailed deer, emerging during early morning and browsing for tender new shoots. Though some luck is required to spot mammals in the pine and savannah woodlands, the wide open spaces are ideal for bird-watching – over 100 species are common. The striking vermilion flycatcher, a sparrow-sized, bright-red bird, is often seen "hawking" or making repeated sorties to nab

nest made the endangered stork easy prey for hunters, and jabiru meat was often peddled in Belize City markets. Now protected, the jabiru's figure graces the back side of Belizean $20 bills.

Mangrove and coastal habitats

Near the coast, savannahs and pine woodlands often blend into brackish water swamps and lagoons shared by mangroves. Though not requiring saltwater to survive, mangroves grow better in salt and brackish water than other terrestrial plants. Long stretches of the Belizean coastline and lower reaches of the rivers are lined by three different species of mangrove.

flying insects on the wing. The fork-tailed flycatcher, another unmistakable inhabitant of the savannahs, has 10-inch (25-cm) long tail feathers called "streamers", which provide increased maneuverability for catching insects flushed up by fires. Often, coveys of quail explode from the tall grasses lining roads in the broken ridge.

By far the most spectacular bird of the savannah and pine habitat is the jabiru, largest stork in the Americas. Standing nearly 5 ft (1.5 meters) tall, the jabiru is entirely white except for a black head and a red band around the neck; it constructs a distinctive 8-ft (2.4-meter) diameter nest atop a lone pine, often visible from a mile away. In pre-protection days, this exposed

The most common and distinctive is the red mangrove, found in frequently or permanently saturated areas. Numerous stilt-like prop roots arch from the main trunk into the soft mud, while aerial roots drip down from the branches, providing additional support in the loose sediments. The red mangrove seed sprouts while still on the tree, forming a 10-inch (25-cm) spear that, when released, embeds itself into the soft mud or sand below.

The black mangrove is found in slightly drier areas. The soft sediment around the tree trunks are punctured with armies of spiky projections (pneumatophores) which rise above the soil or water to assist the plant with gas exchange.

Found on still drier ground are white mangroves, whose oval leaves sport a pair of salt glands for exuding excess salts at their stems. Bunches of wrinkled, grape-sized seeds crowd the outer branches. After dropping, the seeds are dispersed by currents.

The easiest way to see mangroves is by taking a short boat ride up the Belize River from Belize City, where they form a majestic, cathedral-like tunnel over Haulover Creek. But mangroves reach their greatest size along the lower reaches of the remote Temash

MANATEE TOURS

Some of the largest populations of manatee occur off Gales Point near Dangriga, where they are protected by law *(see Travel Tips, Outdoor Activities for details of tours).*

Manatees are vast, docile and amiable creatures that are found all along the Belizean coastline, in lagoons and brackish water. They can easily grow to 15 ft (4.5 meters) and 3,500 lbs (1,585 kg), the only marine mammals that feed primarily on plants. Like most herbivores, they are normally slow and lumbering, but can exhibit tremendous bursts of speed when startled, leaving behind swirls of mud.

A long history of harvesting manatee has led to a general population decline. Manatee was

River in the Toledo District *(see The Far South, page 282).* Here, red mangrove trunks send up 10–15-ft (3–5-meter) high stilt roots, forming open forests of arches.

Manatees and crocodiles

Compared to other ecosystems in Belize, mangrove wildlife is not diverse or abundant. In fact, few terrestrial animals are restricted only to mangroves. Yet two endangered animals, the American crocodile and the West Indian manatee, rely on the mangrove environment.

once an ingredient in the diet and ceremonial activities of the Maya. In the 1800s, logwood cutters relished the manatee meat; the tails were reportedly pickled and eaten cold, while the tough skin was made into durable boot soles. As recently as the 1930s, manatee meat was sold in local markets.

Today, manatee enjoy special protection, and the population is no longer declining: in fact Belize has the largest population in the Americas. But, while hunting has been controlled, water and noise pollution are taking their toll: increased boating and fishing activities have damaged the coastal habitat and are affecting manatee numbers.

LEFT: spotted skunk and American crocodile.
ABOVE: the speckled racer, a non-poisonous snake.

Hunted reptiles

The other endangered animal in the Belizean mangroves is the American crocodile. Feeding on fish, crabs, birds and small mammals, this species can grow to lengths of 22 ft (7 meters). During the dry season, females build nesting mounds, depositing up to 60 eggs inside. The eggs hatch near the start of the wet season and the parents often feed and protect the newly hatched young for some weeks after.

The American crocodile is much less aggressive than its much-maligned cousin, the American alligator, which has overrun southern Florida. The crocodile typically shuns human

aerial combat. Fiddler crabs and 1-ft (30-cm) long great land crabs continually churn up the nutrient-rich soil. Though relatively poor in diversity, a mangrove forest remains a crucible of birth and decay.

Small but nasty

Not all wildlife in Belize is a wonder to behold, in particular some of its insects, though they are not generally the holiday-destroying nuisance they can be in other parts of the tropics. Most insect problems are solved by applying insect repellent during the day and draping mosquito netting around you while sleeping.

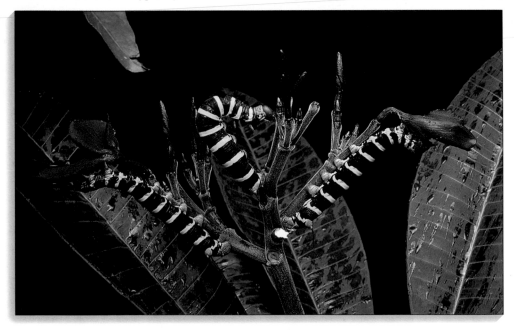

activity. But despite its shyness and a thick hide which protects it from most natural predators, the American crocodile is threatened across its range by hunting and habitat destruction. The mangrove and coastal habitats of Belize are one of the last remaining strongholds of this magnificent reptile.

Other above-water life in the mangroves is not quite as spectacular. The mangrove warbler, a tiny yellow bird with a rust-colored head, hops from roots to branches, picking up ants and flies. Nephila spiders (3 inches/7.5 cm long) spin golden webs to capture the abundant flying insects, while clouds of dragonflies dart through the open spaces as though locked in

Lightweight, long trousers and shirts will protect you from insects and the occasional scrape – infections thrive in the humid tropics.

Finally, always check your shoes or boots and shake out your clothes before dressing: scorpions, though generally rare, can be locally common, especially around San Ignacio. Some of these are about 6 inches (15 cm) long and shiny, metallic black – but are not deadly. This may not be much comfort if one strolls into your room at night, and even the most avid ecotourist has been known to pick up a heavy book and crush an intruding scorpion. ❏

ABOVE: sphinx moth larvae.

Jaguar

The jaguar, largest cat in the Americas and largest spotted cat in the world, is a superbly adapted predator whose legendary stealth in the rainforest has allowed it to stay at the top of the food chain while remaining largely an enigma.

Each part of the jaguar's anatomy plays a role in the hunt. The body – with oversized head, short back and legs, and large, steady feet – is built for power rather than speed. The dish-like eyes, which see color, provide unusually sharp binocular vision to accurately track and seize prey. Within the shadowy habitat of the rainforest floor, the jaguar's sight is six times more acute than a human's.

Long, pointed canine teeth, specialized for crushing bone, complement a set of blade-like premolars to shear meat. The lithe body, sharp retractile claws, and strong shoulders allow the jaguar to grasp and immobilize a 600-lb (240-kg) tapir. Even the name, derived from the Amerindian word *yaguar*, meaning "he who kills with one leap", attests to this animal's great hunting skill.

Because of these fearsome qualities, jaguars are often depicted as vicious and cruel by people who equate anger and murder – as manifested in man – with aggression and killing of prey in cats. On the contrary, there is nothing vindictive in a jaguar killing its prey, any more than in a deer decapitating a plant stem. Each requires food to survive. And, contrary to legend, there is little evidence of jaguars attacking man.

But decades of bad press, bounty hunting and fragmentation of the forest habitat have left the jaguar an endangered species. Once ranging from Arizona south to Argentina, only isolated populations now survive in Central America and the Amazon. Belize supports the largest concentration of jaguars north of the Amazon Basin.

Some of the first behavioral data on the large cat in Belize was collected by New York Zoological Society researcher Alan Rabinowitz, who headed into the Cockscomb Basin (now the jaguar reserve). Rabinowitz found that most male jaguars lead rather solitary lives, ranging within an area of about 13 sq miles (33 sq km). While many other male cats in the wild, such as the tiger and puma, maintain exclusive territories, the jaguars in Rabinowitz' study shared up to 80 percent of their territories with neighboring cats. Yet there was little evidence

RIGHT: the jaguar, revered by the ancient Maya.

of aggression between males. Only one captured jaguar showed signs of facial scars, which would indicate aggressiveness.

Avoiding potentially deadly encounters requires some form of communication between cats with overlapping territories. Rabinowitz found that jaguars use visual and olfactory cues in the form of feces, urine and scrapings. Such signs were found most often where the adult male's ranges overlapped (they are also about the only evidence of a jaguar's presence that most visitors to Belize will see, outside the zoo). Besides providing clues to the jaguar's social behavior, the collected scat provided clues to the great cat's diet. The jaguar is a

nocturnal hunter. It is not surprising, then, that armadillo, paca (a rabbit-sized rodent) and red brocket deer, all nocturnal creatures, make up over 70 percent of the jaguar's intake. More important, the jaguar is an opportunist, eating whatever prey is available, provided it can be caught easily.

The almost mystical hunting skills of the jaguar weren't lost on the ancient Maya. "Our ancestors considered jaguars as living symbols of the gods and their power," says Cockscomb Basin Wildlife Sanctuary director Ernesto Saqui. "The skin was prized as much for what it stood for as for its beauty. Today, we consider the jaguar an intricate part of our lives. By protecting it, we maintain a window to the health of the forest." ❑

SETTING A STANDARD FOR ECOTOURISM

Belize offers some of the most pristine habitats in Central America. But how do you exploit such a bountiful legacy without ruining it in the process?

Belize's barrier reef, atolls, rivers, mountains and tropical forest along with its imposing Maya ruins and vibrant contemporary culture make it ideal for the development of ecotourism. This small Central American state of only 220,000 people has a low population density that has allowed a combination of state and private reserves to protect more than 40 percent of Belize's territory.

TOURISM WITHOUT TEARS

In the mid-1980s, the government recognized that small-scale, low-impact tourism was the way to provide stable economic growth while still safeguarding the environment. Rather than follow the mass-tourism path of Cancún 250 miles (400 km) to the north, Belize decided to follow one that would allow as many Belizeans as possible to participate in the tourism industry as stakeholders.

The development of a small number of up-scale lodges in the spectacular interior of Belize has provided a model of sustainable tourism that has both set standards and inspired many Belizeans to develop a network of accommodation and services to support the burgeoning industry.

Tourism is now Belize's number one foreign revenue earner. And strict governmental guidelines, environmental education and enthusiastic co-operation with international conservation organizations such as WWF and The Nature Conservancy promise a bright future for both Belize's environment and its pioneeering ecotourism

△ **PROUD HERITAGE**
Belize's numerous reserves and parks make it an ecotourism paradise – and a fine role model.

△ **RARE BIRDS**
Habitat loss and poaching has meant only isolated pockets of the magnificent scarlet macaw survive.

◁ **BIG CATS**
The *Panthera Onca*, or jaguar, largest of the New World cats. Rare in Central America, Belize supports healthy numbers.

▷ **TRAIL BIKING**
Cayo District's Mountain Pine Ridge is ideal terrain for adventurous cycling expeditions, with many hilly forest tracks.

△ CORAL KINGDOM
The Belizean coast is home to the longest barrier reef system in the western hemisphere.

▷ WELCOME TO BELIZE
Visitors can be sure of a warm welcome and wonderful hospitality from the friendly, easygoing people of Belize.

▽ BELIZE ZOO
The Belize Zoo mixes fun and education to promote the conservation of endangered species and critical habitats.

▽ ON THE TRAIL
With the help of a local guide, trail systems can be explored throughout Belize on horseback, by mountain bike or on foot.

WORLD-FAMOUS COCKSCOMB BASIN

Established in 1984 as a small forest reserve, the Cockscomb Basin Wildlife Sanctuary soon evolved into a reserve of over 100,000 acres (40,500 hectares). Made famous by the Wildlife Conservation Society's Alan Rabinowitz's study of jaguars, this world-reknowned sanctuary is a haven for many rare and endangered species such as puma, ocelot, margay, tapir, otter and scarlet macaw. Lodging facilities are available at the park administration center and well-maintained trails are constantly being expanded. Trekforce Expeditions recently finished a trail that leads through the tropical forest for several days to the jagged granite summit of Victoria Peak, a hike that is gaining popularity as one of the most adventurous challenges in the whole country *(see pages 260–261 for details)*. Many of the park rangers are from nearby Maya Center, which has a community guest house project, medicinal plant trail and crafts shop, while villagers act as nature guides and porters for expedition trips.

A BIRD-WATCHER'S PARADISE

Belize's tropical location and wide range of pristine habitats

attract a remarkable number of bird species

The calm in the forest was broken by a sudden, excited declaration: "a harpy eagle, that's what it is alright!" Through the viewfinder of their camcorder a group of bird-watchers from Tucson, Arizona, had been birding in the Chiquibul Forest in western Belize, led by a tour guide from Arizona and a local guide from Cayo District.

They quickly reported their find – and gave a copy of their film – to the Belize Audubon Society. A few days' later, the eagle displayed its characteristic crest and huge wingspan (up to 7 ft/2 meters on some of the birds) on Belizean TV's nightly news.

The incident highlighted the growing importance Belize is placing on bird-watching and it is a vivid reminder that even the most ordinary day out in the Belizean bush could turn into a remarkable – even historical – experience.

But you don't have to tramp deep into the Chiquibul to enjoy the the birds of Belize. Your hotel in Belize City, on the Belize or Macal rivers, or even at Caye Caulker, might just be smack in the middle of prime bird territory. Armed with little more than a pair of binoculars, a *Peterson's Field Guide to Central American Birds* and some good walking shoes, you can start your quest. There are nearly one hundred species of birds in Belize City alone. Favored locations are the Fort Point area by the Baron Bliss Lighthouse, the marshy lands around St. John's College, wetlands by the Port Authority and Customs, or the grounds of the House of Culture (former Government House). It's even more fun when you learn the local creole names like "georgie bull," "pyam-pyam," "banana bird" or "shaky batty" (a little bird which bobs its rear end up and down).

With relative ease, you may see everything from ordinary blackbirds (or grackles) to the vibrant banana birds (known elsewhere as orioles). These beautiful little birds are hard to find in the trees; you're more likely to spot one as it swoops down to catch an insect.

You'll probably hear the pyam-pyam (brown jay) before you see him because this bird is a real busybody, chattering or "talking" whenever someone passes by. In Belize, anyone who

talks a lot, or makes comments about others is said to be "going on like a pyam-pyam." The tropical mockingbird is also very noisy and is very protective of its young. During the nesting season, they have been known to dive-bomb small children and people with light-colored hair, so watch out.

Like the mocking-bird, the georgie bull (jacana) can be very aggressive, but only with males of his own species. These birds have spurs on their wings, rather than on their legs, so that when two males fight they look like they are boxing. But these macho creatures also have a softer side, for it is the male, not the female, that hatches the eggs.

PRECEDING PAGES: tricolored herons perched on red mangrove, Shipstern Caye.
LEFT: great egret on the lookout.
RIGHT: brown booby, a resident of Man O' War Caye.

Also common within the city limits are several species of humming-birds, giant flycatchers (kiskadee), royal and sandwich terns, brown boobies, little blue herons, gaulins (egrets), scissor-tails (magnificent frigates), laughing gulls (sea gulls), and kites.

Into the countryside

If you want to join a tour, or take a drive out of town, you can find hundreds of birds along the Northern Highway en route to the Maya ruins at Altun Há and the Community Baboon Sanctuary in

> ### CHRISTMAS ROLL-CALL
>
> In recent years, the Belize Audubon Society's highly popular Christmas bird count has recorded an amazing 600 species, one third of which are migrants.

Bermudian Landing. This is the area in which the Belize Audubon Society conducts its annual Christmas bird count (see BAS feature on page 133 for details).

From the road and down by the Belize River, you're sure to see gaulins (egrets), with their long white necks, and several species of hawks and kites circling above, looking for live prey.

The John Crow (king vultures) are also common in this area. Four species may be spotted along the highway alone. Because they live on garbage heaps and hover near rotting animal carcasses, these ugly birds are so scorned by Belizeans they are even the subject of several piquant creole proverbs (for example:

Ebrey John Crow tink 'e picney white – Every black bird thinks his children are white or, No one sees the flaws in his own child). Any chicken or game bird that tastes tough is also ridiculed as being "John Crow." Nevertheless, the unsightly vultures are essential in maintaining the web of life, just as much as the most flamboyant bird species.

The **Crooked Tree Wildlife Sanctuary** (also off the Northern Highway, see North to Altun Há, page 193) is a truly great place to find birds since the nearby lagoon attracts hundreds of migratory and resident species. This sanctuary is a special treat in the springtime, when waterways begin to shrink, serving to concentrate large numbers of birds. The brightly colored jacana can walk upon the softest mud with its extraordinarily long toes. Migrant white pelicans mingle with tiger herons, limpkins and hordes of great egrets.

Guanacaste National Park near Belmopan is another favorite stop for naturalists and bird-watchers (see West to San Ignacio, page 218). Just off the Western Highway and easily accessible by car or bus, Guanacaste has many varieties of hardwood trees and hundreds of birds including flycatchers, tanagers, yellow bill cacique and bamboo clappers (motmots).

Motmots can also be found at just about any archeological site because they dig their nest burrows in the limestone "hillsides" formed by unexcavated Maya temples. A nesting motmot burrows a tunnel, then turns 90 degrees and makes a cavity in which to lay her eggs. (If you're lucky, you may see one of these little birds poking its head around the corner.)

Glories of the toucan

Keel-billed toucans and their smaller cousins, the toucanets, are also common near archeological sites and wooded areas. Belizeans love this colorful creature so much they have made it the national bird.

The toucan's image is everywhere, from billboards to T-shirts. There's even a brand of matches bearing the name. The most famous toucan of all is Rambo, a charming fellow who roams freely at the Belize Zoo, captivating the nation's children with his multicolored beak and sociable nature.

Although images of majestic red and blue

macaws are also plentiful in the commercial art of Belize, seeing the real thing is a little more difficult. These long-tailed birds reside mainly in the forested areas of the Maya Mountains, accessible via the Mountain Pine Ridge Road, or the back country of the Cockscomb Basin Wildlife Sanctuary; however the best place to see them is in the area of the Maya village of Red Bank in the southern Stann Creek District. It is best to rely on a guide to help you find them between late December to late March, while they feed on the copious fruits of the area. There are reportedly less than one hundred pairs of these brilliant-plumaged yet raucous-

dusk so Belizeans describe a job requiring long hours as "working from polly to polly." These smart birds take advantage of nests or holes created by other animals such as termites: often they simply enlarge an existing nest in a dead tree to suit their own purposes.

While it is not illegal in Belize to take parrots from trees to keep in the home, it is against the law to take a polly out of the country. But because they are so popular in the United States, there have been horror stories of smugglers drugging the birds and trying to pass them through American customs in everything from suitcases to plastic piping. Although there are

voiced members of the parrot family remaining in Belize. If you want to stay in Red Bank, you could contact Program for Belize, the wildlife association, who have a tourist facility here, with lodging and good local food.

The other eight species of parrot, including the tiny aztec parakeets (actually conures, to be correct), are generally more common, with the exception of the endemic Yucatán parrot, which may only be seen in the far north of Belize. In the wild, parrots are active from dawn until

LEFT: the endangered agami heron.
ABOVE: jabiru storks.
RIGHT: scarlet macaw.

BIG BIRD

Belize's largest bird, the jabiru stork, stands about 4 ft (1.2 meters) tall and, with its wide wing-span, looks like a small airplane when it is taking off.

Jabiru adults are efficient providers, and have been seen carrying snakes, rats and lizards up to their young nesting in the ceiba trees. They also transport water (siphoning it into their beaks), which they spray on their chicks, or give them to drink. Unlike the adults, which are mostly white, jabiru young have matted gray feathers that resemble those of a sick or dying bird, perhaps intended to discourage predators or in order to blend in more completely with their background.

very stiff jail sentences in the US for wildlife smugglers, the practice has proven difficult to stamp out. The sad fact is that this activity results in considerable mortality to the smuggled birds, while increasing the likelihood of spreading avian diseases such as psittacosis. If you must buy a pet parrot, be sure to buy it from a recognized breeder.

In contrast to the clever parrot, the "who you?" (the common pauraque, also known as the whip-or-will) appears to be rather stupid: these birds like to sit in the mid-

PELICAN PROVERB

The placid nature of the pelican has inspired the creole proverb: *Sea breeze always blow pelikin wey 'e wan go* (The pelican goes wherever the breeze takes him.)

dle of the road and are occasionally hit by cars. You can easily spot them during night walks by holding your flashlight up next to your eyes, thereby catching reflected eyeshine from the birds. Owls and potoos may also be spotted in this fashion.

Wetland birds such as rail species (top knot chick" or "gallinola") are usually a challenge to see due to their secretive habits; however, the large gray-necked woodrail may be observed along riverbanks during canoe trips on various rivers. Other species to look for in the bush are the owl (barn and spectacled), hawk eagles (which are very rare), and the colorful trogons (which are related to the quetzal

of Guatemala), which may sit motionless in a tree and make its distinctively repetitive call. Game birds include the ocellated turkey, the crested guan, and the great curassow. All these birds, save six species, including the latter two, are protected from hunting in Belize.

Curassows and guans are common only in protected areas, where hunting is prohibited; hunters say that the male and female curassow mate for life and are so devoted that when one is shot, the other expires soon after.

Birds of the sea

Along the coast or out at the cayes, you can't miss the brown pelican perched on piers or flying in formation, often riding the wind low and close to the waves.

Laughing gulls (the only gull species common in Belize) are also everywhere, especially in populated areas; piratical magnificent frigate birds – notorious kleptoparasites – occasionally swoop down upon an unlucky tern or cormorant and divest it of its food. The fish-hawk, or osprey, is particularly exciting to watch as he skims the surface of the water to pluck up a fish with his outstretched talons.

The best places to search for sea birds is on Caye Caulker, San Pedro (many migrants stay north of the village) and at Half Moon Caye Natural Monument. Caye bush or littoral forest, and mangroves, are essential habitat for many species of birds, both residents and migrant. Some of these species include the black catbird, Yucatán vireo, white-crowned pigeon, and rufous-necked woodrail. There is even a thriving population of the Cozumel variety of the nectar-feeding bananaquit. Because of the distance and expense involved, the reserve at Half Moon is mostly frequented by divers, but excursions are occasionally available for bird-watchers who want to see the island's huge colony of red-footed boobies.

There are also several small mangrove cayes that have been declared bird sanctuaries because they support nesting populations of wood storks, three species of egrets and two kinds of herons, white ibis, magnificent frigate birds and anhingas. ❏

LEFT: great frigate bird, with extended throat pouch.

The Audubon Society

Bringing educational programs into schools, advocating on important development issues, promoting bird-watching in Belize – these may sound like a full plate for any conservation NGO. However, for the Belize Audubon Society (BAS) it is just the beginning. The major mandate for this highly influential organization is actually protected area management.

Founded in 1969 by a group of Belizean families interested in birds and other wildlife issues, as an offshoot of the Florida Audubon Society, BAS at first provided people with similar interests an opportunity to meet and formulate field trips. However, its mandate grew with the advent of natural history-based tourism, also then known as "ecocultural" tourism. In the early 1980s, BAS received a mandate from the government to manage several protected areas in the country, as Belize, a developing nation, found it impossible to pay for protected area infrastructure and staff. This work was all done voluntarily by committee members of the organization's Board of Directors.

In the early years, funding was slow to arrive; as the number of protected areas grew, so did their needs – Belize did not want to be home to "paper parks" (sanctuaries that exist in laws but have no on-site management). In the late 1980s funding to run the office itself finally came through from Massachusetts Audubon Society and Programme For Belize. At last the office could be run with more than one manager and a secretary. The Belizean Government awarded a house on North Front Street to serve as headquarters for the organization, which was suffering from lack of space for its library, staff and equipment.

One of the most important attributes of BAS' policy is its commitment to local recruitment, and involving them in sanctuary management. This is in an effort to learn from the mistakes made by early conservation attempts that tended to disregard local people, who thereby had little incentive to abide by management strategies.

A notable tradition maintained by BAS from its inception is participation in a Christmas Bird Count. These counts are accomplished by Audubon Society members far and wide, from Nome, Alaska, to Panama, and can provide interesting data on general bird population trends over the long term in

RIGHT: watching the wildlife – BAS's core activity.

addition to providing members and interested guests with an excuse to spend an entire day in search of birds. Count areas are circles of 15 miles (24 km) diameter, broken up into sections to be covered by counting parties. Coverage is affected by such factors as number of participants, accessibility of areas and transportation.

The first area to be set in Belize begins roughly 12 miles (19 km) up the northern highway and includes diverse habitat such as farms, forest, creeks, and coastal mangroves and forest. The second includes portions of the Western and Hummingbird Highways, with both forested and farmed territory. Another area is centered at Gallon

Jug, within the Río Bravo Conservation area, comprising high forest and some open agricultural land. The most recent count area is Punta Gorda, which frequently boasts the highest number of species recorded.

Since its inception, BAS has vastly improved its management presence and techniques, assisted by finance from the European Union. A growing number of national parks and other protected areas in Belize are managed by BAS; contact the society before your trip to learn about these outstanding examples of Belizean habitat. BAS also welcomes foreign membership and participation in Birdathons, held during spring and autumn migrations. *(For details on BAS, see Ecotourism, Travel Tips).* ❑

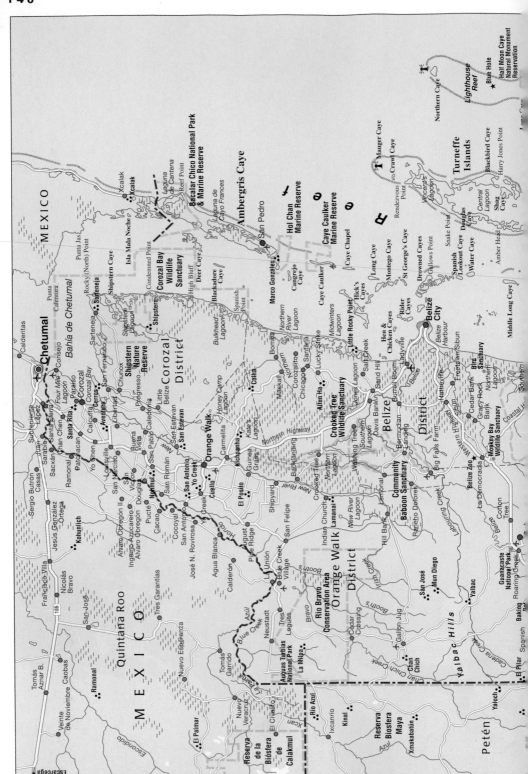

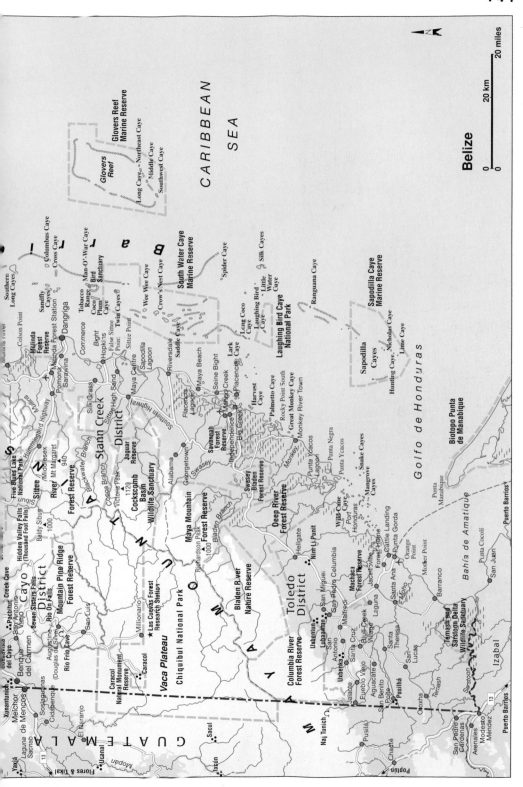

PLACES

A detailed guide to the entire country, with principal sites clearly cross-referenced by number to the maps

Old travel hands like to say that Belize has the look and feel of the Caribbean in the 1950s, before it was "ruined" by commercialism. Everything is small-scale in Belize: the biggest hotels rarely have more than a couple of dozen rooms, and, although this is a tiny country, transport can be tortuous. Only the few major highways are paved; traveling up and down the coast is best done by small, 10-seater propeller plane; getting out to the off-shore cayes is often in small, high-speed motor boats bumping across the waves.

No matter which part of the country you visit, most journeys begin at the least appealing point: Belize City, a ramshackle outpost that is grubby, noisy and troubled by petty street crime, but which still retains a fascinating atmosphere of *Casablanca* intrigue.

Most visitors head quickly to Belize's other attractions (often hopping a light plane directly at Belize City airport). Best known are the 200 or so small islands or cayes (pronounced *keys*) dotted along the Barrier Reef. Some are tiny and uninhabited, with only a few palm trees; Ambergris Caye (San Pedro) is the American-style luxury getaway venue; Caye Caulker has a more authentically Belizean atmosphere, downscale and laid-back.

Back on the mainland, Belize's menu of ecotourism attractions are often combined with visits to remote Maya ruins. North of Belize City lie both the Community Baboon Sanctuary and ancient ruins of Altun Há; a visit to the ancient city of Lamanai includes a river trip through pristine savannah. Further north, the little-visited Orange Walk and Corozal districts have a distinct Mexican flavor.

The center for the ecotourism movement remains San Ignacio, in the rainforests of the Maya Mountains close to the Guatemalan border; comfortable, thatch-roofed jungle lodges have spread across this remote countryside, which are riddled with nature walks to waterfalls, underground caves and jungle-covered streams. En route to San Ignacio is the nation's capital, Belmopan; further into the wilderness lies Caracol, Belize's most significant Maya site.

South of Belize City, the first major attraction is Dangriga, center of Garifuna culture; next is Placencia, a tiny fishing village shaping up as a laid-back coastal resort; third, for the committed ecotourist in search of the truly remote, is Punta Gorda, the base for exploring the far south, with fascinating Maya villages in the forests, unspoiled offshore cayes, and excellent fly-fishing opportunities.

Last but not least, almost all visitors to Belize now take advantage of daily tours to Tikal in neighboring Guatemala, considered the most spectacular of all ancient Maya cities. ❑

PRECEDING PAGES: tropical tranquility, Belize City; enjoying the cayes; back road in the Cockscomb Basin Wildlife Sanctuary.
LEFT: calm evening on the Belizean Caribbean.

BELIZE CITY

*Raised from the swamp on a bed of empty rum bottles
and regularly ravaged by hurricanes, Belize City has a
rough and ready appeal all its own*

**Maps:
Area 140
City 148**

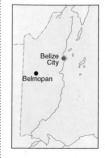

Amandalaaa! Amandalaaa!" shout the newspaper boys as they push through the crowds with the latest edition. Street vendors' carts, loaded down with fruit and cheap Guatemalan goods, squeeze pedestrians on to miniscule sidewalks or force them to step into the traffic. Drivers curse as bicycle riders cut recklessly in front of them; taxis stop without warning in the middle of the street. As the sweat pours down their faces, all many can think about is the air-conditioning in the bank a few blocks away.

It's always the same in Belize City – congested and hot (or raining) – yet in this small place, where everyone seems to know everyone else, friendliness prevails and business still takes a back seat to pleasure. From shop clerks to bank executives, no one is too busy to inquire about the family or exchange a bit of gossip. Friday afternoons are downright festive as everyone discusses weekend plans, keeping one eye on the clock and the other on the cash box.

People move slowly in Belize City, and so does everything else. The heat sets the pace, regulating everything from business hours to just how long it will take the clerk at the income tax department to answer the phone. Visitors are invariably frustrated by the interminable wait at the traffic lights and ready to walk out of restaurants where the simplest order – and often the check – seems to take an eternity. But everyone else is on Belize Time (meaning you're lucky if they show up on the same day, let alone at the right hour) and they're rarely annoyed by delays.

Nor does anyone seem particularly distressed by the city's *brukup* – or dilapidated state. This is not to say the citizens don't "rail up", or complain, about the stench emanating from open sewerage canals or poor water pressure (so low at times they can't bathe or flush the toilet). It's just that most have learned it's useless to expect those in authority to do anything – at least not until election time rolls around again.

Housing shortage

While the more affluent areas of Belize City have large, gleaming cement structures sitting well back from the street and their neighbors, the rest of the town is a hazardous fire trap. Small wooden buildings, many built on stilts to avoid flood waters and catch more breeze, are crowded closely together on narrow streets. Demand for housing far exceeds supply, every bank is inundated with requests for building loans, and desperate families have squatted in outlying areas far from water and electrical lines. Not surprisingly, housing is a recurrent election issue in Belize City, with every candidate vowing to build more low-cost homes, fix the streets, dig more drains and fill more land – but few keep their promises.

PRECEDING PAGES:
the Belize River
waterfront.
LEFT: aerial view of
the city center.
BELOW: new tricks
by an old building.

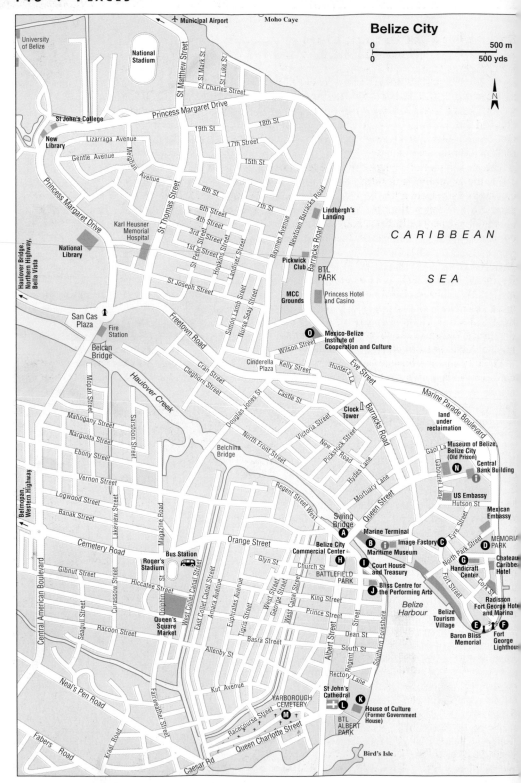

Belize City

Municipal Airport

Moho Caye

0 ————————— 500 m
0 ————————— 500 yds

N

CARIBBEAN

SEA

University of Belize

National Stadium

St Matthew Street
St Mark St
St Luke St
St Charles Street

Princess Margaret Drive

St John's College

New Library

Lizarraga Avenue

Gentle Avenue

Meighan Avenue

18th St
19th St
17th Street
15th Street
8th St
7th St

Karl Heusner Memorial Hospital

Haulover Bridge, Northern Highway, Bella Vista

National Library

Princess Margaret Drive

St Thomas Street

6th Street
4th Street
3rd Street
1st Street

St Peter Street
Hopkins Street
Landivar Street

Baymen Avenue

Newtown Barracks Road

Barracks Road

Lindbergh's Landing

Pickwick Club

BTL PARK

MCC Grounds

Princess Hotel and Casino

San Cas Plaza

Fire Station

Belcan Bridge

Freetown Road

Simon Lamb Street
Nurse Seay Street

Wilson Street

Cinderella Plaza

Kelly Street

Hunter's La.

Mexico-Belize Institute of Cooperation and Culture

O

Eve Street

Marine Parade Boulevard

Haulover Creek

Mopan Street
Sarstoon Street

Mahogany Street

Nargusta Street

Ebony Street

Vernon Street

Logwood Street

Banak Street

Cran Street
Cleghorn Street

Castle St

Douglas Jones St

North Front Street

Belchina Bridge

Victoria Street

New Street

Clock Tower

Pickstock Street

Hydes Lane

Barracks Road

land under reclaimation

Museum of Belize, Belize City (Old Prison)

Gaol La.

Gabourel Lane

N

Central Bank Building

i

US Embassy

Hutson St

Mexican Embassy

Belmopan, Western Highway

Cemetery Road

Lakeview Street

Magazine Road

Regent Street West

Mortuary Lane

Queen Street

Swing Bridge

A

Marine Terminal

Eve Street

North Park Street

MEMORIAL PARK

D

Central American Boulevard

Gibnut Street

Curassow Street

Seagull Street

Hiccatee Street

Dolphin Street

Bus Station

Roger's Stadium

Orange Street

Glyn St

Belize City Commercial Center

H

Church St

BATTLEFIELD PARK

B

Maritime Museum

i

Image Factory

C

Court House and Treasury

I

G

Handicraft Center

Chateau Caribbean Hotel

West Collet Canal Street
East Collet Canal Street

Amara Avenue

Euphrates Avenue

Tigris Street

West Street
George Street
West Canal Street

King Street

Prince Street

Bliss Centre for the Performing Arts

J

Belize Harbour

Fort Street

Cork St

Radisson Fort George Hotel and Marina

Queen's Square Market

Racoon Street

Basra Street

Allenby St

Dean St

South St

Albert Street

Regent Street

Southern Foreshore

Belize Tourism Village

E

Baron Bliss Memorial

F

Fort George Lighthouse

Neal's Pen Road

Fairweather Street

Kut Avenue

Racecourse Street

YARBOROUGH CEMETERY

M

St John's Cathedral

L

K

House of Culture (Former Government House)

BTL ALBERT PARK

Fabers Road

Kraal Road

Queen Charlotte Street

Caesar Rd

Bird's Isle

Rectory Lane

Rebuilding after the hurricanes

Although they may have seen better days, most of the city's 65,000 or more inhabitants say they wouldn't live anywhere else in Belize. Such loyalty flies in the face of bitter experience: residents had to completely rebuild their city twice in the 20th century, after hurricanes literally turned it into a pile of wooden sticks. The 1931 hurricane leveled almost 80 percent of Belize City and claimed thousands of lives (including those of virtually all the East Indians in Queen Charlotte Town). Exactly 30 years later, Hurricane Hattie demolished the town for the second time.

The present face of Belize City is the result of a massive rebuilding effort. In 1971, the government decided to avoid further destruction by relocating the capital to Belmopan, a newly built city 52 miles (84 km) inland. To date, few people have been willing to move. While Belmopan, with its population of around 6,000, may be Belize's political capital, Belize City remains the nation's commercial, social and historical center.

The view from downtown

For many, Belize City's main attraction is economic. Every morning, lunchtime and evening, the streets fill with professional women in their color-coordinated uniforms and men in freshly starched shirts, all making their way to and from their respective offices downtown. There is no shortage of opportunities for domestics and shop assistants, and the city's construction boom also attracts manual laborers from all over Belize, as well as from neighboring republics.

The city center's busiest hub is the **Swing Bridge Ⓐ**, one of three bridges connecting the city's south and north sides, which was renovated in 1998.

Maps:
Area 140
City 148

Popular legend has it that thousands of broken rum bottles were used as a foundation to raise Belize City above its natural swamp bed.

BELOW:
ferries off-loading from the Cayes.

ELEGANT ORIGINS

Hot and humid Belize City was never supposed to be located here on the seafront at all. The original 18th-century settlers preferred the cool, mosquito-free life on St. George's Caye, a few miles offshore, but the expanding logwood trade required a camp closer to the river. Belize was established at the mouth of Haulover Creek only as a temporary solution. But as the years passed, permanent wooden structures became more common, while swampland north and south of the river was reclaimed and connected by a bridge.

It may be hard to imagine today, but journal accounts from the early 1800s describe the settlement as positively charming, the streets lined with gracious colonial homes and lush gardens. Only the privileged few were part of such a genteel picture; the African slaves who made possible the white and upper-class creoles' pampered lifestyle lived in places like Eboe Town, where Yarborough or "Yabra" now is. This was composed largely of "negro houses:" long rows of separate rooms sharing a single roof. Indentured servants from India and Garinagu (Garifuna) settlers also occupied less than idyllic quarters in an area known as Queen Charlotte Town, or Frenchmen Town, which was located east of today's Caesar Ridge Road.

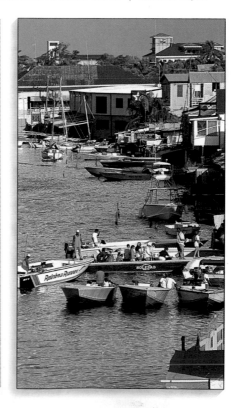

Constructed in 1922 for what was then primarily pedestrian traffic, the bridge is notorious for its narrowness and steep incline and can hardly accommodate today's heavy traffic. The biggest drawback, however, is that the bridge must be manually swung open every morning and evening to allow sailboats and other large craft to exit or enter the river, stopping traffic on both sides for some time. Plans are underway for an automated replacement, but many city residents will be sorry to lose this old veteran, which weathered both the 1931 and 1961 hurricanes (although it had to be retrieved from some way up the street in 1931).

One of Belize City's first cars, a model-T Ford owned by a doctor, always rolled back down when it tried to cross the steep Swing Bridge, unless it was given a push by helpful bystanders.

Belize City's Nob Hill

Across the Swing Bridge is what the district residents call, logically enough, "the northside," where many of the city's hotels and nicest mansions can be found.

Along North Front Street stands the **Biddle Building**, a lovely old structure with lots of Victorian gingerbread trim, which used to be a popular shoe store but has also been appropriated by the post office for parcel post service.

The old **Fire Station** across the street on the riverfront houses many antique examples of firefighting equipment all still in use. The building now houses the **Maritime Museum B**, and the **Marine Terminal**. Examples of old Belizean watercraft as well as fish species and corals are on display and a handmade dorey hangs overhead. Upstairs are exhibits charting the maritime history of the region, with a small collection of memorabilia dedicated to Baron Bliss, Belize's foremost 19th-century philanthropist. Children especially enjoy this well laid-out little museum and it's a pleasant place for adults to spend a half an hour while waiting to take a water taxi (Mon–Sat 8am–4.30pm; small entry fee). You can also grab a cup of coffee and a piece of local pastry at the

BELOW: a lull in the traffic flow on the Swing Bridge.

Riverview Café, also in the terminal, and browse the surrounding stalls for T-shirts, hats, beach towels and other souvenirs.

Just up the street from the Marine Terminal, heading away from the Swing Bridge is the **Image Factory** . This is one of Belize's first real art galleries and it's still one of the few where you are sure to find a good show most of the year. The Image Factory was started by Yasser Musa (son of the current Prime Minister Said Musa) in the early 1990s and features the work of local artists and visiting talents, as well as educational exhibits on natural and cultural history. Musa and Gilvano Swasey, both artists, curate most of the shows and foster the work of younger or newer talents through the Image Factory Foundation. A portion of the gallery is reserved for the sale of local work (Mon–Fri 9am–6pm; free entry but donations welcome).

Continuing up North Front Street is The Fort. This area was formerly Fort George Island; it did have a fort until 1803 and was separated from the rest of the city by a creek.

Memorial Park

In 1924 an American construction company reclaimed the land and built some lovely homes on Cork Street and facing **Memorial Park** , which commemorates the Battle of St George's Caye in 1798 *(see page 38)* and Belizean servicemen who served in World Wars I and II. The park is used for open-air concerts and while the facilities themselves have seen better days, it's still a favorite gathering spot during the September Celebrations. The Belize Tourism Board and the City Council set up a makeshift "Tourism Village" in the park on "Cruise Ship Days" where local vendors sell everything from T-shirts and

Belizeans are very proud of their postal service, and their stamps are prized by collectors.

BELOW: colonial architecture on Cork Street.

carvings to home-distilled cashew wine. A few of the city's more graceful colonial homes surround Memorial Park, but like the park itself, some are in real need of loving care. Those in better shape are generally rented out to foreign embassies, UN agencies or other businesses. The Fuller family, however, has taken pride in preserving their home. Carlos Fuller, the government's chief meteorologist who also serves as "weatherman" on radio and TV says his father told him the house, which is located at the "V" or entrance to the park, survived the 1931 hurricane almost intact by floating off its foundations and ending up across the street; it still contains about 90 percent of its original interior woodwork.

Luxury hotel zone

With several guesthouses and one of the city's largest hotels, **Radisson Fort George Hotel and Marina**, the tip of the northside – known as the Fort – may have more tourist accommodations than anywhere else in town. Locals also enjoy the view from the Fort, particularly on Sunday afternoons when families and lovers take a walk out to the lighthouse, past the **Baron Bliss Memorial E**. The Baron, a wealthy British invalid who fished Belizean waters for several weeks and then died aboard his yacht in 1927, left the bulk of his estate to the Belizean people in gratitude for their hospitality during his final days.

The **Fort George Lighthouse F** is one of the last things visitors see when leaving the city by water taxi and it is still a welcome site to boaters when they approach the mouth of the Haulover Creek. The Baron Bliss Day harbor regatta (generally held on March 9 holiday weekend) takes place in the sea near the Fort and spectators crowd the area for a wreath-laying ceremony and to watch the sail boats.

LEFT: the Belize City Commercial Center.
RIGHT: taking produce to the streets.

The lighthouse and children's park across the street were built for public enjoyment with funds from the Baron's Trust, as was the Bliss Institute, on the Southern Foreshore, which contains a library, an art gallery and auditorium.

Map on page 148

Handicrafts and market

On your way back from the Fort, in the old customs area on the waterfront, is the **Belize Tourism Village**, a shopping mall and entertainment complex that caters for the vast number of cruise ship visitors. This is the first place that the thousands of cruise ship passengers see as they pass through from the dock. Most head straight out to the waiting tour buses ready to take them to the Maya ruins, the zoo, or perhaps on a tour of Belize City. A few blocks over, near Memorial Park, is the **Chamber of Commerce Handicraft Center G**. It is only open during the week but you can find anything from tiny stone-carved Maya pendants to wooden furniture made by local artisans. Prices are a little higher than buying directly from the artists, but the Center was one of the first successful attempts to help Belizean craftspeople market their products.

Speaking of markets, the **Belize City Commercial Center H**, which replaced the "Old Market" at the foot of the Swing Bridge on Regent Street, was one attempt at urban renewal, but the marble-floored high-rise – high for Belize City, at least – has always been the focus of controversy. Few Belizeans wanted to lose the Old Market, a steel-arched structure built in 1845 that was one of the few of its kind left in the Caribbean; meanwhile, the circumstances surrounding the building contract with an Italian construction company were dubious. Public outcry led to the Old Market being carefully dismantled and stored away, to be rebuilt sometime in the future as part of a proposed tourist center. But, as with many Belizean development schemes, the resurrection remains uncertain.

The Commercial Center still houses vegetable vendors on the lower level (jewelry stores and music shops are now the street level tenants) while the upper floors are rented by boutiques and government offices.

TIP

Big Daddy's restaurant on the top floor of the Commercial Center offers the best rice and beans in town, along with a great bird's-eye view of the river while you eat.

BELOW: the Fort George Lighthouse.

Legal eagles and political scandal

Also on Regent Street is the **Court House I**, where lawyers and judges still wear British-style robes while working in the building constructed in 1926. It replaced the one destroyed by fire in 1918. The clock tower was erected in memory of the colonial governor, Hart Bennett, who was fatally wounded by a falling flagpole during the disaster. January visitors may be lucky enough to watch the ceremonial opening of the first Supreme Court session of the year. The Belize Defense Force Band provides the marching music and the justices, in full British judicial regalia (including white wigs) stand on a platform surrounded by all of the attorneys-at-law. The proceedings on the front steps last only a few minutes, then the entire group retires to one of the courts for a speech by the Chief Justice, which is closed to the public. **The Public Building**, on the same compound, used to be the seat of the Legislative Assembly until it moved to Belmopan in 1971; it is used by several government offices, including the Treasury and Office of the Prime

Minister (on Wednesdays, anyone can walk in without an appointment and wait their turn to voice their concerns or ask for favors.)

Facing the Court House, **Battlefield Park** seems quiet now; it got its name in the 1930s and 1940s for the heated political arguments that took place there. A labor organizer, Antonio Soberanis – whose likeness has been erected in the park – and political activists like George Price and Philip Goldson attracted crowds with their emotional speeches on social justice and self-government.

Bliss Institute

Just around the corner from the Court House, facing the sea on the foreshore is the **Bliss Institute ❶**. Built with funds from the Baron Bliss trust, the building houses the Belize Law Library, as well as the Belize Arts Council, an auditorium for performing arts, and the Belize Art Gallery. Belize City residents of all ages have a real fondness for the place whether they remember the venerable old librarian and poet Leo Bradley helping them to find books for a school project, or because it was where they had their first taste of show business as a performer in the annual children's festival of arts. As part of the Museum of Belize Project, the Bliss was renovated to make it a more comfortable place to enjoy local theatre, dance or music. The art gallery facilities have also been improved.

The **House of Culture ❿**, formerly the Government House, completed in 1812, is also being refurbished and its gallery spaces improved. Located at the end of Regent Street, this spacious colonial mansion was home to British governors appointed to Belize. In colonial times Belizeans could only enter the mansion and the grounds through special invitation, but today they are open to the public. The House of Culture offers art and music classes, and hosts concerts,

BELOW:
the Court House.

plays and even fashion shows. The beautiful grounds are available for weddings and other special events and are open from 8am to 4pm on weekdays. Local plants along the nature trail are clearly labeled and a variety of birds either make the garden their home or stay for the winter months.

Map on page 148

St. John's Cathedral

Just across the street from the House of Culture and the BTL park is the oldest Anglican church in Central America, **St. John's Cathedral** ❶. Built by slaves using bricks brought to Belize as ship's ballast, the building was completed in 1820 and became the coronation site of four Mosquito Kings, whose people (Native Americans who once inhabited the Mosquito Coast, in what is now Nicaragua) maintained good relations with the British government in Belize, even though they eventually came under Spanish rule. The interior of the church contains wall plaques commissioned by the families of some of the earliest parishioners, and a more recent wooden sculpture depicting the dove of peace by one of Belize's most revered artists, George Gabb. The original roof was replaced after it was damaged by fire in 2002. Fortunately inside was virtually unscathed.

City bus driving past Yarborough Cemetery.

Lying opposite the cathedral is **Yarborough Cemetery** ⓜ, named for the land's owner, the magistrate James Yarborough. It was used from 1781 to 1882, first as a burial ground for the colony's more prominent persons and later opened to the masses. There are no mourners these days, but you may find groups of school children scampering over the graves deciphering the intriguing tombstones or playing ball. Not too far from the graveyard is a statue of the first self-made Belizean millionaire, Emmanuel Isaiah Morter, a devotee of Marcus Garvey, who owned a great deal of property along Barracks Road and donated much of his fortune to the UNIA (United Negro Improvement Association). The monument also marks the entrance to what was Eboe Town in the 19th century.

BELOW: a slice of tropical sunshine, served with a smile.

Regent Street

Heading back down Regent Street, leaving St. John's Cathedral and the House of Culture, are many of the city's best-preserved examples of 19th- and early 20th-century architecture. Regent Street is generally quiet, with doctors, lawyers and accountants renting many of the old homes for offices. But some families still live on what used to be known as "Front Street" since it faced the sea at one time, before the southern foreshore was developed. Several structures survived the hurricanes because they were made of bricks. The bricks date these buildings to the early 19th century; iron slave shackles can still be found embedded in some of their interior walls (including the building at the corner of Prince Street), a startling reminder of the darker side of Belizean history.

While Belize City has no organized building preservation effort, most historically significant structures are maintained simply because they are still in use. Parallel to Regent Street is Albert Street, the commercial hub of downtown. There are no skyscrapers but there is cement, plenty of it. If there were old brick buildings, they have long burned down or been knocked down to make way for East Indian, Lebanese

Belize City's Haulover Creek was so named because cattle had to be "hauled over" to the other side before a ferry service was introduced.

and Chinese shops that sell everything from shampoo to mattresses. The major commercial banks are also located here as well as two competing supermarkets, Romac's and Brodies. If one doesn't have what you want, just walk across the street to the other. Central America fruit vendors are also out in full force on Albert Street. The street is at it most active on Fridays and becomes eerily vacant on Sunday afternoons when everything is closed.

Gabourel Lane

Queen Street, back over the Swing Bridge, is similar to Albert Street, both in terms of economic activity and hustle and bustle. The main police station, Eastern Division headquarters is on Queen Street, which ends on Gabourel Lane. Gabourel Lane is another part of town worth exploring: home of the **US Embassy**, housed in a beautiful colonial building dating back to the early 20th century. Although there was an abundance of the finest wood in the world in Belize at that time, the Americans built their consulate in New England and shipped it to Belize City.

At the end of the street is Her Majesty's Prison, which was in use until the early 1990s, and has been transformed into the **Museum of Belize N** (open Mon–Sat 10am–6pm; entrance fee). One prison cell has been preserved and the exhibits recount the history of Belize City. However, the main focus of the museum is the stunning ceramics and jade jewelry from Belize's Maya culture. Behind it, on the same grounds, is the Central Bank of Belize, built in a style reminiscent of Maya temples, which also houses the headquarters of the **Belize Tourism Board**. Beyond the museum the entire seafront is being developed. Land has been reclaimed and the seawall and pedestrian promenade extended.

BELOW: St. John's Cathedral.

Into the suburbs

The modern areas of Belize City are more spread out, and while you can walk, a taxi may make the heat more bearable. A taxi ride can be quite an adventure in Belize City as cabs speed through traffic, brushing past pedestrians, and sail over bridges apparently defying the laws of gravity.

If you decide to catch a cab tell the driver to head for the Newtown Barrack and Princess Margaret Drive. You'll pass Sandlighter's Promenade, a tiled walkway that runs along the sea wall up to the Princess Hotel and Casino. The area is dedicated to the sandlighters, or small sailboats that used to pull up and unload the sand their crews had dug up at the various coastal sandbars and then brought to town for use as landfill or for construction.

Across from the promenade where people gather in the evenings to "catch the breeze" is the **Mexico-Belize Institute of Cooperation and Culture** (open from 8am to 5pm weekdays). It was established in 1993 by the Mexican government to enhance relations with Belize. As well as hosting exhibitions of both Mexican and Belizean artists the center sponsors films and lectures. More importantly however, it offers classes in Spanish for a modest fee. The courses are almost always filled by Belizean students and professionals who see the growing need to become bilingual.

Around Princess Margaret Drive is the area of Belize City the more prosperous call home – named, appropriately enough, King's Park. Here and in the adjacent West Landivar are also many of the city's schools, the oldest of which is St John's College, established by Jesuits in 1887. Nearby are the University College of Belize and the Belize Teachers' College.

It's obvious to anyone who spends any time in Belize City that there is no room for expansion in the city itself. But as it is reclaimed swamp, and bordered by swamp to the north and west, and sea on the east and south, there is also a shortage of usable land on the outskirts.

Housing developments such as Bella Vista and Belema have sprung up immediately outside the entrance to town by the northern highway, but the area is subject to flooding, as many proud new homeowners found out during the weeks following Hurricane Mitch in 1998. The northern highway, which occupied a thin strip of land all the way to mile ten is bounded by the river on one side and the sea on the other, and came dangerously close to being cut off entirely during the Mitch evacuation.

A real building boom is going on in the town of Ladyville and sister village of Lord's Bank, as well as on the land near the international airport. The sleepy hamlets that used to be inhabited by the airport or Belize Defense Force Camp employees now have luxury as well as middle-income homes at Vista Del Mar and the highway is becoming crowded with commuters. The distance from town is more psychological than actual – its only ten minutes by car – but city folk tease Ladyvillians about moving "up the road" or "living in the bush." All agree the suburbs have their advantages, the greatest of which is the escape from the noise and confusion of the city. And – so far – the neighborhoods are far less prone to crime. ❑

 TIP

A good spot to spend a few hours, cooled by welcome sea breezes is the **Belize Telecommunications Park** (BTL), which has picnic tables and a playground.

BELOW:
giving a little lip.

BELIZE ZOO

Famous throughout the Americas for its educational facilities and its preservation programs, the Belize Zoo offers the perfect introduction to some of the country's indigenous wildlife

Map
on page
242

What many people fail to realize when they come to Belize is that their chances of seeing the larger land animals are limited. The tangle of vines and thick foliage makes it difficult to see even a few feet off a forest path or road. Also, many tropical creatures are nocturnal, finding safety under the cloak of night. Except for a flash of fur dissolving into the bush, or the snap of branches and rustle of leaves, most visitors will end up experiencing the habitat where wildlife live instead of viewing the creatures themselves.

But there is one place where you are assured of seeing a jaguar or a tapir in a natural setting. The **Belize Zoo** is an oasis of ponds, forests, and flowers among the sprawling savannahs 29 miles (47 km) west of Belize City.

Natural comforts

Over 60 indigenous Belizean animals are comfortably harbored in large, naturally vegetated enclosures. In fact, during the heat of the day, many of the animals are difficult to see because of the thick cover. This is because the welfare of the animals takes precedence over the viewing ability of visitors. You will often feel that you are in the forest, peering through a tangle of vines and shrubs to catch a glimpse of a jaguarundi or ocelot. Just as when searching for wildlife in the rainforest, patience and persistence are necessary to view the beauty of the creatures at the Belize Zoo.

The animals and grounds are meticulously cared for by the Belizean staff. Shiny pelts, bright eyes and, in most cases, pleasant dispositions attest to the health of the animals. Raised gravel paths lead from exhibit to exhibit through natural savannahs and pine ridge vegetation, as well as transplanted rainforest. Hand-painted signs call attention to the natural habits of each animal and its endangered status, reminding Belizeans and visitors that "Belize is my home too!"

Sharon Matola, the North American founder and driving force behind the zoo, arrived in Belize after a colorful career that included a stint with a Romanian lion-tamer and a circus tour in Mexico. Today, she often recounts an incident that helped convince her she was on the right track during the zoo's difficult founding years of the early 1980s. A very old man showed up at the gate after closing. At the time, Matola was keeper, janitor, tour guide and accountant rolled into one, so she let the man in and gave him a personal tour. At first the old man commented freely at each cage about well-entrenched Belizean myths – how ant-eaters kill dogs with their tongues, or that boa constrictors are poisonous during the day. Soon he grew silent. Finally, as they stood in front of a sun-lit

PRECEDING PAGES: sunset on the Belize River.
LEFT: the puma is no pussy cat.
BELOW: interactive sign at the zoo.

Scarlet macaw, one of Belize's rarest birds.

BELOW: the zoo animals speak for themselves.

jaguar, Matola noticed tears in the old man's eyes. "I'm very sorry, Miss," she recalls him saying. "I have lived in Belize all my life and this is the first time I have seen the animals of my country. They are so beautiful."

That was in 1983, when the zoo consisted of chicken wire cages sheltering animals left over from a natural history film. Matola was hired by the film maker to care for the animals, and when the film was completed, she was left to decide how to dispose of them. Many were tame and unaccustomed to life in the wild, so the idea of an unusual zoo cropped up. Matola hung signs beside the cages soliciting funds to buy feed; she visited schools around the country to raise awareness about the wealth of Belizean wildlife and its deteriorating habitat; and she went outside Belize to raise money from environmental groups.

Educational activities

Today, the Belize Zoo covers 30 acres (12 hectares), employs 17 Belizeans and is part of a larger complex that includes a Tropical Education and Research Center. It is the focal point for environmental awareness in Belize. An innovative visitors' center features the artwork of local schoolchildren, freshwater aquariums, and explains the zoo's sophisticated solar system; there is also a children's playground with natural motifs.

And while it may have been an old Belizean man who encouraged Sharon Matola to develop the zoo, it is the children who have made it one of the most popular places in the country. Besides the busloads of children arriving on school field trips, every year the zoo celebrates April the Tapir's birthday and the whole country is invited to party. Whether they are from the more exclusive private schools in Belize City or the tiny government schoolhouse up the road,

the kids crowd around to help feed her a cake made of vegetable mash. Rambo the toucan is another favorite who has become a minor celebrity, and Hoodwink the owl, a fictional cartoon character, has his own story and coloring books. The zoo and tropical research center sponsors an annual environmental fair and the nation's primary schools eagerly compete for computers and other prizes.

These efforts have done much to create awareness of the need to preserve Belize's wildlife and the zoo itself is probably the most child-friendly attraction in Belize. From the humorously written signs to the interactive information displays near the exhibits, the zoo caters to the very young in the hope they will learn to respect their country's animal life. It seems to be working – just watch them hold their noses by the pungent peccaries, roar back at the howler monkeys, or cautiously approach that beautiful but terrifying jaguar sitting oh so close to the fence. Just like the visitors to their country, they know the Belize Zoo is probably the only chance they will have of seeing wild animals up close.

You don't have to travel for hours to get that close-up view. Going to the zoo is easy: just catch a Belmopan-bound bus, get off at the zoo entrance by the side of the highway and walk the few hundred yards to the main gate. Belize City taxi drivers generally charge about BZ$80 for a half-day trip. But the zoo is hot, and while the animals enjoy the shade, you'll have trouble finding it on the loose stone paths. Avoid the midday heat and take a hat and bottled water, you're going to need them both. Insect repellant is a good idea or the jaguar won't be the only one with spots on his arms and legs! The zoo is open daily, from 9am to 5pm, BZ$15 for adults, BZ$7.50 for children. It has a nice little gift shop, but no restaurant. Ten minutes or so up the highway are Cheers and JB's, which have great hamburgers and local food and accommodation too. ❏

Map on page 242

The Belize Zoo is as much a botanical garden as it is a zoological park. The message: we need to save the habitat to save the animals.

BELOW: look into my eyes…

Map on page 168

NORTHERN CAYES

From the spectacular Blue Hole to the lively resorts of Ambergris Caye, the string of cayes in the north of Belize are among the country's leading tourist attractions

While most visitors to Belize simply hop on a plane and go straight to a hotel on San Pedro, Ambergris is by no means the only caye in Belize worth exploring. Each of the northern islets offers something unique, although getting to them can be an adventure in itself. Air travel is possible only to a few spots, but water taxis (speed boats which leave **Belize City ❶** at regular intervals and charge a fee) and boat charters from a hotel or tour operator can take you just about anywhere.

Not all cayes in Belize are the beautiful coral islands featured in travel brochures. Many are little more than a muddy tangle of mangrove trees. Yet even the most homely cluster of roots plays a vital role in the coastal eco-system; for fishermen, they are small paradises, and sportsmen from around the world now come to fish for snook, tarpon, bonefish and snapper.

Founded by pirates

Many of the cayes' names date back to the days of pirates and buccaneers. Near Belize City, for example, the **Drowned Cayes ❷** contain such evocative titles as Frenchman's Caye and Spanish Lookout; Bannister Bogue is a channel named after a pirate who later became a logwood cutter in the late 1600s; while Gallows Point was where criminals and freebooters were hanged. The pirate John Colson anchored his ship at **Colson's Cayes ❸** further south, but today lobster fishermen use these mangroves to collect booty of a different sort. **Robinson's Point** was once the center of Belize's boat building industry with a shipyard run by the Hunter and Young families; all that remains is an old lighthouse.

However, if you want to get the feel of why pirates used to love the Belizean – at that time the Bay of Honduras – coastline and secluded cayes, you hardly have to leave Belize City. **Moho Caye ❹**, a short hop off the coast to the north of Belize City (behind St. John's College) is a little C-shaped caye that is now used as a boat marina. The caye has changed owners several times in recent years, but the lodge is still open and the restaurant and bar are an intriguing little hideaway spot to cool off in the evening and on weekends. (Bring repellant though.)

A skiff ferries passengers to and from Belize City every half hour and in the meantime you can wait on an interesting little dock built right on top of mangrove roots along the shore.

There's another little watering hole not too far from Belize City, but the "regulars" are not people, they're manatees. Although **Swallow Caye ❺** sounds like it is a haven for birds – and you'll see plenty of these too – it's the manatees who enjoy the warm-water sink-

PRECEDING PAGES: the Blue Hole. **LEFT:** relaxing at Caye Caulker's Cut. **BELOW:** traditional cargo sailboat.

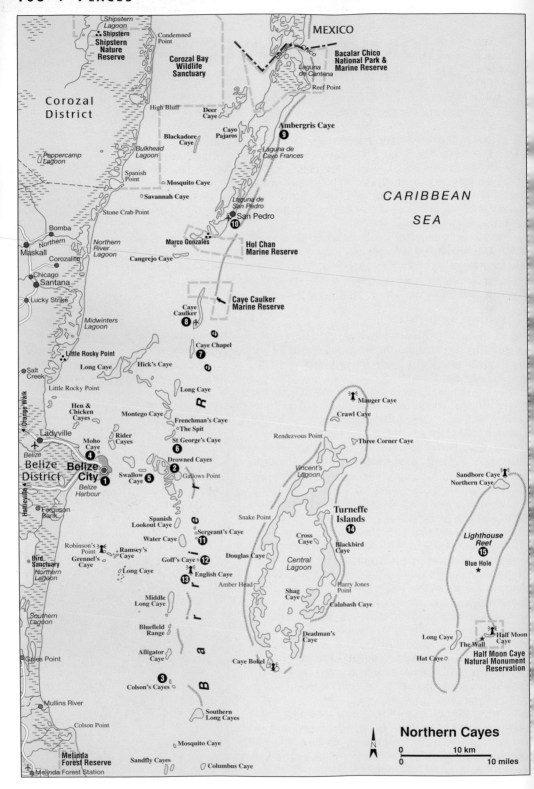

Northern Cayes

0   10 km

0   10 miles

N

Map on page 168

hole that draw the crowds. For years the spot was a secret enjoyed only by those lucky enough to have Chocolate Heredia as their guide (he's in the Caye Caulker section of the phone book under "C" for Chocolate) or be in the company of a handful of other Belize City fishermen who know the coastal waters.

But now the word is out and so many manatee watchers come to the sinkhole, now a protected reserve, signs have been posted to warn boats to slow down and keep their distance. Although it is tempting to hop overboard and swim with these gentle creatures when you see their snouts peek above the water, it's not allowed, or appreciated by those who are trying to protect this endangered species.

Don't expect to see much more than their nostrils blowing air, and some days they can't be seen at all, although they are probably feeding on plants on the sea floor. Or maybe they have just grown tired of visitors. But when you do see their large shadowy form, its something you will remember *(see page 273 for more information on manatee watching)*.

Site of the first settlement

Just 9 miles (14 km) from Belize City, crescent-shaped **St George's Caye ❻** is the most historic of all the offshore islands. It was here that the British buccaneers established the territory's first real settlement around 1650; a century and a half later, they defeated Spanish invaders in the famous Battle of St George's Caye in 1798 *(see Buccaneers and Baymen, pages 33–38)*.

One account, written by a traveling Spanish cleric, reveals that in the mid-17th century, the British pirate Bartholomew Sharpe used St George's Caye as a command center for an impressive fleet of 23 vessels manned by several hundred buccaneers. The priest reports that he was captured by Sharpe's men and taken to the caye, but since he didn't speak any English and Sharpe didn't speak any Spanish, the two communicated in Latin. (Sharpe is reported to have acquired the language in Britain while he himself was training to enter religious orders.) Fortunately for the Spaniard, the gentleman pirate spared his life but put him to good use conducting Mass and hearing confessions, until he was released a few months later.

Today the only reminders of these colorful times at St George's Caye are a mounted cannon on the beach and a small **graveyard** near **St George's Lodge**. A white picket fence encloses what little is left of the cemetery; the elaborate tombstones and many graves of the caye's early settlers were carried away during the 1961 hurricane. The rest of the island is occupied by the vacation homes of Belize's more affluent families, two small hotels and several fishermen's homes.

The caye is very quiet during the week, but on the weekends many Belize City residents come out for fishing and water-skiing, or sunbathing on the kraals (an old colonial system of enclosing an area of sea water, supposedly to protect swimmers from sharks). A mile (1.6 km) offshore is an area of shallow water called **The Spit** (or Miami Beach), a great place to anchor a boat and hop over the side for a swim. The water is only about 1 to 3 feet (0.3m to 1 meter) deep and the sand is completely free of sea grass and other vegetation.

Colorful cafés line Caye Caulker's sandy walkways.

BELOW: the laid-back pace of Caye Caulker.

The only hotel currently operating on the island, St George's Lodge, caters mainly to scuba divers. The British Army Training Support Unit, BATSUB, has its rest and relaxing station at St. George's Caye and the soldiers enjoy windsurfing and other sports.

Spaniards' graveyard turned golf course

Although it has never been verified by scientific research or excavation, legend has it that **Caye Chapel ❼** got its name because the Spanish buried their dead here after the battle of St. George's Caye in 1798.

We may never know for sure because the caye, lying 7 miles (11 km) north of St. George's Caye, is being converted into an exclusive golf resort, which may at some point include casino gambling. To extend the golf course, a long sea-wall was built out into the sea and the island was made larger. This instantly caught the attention of environmentalists who feared the work would threaten lobster hatching grounds between Caye Chapel and Caye Caulker and are against the use of pesticides to maintain the grounds saying these will run off into the water and damage the nearby reef. In what appeared to many as an apparent attempt to counteract adverse publicity about the project, the American owner of Pyramid Island Resort, Larry Addington, donated US$1 million-worth of brand new pick-up trucks to the Belize Police Department. No more was said about the development; although the Ministry of Natural Resources determined the lobster hatching grounds were not being disturbed, local environmentalists remain concerned about the project. While the donated police trucks are being used on the mainland, these days Pyramid Island seems to be doing some policing of its own. Warning signs are posted at the water taxi drop-off

BELOW: sea kayakers getting ready to roll on St. George's Caye.

point on the rear of the island clearly stating that armed guards patrol the island and only registered guests are allowed to come on shore. It is not clear what has prompted the beefed-up security, but the sign, graphically illustrated with the image of a handgun, is not exactly a warm welcome and indicates that neither local nor foreign drop-in visitors are welcome.

Fishing village cum tourist mecca

One of the most popular northern cayes is **Caye Caulker** ❽, just a few minutes north of Caye Chapel. This working fishing village was originally settled by *mestizos* (of mixed Spanish and indigenous blood) fleeing the Caste War in Mexico's Yucatán in the late 800s; today it has about 1,000 year-round residents, mostly of *mestizo* descent. The population swells considerably on weekends and holidays, when hundreds of Belize City residents descend on the island's small guesthouses and hotels. Easter is the busiest season and those who arrive without advance reservations may well need to search around for a friend to give them some floor space in their room.

Many Belizeans prefer Caye Caulker to San Pedro on Ambergris Caye, and not just because hotel rates are lower (although you may have to share a bathroom). Most importantly, they feel more at home here than in the Americanized San Pedro on Ambergris Caye. Caulker has a typically Belizean atmosphere, with many of the restaurants and sidewalk stands offering local cuisine and the bars providing raucous nightlife. Drinking is a favorite pastime (except on Good Friday or election days when no liquor can be served), and there's usually a live band. It's not uncommon to see tourists and Belize City visitors struggling to find their way home through the sand, or taking a snooze in a beached dory.

Map on page 168

TIP

As in all Belizean waters, divers and snorkelers are warned not to touch the delicate coral or remove any marine life from anywhere on the reef, particularly now that it has protected status as a marine reserve.

BELOW: wreck on the reef at Half Moon Caye.

A dreadlock-shaded smile on Caye Caulker.

BELOW: conch shell mountain.

(Visitors are asked to remember that Caye Caulker is not a resort community but a working village and people who live here have to get up and go to work or school, so try to keep the noise down on your way home in the evening.)

Sand dredged from the back of the island and pumped to the front creates a lovely – but artificial – beach several metres wide along the seaward shore. **The Cut** (more popularly known as The Split), at the north end of the village, a channel through the island made by Hurricane Hattie in 1961, may be the most popular gathering place on the island, with a nice swimming area (be careful of the strong current and speedboats, however) and an open-air bar. European tourists who like topless sunbathing are often the cause of some excitement at the Cut, but unless a policeman strolls by, no one is likely to tell them that it's illegal in Belize. Day trips to the reef for diving and snorkeling are also available and water taxis make runs to San Pedro throughout the day.

Children like the Split because the water is shallow for a good stretch in front of the sea wall and the sandy bottom is free of rocks. Little fish, crabs and starfish along the wall also provide hours of entertainment and island children are eager to demonstrate to the city kids and tourists how to get in and out of the water without a ladder, since there is rarely one in place.

Because of its relaxed, Bohemian lifestyle, some visitors like Caye Caulker so much they never go home. As a result, the caye now has a number of expatriate artists, and several restaurants and gift shops are run by gringos determined to find their own piece of paradise. Pleasant as it is, though, the island has its share of problems – including a rising crime rate and reputation as a haven for drug traffickers. Determined not to let their island be overrun by criminals, residents frustrated by police inactivity have organized an extremely successful citizens' patrol program, similar to one pioneered at San Pedro. At the other end of the social scale, residents want to ensure that tourism growth is controlled and the island does not become over-commercialized.

Growing tourism has also meant growing pressure on the nearby reef. After a decade of requests from local fishermen and environmentalists, in 1999 the government gave reserve status to most of the reef in front of the caye. The Belize Fisheries Department is developing the proper regulations in consultation with local fishermen and conservation agencies. In the meantime, national fishing regulations apply to everyone, including open and closed seasons for lobster and conch.

The northern tip of the caye forms the terrestrial part of the Caulker Forest and Marine Reserve. This protective measure became necessary after developers began denuding the caye of native tree species and leaving only coconut trees, and organizations such as the **Siwa-Ban Foundation** of Caye Caulker raised the alarm about overdevelopment. Ellen McRae is one of the island's most active conservationists and is an avid birder. She will tell you anything you want to know about Caye Caulker and is a walking field guide of avian facts and figures. As much as she loves Caye Caulker, every year in December and January she spends her weekends on the mainland joining the Belize Audubon Society's Christmas bird count.

Hispanic Ambergris

On a typical Saturday night in the village of **San Pedro**, a crowd gathers outside the local church. The event seems to be a typical wedding, with a girl dressed in white and her groom in a black tuxedo as the centers of attention. But, after the service, the happy couple hops into a golf cart decorated with palm leaves; the rest of the church party follows in a train of bouncing buggies, the main form of transport on this almost car-free island. The reception is nearby, in a canopy-covered basketball court; in the center stands a huge white cake, decorated with 30 plastic dolls.

The event, it turns out, is actually the girl's *Quince Años*, or 15th birthday – an old Mexican tradition that is celebrated with 15 other girls and boys about the same age. The festivities bring half the population of San Pedro together and carry on late into the night – part of the strange innocence that still permeates Belize's most popular tourist resort, **Ambergris Caye** .

It's not surprising that Mexican is the predominant influence on Ambergris Caye and San Pedro (the only settlement here, effectively synonymous with the caye). In fact, Ambergris is technically not an island at all, but a 25-mile (40-km) peninsula extending from the Yucatán and separated from Mexico only by a small channel originally dug by the ancient Maya.

In the early 1980s, fishing was still the major industry at San Pedro – which is why the town and church were named after St Peter. Now many of the fishermen use their locally made mahogany boats to take tourists to the Barrier Reef that parallels the island. But although this is the most touristy part of Belize, the population is still only 4,000. If you like your tourism slick and well-orchestrated, with raging nightclubs and elegant dining, this may not be the place for you. San Pedro and the Caye have lots of charm, but sometimes the eyes and the heart need to make the distinction between run down and quaint.

The population of San Pedro is determined not to become one more high-rise Caribbean resort: laws have been passed prohibiting any building more than three stories tall. The idea is to maintain the small scale of Ambergris and give owners of small hotels a chance to stay in business.

There is plenty to enjoy in Ambergris, where the living is so casual that going barefoot is appropriate just about anywhere. The streets of San Pedro are of soft, foot-friendly dirt. Many bars, restaurants, and stores have soft sand floors. Like their counterparts in Placencia, Caye Caulker and just about any other sand-based town, residents go barefoot most of the time. The women may wear high heels for special occasions like weddings and graduations, but the pretty shoes are usually kicked off moments after the ceremony ends.

But while the sand is soft (if scorching hot on the soles of your feet at noon) it doesn't always stay on the ground. With over 200 vehicles on the island and numerous golf carts, its hard to avoid swirling whirlwinds of it stinging you in the eyes. Tropic Air recently helped to lay clay tiles on the busiest road near the airstrip and many villagers wish there were enough money in the council coffers to pave the entire island!

Ambergris Caye is thought to have gained its name when quantities of ambergris (a substance secreted by sperm whales), appeared on its shores during the 19th century.

BELOW: a wary moray eel eyes an approaching scuba diver.

The sand also combines with the sea salt to create problems for the power company, Belize Electricity Limited. After investing millions in a submarine cable to provide a booming San Pedro with more efficient electricity, the company was suddenly faced with extensive and costly "blackouts" when equipment on the poles was unable to handle all the salt and sand buildup. BEL had to wash off power lines and import special coverings from abroad. They also had to compensate some residents and resorts for damaged electrical appliances.

But San Pedranos tend to take such inconveniences in their stride. Life is pretty mellow here, so much so that you will notice a fair amount of resident North Americans running hotels, gift shops and restaurants. Some older San Pedranos resent what they see as the Americanization of San Pedro, but the younger folks don't seem to mind. The local high school students are just as inclined to speak with an American accent as they are to switch back and forth into creole or Spanish.

Belize's largest caye

Ambergris, 35 miles (56 km) from Belize City, can be reached by water taxi in two hours or small propeller plane in about 20 minutes. San Pedro's airport has a rugged appeal to it, far removed from the crowded world of international terminals. The airport has an air-conditioned terminal and outdoors is a white wooden bench, which served as a "waiting room" for years. Dogs snooze beneath the parked planes and, between arrivals and departures, kids ride their bikes across the lone runway – even though they shouldn't.

BELOW: Barrier Reef Drive, San Pedro's main street.

Located near the southern edge of San Pedro, the airport is a good orientation point. Facing the road that parallels the landing strip, the town proper is to the

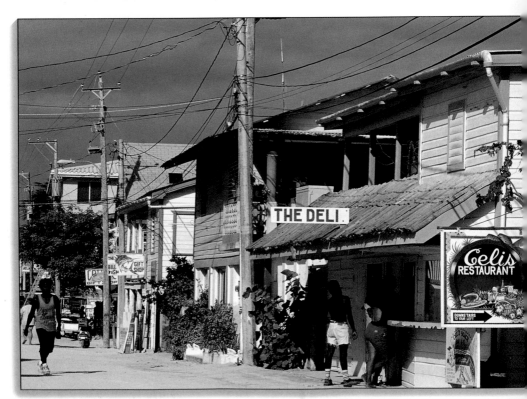

immediate left; to the right, the road leads through the quiet resorts of the south. Straight ahead, beyond a few buildings, is the Caribbean; behind is the lagoon.

Three streets run north–south through **San Pedro ❿**: shoreside Barrier Reef Drive; Pescador Drive, in the middle; and, lastly, Angel Coral Street. The heart of town is midway along Barrier Reef Drive. On one block, there is the **Town Hall** and **police station** (the police have little to do except remind tourists to turn on their golf cart or bicycle headlights when driving at night). On the next block is **San Pedro Church**, an airy building whose large windows have jalousies so that the congregation can be cooled by the Caribbean breeze.

Opposite the church is **Plaza Park**, an open-air, concrete space, with a painted bust of a Maya chief, not too far from the churchyard's painted statue of St Peter. Neither statue could qualify as great art, but both have a naïve charm. The park also has a basketball court, played on every night. People gather to watch the games, if for no other reason than to take advantage of the sea breeze: games are subject to being interrupted during the rainy season by sudden storms.

Evening vibrations

Directly down on the beach from here is the center of the caye's nightlife. The **Pier Lounge** is known for its promotional gimmicks, especially the Chicken Drop Contest on Wednesday night, where you can place a bet on which numbered square a chicken will defecate on. The Pier also holds the annual Beach Queen contest, in July.

While strolling along Barrier Reef and Pescador drives, step back and look at the buildings themselves; many are classic versions of Caribbean architecture.

Maps:
Area 168
City 175

BELOW: Ambergris dreaming.

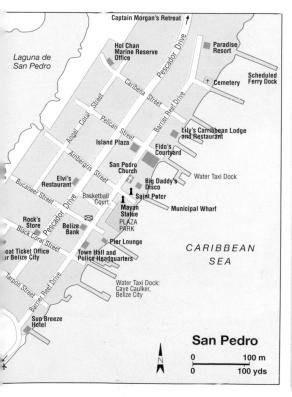

The painted statue of a Maya chief in San Pedro's Plaza Park.

The **Barrier Reef Hotel** is perhaps one of the most splendid examples, it is one of the oldest houses in San Pedro, but even some of the apparently decrepit wooden houses are still architecturally interesting. Some visitors to San Pedro have been looking down instead of up: in a lot on Pescador Drive, across the street from Elvi's Restaurant, a team of archeologists has been spending summers sifting and digging, gradually finding relics from the island's remote past as a Maya settlement.

The undeveloped north

Many of the local inhabitants live towards the north end of town, some in the vicinity of an unsightly landfill. Beyond this, the island is divided by a stream, known locally as The River: a hand-pulled barge ferries people across to the northern part where the development is less rampant and the mood, if possible, even more laid back.

This is the place for those who find even the subdued village life of San Pedro too much and who really, really want to get away from it all. A rugged sand path runs along the shore, which can be traveled by foot or bike. But the preferred way to head north of San Pedro is by boat. There are no towns here, so activity centers around several resorts, including **Journey's End**, and some good restaurants such as Capricorn.

The northern end of the caye may seem quiet, but when a shrimp farm began to install a pipe out into the sea near the reef, San Pedrano tour guides and fishermen staged a protest forcing the company to revise its plan. Large-scale tourism development has been proposed for this part of the caye for years, but so far nothing concrete has happened.

BELOW:
T-shirts for sale.

Map on page 168

The road south of San Pedro

Ambergris Caye owes much of its physical existence to the mangrove, which can be most easily seen to the south, following the sand road from the airport. Untouched except for the occasional plastic wrapping or old shoe washed in by the gentle waves, the mangrove swamp is like a trip into the womb that gave birth to the island.

Before the mangroves is a clearing developed as a park by the local Lions' Club. The area was used as a set for some of the scenes in the Harrison Ford movie, *The Mosquito Coast*. There's no shortage of the devilish insects here, and having repellent on hand is a good idea, especially at night. Mosquitoes are seldom a problem on the beaches, however, from which they are pushed back by the steady trade winds.

Back in the direction of town is the **Belize Yacht Club**, which is not a yacht club at all but a condominium development with a good marina. (Local officials aren't enthusiastic about vacation condo complexes, which create few jobs; rents usually go to out-of-town owners rather than circulating in the economy.) For an island with few gas-driven vehicles, there is an extremely attractive Shell gas station located at the front of the Yacht Club. It is built in Spanish colonial style and features a mahogany door with Maya relief figures.

Into the Caribbean

Like any other self-respecting tropical island, Ambergris Caye looks to the sea. The island is set in the Barrier Reef, and it is off-shore that one heads for swimming, fishing diving and snorkeling.

There are no real beaches or even waves along Ambergris' shoreline. Most of the water between the coast and the reef is shallow and grassy – a shoreline for lounging, not surfing.

It was the Maya who discovered a natural cut in the reef, which attracted a wide range of marine life. They called it "Hol Chan," Little Channel. In 1987, the area around the cut was declared the **Hol Chan Marine Reserve** – only 10 minutes away by boat, it is Ambergris' principal local site for snorkeling and scuba diving.

Snorkelers look for the beautiful coral formations along the reef and for fish, many of which like to congregate beneath the anchored boats, while scuba divers are attracted to a sinkhole and an underlying cave *(see "Beneath the Waves," pages 103-107, for details on Belize's marine life.)*

Fishing is not permitted in the reserve, but there's plenty of sea left for that. Most fishing consists of either trawling in the open sea or dropping anchor in one of the larger lagoons, where the water is calm.

Snappers and groupers are plentiful, and an occasional barracuda puts up a good fight. The sea also provides a lobster industry. Over the years, however, the lobsters have been over-fished, and between March and July the crustaceans are off-limits.

While San Pedro is the ideal base if you're planning to visit Hol Chan, many dive and snorkel operators from Caye Caulker will also take you there. Snorkeling along the reef is fun, but the truly adventurous

BELOW: a burst of energy on court.

TIP

There are no ferry services to the cayes south of Belize City, such as Goff's and English Cayes, but boats can be hired for the trip from several companies *(see Travel Tips, Outdoor Activities, for details)*.

will want to take the plunge at Shark Ray Alley. This is only 1 mile/2 km south of Hol Chan and offers the unique experience of diving or snorkeling with stingrays and sharks; well, nurse sharks. Although they seem fairly harmless (but don't look that way at feeding time) this is not a swim for the fainthearted. You may jump into the water fairly confident but suddenly start feeling a little nervous when the wings of the ray brush against you. You can only visit Shark Ray Alley with an experienced guide. The responsible guides do not pick the rays up out of the water or try to get the nurse sharks excited by feeding them before you get into the water.

Ambergris Caye exists in a fragile ecology, both socially and biologically speaking. Its future faces the same challenge as most of the world's tourist areas – to be able to develop its resources, while – in the ways that are fundamentally important – remaining the same.

Back south

Returning to the waters south of Belize City, there are some lesser-known cayes, where you can find a little piece of tropical paradise all to yourself. Tiny **Sergeant's Caye ⑪**, named for an 18th-century merchant, is almost always deserted except for five guardian coconut trees. **Goff's Caye ⑫**, just to the south has more shade, but also more people, especially at weekends. To protect visitors from too much sun or a sudden downpour, a large thatched roof has been erected over a cement slab, but there are no picnic tables or benches, so it's a good idea to bring a folding stool or a hammock if you need creature comforts.

Goff's Caye may be small, but it is ever-changing. The sands shift around, constantly altering the shape of the island. Sometimes your boat can dock right

BELOW:
shooting the surf.

off the pier for easy unloading of passengers; at other times the pier is marooned offshore and you have to wade in holding your picnic basket over your head. The sand may move but the coconut trees stay put and so does the reef. The snorkeling around Goff's Caye is consistently good and the tide pools where the reef meets the sand are always full of the same shy little fish and crabs that have amused generations of children. Although the water taxis have so far not added this caye to their normally scheduled runs, a number of charter boat agencies will do it and some include lunch in the package. Rates are better if you can get a group together. If you only have time to visit one caye from Belize City, this has got to be it – so it's worth the extra effort to get there.

English Caye ⑬, further down the line, sits alongside the main shipping channel. Its steel frame lighthouse, built in 1935, marks the entrance to the channel for deep draft vessels coming into the port of Belize City. There are also several homes here.

Beyond the Barrier Reef

Diving and fishing enthusiasts may venture further into the Caribbean to Belize's three coral atolls. Although most watersport activities take place from charter boats, a surge of interest has fueled the development of a few island-based resorts. Two of these atolls, the Turneffe Islands and Lighthouse Reef, can be reached from Belize City; the third, Glover's Reef, is off the coast from Dangriga, *(see South to Dangriga, pages 241–251)*.

The **Turneffe Islands ⑭** are the surface elements of Belize's largest atoll running some 30 miles (48 km) from north to south; it has several shallow lagoons, a couple of upscale resorts and two lighthouses. The northernmost beacon, built

Map
on page
168

TIP

Two of the best diving and snorkeling sites off the Turneffe Islands are **Elbow Reef** and **Black Beauty**, an area known for its black coral (a false coral, popular in local jewelry, but a practice that is frowned on by conservationists).

BELOW: snorkelers taking the plunge at Hol Chan Marine Reserve.

Map on page 168

Diving through nooks and crannies near Half Moon Caye.

BELOW: sharing a romantic sunset. **RIGHT:** aerial palm mosaic.

in 1885, is on **Mauger Caye** ("Skinny" in creole) while a second lighthouse can be found on **Caye Bokel** ("Elbow" in Dutch) at the southern tip of the atoll.

Almost all the major charter boat and dive services arrange trips to Turneffe, but guests at the various fishing and vacation lodges are usually picked up by the lodge's own transportation from Belize City.

Lighthouse Reef ⑮ is another atoll with a treacherous boundary of coral. Like Turneffe, there are also two lighthouses here, one on **Sandbore Caye**; the other, first built in 1828 and replaced in 1848, is on **Half Moon Caye**, a crescent-shaped island that is easily one of the most beautiful places in Belize. The abundance of nesting sea birds and marine life made Half Moon Caye and its surrounding waters a natural choice for the nation's first Natural Monument in 1982. Around 4,000 red-footed booby birds nest on the island; the population is unusual for being white instead of the usual dull brown (the only other similar booby colony is near the island of Tobago in the eastern Caribbean). An observation platform allows unrestricted viewing of the boobies, along with some of the 98 other species of birds that have been recorded on the island. Lighthouse keeper John Lambey is happy to chat with visitors about the endangered sea turtles that have chosen this beach as a nesting site.

Forests of black coral sprout like weeds from **The Wall** near Half Moon Caye. This vertical drop-off is sliced by canyons and narrow passages, many of which have overhangs that often coalesce into short caves wide enough for divers to swim through. Closer to shore lies a wide sand bank covered with thousands of garden eels swaying in the current, where they feed off passing plankton. These creatures are extremely shy, quickly pulling back, tail first, into their holes in the sand, at the approach of a diver. ❑

THE BLUE HOLE

Lying just 7 miles (11 km) north of Half Moon Caye is one of the world's most famous dive sites, and one of the most beautiful natural wonders in Belize: the Blue Hole.

Looking from the air like a dark blue pool in a field of turquoise, the site gained fame in 1972 when Jacques Cousteau maneuvered his ship *Calypso* through narrow coral channels to moor and film inside. The Blue Hole is actually a sinkhole created by a collapsed underground cavern; over 980 ft (300 meters) across and 445 ft (135 meters) deep, with huge stalactites hanging from offshore caves at depths of 100 to 150 ft (30–45 meters).

Sharks and turtles abound here, though their presence is rarely predictable. This dive is usually reserved for the more adventurous and experienced, under the strict supervision of a dive master. It is definitely not a plunge to be attempted by the novice.

The Belize Audubon Society and the Forestry Department manage the Blue Hole National Monument at Lighthouse Reef, which covers an area of 1,023 acres (414 hectares) with the Blue Hole at the center. No fishing, polluting or disturbing of the marine or plant life is permitted, but there has been some trouble with fishermen moving the buoys marking the four corners of the site.

A PRECIOUS STRING OF PEARLS

Belize's Barrier Reef is attaining protection as a chain of sanctuaries designed to safeguard and showcase its precious marine habitats

Belize is endowed with a rich diversity in its marine habitats, sufficient to warrant World Heritage status. A growing number of offshore areas are being set aside as preserves, helping to ensure their survival – and balance the demands of tourism with preservation.

FROM NORTH TO SOUTH

This is a selection of some of the country's best marine areas (with details of how to get there in the Travel Tips section at the back of the book.) Northernmost, **Bacalar Chico National Park** matches its counterpart in Mexico, protecting wetlands, forest and reef. It is here that the Barrier comes closest to the land.

Next in line is **Hol Chan Marine Reserve**, off Ambergris Caye. This multihabitat (reef, seagrass, mangroves) Marine Protected Area, or MPA, was the first on the reef in 1987, and has provided a stimulus and model for subsequent MPAs.

Continuing south, **Caye Caulker Marine and Forest reserves**, a hard-won twin MPA that runs along the reef and seagrass in front of the caye, together with mangroves, lagoons and littoral forest of the north point of the caye.

Near Dangriga is the **South Water Caye MPA**, encompassing a vast area of reef and lagoon, including northern faroes. Near to Punta Gorda, is **Port Honduras MPA**, consisting of near-shore cayes and adjacent mainland wetland. **Sapodilla Cayes MPA** protects Belize's southernmost cayes.

△ **FRIENDLY NURSE SHARKS**
Nurse sharks are relatively easy-going (for a shark, that is) and often show a harmless curiosity in their visitors.

▷ **RICH HABITATS**
Multihabitat areas, such as Bacalar Chico, are chosen for their biodiversity, sheltering a wide range of marine life.

▷**SMALL FOOD FISH**
The smaller reef fish, such as these striped spadefish and blue-striped grunts, provide important food for the larger inhabitants.

◁ RESEARCH INSTITUTE
The Smithsonian Institute runs a research station on Carrie Bow Caye, which may be visited by appointment.

△ SKIMMING THE SURFACE
Snorkeling over the top of the reef can be a delight of discovery, as many of the most colorful fish and coral live close to the surface.

▽ HAWKSBILL TURTLE
Belize's most endangered sea turtle is protected by law, but you may be lucky enough to see one along the reef.

▷ COLORFUL TUBES
Inhabiting the ocean depths off the reef, sponges are colorful but simple life forms, which feed by filtering plankton from the water.

◁ DELICATE DELIGHTS
Corals are highly fragile and should never be touched, let alone removed – some can even cause a nasty rash if you get scratched.

PLUMBING THE REEF DEPTHS

Belize's superlative marine environment offers exciting appeal for every diver and snorkeler. While you're enjoying your reef adventure, however, you should also be aware that the reef is vital to the well-being of the country itself.

The reefs, particularly the Barrier Reef, absorb most of the surf shock from hurricanes, which annually sweep across the Caribbean causing mass injury and devastation.

Follow a few simple rules to help preserve the reef:
● Stay at least at arm's length from coral, to protect both it – and your skin – from possible scrapes.
● Remain horizontal while swimming over coral so as not to raise sediments, which may suffocate it or introduce diseases.
● Keep plastic, cigarettes and other waste products inside your boat.

NORTH TO ALTUN HA

Map
on pages
188–9

Besides the impressive Maya ruins of Altun Há,
within a few hours' drive north of Belize City there are pioneering
nature preserves and luxurious jungle resorts

Whether or not they know the archeologists' name for it, everyone in Belize recognizes the Temple of Masonry Altars at Altun Há. The image is on the paper money, school textbooks, perhaps even most importantly for some, it was chosen for the logo of the national beer, Belikin.

The ancient Maya site is the centerpiece of northern Belize District, a classically Caribbean landscape of rich, humid, rain-soaked lowlands. The villages here are tiny, usually no more than a few brightly painted wooden houses on stilts clustered along a small roadway, perhaps with a tin-roofed church from which the sound of hymns will drift on a Sunday morning. A few are still without electricity or running water, sharing a hand pump. But although the atmosphere is languid, even soporific, this is one of the most visited parts of the country, easily reached by car from Belize City.

This is also the first part of Belize that many travelers see. **Phillip Goldson International Airport ❶**, near the village of Ladyville, lies 10 miles (16 km) north of Belize City on the Northern Highway. There are a couple of box-like hotels near the airport, as well as the airport camp, headquarters for the few British forces remaining in Belize. The Northern Highway is well paved and runs more or less unbroken up to the Mexican border.

PRECEDING PAGES:
Altun Há's Temple
of the Masonry
Altars; **LEFT:** young
howler monkey.
BELOW: two Maya
generations.

Wine and baboons

Only 5 miles (9 km) north of the international airport is a rougher dirt road turning off to the left; it continues through the villages of Burrell Boom and the poetic-sounding (but nearly non-existent) Scotland Halfmoon. At **Burrell Boom ❷**, one of the key communities in the old logging days, some enterprising villagers are also trying to woo visitors with their homemade wines. The potent beverages, made from ginger, sorrel, cashew and assorted fruits, have long been Belizean favorites, especially at Christmas. If you buy a bottle, watch out, the concoction may taste sweet and innocent but a little goes a very long way – all the way to tomorrow morning if you're not careful. Follow the bends in the river road until you see the signs to the winery. Burrell Boom also has a comfortable hotel and a bar.

After 13 miles (20 km) from the turn-off, you come to the **Community Baboon Sanctuary ❸** – one of the most popular and successful conservation projects in Belize. Founded in 1985, the Baboon Sanctuary is a co-operative effort between environmentalists (aided by the World Wildlife Fund under the auspices of the Audubon Society) and local creole landowners to save Central America's declining population of black howler monkeys, known as baboons in Belize. Apart from Belize, this sub-species is only found in the river lowlands of Guatemala and southern Mexico, where the rainforest has been shrinking at such a rate that extinction was becoming probable (for more on the howler monkey, see In the Wild, pages 115–122).

A zoologist from the University of Wisconsin, Dr Robert Horwich, initially signed an agreement with 16 local farmers along the Belize River: while still working their agricultural lands, the farmers pledged to follow a management plan that would help protect the howler monkeys.

We're for the baboons!

The agreement covered topics as diverse as a co-ordination plan for cutting and burning local plantations, to the building of "baboon bridges" – rope and wood ladders hung across roadways to allow monkeys safe crossings. The program was an instant success and has been the basis for other community-based reserves around the world. Since 1985, the number of participating farmers has gone up to nearly 100, allowing the sanctuary to cover 20 miles (32 km) along the Belize River.

Villagers have profited from the rise in tourism, and have taken up the creole slogan *Baboon ya de fu we* ("literally translated as "The baboons here are our responsibility.") Howler monkey numbers, initially estimated at 800, are now around 1,200 and rising. The program has also had an impact elsewhere in the country with howler monkeys being successfully relocated to the Cockscomb Basin Wildlife Reserve by a team of American scientists aided by Belizean volunteers. The new "colony" is said to be doing well.

The sanctuary's service village is **Bermudian Landing**, a British logging camp in the 1600s and today a relaxed creole outpost. Check in at the visitors' center here – there are some places to stay, some flat ground for tents, or the station manager can arrange for accommodation with local families. A small museum, opened in 1989, was Belize's first devoted to natural history, and an interpretive trail can be followed. Canoe trips, horseback riding and crocodile-watching tours are also available. There is also a jam fac-

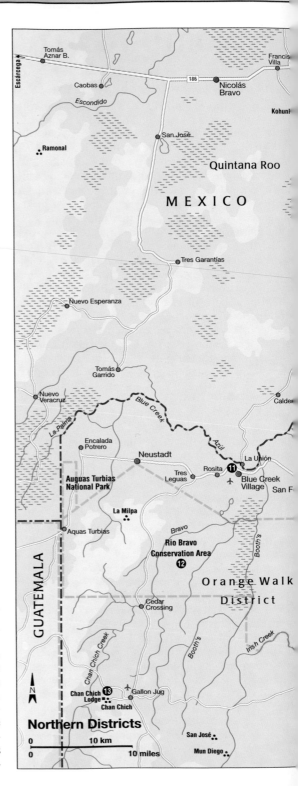

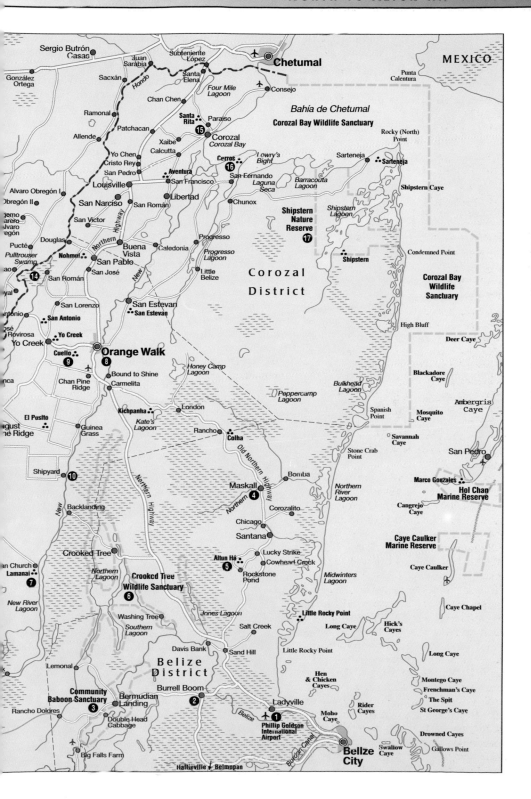

The tall jabiru stork, a distinctive sight at the Crooked Tree Wildlife Sanctuary.

BELOW: the old Northern Highway.

tory and a Creole Cultural Center. All visitors are asked to register at the Community Baboon Sanctuary Museum, open 8am–5pm daily. The regular nature trail costs BZ$10 per person and night hikes are available for BZ$20.

The Sanctuary is 26 miles (40 km) from Belize City and most taxi drivers will take you there for around BZ$100. The bus service is cheaper but a little trickier. The smaller companies that service the route leave Belize City early in the afternoon or evening, and don't return until the next day. There is no service at all on Sunday, so be prepared to spend the night, or maybe the entire weekend, with a local family bed and breakfast. Advance arrangements are recommended; contact the Belizean Audubon Society.

Viewing the wildlife

Local guides can be hired at the Visitors' Center for walks through the sanctuary. As with any animal-watching in Belize, the best time to visit is around dawn or dusk, when the cacophonous shrieks of the howler monkeys echo along the Belize River. The sanctuary is also home to more than 200 species of bird and the usual menagerie of Belizean wildlife, including deer, iguanas, jaguars, anteaters, coatis, turtles and peccaries. Although classified as riverine rainforest and cohune palm forest, the landscape can be surprisingly dusty and scrubby, especially at the end of the dry season. Having been logged steadily for some 300 years, the forest in the sanctuary is mostly secondary growth dating back no further than the turn of the 20th century.

A rough dirt road leads south from the sanctuary to the Western Highway, past villages like **Willows Bank** and **Double Head Cabbage** (whose names are the most interesting thing about them). These areas have been depressed econom-

ically for years, with many of the younger folk leaving to seek work in Belize City or in the United States, but some community leaders have recently formed the Belize River Valley Development Association to try and create jobs. BelRiv is promoting small-scale fish farming using native river species, subsistence farming and preserve processing. Non-governmental organizations have also been training local fishermen in techniques to try and "catch" some North American anglers who enjoy fishing Belize's inland waterways for snook and tarpon.

Alternative route to Altun Há

Heading north again on the new Northern Highway, via Burrell Boom, the turn off to the right after passing through Sand Hill (6 miles/10 km) is the rather rougher Old Northern Highway. The tiny villages of Cowhead Creek, Lucky Strike and Santana pass by in a colorful blur – the houses all seem to be painted baby blue or frou-frou pink, framed by the lush green of surrounding palm trees.

Maskall ❹, although it is no more impressive than the other villages on the highway, functions as the region's local administrative center. The village may have only received 24-hour electricity a few years ago, but they have already declared their intention to be on the tourism fast track. After all, they are strategically located. Everyone who wants to get to Altun Há has to pass through Maskall. Even boat operators from San Pedro have to come down the Northern River that runs through the town to bring visitors arriving from the caye on day-trips. Villagers are hoping their local crafts, woodcarving, produce and home-cooking will encourage the tour buses and rental vehicles to make a quick stop. As one aspiring carver put it, "We want to see the tourists' faces up close, not through tinted windows!"

Maps:
Area 188
Site 191

TIP

The luxurious Maruba Health Resort is a surprising attraction in this undeveloped area. Marked at Mile 40.5 on the highway, the hotel offers a range of therapeutic cures, as well as an excellent restaurant for those opting for regular self-indulgence

BELOW: one of the rebuilt pyramids of Altun Há.

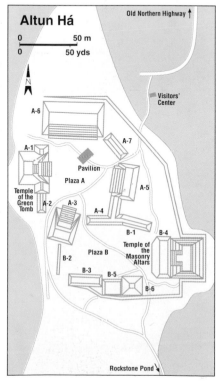

Altun Há

Only a short drive away are the impressive Maya ruins of **Altun Há ❺**, a Classic Period ceremonial center with two large plazas (large enough, in fact, that kids from the nearby village of **Rockstone Pond** are often found playing football in them) and 13 ancient structures, which were probably occupied from 1100 BC to AD 900. Some 3,000 Mayas are believed to have lived here, mostly supporting themselves by farming and trading. Excavation of the site began only in the mid-1960s. The dominant pyramid of Plaza A, known as the **Temple of the Green Tomb**, is actually several temples built on top of one another. Around 300 artifacts have been found inside it, from skins to jewelry, stingray spines to parts of an ancient Maya book.

Vast quantities of jade jewelry have been found at Altun Há.

The tallest structure at Altun Há, the **Temple of the Masonry Altars** (also known as the Temple of the Sun God) looms over Plaza B at a height of 60 ft (18 meters). Five of the seven tombs found in the pyramid had already been ransacked, but in 1968 archeologist David Pendergast discovered the untouched remains of an elderly priest.

Other digging at this temple showed that local priests indulged in an unusual form of sacrifice, whereby beautifully carved jade objects were smashed and flung into fires. And one of its seven tombs showed signs of desecration during the end of the Maya period, which has led archeologists to speculate that Altun Há was abandoned after a violent encounter, possibly a peasant revolt – one more clue in understanding the abandonment of the great Maya cities. David Pendergast is now conducting guided tours of Altun Há and other Maya sites in the region as part of a new trend in educational tourism. Archeologist Michael D. Coe, famous for his work in the Yucatán, leads similar expeditions *(see Travel Tips, Tours Operators, for contact details.)*

BELOW:
replica Maya
pottery for sale.

SACRED MAYA JADE

Buried alongside the remains of a priest found at Altun Há in 1968 by David Pendergast was the jade head of the Maya Sun God, Kinich Ahau. At 5.8 inches (14.9 cm) in height, and weighing 9.75 lb (4.42 kg), this is Belize's most important ancient relic and the largest jade carving found anywhere in the Maya world. It is now kept in a vault in the Belize Bank. A replica of the carving is on display in the Museum of Belize in Belize City.

Jade was the most precious substance to the Maya, as it had been to other pre-Columbian cultures, such as the Olmecs of Mexico. It occurs in various shades, but the Maya prized the green jade most highly, considering it sacred for its glowing green hues that reminded them of the green leaves of maize, their symbol of life itself. For this reason, only kings and deities were allowed to wear jade, as a mark of their status and power.

Jade was traded throughout Mesoamerica; large quantities were extracted from the Motagua River Valley in the southern Guatemalan Highlands. The raw product was exported to the lowlands, where expert artisans fashioned it into delicate and beautiful items of jewelry and ornaments. These artifacts were then re-exported to the highlands in exchange for other local commodities.

But if you just want to sightsee, check in at the visitors' center at Altun Há and pay a $5 fee before entering the site. Bring plenty of water and wear long sleeves and long pants – the insects, and the sun, can be brutal. Altun Há is an easy half-day trip for Belize City taxi drivers and tour operators (*see Travel Tips, Tours, for recommended agencies*) and it is rapidly becoming a popular stop on the cruise ship circuit. Visitor facilities are limited but they should improve as part of a government project to upgrade all Maya sites.

Paradise for birdwatchers

Due west of Altun Há on the new Northern Highway is a dirt road to the left, leading, after 12 miles (19 km) to the **Crooked Tree Wildlife Sanctuary** ❻. This string of four lagoons, connected by swamps and rivers, is one of Belize's richest bird habitats – nesting here are migratory flocks of egrets, tiger-herons, roseate spoonbills and hundreds of other species. Perhaps the most impressive, although elusive, is the jabiru stork, the largest bird in the Western hemisphere, with a wingspan of up to 8 ft (2.4 meters). The wildlife sanctuary was set up by the Belize Audubon Society in 1984 and is now managed by wardens from the village. Before entering, sign in at the tidy visitors' center, just outside the village of **Crooked Tree**, one of the first "Banks", or logging camps, founded by British logwood cutters in the 17th century. Before the causeway was built in the 1980s, the only way to get to Crooked Tree was by boat. The lagoon is a natural reservoir in the Belize River Valley and regularly floods in the rainy season.

The origin of the village's name is the source of local humor, with some swearing it was the site of a huge old crooked tree while others claim it was the hideout for three nefarious buccaneers or bandits (in creole the letters "th" are always pronounced as "t" hence crooked "tree" not "three."). Either version seems plausible since twisted trees still abound and almost all villagers seem to have Tillett, Rhaburn or Wade as a surname.

The manager of the sanctuary can give you a little local history as well as provide information on nature trails and birdlife. The ideal way to visit is by taking a hired boat trip into the swamps and lagoons (call the visitors' center or any of the resorts in Crooked Tree, well in advance of your visit to arrange this, as the village is not over-endowed with boats). Peak birdwatching season is between April and May, when hatching begins (most migratory birds arrive in November, and many leave before the rainy season starts in July). As usual, start at dusk. Check in at the Sanctuary Information Center (the visitors' center), when you arrive. There are four daily buses from Belize City, in the morning and afternoon.

Apart from bird life, the waterways of Crooked Tree have thriving communities of turtle and Morelet's crocodiles; it is also one of the last places in Belize where logwood can still be found. Crooked Tree is not only famous for its birds; to Belizeans the name has long been synonymous with cashews – cashew nuts, cashew wine, even stewed cashew fruit. To celebrate this nifty nut, every May the village holds The Cashew Festival. It features nut roasting and every imaginable cashew-based product, as well as local cuisine and music. ❑

Map on pages 188–9

Thankful for being spared the worst effects of Hurricane Mitch in 1998, the villagers of Crooked Tree sent a large consignment of provisions to the Belizean Red Cross for the storm victims in Honduras.

BELOW: glorious heliconia flowers.

FROM LAMANAI TO COROZAL

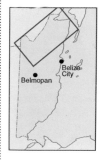

Map on pages 188–9

Northern Belize is strongly Hispanic; its economy is based on sugar cane, but growing numbers of tourists are visiting the area's isolated ruins and its pioneering wildlife preserves

While the Belize district may be considered the stronghold of the creole culture, the northern portion of the country belongs to the Hispanics or Mestizos. Not only do the people of the Orange Walk and Corozal districts speak mostly Spanish, their lifestyles are also very Latin. And very rural. Sugar cane is still king in this region and just about every family is either growing it, trucking it, or processing it.

Tourism is still a sideline, so you won't find San Ignacio's stream of eco-tourists, or the variety of hotels and restaurants available at San Pedro. But if you like your Maya ruins remote and mysterious and your towns and villages untouched and genuine, then you'll enjoy what sleepy Orange Walk, and even sleepier Corozal have to offer.

Lamanai

The trip to **Lamanai** ❼ is often as memorable as the impressive ruins themselves, thanks to the adventurous journey required to get there, via a rugged dirt road or a dreamy river trip through the sinuous waterways of a remote jungle river. Located on the banks of the **New River Lagoon**, it can be reached by easy day trips from Maruba and Orange Walk Town.

A rough but easily passable road runs through the finely named villages of **Dubloon Bank Savannah**, **Bound To Shine** and **Guinea Grass**, into the sugar cane country of the New River. Trucks weighed down with cane lumber by, operated privately by local farmers who are paid by the ton. From the small docks at **Shipyard**, motorboats leave for the hour-long journey along the New River's inky black waters.

The river and surrounding swamp is teeming with wildlife, including a healthy population of Morelet's crocodiles. These gave Lamanai its name – Maya for "submerged crocodile" – and make the prospect of swimming, while safe, rather nerve-racking. Apart from pointing out birdlife, most boat drivers will bump up against gutted tree trunks on the shoreline, waking up a mass of tiny, sleeping bats, and sending them in a cloud over passengers' heads.

The last surviving Maya city

By the time you reach the ruins, you feel like Indiana Jones, and since you may well have the place to yourself, there's nobody to destroy the illusion. A few thatched-roofed houses have been built at the dockside for the ruin's guards, along with an open-air picnic hut and a small museum piled high with Maya artifacts (nothing too valuable, the best pieces having been removed to Belize City). Several paths run through into the dense jungle, which is now being re-

PRECEDING PAGES: Lamanai, tangled up in tree roots. **LEFT:** lush foliage on the New River. **BELOW:** the giant mask of Lamanai.

inhabited by families of black howler monkeys. Only a small part of the ancient city has been unearthed, and workers are constantly having to keep the encroaching vegetation at bay.

A small museum at Lamanai contains an excellent collection of artifacts found at the site.

BELOW:
comfortable boat cruise into the wilderness.

Lamanai's history

Lamanai was first settled some 3,000 years ago and its most impressive temples were built in the Preclassic period around 100 BC. Several centuries later, in the Classic period, the population had increased from 20,000 to 50,000.

What makes Lamanai unique is that it was still inhabited when the first Spanish conquistadors arrived in search of gold here in the 16th century. The population was about a quarter its Classic number, and its most spectacular temples were untended. How Lamanai survived the cataclysm that devastated the other Maya cities is unknown. In any case, Spanish missionaries quickly set about building a church to convert the heathens. The Maya rebelled and burned it in the 1640s, but European-imported diseases soon decimated the community. Even so, there were a few Maya inhabitants here when British settlers arrived in the 1800s; the new colonialists drove them out to Guatemala so the land could be cleared for sugar.

Thomas Gann, a British medical officer and amateur archeologist made the first modern excavations at Lamanai in 1917, but it wasn't until 1974 that large-scale digging was begun by Canadian David Pendergast of the Royal Ontario Museum. His wife, archeologist Liz Graham, worked with him there until the mid-1980s. Dr. Graham, now at London College, heads a study program at Lamanai in conjunction with the Belize Department of Archeology and Lamanai Outpost Lodge (*see* www.lamanai.com *for information on courses*).

Exploring the ruins

The Lamanai pyramids are still known by their dry archeological labels. The first on the path is **P9-56**. While its exterior dates from the 6th century AD, this pyramid was found to have been built over a finely preserved temple from five centuries earlier. The most famous feature is a 13-ft (4-meter) high limestone face carved into its side, now protected from the elements by a makeshift roof: its combination of thick lips, bared teeth, dreamy eyes and elongated forehead (created by the Maya custom of flattening their children's skulls) make the image half terrifying, half serene.

A second statue is known to be on the left side of the temple stairs, but archeologists left it buried to protect it from torrential rains and possible looters.

Lamanai's best-known and most impressive pyramid is **N10-43**, a steep, 112-ft (34-meter) high edifice. It reached its present height by around 100 BC, making it the largest Preclassic structure in the whole of Mesoamerica (although not as tall as the Classic pyramids at Xunantinich and Caracol, it is still considerably higher than any modern Belizean building). Like most Maya structures, it was modified heavily.

The temple's steps are in good condition following restoration and can be climbed for breathtaking views across the jungle canopy and New River, with the cries of birds and occasionally howler monkeys echoing upwards. This makes the perfect vantage point for picturing ancient Maya rituals (priests would take positions on the temple, with the rest of the population gathered below in the plaza); or imagining Maya astronomers gathering by night to contemplate the heavens.

Below pyramid N10-43 is the **ball court**, where the violent *pok-ta-pok* was played; archeologist Pendergast found pottery containing mercury here, the

Map
on pages
188–9

TIP

Like all Belize's Maya sites, Lamanai is open daily, 365 days a year, and a BZ$5 entry fee is charged at the Visitors' Center.

BELOW: P9-56, Lamanai's pyramid of the mask has been restored.

only time the substance has been found at a Maya site. In the makeshift hut nearby is a **stela** carved with hieroglyphics; underneath it was found the bones of six children, assumed to have been sacrificed.

Apart from the Maya structures, at the nearby village of **Indian Church** are the remains of two 16th-century Spanish missions and a ruined sugar mill built by former Confederate soldiers in the 1870s. Despite an influx of squatters escaping from bloody civil wars in neighboring Guatemala and El Salvador during the 1980s, this once-thriving area remains all but uninhabited – and the more mysterious for it.

Orange Walk

Sprawling across to the Guatemalan and Mexican borders, the vast Orange Walk District can be thought of as having two largely unrelated regions. To the east are the urban centers (such as they are), surrounded by endless fields of sugar cane; as in neighboring Corozal District, the agriculture was largely begun by refugees from the Mexican Caste Wars in the 1850s, and today the small villages have a curious mix of laid-back Caribbean and Hispanic flavors.

Meanwhile, lying to the west of Orange Walk District are great swathes of Belize's most remote savannah and rainforests. Until the mid-1980s, these uninhabited lands were entirely owned by a single logging operation, the Belize Estates Company – a million-acre (400,000-hectare) holding that made up one-fifth of Belize's total area. Today the rainforests are being set aside for one of Central America's largest and most ambitious conservation reserves, and include such oddities as a luxurious hotel set in the main plaza of a lost Maya temple *(see Chan Chich, page 205).*

LEFT: Belikin pit-stop
RIGHT: Let God Speak, in Orange Walk Town's main street.

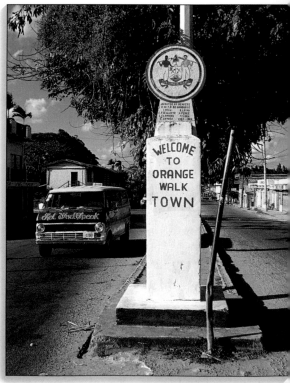

Orange Walk is fighting to overcome a bad reputation earned in the 1980s when sugar prices began to decline, and many farmers turned to growing marijuana for the more lucrative drugs trade instead. The outlaw days didn't last long, however. Stepped-up control measures underwritten by the US Drug Enforcement Agency reduced Belize from the fourth-largest US supplier of marijuana in the mid-1980s to a "marginal producer" by the end of the decade, while cocaine flights (but not the boats) appear to have been curbed.

Forming the hub of northern Belize's main roads, **Orange Walk Town** ❽ is still the most convenient, if not the most interesting or comfortable, base for exploring the north. Although this is Belize's second-largest town, with a population of 12,000, there is very little to see here. It has two forts, **Mundy** and **Cairns**, which were used to fend off Mexican bandit raids in the early 1870s (in one attack, former Confederate soldiers saved the day – *see page 45*).

Orange Walk Town is fondly called "Sugar City" by residents because it is smack in the center of the northern sugar industry. Like lumbering elephants, the cane trucks – seemingly overloaded and about to tip over – dominate the scene, even in the middle of town. Numerous accidents, tremendous wear and tear to the primary thoroughfare as well as cane "trash", the stalks that fall off onto the street, have led the government to propose building a bypass road. You'll see the need for it yourself, especially at night; its not uncommon to find cane trucks parked, not on the side of the road, but barely to the shoulder, with no lights or indicators of any kind. (Sad to say, drunks are also a hazard on Friday and Saturday nights when they stagger down the road through the various villages.)

Folks from the rest of Belize generally whip through Orange Walk on their way to Chetumal across the border in Mexico. But when they do stop in Orange

Map on pages 188–9

BELOW: truckloads of sugar cane heading for the refinery.

TIP

There is an official network of Casas de Cambio where visitors should exchange currency. However, some people still use the services of informal money changers.

Walk Town it's for the country's best corn *dukunu*, *tamales* or *tacos* sold by vendors carrying pigtail buckets in the Central Park. Even though it is prohibited people can change Belizean and American currency to pesos in a more relaxed atmosphere in Orange Walk than at the border. The exchange rate is the same and there is less pressure and competition from the *peseros* (money changers).

While it may not have the mass appeal of Lamanai, the **Cuello** ➒ archeological site on the property of the Cuello rum distillery, some 3 miles (5 km) to the west of Orange Walk Town, is believed to be the oldest Maya ceremonial site in the area, dating back some 2,600 years. Permission must be obtained from the distillery to go onto the property (tel: 322–2141). Today, there is not much to see at the site, with one small pyramid and a few earth-covered mounds. Probably because these modest offerings cannot compete with the likes of Lamanai, Cuello is mainly frequented by serious archeology students.

Waves of migration

Just outside the town is the still-active **Tower Hill Sugar Refinery**. It was built in 1974, and with the closing of Corozal District's Libertad refinery in the mid-1980s, it now handles all of Belize's cane. In the cutting season, all roads leading to Tower Hill are choked with lines of cane-laden trucks and trailers.

The still-unpaved road from Orange Walk to Blue Creek was settled by *mestizos* and Yucatec Maya fleeing the Mexican Caste Wars, and many villages still bear Maya names like **Yo Creek** and **Chan Pine Ridge**. In the 1950s they were joined by a new immigrant group: the Mennonites.

The Mennonites in Orange Walk District have ended up in two settlements, each representing opposite ends of their philosophical spectrum. The most con-

BELOW: young girl with pet coati-mundi.

THE SUGAR CANE INDUSTRY

Sugar cane has shaped the social history of northern Belize since the middle of the 19th century. Local British settlers were delighted to discover that refugees from the Mexican Caste Wars were competent farmers (a trade that creoles have traditionally disdained).

With mahogany and logwood exports declining, the settlers turned to exporting sugar back to England. By the mid-1860s, sugar production had risen to 1 million lbs (450,000 kg) a year and was being turned into 50,000 gallons (230,000 liters) of rum. By the 1930s the enormous Libertad factory was built here; in the 1960s it was purchased by the British firm Tate & Lyle, which set about increasing sugar production to the maximum.

Even small landowners, formerly subsistence farmers, began to grow the undemanding cane, known as "the lazy man's crop." Sadly, US demand for sugar collapsed in the 1970s; although 75 percent of local land was devoted to sugar cane, the Libertad refinery closed in 1986. Having abandoned maize growing and other milpa crops, many small farmers began relying upon relatives abroad or turned to growing the more lucrative marijuana.

While raw sugar cane is still grown everywhere, it is now processed in Orange Walk District.

servative sect lives in **Shipyard** . Known as the Old Colony, this is where the Mennonite women wear long, dark dresses and large beribboned straw hats in a style brought from Europe, while taciturn men wear suspenders or overalls rather than belts *(see The Mennonites, pages 77–79)*.

Along the Río Bravo escarpment in northwestern Orange Walk District, the more progressive Mennonite community of **Blue Creek Village** ⓫ has sweeping views and a prosperous mien. The Mennonites who came here in 1958 split the community when they decided to use heavy machinery, forbidden by conservatives, to clear the jungle. The Blue Creek settlement has a distinctively North American feel, since many of the settlers came from Canada.

Just a stone's throw across the Río Hondo lies Mexico and the small town of **La Unión**. Although it is not an official border crossing, both Mexicans and Belizeans row across the Hondo's shallow waters for shopping excursions. The Mexican government has indicated that they would like to establish a full-fledged border crossing at La Unión to keep better track of arrivals and a tighter lid on the smuggling of goods in both directions. The Belize Customs and Immigration Department has its hands full trying to prevent contraband goods from entering, but manpower is limited and the trade is brisk.

The Mennonites of Blue Creek Village are not opposed to modern technology; they even used parts of a crashed cargo plane to build a small hydroelectric plant.

Unique wilderness experiment

Until the mid-1980s, a million acres (400,000 hectares) of rainforest in Orange Walk District was owned by the venerable, 150-year-old Belize Estates Company. Timber, mainly mahogany, cedar and santa maría, was logged from this remote area. The logs were then transported via a railroad, no longer in existence, to the New River Lagoon at Hill Bank. From there they floated by a circuitous route past Orange Walk Town to Chetumal Bay and finally down to Belize City. The logging was always carried out selectively, leaving these forests roughly 75 percent intact, while most of the rest of Central America's rainforests have been devastated.

Then, in the mid-1980s, Belize Estates Company was bought by Belizean businessman Barry Bowen and subsequently divided into four parcels, one of which was purchased by a consortium of conservation organizations that joined together to form the Program for Belize (PFB). In 1988, this land became the **Río Bravo Conservation Area** ⓬, which now covers some 202,000 acres (80,800 hectares).

In a formal agreement with the government, PFB is holding these lands in perpetual trust for the people of Belize. The aim is to generate income from ecotourism which will provide funds for conservation efforts throughout the country and training for Belizeans. The range and depth of flora and fauna is as impressive as anywhere in the country: the region contains some 200 species of trees, and 400 species of birds; all five species of wild cats found in Belize also flourish here.

Within the area's boundaries are also several Maya sites that are now being studied. **La Milpa** is one of the largest in Belize, with at least 18 plazas, two large reservoirs and 60 major structures, stelae and courtyard groups. It is being excavated by groups from

BELOW: colorful residence in Orange Walk Town.

Map on pages 188–9

Boston University in conjunction with Belize's Department of Archeology. The other parcels of land are also being preserved, in different ways. Coca-Cola Foods came under attack from foreign conservation groups for its alleged plans to clear rainforest to grow citrus trees. In fact, the property under consideration was largely savannah, but being sensitive to public pressure, Coca-Cola donated 42,000 acres (17,000 hectares) of its land to the Program for Belize and to date no citrus development has taken place on its remaining property. In addition to the lands donated by Barry Bowen, PFB has purchased private land through funds provided by supporters in the USA, UK and elsewhere. The Río Bravo field station is used for university wildlife, forestry and archeological study programs, but it also encourages ecotourism. Accommodations include *cabañas* and "green dormitories" near La Milpa (3 miles/5 km from the ruins) and Hill Bank field stations. Prior booking is required from the Programme for Belize Office and applications for field studies and research must be submitted in advance. The Río Bravo management area is 31 miles/50 km from Orange Walk with the main access from Blue Creek Village.

Hotel in a Maya ruin

Just south of the Río Bravo Area lies the **Gallon Jug** parcel, some 130,000 acres (52,000 hectares) of tropical forest retained by Barry Bowen as a private preserve. Intensive farming is carried out in a small area, with corn, soybeans, coffee, cacao and cardamom being grown. Also, an unusual cattle project is experimenting with English Hereford bloodlines to improve local stock.

But the most curious innovation for travelers here is **Chan Chich Lodge ⓭**, a hotel situated – with the Archeology Department's blessing – in the lower plaza

BELOW: mangos ripening in a back-country smallholding.

of an ancient Maya site. Chan Chich Lodge was carefully planned by original managers Tom and Josie Harding to have a minimum impact on the surrounding tropical forest and the Maya plaza (it also protects the site from robbers). It features luxurious thatched *cabañas* and a cozy dining room and bar, paneled in a variety of local hardwoods. There is also a screened swimming pool and Jacuzzi.

As a private preserve protected from hunting, Chan Chich enjoys some of the most abundant concentrations of tropical forest wildlife in Central America. Various tame animals wander around the site, including deer and foxes; there is a wealth of birdlife and jaguar sightings are not uncommon. Other animal encounters are even more bizarre: on one occasion, a boa constrictor was caught in the clothes drier, bringing laundry day to a screeching halt.

With more than 9 miles (14.5 km) of hiking trails and a small cadre of natural history guides, the tropical forests surrounding Chan Chich are unusually accessible. Transportation is available to the resort by air to a private airstrip, or by road via Orange Walk.

Pulltrouser Swamp

Finally, in the remote region north of the Río Bravo area, in the northeast corner of Orange Walk District, the picturesquely named **Pulltrouser Swamp** ⑭ offers an unusual perspective on Maya agricultural habits. Tropical soils are notoriously poor, but the Maya built an extensive canal system here. Raised cultivation fields were built, with waterlilies used as mulch, hints that the Maya were certainly more sophisticated than simple slash-and-burn farmers. Visible signs of the original canals have been identified on satellite images, but nothing can be seen now from the ground.

ABOVE: bean pod of the multi-purpose cohune palm.
BELOW: former mayor Willard Levy in front of Corozal Town Hall's historical mural.

Corozal

The name Corozal comes from the cohune, a large palm that likes fertile soil and was a symbol of fecundity to the Maya (its name is thought to come from the Spanish cojones, *meaning testicles, after the tree's round nuts).*

Tucked up in the northern limit of Belize, Corozal District looks like it has changed little since colonial days – or, by a further stretch of the imagination, the days of the Maya. The district is still only sparsely populated and scattered with small, sleepy villages. Its entire eastern half is swampy savannah, accessible only by an uneven road which roughly traces the New River and Freshwater Creek; the western coast is dominated by sugar cane, and is one of the most intensely cultivated agricultural areas in the country.

Corozal District's population has been largely Spanish-speaking for many generations, thanks to violence across the Mexican border. In the mid-1800s, Mexico's Yucatán Peninsula was wracked by the murderous Caste Wars, waged between enslaved Maya indians, mestizos and whites. After the battle of Bacalar in 1849, thousands of refugees, both indian and mestizo, fled south to the relative safety of British Honduras. While Corozal District shares the mixed ethnicity that so characterizes Belize, many of its people still bear Maya surnames such as Ek, Uck and Tzul.

Only 20 minutes' drive from the Mexican border is the district's urban hub, **Corozal Town ⑮**. The town overlooks Chetumal Bay and most recreational activity centers around the sea wall that winds its way around the edge of the town. It is one of the few places in Belize where you can swim, or bathe right near the side of a main street. You don't need a swimsuit, most people just wade in with their clothes on (the women feel more modest that way and tend to wear a long t-shirt over their swimsuit if they do put one on.)

Because of its proximity to the border, Corozal seems more like a suburb of Chetumal than a Belizean town. Especially since Corozalenos regularly cross over to shop, go to movies or discos, even to buy their groceries. But make no mistake, even northerners with close family ties in Chetumal consider themselves Belizeans through and through and would balk at any insinuation that they share dual nationality.

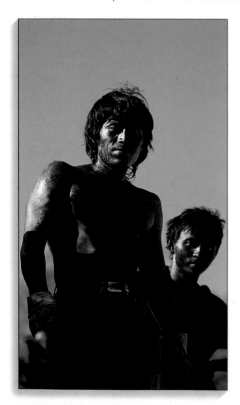

BELOW: sugar cane workers of Mexican descent.

Village life

Those who live in the many surrounding villages are equally, if not more, attached to their home district. Many young people commute two hours each way on a daily basis to attend school or work in Belize City. Even those professionals who later find employment in the larger commercial center or the nation's capital Belmopan prefer to make the pilgrimage home almost every weekend.

And they always return home to vote. Politics is a serious business in Corozal, and the entire north for that matter, with certain party leaders sustaining their reign for decades. Loyalty to color (red or blue) borders on fanatical and campaigning is fierce around the national or local town council elections.

Crime has also taken a foothold in some areas with residents of beautiful little villages with ancient names such as Xaibe and Patchacan living in fear of night-time robberies or drug-related activity and earning the unwelcome sobriquet of "Little Colombia."

But for the most part, traditional family-oriented life continues in the Corozal district on a relaxed, steady and reliable tempo. Villages with Spanish saints' names like San Román, San Narciso, San Estebán and San Joaquín hold annual fiestas. Everyone turns out to attend Mass, followed by a communal feast, Latino music and carnival rides. At such events it is still possible to meet your future husband or wife or show off your new grandchild to the community.

Map on pages 188–9

A brief history

Founded in 1849 by refugees from the massacre at Bacalar, Corozal Town today is neat and clean, designed on a classically Hispanic grid pattern with three parks and friendly, mostly Spanish-speaking people. Until 1955, its homes and buildings were thatch and adobe. But that year, Hurricane Janet tore the town to shreds; rebuilding took the form of the concrete and wood structures that characterize the town today.

There are the remains of a small fort near the main plaza, from the days of the Caste Wars when Mexican bandits regularly crossed into Belize; the town hall has a mural depicting local history, by painter Manuel Villamor Reyes (which includes a scene of the Indian massacre at Bacalar, Mexico).

With 10,000 people, Corozal Town is one of Belize's largest settlements, but it retains the sleepy look of an undiscovered outpost. However, research indicates that the place has been more or less continuously occupied from 1200 BC.

Occasionally protruding from the ground in the northern parts of the city are a series of line-of-stone foundations, the remnants of a Maya settlement called **Santa Rita**. While most Maya structures were elevated, those of Santa Rita were only slightly raised, so subsequent building was made on top of ancient tombs and residential structures. When excavation began in the 1980s, it was

The Mexican-style festive dish served at annual fiestas held in Corozal villages is pibil – a pig roasted underground and served with maize tamales and chimole, a black soup .

BELOW: brown pelican, caught in mid-flight.

found that more than 50 percent of Santa Rita's structures had been paved over by present-day Corozal Town. Some had even been ground up for road fill. Today only one modest structure can readily be seen, near Corozal's bottled drinks distribution center. Interesting finds at Santa Rita included a few gold objects – which suggest possible trade with Mexican civilizations like the Aztecs, since Belize is not a gold producer and gold is not normally associated with other Maya sites in Belize. A skeleton inlaid with jade and mica was another unique find at the site.

Young great egrets.

Cerros

Not far from Corozal Town is the region's best-known Maya ruin, **Cerros ⑯**, which means "hills." It is pleasantly situated on the peninsula between Corozal Bay and **Lowry's Bight**, the gateway at the river mouth into the interior of Belize and northeastern Petén. Evidence of intensive Pre-Hispanic agriculture has been identified along these rivers. Cerros was occupied primarily during the late Preclassic period, roughly from 300 BC to the beginning of the Christian era, with a peak population of about 2,000.

Cerros can be reached by boat from Corozal Town or by land along a rough dirt road (passable only in the dry season). Three acropolises and plazas can be seen, although they are covered by vegetation and the tall masks, depicting people and animals, were plastered over by archeologists to protect them from the elements. Cerros' largest structure, Number Four, is 70 ft (21 meters) tall with a massive base, roughly 175 by 200 ft (53 by 60 meters) and offers a panoramic vista of the coast from its peak. It was possibly abandoned when the Maya started relying on overland trading routes instead of the waterways for which Cerros was strategically located. Cerros is open daily year round, 8am–5pm; entry fee.

BELOW: the julia butterfly (*dryas julia.*)

Sugar and swamps

The paved **Northern Highway** runs south of Corozal Town, through the western half of the district towards Orange Walk Town. The route passes through lands devoted to sugar cane. Five miles (8 km) south is the ruin of the **Aventura Sugar Mill**, one of the oldest in the district. Only one chimney remains standing. Local villages are still geared to producing cane, although its value is much reduced and it has to be sent south to Orange Walk for processing.

This is one of the least developed parts of Belize, and until very recently was difficult to reach by car (a better road has been put through, although still dodgy in the wet season – four wheel drive is advised). Small villages like Little Belize and Chunox dot the way, and at the end of the road is the fishing village of **Sarteneja**. The name means "hole in a flat rock," referring to a *cenote* or well. This certainly must have been an attraction to the ancient Maya in this low rainfall district, with levels of precipitation well below the rest of Belize.

Sarteneja is a pleasant enough place to pass an afternoon. The buildings' pastel colors are drained by the fierce sun, and you can go swimming right off the main pier in waters that range from milky to clear.

Often local builders can be seen repairing or building boats in dry dock while fishermen cruise in with their catch of lobster, conch or fish. With only one bus service a day, many Sartenejans find crossing the bay by boat to shop in Chetumal in Mexico cheaper and more convenient than traveling to Belize City.

Just outside Sarteneja – and the main reason for coming to this remote corner – is the **Shipstern Nature Reserve** , founded in 1988. It was originally a self-sustaining business devoted to exporting butterflies to Europe and the US; the profits were used to finance the nature reserve and preserve 22,000 acres (8,800 hectares) of coastal savannah.

The reserve features an extensive, shallow, brackish water lagoon system, home to breeding colonies of many varieties of birds like the reddish egret and the wood stork. The latter is rapidly disappearing in both North America and Belize – near Shipstern, one of the last remaining breeding colonies of wood storks was almost destroyed by Mexican poachers, who like to barbecue the fledgling young. Today a watchman is stationed in a remote camp in Shipstern to guard a nesting colony of these stately birds, and numbers of successfully fledged young are rapidly increasing.

Shipstern Nature Reserve headquarters feature a few neat stuccoed buildings. Although butterflies are no longer exported, flight cages filled with colorful species are still on view; visitors are treated to a pleasant tour and a visit to the botanical collection. In 1990, the Reserve's Chiclero Botanical Trail opened and one can take a pleasant stroll through dense forest and find labeled trees common to this coastal forest type.

The reserve produces a newsletter, *Paces*, which discusses local environmental concerns and is distributed throughout Sarteneja village. Sunny days are the best time to visit the reserve as the butterflies are most active then, whilst on overcast days, they tend to hide amidst the foliage. For more information on the reserve or about accommodations contact the Belize Audubon Society *(see Travel Tips, Ecotourism, for contact details)*. Entry fees are BZ$5 per person.

Onwards to Mexico

The border crossing into Mexico is just north of Corozal Town, at **Santa Elena** on the Río Hondo. Regular buses run to the Mexican town of **Chetumal** (passengers disembark for border formalities and walk across the small bridge, where the bus is waiting for them on the other side). Many Belizeans make the trip in a day for a taste of the distinctly different atmosphere of Mexico and to take advantage of the prices in Chetumal's many duty-free stores. In an ironic twist to Belize-Mexico relations, the recently established Corozal Free Zone in Belize is starting to create some resentment among the Chetumal business owners. While they welcome Belizean consumers, they are now seeing thousands of Mexicans lining up, bumper to bumper crossing over into Belize (taking their pesos with them) to purchase duty-free gasoline, name-brand clothing and other luxury goods. Economic developments in the CFZ, and its impact on both sides of the border, promise to be an interesting study for some time to come. ❑

Map on pages 188–9

TIP

The small fishing village of Consejo is the northernmost coastal settlement of Belize, with a few holiday homes and the Adventure Inn, a popular resort for fishermen *(see Travel Tips, Where to Stay, for contact details)*.

BELOW: mossy stream bed in the forest.

WEST TO SAN IGNACIO

From its bland capital Belmopan, to the heartland of Belize's ecotourism around San Ignacio, the west of the country has vast tracts of wilderness, tamed only by luxurious jungle lodges

Map on page 214

When travelers talk about visiting the interior of Belize, they are usually refering to the lush, mountainous rainforests around the town of San Ignacio – heart of the country's booming new "ecotourism" trade. The region is a nature-lover's fantasy come true. Spread out across a remote sub-tropical wilderness are dozens of cabaña-style lodges, many of them quite luxurious. Within striking distance – by car, horseback, canoe or foot – are secluded, jungle-rimmed swimming holes, enormous limestone caverns, Belize's most significant Maya ruins and Central America's highest waterfalls. The constant background music is the shriek of tropical birds, while iguanas, gibnuts and skunks habitually stroll across the well-marked nature trails.

Meanwhile, the rainforests are surprisingly free of Belize's least popular life form, the mosquito – the higher altitude makes days around San Ignacio hot without being overwhelming, while evenings can almost be described as cool.

On the frontier with Guatemala, this is also one of the most Hispanic parts of Belize, populated largely by Spanish-speaking mestizos and Maya farmers; second in numbers come creoles, followed by a classically Belizean smattering of East Indians, Chinese and Lebanese. A few British soldiers still train here, while several large communities of Mennonites farm the rich land and can be seen clattering along the highways in horse-drawn carriages.

The journey west is itself an interesting one, with the Belize Zoo *(see page 161)* just 15–20 minutes before you reach Belmopan on the Western Highway, Guanacaste Park literally on the doorstep of the capital and St. Herman's Cave and the inland version of the Blue Hole just a few miles past Belmopan. All are popular, and worthwhile, detours. For curiosity's sake, you can, of course, stop in the new capital city, although after three decades it is still best described as a work in progress.

Belmopan

Founded in 1971, **Belmopan ❶** is the Brazilia of Belize: an artificial capital that has never quite caught on. In fact, it is still one of the country's smallest towns, although it officially became its second city in 1999. Government ministries are based here, but most politicians would rather commute from Belize City than take up permanent residence; the bulk of the workforce may be employed by the government, but few people are interested in party politics.

Belmopan was former Prime Minister George Price's vision of "a modern capital for an emerging nation." The idea of an inland location had first been fielded after Belize City was devastated by Hurricane Hattie in 1961. Price hoped that a planned city would attract Belizeans from all over the country, and

PRECEDING PAGES: morning mist over the Macal River. **LEFT:** Belmopan's National Assembly. **BELOW:** jogging on the empty roads.

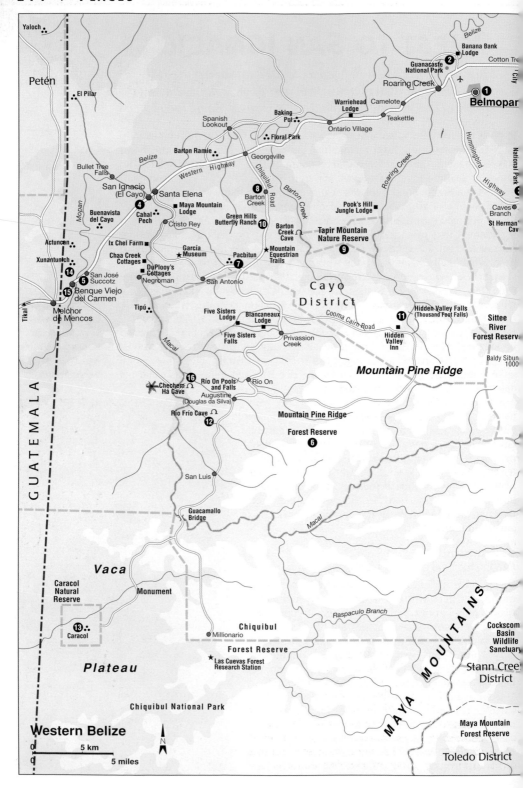

Yaloch

Petén

El Pilar

Banana Bank Lodge ②

Cotton Tre

Belize

Guanacaste National Park ②

Roaring Creek

Belmopan ①

Warriehead Lodge

Camelote

Baking Pot

Teakettle

Spanish Lookout

Floral Park

Ontario Village

Hummingbird Highway

National Park

Barton Ramie

Georgeville

Caves Branch

St Herman' Cav

Belize

Western Highway

Chiquibul Road

Barton Creek

Roaring Creek

Bullet Tree Falls

San Ignacio (El Cayo)

Santa Elena ④

Barton Creek ⑧

Pook's Hill Jungle Lodge

Buenavista del Cayo

Maya Mountain Lodge

Cahal Pech

Cristo Rey

Green Hills Butterfly Ranch ⑩

Barton Creek Cave

Tapir Mountain Nature Reserve ⑨

Actuncan

Ix Chel Farm

García Museum

Pacbitun

Mountain Equestrian Trails

Cayo District

Xunantunich ⑭

Chaa Creek Cottages

DuPlooy's Cottages

Pacbitun ⑦

San José Succotz ⑤

Benque Viejo del Carmen ⑮

Negroman

San Antonio

Melchor de Mencos

Tipú

Five Sisters Lodge

Blancaneaux Lodge

Cooma Cairn Road

Hidden Valley Falls (Thousand Foot Falls) ⑪

Sittee River Forest Reserv

Tikal

Macal

Five Sisters Falls

Privassion Creek

Hidden Valley Inn

Baldy Sibun 1000

Mountain Pine Ridge

Chechem Há Cave ⑯

Río On Pools and Falls

Río On

Augustine (Douglas da Silva)

Río Frío Cave ⑫

Mountain Pine Ridge

Forest Reserve ⑥

GUATEMALA

San Luis

Guacamallo Bridge

Macal

MAYA MOUNTAINS

Vaca

Caracol Natural Reserve

Monument

Raspaculo Branch

Cockscom Basin Wildlife Sanctuary

Caracol ⑬

Chiquibul

Millionario

Forest Reserve

Stann Cree District

Plateau

Las Cuevas Forest Research Station

Chiquibul National Park

Maya Mountain Forest Reserve

Western Belize

N

0   5 km

0

5 miles

Toledo District

Map on page 214

eventually replace Belize City as a commercial and cultural center. He also hoped it would centralize the government by bringing each ministry together on the same compound with new, efficient facilities.

Things didn't go quite so smoothly as on paper, however. The new government offices, designed to resemble a Maya temple and plaza, were much too small, so today many offices are located away from the center of town. Instead of cutting red tape, the move to Belmopan created it. Citizens had to travel all the way to the capital to have documents signed or obtain permits. This proved very time consuming, especially when officials missed appointments or demanded multiple trips: before long, government branch offices in Belize City and other towns were given the same power as the head office in the capital.

The biggest problem of all was that Belizeans weren't willing to move to Belmopan – and most still aren't. After nearly 30 years, Belmopan has fewer than 4,000 inhabitants, most of whom are refugees from neighboring countries in Central America. Of the Belizeans who work here, almost all commute the hour or so each way from Belize City or San Ignacio rather than live here full time. Even after Hurricane Mitch miraculously bypassed Belize in 1998 and forced thousands to bunk in with Belmopan relatives, there was no mass rush to move out of Belize City into the new capital. In fact, only the phone company moved its overseas operators to a new facility there. After considerable pressure from the government, the University College of Belize (now the University of Belize) finally agreed to expand its existing Belmopan Junior College and vacate most of its Belize City classrooms. The student body, mainly from the districts, is not pleased.

It's not that Belizeans don't like Belmopan, its just that they find the town quiet – in fact, dead. With only three hotels and a few restaurants, there isn't much for the predominantly young, single, government employees – and now students – to do for excitement. The biggest event of the year is the National Agriculture and Trade Show, held in late April at the fairgrounds, which draws thousands for three days of exhibitions and socializing. For the rest of the time people have to rely on house parties, playing cards, and a handful of bars for entertainment. Belmopan's searing temperatures don't help lure anyone to settle here either: in the middle of the day, it's rarely below 100°F (40°C) and hauntingly still.

BELOW: restaurant on the Western Highway decorated with British Army memorabilia.

Apolitical center of politics

On the other hand, the few who choose to live in Belmopan enjoy well-maintained roads, clean neighborhoods and a low crime rate. Unlike Belize City, there is ample room for expansion.

Perhaps because of the heat, the capital's inhabitants are not easily ruffled. In a nation where just about everything is political in some way, Belmopan's government employees remain uninterested in the activities of either party. The only time many of them express any opinion at all is when a salary cut or increase is proposed. When the rest of the country may be heated up over some election issue or political scandal, clerks in the Belmopan ministries remain cool; the mere suggestion of anything as radical as a strike is met with laughter or disdain, and they are seldom shocked by charges of political corruption or high-level romantic intrigue. Government officials may come and go, but public servants generally stay put.

Belmopan residents also take in their stride the numerous Central American refugees in settlements like **Salvapan**, **Las Flores** and **Ten Cents Creek** on the outskirts of town. The immigrants here have fitted in more easily than in other parts of Belize, taking jobs as domestic laborers, construction workers, street vendors or milpa farmers, and sending their children to school. Belmopan's hard-pressed merchants and liquor vendors welcome the new business. Except for an occasional immigrant-related "chopping" (an assault or murder by machete), there is rarely any news from the settlements. The residents of the outlying areas voted overwhelmingly for cityhood because of promises their living conditions would improve. Now most houses have electricity and running water, there are even a few paved streets.

Exploring the mini-capital

Driving into Belmopan for the first time can be a baffling experience: the wide, roundabout **Ring Road** seems to circle great patches of emptiness. If you arrive in the middle of the day, even the built-up area seems like a ghost town, as everyone cowers indoors from the punishing sun.

It's true that there's not a lot to see in Belmopan. There are no historical monuments, and most of the buildings are dull administrative offices. In 10 minutes on the Ring Road, you can take in all the sights. But if you have to go to Belmopan on business, or are making a stop en route to somewhere else, there are a few pleasant places to spend a couple of hours.

BELOW: stark government offices.

The best place to start is **Market Square**, which at any given moment is usually the busiest place in town: buses en route to destinations all over Belize stop here and there are several banks, the Caladium Restaurant, smaller food stalls, and shops nearby. Central American street vendors, many of them children, sell corn and chicken tamales, chewing gum and snow cones.

Map on page 214

Department of Archeology

Follow a path behind the square to the Maya pyramid-inspired **National Assembly**, flanked by government offices. Besides the Ministry of Health, Social Services, Department of Women's Affairs and so on, these buildings also hold the **Department of Archeology**, where hundreds of Maya artifacts are kept in a giant bank vault. The vaults are no longer open to the public, but glass cabinets lining the corridors contain excellent examples of Maya ceramics and jewelry. Even better displays can be seen in the new Museum of Belize *(see page 156)*. At other times, the department's employees are usually happy to give you information on various sites throughout Belize. The **National Archives**, used mostly for research, contain old government documents, newspapers and photographs. The Governor General stays at **Belize House**, near the National Assembly.

By following the Ring Road you can find Belmopan's best hotel, the Bull Frog Inn. This is a good place to sample local cuisine or revive yourself with a cool drink *(see the Where to Stay section of the Travel Tips for contact details)*. Most of the Ring Road runs past housing developments, with modest homes on streets named for Belize's wildlife and plants. The **Belmopan Hospital** is the only emergency facility between San Ignacio and Belize City.

BELOW: time for a quick bite in transit.

BELOW: San Ignacio's Hawkesworth Suspension Bridge.

Back to nature

If you haven't found somewhere to eat inside Belmopan proper, the Oasis, just off the main entry road, is welcoming. The food is generally good and the large attractive thatch hut is surrounded by gardens.

After a quick tour of Belmopan, the **Guanacaste National Park** ❷ makes a good place to freshen up, right at the intersection of the Western Highway. Not only does Guanacaste have magnificent trees and nature trails, but not too far from the main road there is an incredible swimming spot on the river. The current is very slow here as the water cascades gently over the rocks; locals wade right in with their clothing on, so there's no need to miss the refreshing cold water just because you forgot a bathing suit. A bus from Belize City, Belmopan or points south can drop you right at the entrance to the park making it one of the most accessible natural reserves in Belize (entry fee).

Heading west from Belmopan, 13 miles (21 km) down the Hummingbird Highway is the **Blue Hole National Park** ❸. There is one entrance near the Blue Hole itself (at the bottom of a long flight of steps) and another at the visitors' center near St. Herman's Cave. The blue hole is an astonishing sight: it's truly blue, with just a touch of green at the edges of the 30-ft (9-meter) diameter pool. The natural wonder is actually a collapsed karst sinkhole, estimated to be about 100 ft (31 meters) deep. In the dry season the water is extremely cold because it is cooled by the underground limestone. The Belize Audubon Society manages the park, which also contain over 250 species of birds and other animals. There are self-guided trails near the cave, which is one of few in Belize that can be entered without a special permit from the archeology department. Camping and caving equipment can be rented at the visitors' center (small entry fee.)

LA RUTA MAYA RIVER CHALLENGE

Before Cayo District was linked to the coast by road, the only way to reach Belize City was via epic, 10-day boat journeys down the Macal and Belize rivers.

Recreating those pioneering days, La Ruta Maya River Challenge is an annual canoe race, which starts at the Hawkesworth Bridge in San Ignacio and travels downstream, all the way into the Haulover Creek at Belize City, drawing attention en route to the natural beauty of the area, as well as its cultural history.

The event was first organized in the late 1990s and is held every March, usually around the 9th. In a relatively short time it has become one of Belize's biggest sporting events, eclipsing even the Baron Bliss Regatta with paddlers from Placencia and points south going shoulder to shoulder against teams from the west as well as the UK, and other countries. If you're in San Ignacio when the three-day race kicks off, it's well worth getting up early to watch from the mist-covered banks of the river.

If you'd like to actually take part in the event, you'll need a three-person team (both women's and men's teams race together), a canoe and personal supplies. There is a registration fee and some advance training on the river is strongly recommended.

Cayo District

If you manage to tear yourself away from the blue hole or have spent your morning stalking animals with your camera at the zoo, the Maya ruins and pleasures of the Mountain Pine Ridge still await you further west. Get back on the Western Highway and head for San Ignacio, the base for all ecotourism activities in the Cayo District.

Historically, the region around San Ignacio has always kept to itself. Maya armies here put up one of the longest struggles against the Spaniards in the Americas. The Spanish conquest of the 1540s never reached this remote region, and later news that the Castilian king expected them to pay taxes, obey Spanish laws and worship the Christian god was poorly received. Newly built churches were burned in rebellion, and, according to the chronicles, several captured soldiers and missionaries were sacrificed.

The inhabitants of Tipu, a city on the **Macal River** (possibly where a farmhouse now stands in the village of Negroman), led the resistance. Two Franciscan friars thought that they had converted them to Christianity in 1618, only to find a year later that the entire population was secretly practicing idolatry. Twenty years later, the same friars were received by pagan priests who performed a mock Mass with tortillas as the eucharist. The Maya then smashed the crucifix, roughed up the friars and sent them packing back to the coast.

European diseases like smallpox eventually all but wiped out the Indian population, and by the early 1700s the Spanish were able to assert control and resettle many survivors in Guatemala. British and creole lumbermen arrived, setting up logging camps and bringing with them the power of the British Crown. They quickly sold off Maya land and drove the last dispirited natives into easily manageable towns. San Ignacio started off as the major loading point on the Macal River for mahogany and chicle, growing slowly to its role today as the agricultural center of the region.

Confusingly enough, the district around San Ignacio became known as **Cayo**, after the Spanish word for cayes – coral islands off Belize's coast – while San Ignacio itself is also known as **El Cayo**. The name may be a reflection of the isolation early settlers felt from the rest of the world before a roadway was first pushed through in the 1930s. Until then, boat trips to Belize City took about 10 days, horseback journeys anywhere from two weeks to a month.

San Ignacio

Today, however, thanks to the country's best paved road, the **Western Highway**, San Ignacio can now be reached in a mere 90 minutes (for most of the year) by car from Belize City. En route from Belmopan are the tiny villages of **Teakettle** and **Georgeville**. The northern turn off to **Spanish Lookout** leads into the most populous Mennonite area. These Mennonites are by no means traditional, driving around in pick-up trucks, using telephones and mechanical machinery. Pancake-flat and rich brown, the country seems indistinguishable from, say, Ohio.

Built in a spectacular valley, on the edge of a ravine above the Macal River, the town of **San Ignacio** ❹ is

Map on page 214

TIP

A good and easy walk from San Ignacio, taking about half an hour, is due north along the Macal River to its meeting with the Mopan River at Branch Mouth. A pleasant swimming spot here will help you cool off.

BELOW: welcome to Eva's Restaurant and Bar, the social hub of San Ignacio.

separated from the neighboring village of **Santa Elena** by the **Hawkesworth Suspension Bridge** – a miniature model of the Brooklyn Bridge. Although it only has one lane, for west bound traffic, it remains one of the more impressive engineering feats in Belize. (Traffic heading in the other direction crosses the river further downstream over the Low Water Bridge.)

San Ignacio was the last frontier in one of the most obscure corners of the British Empire, and several of its buildings retain a faded colonial charm. The police station, for example, perched above the bridge, looks like it belongs in an Indian hill station or a lost provincial outpost in a Somerset Maugham short story. The narrow streets are quiet to the point of somnolescence – although the combined population of San Ignacio and Santa Elena is around 8,000, making this the metropolis of western Belize, hardly any of them are out by day. The exception is on a Saturday, when local farmers flock to the **market** with their produce.

The social hub of San Ignacio (and the unofficial tourist information office) is **Eva's Restaurant** on Burns Avenue, run by wiry Englishman Bob Jones. At lunchtime, when the rest of San Ignacio seems a ghost town, Eva's is hopping: travelers, locals and expats gather here for chile con carne and *Belikins* every day, and for information on every corner of Cayo district. Eva's also has a couple of computers connected to the internet and everyone from local high school students applying for university studies abroad to visiting archeologists and naturalists logging on to receive and send their email.

Around Eva's are most of the cheap hotels in San Ignacio, and across the street is **Serendib**, the only Sri Lankan restaurant in Belize (and perhaps all of Central America), serving tasty and reasonably priced curries.

San Ignacio is the gateway to the vast Mountain Pine Ridge Forest Reserve.

BELOW:
San Ignacio's police station.

Cahal Pech – the ruins and the tavern

Just off Buena Vista Road are the ruins of **Cahal Pech**. Although quite important for Belizean archeology, the main temple has been "restored" for tourists, with crudely plastered carvings in a Disneyland style (and unlikely to impress anyone unless it's their first Maya ruin). Cahal Pech was populated around 1,000 BC until AD 800. The name means "Place of the Ticks" – given in the 1950s when the area was used as a cow pasture.

More impressive than the ruins, in its own way, is the neighboring **Cahal Pech Tavern**, a large shed that houses San Ignacio's most popular bar and nightclub. The town's dreamy calm breaks after dark on Friday and Saturday nights when local workers let loose in a frenzy of live *Punta* music. Downtown, the Blue Angel disco turns into a raucous all-night party with a nod towards Bohemian scenes in larger world cities; amongst the usual crowd in shorts and singlets, you might see a character wearing a purple tuxedo with ruffled shirt, or a blonde woman in a slinky black number, hobbling along the broken streets in high stilettos. (A word of warning: the scene gets increasingly rough as the night goes on, and locals insisted that wire grilles were put over the second-story Blue Angel's windows because too many people were being thrown through them in drunken brawls.)

Maya carvings and pyramids

Back on the Western Highway, some 8 miles (13 km) southwest of San Ignacio is the village of **San José Succotz** ❺, by the rapids of a lush river valley where Maya women wash clothes on the rocks. A small sign directs visitors to the house of Maya artist David Magaña, who sells his own and his wife's fine carv-

Map on page 214

TIP

Horses or mountain bikes can be hired in San Ignacio to visit the village of **Bullet Tree Falls** and the ruins of **El Pilar**, which also have nature trails, with excellent birdwatching opportunities.

LEFT: young Maya artisan with a replica stone frieze.
RIGHT: Maya-style resort near San Ignacio.

The Mountain Pine Ridge Forest Reserve has many excellent trails for mountain biking expeditions.

BELOW: Butterfly Falls, Mountain Pine Ridge Forest.

ings and paintings. The designs are taken from a faded academic textbook of ancient Maya culture. "My people used to be amongst the greatest artists in the world," he explains, "and I want to show people that we can live using the lost skills." In cooperation with Maya Mountains Lodge, Magaña and his wife are working on a textile course with local women.

Chaa Creek

If you want a taste of Belizean wilderness without having to go too deep into the "bush", only 5 miles (8 km) west of San Ignacio is a turn off that follows a tributary of the Macal River, **Chaa Creek**, to the heart of cabaña country. The best-known lodge here, the **Lodge at Chaa Creek**, also has one of the best locations, nestled amongst rainforest-covered hills in the Macal River valley. Strict ecotourists might object to the manicured, flower-filled grounds, but most visitors allow themselves to be seduced by what might be termed "rustic luxury."

Each room is a separate cottage, decorated with Guatemalan handicrafts and using kerosene lamps for light at night. Cool breezes waft through large open windows facing down on the luscious river valley, and although there are not even mosquito nets, nothing more meddlesome than a flying beetle comes into the room. The all-inclusive resort has its own natural history center and butterfly farm, and offers a wide range of adventure activities in the area; horseback riding, canoeing, hiking, bird-watching and mountain-biking. There is even a fully equipped spa, with massages and other therapeutic treatments, which presumably helps guests to recuperate from all their other activities.

In this same district are a half dozen other places to stay, including the no less comfortable **DuPlooy's Riverside Cottages**, with their own white-sand beach

MEDICINAL PLANT PROJECT

Connected to the Lodge at Chaa Creek is the Ix Chel Farm, a unique facility devoted to researching the healing powers of tropical plants. Ix Chel (the name comes from the Maya goddess queen, a symbol of healing) was founded by Chicago-trained herbalist Rosita Arvigo, who convinced a local Maya shaman, Don Eligio Panti, then in his late eighties, to pass on his learning. This ongoing ethnobotany project has collected and classified numerous plants from the neighboring forest that may help in the treatment of a variety of ailments including Aids. In the past, tropical plants have been used in western medicine against malaria (quinine), for anesthesia (curare), treating leukemia (vinblastine) and as ingredients for contraceptive pills (periwinkle flower extract).

Rosita runs a small shop, Rainforest Remedies, she produces tinctures, salves and herbal oils from the medicinal plants of Belize, which are available in Belize and by mail order (www.rainforestremedies.com). Herbal teas and elixirs treat everything from bladder disorders to menstrual pains and impotence. A popular item is Traveler's Tonic – an effective preventative and treatment for the ever-present threat of diarrhea. Rosita also organises workshops and seminars on Maya medicine and spiritual healing.

by the River Macal. DuPlooys' owners have established the **Belize Botanic Gardens** (open daily 8am–5pm; entry fee; tel: 824-3101) in 50 acres (20 hectares) of their property, developed after more than 10 years of reforestation work, planting some 2,500 trees. The impressive grounds include hundreds of species of native trees, orchids, and a network of nature trails. A wildlife expert offers guided tours of the gardens (which attracts local bird life), or you can explore it on your own. The legacy of the late Ken Duplooy, who founded the garden, continues to inspire: fourteen new species of orchid have been discovered and one, *Pleurothallis duplooyii*, with tiny purple blooms, has been named for Duplooy.

Into the wilderness

Responding to the surge in ecotourism, the latest immigrant wave seems to be North American environmentalists and hoteliers, who have colonized the countryside. Comfortable – sometimes very luxurious – cabañas have spread rapidly across the hinterland (tourism authorities say the number leapt in one year from 14 to more than 50). This means that, while having your own car to explore is an advantage, it is by no means necessary: most lodges organize tours to every corner of the district (or tours can be arranged through Eva's in San Ignacio).

The most popular excursion in the region is due south of San Ignacio to the **Mountain Pine Ridge Forest Reserve ❻**. The sudden appearance of the pine forest, looking as if it is straight out of Vermont, is one of Belize's more peculiar geological anomalies. Geologists explain that the unique granite base and nutrient-poor soil content of the area was either thrust up from below Central America countless millennia ago or was a Caribbean island that was effectively pushed on top of the rest of the isthmus during its formation.

BELOW:
Vermont comes to Central America: the Mountain Pine Ridge how it used to be.

Two access roads run into the ridge from the Western Highway. The first is the Cristo Rey road from Santa Elena, not far from the San Ignacio bridge. This is the same turnoff signposted to **Maya Mountain Lodge**, a well-maintained group of cabañas nestled in the forest. Billing itself as an Educational Field Station, the lodge is a family-style place run by two American members of the Bahai faith, Bart and Suzi Mickler, who take their ecotourism seriously.

Maya handicrafts

The uses of the chicle gum tree have been known since the days of the ancient Maya; see The Chicleros, *page 39, for a history of the fascinating "gum gatherers."*

The Cristo Rey road runs through the one-horse village of **San Antonio**, one of the few places in Belize where Maya is still widely spoken as a first language (the dialect is Mopan). Just north of town is the house of the **García sisters**, who sell slate carvings and other Maya handicrafts. Unlike the Maya of neighboring Guatemala, the Belizean Maya have only recently started marketing such wares to tourists. The two sisters were taught by their father, a former *chiclero* (chicle gum base tapper). They have also opened a small museum of Maya culture in a traditional thatched hut, full of scattered odds and ends. Starting with a small, cottage craft operation, the sisters have built up their small empire over the years with what is, by Belizean standards, hard-nosed business sense.

Pacbitun and Barton Creek

BELOW: the Lodge at Chaa Creek, one of the region's leading "eco-resorts".

Two miles (3 km) to the east of San Antonio, on private land, are the ruins of **Pacbitun ❼**, one of the oldest Preclassical Maya sites (it dates from 1,000 BC and flourished as a trading center into the Late Classic period, around AD 900). Local farmers knew about Pacbitun's existence for generations, but it wasn't until 1971 that the first archeologists made studies here. They found 24 pyramids

(the highest is 55 ft/16.5 meters), eight stelae, several raised irrigation causeways and a collection of Maya musical instruments. The name means "Stones Set in the Earth." Permission to visit must first be obtained from Mr Tzul (you'll find his house on the turn off to Pacbitun. The site is becoming overgrown).

The second access road heads south from Georgeville through the traditional Mennonite community of **Barton Creek ❽**. This is a breakaway group from the modernized community around Spanish Lookout: you feel as if you've wandered into the 19th century as men walk by with flowing white beards, hats and overalls, while the women wear long black dresses with hats. There is no problem about visiting the Mennonite farms (the elders, who usually speak English, are happy to explain their religion), but remember that they do not like being photographed.

Tapirs and butterflies

East of here, between Barton and Roaring creeks, is the **Tapir Mountain Nature Reserve ❾**, a highly protected area of humid forest in the foothills of the Maya Mountains, run by the Belize Audubon Society (BAS). This pristine block of tropical forest, stretching across dramatic limestone karst formations, was given its heritage listing thanks to the efforts of its German owner, conservationist Svea Dietrich-Ward. The reserve is home to a rich selection of bird species, including the keel-billed toucan, as well as Baird's tapir, both animals revered as national symbols. However, the reserve is so private that it is not open to the public at all, but only accessible to qualified naturalists and serious researchers with prior permission from the Belize Audubon Society. Further south is the ranch **Casa Cielo**, run by **Mountain Equestrian Trails**, which offers horse riding for all abilities. MET also arranges trips to the privately-owned **Slate Creek Reserve**.

By contrast everyone is welcome at the **Green Hills Butterfly Ranch ❿**, where you can walk through a butterfly enclosure and view an impressive botanical collection. Butterfly breeding has become a booming business in Belize in recent years, with six such operations throughout the country, three of them in Cayo District. Besides their obvious attractions to tourists, the butterfly farms send pupae in crates to the US and Europe, where they are highly prized – particularly the famed Blue Morpho – by collectors and zoos. Green Hills is at mile 8 on the Mountain Pine Ridge road, near to Pacbitun, and can be reached by coming through Georgeville or from the Cristo Rey road.

Owner Jan Meerman has been studying butterflies in Belize since 1989 and he is eager to share his passion for these beautiful insects and explain what he has learned about their behavior and communication abilities during a guided tour. Green Hills is open from 9am to 4pm daily with guided tours lasting about an hour. Drop-ins are fine, but only between Christmas and Easter. At other times you are asked to call 820-2017 for an appointment. Entry fee is BZ$10 and group rates are available. Guided tours of the Botanical collection need to be arranged in advance. Take plenty of film for your camera and comfortable and strong walking shoes.

Map on page 214

TIP

Near to the Thousand Foot Falls is the **Hidden Valley Institute for Environmental Studies**, which runs educational field trips for Belizean schools and produces area research studies.

BELOW: hard work on the Macal River.

Heart of the ridge

After you enter the pine ridge itself, the vegetation changes abruptly to pines, mixed in with bromeliads and wildflowers; the bird life is rich here and the air slowly becomes cooler. A ranger stops traffic at a checkpoint barrier marking the entrance to the **Mountain Pine Ridge Reserve**, registering names and vehicle license plates to control illegal camping and logging, as well as to keep a record in case of accidents.

Two miles (3 km) further along Baldy Beacon Road you'll come to the turn off to Cooma Cairn Road. After about another 4 miles (7 km), a short track on the left leads to **Hidden Valley Falls** ⓫. These are also known as **Thousand Foot Falls**, although they happen to be 1,600 ft (480 meters) high. From the picnic ground you can watch the thin plume of water stream down a cliffside and disappear into the lush forest below. In the vicinity are many smaller but arguably more beautiful falls, including **Big Rock Falls** and perhaps the most charming, **Butterfly Falls**.

Eleven miles (18 km) further southwest (marked on the left) are the **Río On Pools**, natural rock pools and little waterfalls formed by enormous granite boulders, in a serene open setting – also ideal for a swim.

Five miles (8 km) south is the turn off to the **Río Frío Cave** ⓬, the largest cave in Belize and the most accessible. During the dry season, it is possible to follow the river into the cave's enormous mouth and out the other end (about 870 yards/800 meters). The rocks are a little slippery, but not unmanageable; inside are unusually colored rock formations, stalactites, and the odd colony of bats. There is also a 45-minute outdoor nature trail for the energetic.

The road now leads a short way to **Augustine**, the only settlement in the

BELOW:
the restored frieze
of Xunantunich.

nature reserve, where camping is permitted and several new tourist accomodations have been set up (including a lodge being built by the Hollywood film director Francis Ford Coppola, whose impressive figure can sometimes be spotted here).

Maps:
Area 214
Site 227

South to Caracol

Call in at the ranger station in Augustine for access further south: passage into **Chiquibul Forest Reserve**, populated only by a few loggers, tree-tappers and archeologists, is closely monitored.

The main attraction for most travelers in this remote region is the ruined Maya city of **Caracol ⓭**. Until 1993, Caracol was only accessible by one of the worst roads in Belize, and archeologists still tell tales of their four-wheel drives becoming mired in mud for three days at a time. A new road has cut the driving time from Augustine down to two hours but, despite continual improvements, the going can still be rough and it's sometimes completely closed when it rains.

The route runs into the **Vaca Plateau**, with a return from pines to the more familiar rainforest foliage and some spectacular views over mountains and river valleys. The only other traffic is likely to be logging trucks and British troop carriers – the British Army still maintains a jungle training camp here, and it's not unusual to run across a few dozen likely lads standing stark naked in a river after a grueling hike.

Beneath the Vaca Plateau are a series of great cave complexes, including the Chiquibul, which may be the largest in the western hemisphere. It was only found by modern spelunkers in the 1970s and remains little explored – although tales of prehistoric fossils being discovered there have caused new interest.

BELOW: El Castillo, Xunantunich's tallest pyramid.

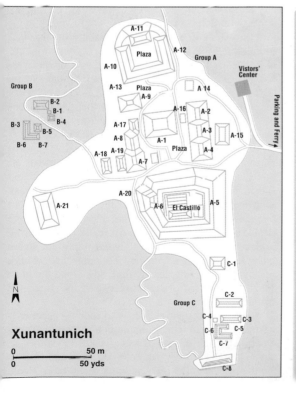

Xunantunich

0 ——— 50 m
0 ——— 50 yds

STRUCTURE A6
"EL CASTILLO"

At 130 feet, this structure remains the tallest buildings in Belize today. It is located at the center of the ancient city and functioned as the primary focus for the Xunantunich ruling fa

The road becomes progressively more bone-shaking until the ruins suddenly appear – a Maya pyramid, only recently hacked from the jungle, glimpsed through a gap in the vines *(see Caracol, pages 233–239)*.

The Belize government and the Tourism Board are spending millions of dollars upgrading the road, facilities for visitors and the site itself. They want to make Caracol the "centerpiece" of Belize's Maya sites, and hopefully keep some travelers who are presently going on to Tikal in Guatemala in Belize, as well as attract Guatemalan visitors.

Xunantunich

Ancient Maya pottery in Chechem Há Cave.

BELOW: Vaca Waterfalls, Mountain Pine Ridge Forest

San José Succotz, a village a few miles/km southwest of San Ignacio is the jumping-off point for the Maya ruins of **Xunantunich** ⓮, one of the biggest attractions in the Cayo District, and one of the most impressive Maya sites in all Belize. The ruins are reached by crossing the Mopan River on a hand-winched ferry (there's a boatman paid to work the pulley full time, although he gladly accepts volunteers; the ruins are a couple of miles further on). In contrast to Cahal Pech, the Maya site of Xunantunich is inspiring, and the view from the top of the highest structure is breathtaking. The view of the Macal River from the ferry on the way over is itself memorable.

One of the most famous of Belizean ruins, Xunantunich was a major ceremonial site in the Classic Period, collapsing some time in the 10th century. It was first worked in the late 19th century by a wandering British medical officer; since then, archeological expeditions have worked on the site sporadically, while looters have made their own marks. Digging is still going on, although only a fraction of the site has been unearthed – once work is done, archeologists are hoping to find valuable clues as to why the Maya city-states collapsed.

Xunantunich is best known for the towering pyramid known as **El Castillo**, or **A-6**. At around 130 ft (40 meters), this was considered the highest structure in Belize until the recently measured pyramid at Caracol was found to top it by a few feet. The site's name "Stone Woman," or Maiden of the Rock was given recently, but archeologists admit a connection between its phallic structure, the Maya warlords' assertion of power and the fertility of the earth for producing maize. Two temples have been revealed at its summit, the later built over the first: half-way up on the eastern side of the older temple is the famed **frieze**, restored in the early 1970s. The central mask with ear ornaments represents the sun god, flanked by signs for the moon, Venus and different days. There is also a headless man on the frieze, although why he is decapitated is unknown. Several important **stelae** have been unearthed here, now housed in a new building by the guard's house. Paths lead beyond the main plaza to **residential structures** used by upper and middle-class Maya.

Because it is relatively easy to reach – especially compared to Caracol, Xunantunich is a popular destination for school groups and cruise ship visitors, so it can get a little crowded. You can walk a mile or so up the hill from the ferry, along a paved road, if you are in fairly good shape, but if not, drive up as far as you can – there is a parking lot just below the entrance at the top. The site is open daily year round, 8am–5pm, and there is a BZ$10 fee, payable at the visitors' center at the top.

Maps:
Area 214
Ruins 227

West towards the border

But if you are bound for Guatemala, or just want to get the feel of western border life, the Western Highway proceeds on to **Benque Viejo del Carmen** ⓯, a sleepy village founded by Guatemalan refugees in the 1860s. Not much goes on in Benque apart from an annual three-day fiesta in mid-July; and *Las Finados*, the Day of the Dead celebration at the end of October and beginning of November. *Los Finados* includes offerings of food and favorite liquor to the souls of the departed and a candlelit procession through the streets of Benque to the pretty little cemetery at the edge of town.

Unless they have relatives in Benque or it's fiesta time, most people pass straight through en route to the Guatemalan border nearby. Like their counterparts in the northern town of Corozal near the Mexican border, Benquenos travel easily back and forth to the Guatemalan border town of Melchor de Mencos, sometimes too easily. Immigration has a hard time controlling the flow of people (and goods) in either direction since many simply bypass the official crossing and wade across the Macal River.

Chechem Há Cave

A new road has been driven south of Benque into the Vaca Plateau to service a projected hydro-electric dam (environmentalists are concerned about the damage this will cause, but are resigned to its construction). Coincidentally, the road has provided access to one of Belize's more off-beat and exciting archeological visits, **Chechem Há Cave** ⓰, at **Chemauch farm** (follow the winding dirt road through the mountains for half an hour until a small yellow sign directs you onto a hair-pin turn off). Several years ago, owner Antonio Morales set up a few rudimentary cabañas on the edge of a ravine overlooking the Macal River – possibly the most spectacular setting yet in the San Ignacio region (although the lack of running water makes staying there only a notch above camping). Then, while chasing some stray cattle through the rainforest, he came across a cave on his land. Going inside, he found an extensive catacomb with niches full of ancient Maya pots.

Archeologists from Belmopan removed a few of the most important pieces for study, but decided to leave the rest intact. Morales now leads small tour groups into the cave, passing by torchlight through the winding caves once used by Maya as a storehouse and refuge. Makeshift ladders and ropes lead into corners crowded with pots (one even contains some decomposed maize); the climax of the visit is a chamber once used as a ceremonial center. However, it's not for the claustrophobic: turning off the flashlights, you're left in total darkness; the only sound is your own thumping heart.

And if that doesn't get your historical imagination going, nothing will. ❏

BELOW: El Castillo, Xunantunich.

CARACOL

Belize's biggest and most important Maya site is also its most inaccessible, but it promises a rewarding experience for the adventurous visitor

Maps:
Area 214
Site 234

Guatemala has Tikal, Honduras has Copán and Belize has Caracol. But like so many things in Belize, the true value of the Maya site, both culturally and economically, is only just being realized. The ancient Maya city of Caracol was a massive and sophisticated metropolis that remained hidden from the world under a blanket of rainforest for nearly a millennium. Rediscovered half a century ago, it was dismissed as a minor site. But in recent years, archeologists have realized that Caracol was far more important and powerful than they had guessed: the lost names of Caracol's heroic kings and their legendary battles are now being triumphantly returned to their place in history books.

Misconceptions about its archeological significance and Caracol's remote location on the western edge of the Maya Mountains (within the Chiquibul Forest Reserve) means relatively few people have been there. Visitors to Belize have been far more likely to go to Altun Há, just minutes from Belize City, Xunantunich just a ferry ride away from San José Succotz in Cayo or Lamanai in Orange Walk, than to drive several hours to Caracol.

However, Caracol's absence from the tourist circuit is soon to be a thing of the past: with funding from the European Union, a new visitor center has been built and the access roads improved. Now the site is accessible year round. It's still a good idea to go there by four-wheel-drive as, even on the upgraded road, the going can be difficult in places, especially during heavy downpours of rain, which can occur at any time of year.

While Caracol may only now be capturing the public imagination as a major site in *El Mundo Maya*, in its heyday, for over a century in the Classic Period, Caracol controlled the rainforest Petén region (now in Guatemala), possibly even including the great – and today much more famous – city of Tikal. Continuing excavations of Caracol's monumental architecture and sculpture are slowly confirming proof of the city's past glory.

Re-emerging from the rainforest

In 1937 a mahogany logger, Rosa Mai, reported the discovery of the ancient city to archeology officials in what was then British Honduras. The top archeological official, A.H. Anderson, first visited the site in 1938 and discovered some stelae and the Temple of the Wooden Lintel, the only building then visible.

Anderson named the site "Caracol", which means snail in Spanish, but more recently the hieroglyphic site identification symbol, or emblem glyph, has been translated to mean "ox witz ha" or "place of three hills." Another translation is "ku kau tu mak" the meaning of which is not yet known.

The world's view of Caracol for the next three

PRECEDING PAGES:
Maya frieze
from Caracol.
LEFT: pyramid in
the rainforest.
BELOW: local
site excavator.

Iguanas love to bask on the hot stonework at the ruins.

BELOW:

Caracol's vast Caana complex.

decades was formed in three short field seasons in 1950, 1951 and 1953 by the University of Pennsylvania. Several stelae and altar groups were uncovered – and removed. For two seasons Anderson led his own excavation at the site, but in 1961 Hurricane Hattie destroyed most of Anderson's notes and drawings in Belize City.

Archeologists avoided Caracol, which they considered a medium-size site dominated by Tikal. But in 1983 Paul Healy of Trent University, Ontario, reported that agricultural terracing outside of Caracol's center once supported a much heavier population density than once thought. And, recent research indicates Caracol may have actually controlled Tikal for a time. In the 1980s and early 1990s the Caracol Project was run by Arlen and Diane Chase of the University of Central Florida. There was a continuous series of breakthroughs, including the discovery and translation of an altar that describes a military victory over Tikal in the 7th century, as well as one major and 50 lesser tombs. (No one is working at the site at the moment, however.)

The site of Caracol was settled by a well-organized Maya group in around 300 BC in the Preclassic period. The city's epicenter was built on a plateau 1,600 ft (490 meters) above sea level, without a natural water source but protected by surrounding hills. The population depended on human-made *aguadas*, or reservoirs, the remains of which can still be seen (one is used by Caracol Project members for reconsolidation of cement and bathing water).

Stelae show a royal lineage entrenched in Caracol by the 5th century AD, reaching its first peak in the year 562, when the ruler Lord Water defeated Tikal. The city subsequently prospered and grew to its ultimate population of about 180,000 people in AD 650. One of Lord Water's sons, Lord K'an II, continued

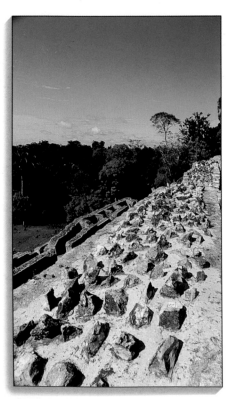

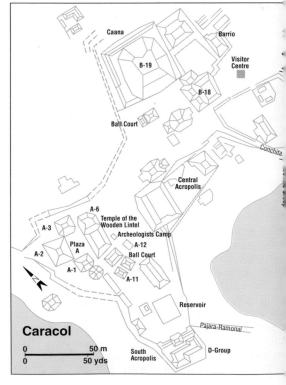

Caracol

Caana

Barrio

Visitor Centre

B-19

B-18

Ball Court

Conchita

Central Acropolis

A-6

Temple of the Wooden Lintel

A-3

Archeologists Camp

A-12

Plaza A

Ball Court

A-2

A-1

A-11

Reservoir

Pajara-Ramonal

Caracol

0 ——— 50 m
0 ——— 50 yds

South Acropolis

D-Group

Map on page 234

his father's success with a victory over Naranjo in AD 631. A 9th-century renaissance under Lord Makina-hok-kawil brought tremendous construction and expansion to the epicenter and particularly Caana.

Visitors will encounter a rainforest environment nearly identical to Tikal. There are grand ceiba trees, cohune nut palms (which provided the ancient Maya with nuts) and escoba trees covered with toothpick-sized spines. Wildlife includes parrots, ocellated turkeys, yellow-billed toucans, red-crowned woodpeckers, a few mot-mots and the occasional howler monkey. Caracol is a designated National Monument Reserve, so the beauty of the rainforest and its ruins will not fall to developers.

Exploring the site

Visitors today arrive by road at the epicenter of the ancient city. This is the nexus of Caracol's *sacbe*, or causeway, a system widely used throughout ancient Mesoamerica, from which at least seven raised roads radiated like the spokes of a bicycle wheel. With names like **Conchita**, **Pajara-Ramonal** and **Retiro**, the causeways lead to spectacular architectural groups up to 5 miles (8 km) away, which possibly defined the geographic borders of Caracol. Along many of these causeways are agricultural terraces that supplied the city with either food or cash crops – such as cacao and cotton – used in trade.

The **South Acropolis**, on the edge of the site, is thought to be an elite residential complex, including an amazingly preserved Late Classic tomb with a corbelled vault. Some tombs at Caracol have the closing dates painted in hematite-red still visible on the bottom-side of the central capstone.

Nearby are the **ballcourts**, where Caracol's athletes played the traditional

BELOW:
four-wheel drive transport to the ruins.

One of the mysteries of Caracol is how its residents survived here with no reliable water supply. The Maya engineers must have built extremely efficient reservoirs and irrigation systems to supply the site throughout the long dry season.

BELOW: a gardener keeps the jungle under control.

ball game. In the center of the main court lies a marker, discovered in 1986, which dates to 9.10.0.0.0. (AD 633). It was dedicated by Lord K'an II in honor of his father, Lord Water, who defeated the rulers of Tikal in AD 556 and again in AD 562. The discovery has helped to explain a century-long hiatus in Tikal, when no stone monuments or new architecture were erected. It was a lucky find: for many years the treasure lay underneath a log trucking road.

Plaza A was the city's cultural focus, containing the largest concentration of stelae and altars. The placement of the **Temple of the Wooden Lintel** and its flanking structures are modeled after the astronomical observatory (**Group E** buildings) at **Uaxactun** – where two stelae markers on either side of the plaza would line up with the rising sun during the winter and summer equinoxes. The Temple of the Wooden Lintel's original *zapote*, or sapodilla, wood beams in the back room are carbon-dated to about AD 50. Thorough trenching through the center of the building exposed earlier versions of the temple from before 300 BC, the earliest Preclassic days of Caracol. A cache uncovered here yielded a container of liquid mercury, possibly used during a religious ritual.

Structure A2 is 82 ft (25 meters) high and supports stela 22, which has the longest glyphic text in Belize. It was also dedicated during the reign of Lord K'an II in the 7th century. Although you can no longer see the bright colors, structure A3 was originally covered in red stucco. A tomb inside dates from AD 696.

The well-preserved palaces of **Barrio** were built in the 9th century above earlier buildings. A major drop to the south and east of the plaza indicate how much it was artificially raised.

Plaza B, on the north side of the site, is its most massive complex. **Altar 24** in Plaza B has a fascinating relief depicting two stout men facing each other

their hands bound behind their backs and their hair bound in a knot. Save for a loincloth, these royal figures wear no clothing and are stripped of jewelry (papyrus strips have been placed in their ears instead of jade ear flares). The glyphs explain that the man on the right is a hostage from the site of Ucanal, the man on the left from the unidentified site Q.

Map on page 234

Pinnacle of ancient Caracol

In Plaza B you will find the massive **Caana complex**, or "sky place", which is counted among the greatest Maya structures of Mesoamerica. It contains palaces, courtyards, pyramids and other buildings whose exact purpose is still unknown. There has been speculation that the rooms at the very top were the royal family's residential chambers. The base of Caana is above a natural limestone hill and measures 330 by 395 ft (100 by 120 meters). The length of the rooms on the middle level facing the plaza are all similar, each with a wide front entrance and a large, often U-shaped bench. These rooms were designed for a specific purpose – either as a seating area to watch the plaza (like luxury boxes at a baseball stadium) or a place to display prisoners or royalty to the people gathered in the plaza below. To the west archeologists discovered a special staircase to the next level, which could be ascended and descended hidden from the plaza view.

Detail from the intriguing relief on Plaza B's Altar 24.

An open room on the eastern side has special entrances to side rooms – Lilliputian "dwarf" doors that lead to bare rooms with air vents. These rooms might have been used for prisoners, children, animals, storage or any other practical purpose. Soldiers posted at either end possibly guarded access to the second level – which contains magnificent architecture that was surely the pin-

BELOW: excavation work on the huge Caana complex is complete.

Map
on page
234

nacle of ancient Caracol. Visitors enter through a special doorway, with a bench on either side (probably a place to catch one's breath). A central plaza is surrounded by three 40-ft (12-meter) pyramids (they were much taller when complete) and a long rectangular building.

Directly in front of the northern pyramid, **B19**, lie stairs specially built to give access to a tomb buried in an earlier building (**B19-2nd**). The large chamber once contained the body of a very important woman from the 7th century, but scholars are still determining her identity although some believe she was Lady Batz' Ek who married Lord Water in AD 584. Glyphs in the tomb bear the date AD 634, which may or may not be her date of death; the tomb may have been commissioned some years later as recorded on other monuments by Lord K'an II's artists.. Between B19 and the eastern pyramid, **B18**, is the entrance to a palatial courtyard surrounded by large rooms. The stucco molding against the south side of B18 represent a weave design used by the royalty.

Looters found three major tombs in the rear of the western pyramid, **B20**, which can be visited via a trail around Caana. In the second tomb, a painted text on the back wall was destroyed.

An earlier version of this pyramid, **B20-2nd**, began more than 13 ft (4 meters) below the current plaza. A 10-ft (3-meter) earth monster mask stood at the base, with an entrance through the mouth (representing the gateway to the Underworld or *Xibalba*). Inside, excavators found a small room with a burned body and graffiti depicting a procession, with a bound prisoner marching ahead of a ruler carried on a litter. The smoke from this room – either from incense or charred corpses – once billowed out through the eyes of the monster mask, a dramatic device intended to produce fearful awe among the faithful throng.

BELOW: ocellated turkey, one of Caracol's protected residents.

HEAVEN AND THE UNDERWORLD

According to Maya beliefs, heaven was composed of 13 different levels. In the topmost layer lived Itzamna, the "celestial dragon" or serpent, the male figure who was the god of creation, of agriculture, writing, and the all important calendar. Itzamna was also identified with the sun, with maize and semen, and with blood. His companion was Ixchel (Rainbow Lady) who was also identified with the moon. All the other gods in the Maya pantheon were the offspring of these two.

Each of the 13 layers was identified with a particular god, among whom were the north star god, the maize god, and the young moon goddess. The benevolent rain gods, or Chacs, were also to be found at the four corners of the earth, together with the Bacabs.

The exact number and attributes of these gods is difficult to ascertain. It seems that each of them had four different aspects, corresponding to the colors of each corner of the world. Then, too, they all seem to have had a counterpart of the opposite sex, reflecting the dualism that underlies much of Maya thought. To complicate matters still further, it is thought that the Maya gods had a double in the layers of the dark underworld where, like the sun, all the gods had to pass in order to be reborn.

Caves

Much of the geological structure of Belize is porous karst limestone. This makes it ideal for the formation of underground caves and rivers, and the south of the country is dotted with them. Although many caves have been known of for years, new ones – including some of the most extensive systems in the whole of Central America – are still being explored.

The Maya peoples who first inhabited Belize were particularly in awe of these underground caverns. For them, they were the entrance to the underworld, which they called **Xibalba**, or the Place of Fear. The Maya saw the surface of the planet on which they lived as being sandwiched between many other levels in which the souls of the dead, spirits, and their gods lived. There were nine levels beneath the earth, and caves gave a privileged if frightening access to this lower world. At many sites in Belize, you can still see the cave-paintings, the pottery shards, the remains of fires and even occasionally sacrificial skeletons still wearing their jewellery and other finery.

Underground attractions

The caves in Belize are registered archeological sites, which can be entered only with a licensed guide. Among the cave systems you can visit, the most impressive include the **Caves Branch Jungle Lodge**, 13 miles (21 km) south of the capital Belmopan on the Hummingbird Highway. The lodge, on the bank of the Caves Branch River, is halfway between the immense **St. Herman's Cave** and the **Blue Hole National Park**. Both St Herman's Cave, a sinkhole which continues underground for a quarter of a mile, and the Blue Hole itself, which is another collapsed underground river channel, are worth the visit.

Also increasingly popular are the Cayo District caves. These include the **Barton Creek Cave**, where you can take a mile-long canoe ride along Barton Creek after it dives into the cavern in the midst of luxuriant vegetation. Even more interesting are the Maya artifacts to be found at the nearby **Chechem Há Cave**

(at the turnoff at mile 8 on Hydro Dam Road out of Benque Viejo). This was apparently used to store grain and as a religious center. The different parts of the cave still house many intact pottery urns and other vessels.

There are organized tours at **Río Frío**, in the Mountain Pine Ridge Forest Reserve. A huge opening leads into the caves, with a stream flowing through the middle – and the exit leads to a nature trail that goes on to the equally impressive **Cuevas Gemelas** (Twin Caves) and other caves well worth exploring.

The latest and perhaps most exciting cave discoveries are still very much for the professional speleologist. Cave divers sponsored by the National Geographic have found Central America's longest cave system, on the **Chiquibul River** bordering Guatemala in the Maya Mountains. Here there is evidence that the Maya used them for their ceremonies: pots, clay whistles, incense burners, grinding stones and stone altars have been found, from a time when the rainforest above the caves was home to tens of thousands of people, not almost deserted as it is today. ❑

RIGHT: entrance to Hokeb Há Cave, Blue Creek.

SOUTH TO DANGRIGA

Stann Creek District is the home of the Garifuna culture, famous for its arts and Punta Rock music. You'll also find some superb caves inland and idyllic cayes out on the reef

Map on page 242

The Hummingbird Highway, running from Belmopan to Dangriga, has a beautiful name, amply justified by the surrounding scenery, which is among the most spectacular and tropical of southern Belize. The road – now fully paved as part of a national road-building program – passes through a magnificent forest of cohune palm: Cohune Ridge, as it is known locally. This ridge, which once ran continuously for 30 miles (50 km) or more, fringing the base of the misshapen limestone hills known as karst, on the eastern fringe of the Maya Mountains, has been reduced by road building, hurricane destruction and farming. Large numbers of Central American immigrants have moved into this area in recent years, establishing their own Spanish-speaking communities such as Armenia and Santa Marta, growing vegetables and citrus fruit to sell at the nearby Belmopan market. Throughout the Stann Creek Valley these immigrants form the greater part of the workforce for the citrus growing and processing industry.

The Blue Hole and Five Blues Lake national parks

The first major place of interest you'll come to, some 13 miles (20 km) south of Belmopan, is the **Blue Hole National Park ❶**, centered around a beautiful, circular swimming hole that is surrounded by dripping forest. The waters come from an underground river, making them unusually cool (intrepid scuba divers have explored it for several hundred meters). Those unafraid of heights can also dive 25 ft (8 meters) from an overhanging cliff. A half-hour walking trail leads from the highway near here (watch out for the sign) to **St. Herman's Cave**, which is one of the largest and most accessible in Belize. There is a visitors' center (where you pay an entrance fee) ten minutes' walk from the cave, as well as a nearby campsite. You can wade through the river into the cave with a torch (carry a spare) for about twenty minutes, but to penetrate further you have to take a guided tour, which can be organized at various hotels in San Ignacio.

Continuing south, the road climbs through mature hardwood forest before passing the citrus groves that dominate the Stann Creek Valley. Ten miles (16 km) from the Blue Hole is a track to the **Five Blues Lake National Park ❷**. The lake is so named after the different shades of blue that light conditions produce. The lake is in a beautiful, natural clearing in the jungle and is a *cenote* created by the collapse of a cavern roof. There are forest trails and caves, also containing evidence of Maya occupation, and you can swim and canoe on the lake. Lodging in private houses is available in nearby St. Margaret's village.

LEFT: taking to the streets in Dangriga.
BELOW: local artist, Benjamin Nicholas.

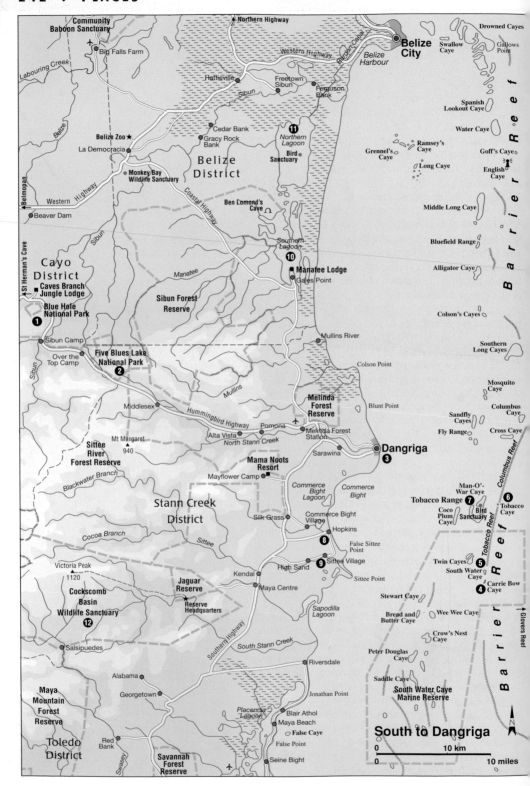

South to Dangriga

0   10 km

0   10 miles

South of here, the Hummingbird Highway enters Stann Creek District. Citrus is to Stann Creek what steel once was to Pittsburgh. A few visionaries gave birth to the industry in the mid-1920s by planting 13 trees a few miles west of Dangriga in the rich alluvial soils of the North Stann Creek River.

Today the citrus industry is one of Belize's top three foreign exchange earners. Two modern processing plants service 60,000 acres (24,000 hectares) of citrus groves in Belize (almost 50,000 acres/20,000 hectares in this valley alone), transforming 6 million boxes of oranges and grapefruit a year into concentrate and juice. Production has increased considerably during the 1990s and is projected to increase to 10 million boxes by 2004. This increased production has helped to compensate for the depressed world price for citrus over recent years largely due to competition from the big citrus-producing countries.

Map on page 242

Garifuna heritage

The largest town in Stann Creek District, **Dangriga** ❸ takes its name from the local Garifuna language, loosely meaning "standing waters." It lies peacefully along the banks of the North Stann Creek River, whose water is legendary: the town's drinking supply is refreshingly cool and arguably the best-tasting in Belize. A well-known Belizean saying warns that once you drink from gumaragaru (the Garifuna name for the North Stann Creek River), you must come back to Dangriga. And a famous Belizean song by Lord Rhaburn, Belize's king of calypso, chants, "Gumaragaru water, sweet sweet water."

Of all the larger settlements in Belize, Dangriga has most obviously resisted the unrelenting pull of the present. It was settled in the early 19th century by the Garifuna (also known as Garinagu or Black Caribs), a cultural hybrid of escaped African slaves and Caribbean Indians *(see Garifuna Odyssey, page 252)*. The town's dreamy atmosphere still harks back to a past age. The houses are made of weathered wooden planks and raised on stilts (the founding townspeople quickly learned that raised houses caught the evening sea breeze in this otherwise stiflingly hot location, and saved them from the occasional flood in the rainy season). Old fashioned wooden fishing dories lie tied up along the banks of the 100-ft (30-meter) wide river, beside canopied ferries with hustling fishermen unloading their day's catch. A number of high-powered passenger boats are also parked along the river preparing for a charter to carry tourists to the nearby cayes. Vegetable and fruit stalls and clothing bazaars crowd the narrow streets near the riverside market; newly arrived Central American refugees display their wares alongside their Garifuna neighbors.

Of course, the modern world has crept in. Instead of pursuing traditional fishing and farming, many Garifuna have become teachers and civil servants. Cable television has arrived in Dangriga, and a steady flow of cash from large expatriate communities in the US has allowed some wooden houses to be replaced with the cold practicality of concrete. Youngsters sporting BZ$200 tennis shoes and mountain bikes now speed past graying Garifuna women carrying firewood or plastic buckets of water on their heads.

BELOW: sunrise at the Pelican Beach Resort, Dangriga.

Between the slow pace of traditional subsistence living and the headlong rush for materialism, little attention has been paid to promoting tourism in Dangriga. The town itself has few obvious attractions, although it is pleasant to stroll around. It is divided in half by North Stann Creek, crossed by a bridge; on the north side are the town hall and small market, on the south the post office. There are a few cheap hotels, restaurants and raunchy bars in the center of town (if you're up for some local color), as well as the Round House disco on the northern side. Two miles (3 km) out of town is a toweringly ugly monument to the Garifuna, known as the Chuluhadua (a Garifuna word, meaning "we have arrived", built by local politician Dr. Theodore Aranda.

Afro-Caribbean culture

Most people come to Dangriga as a base for exploring the rest of Stann Creek District, including the offshore cayes, or getting to know the unique Garifuna culture. Despite the changes, it is the devotion of the Garifuna to their roots that sets them apart from other ethnic groups in Belize.

A mystical spiritualism is the glue that holds the culture together: although the Garifuna religion shares similar West African roots to voodoo practices found in other parts of the Caribbean, it has developed into something quite distinct. Central is the magical practice of *obeah*, whereby forces of good and evil are directed towards individuals through spells. The assistance of a *buyei*, or shaman, is necessary to guide the way through a complex series of rituals and use of talismans that can take many hours. Great care and thought is needed, because the spells cannot easily be broken. In fact, if the person placing the spell on someone else dies, it can never be broken.

BELOW: finest Sunday best.

Family ties

The basis for the religion is the powerful spiritual bond between past, present and even future members of any family group. In a ritual called *adugurahani* or *dugu*, people communicate with their deceased relatives. Outsiders rarely observe the ritual, which contributes to misconceptions and conjecture. Though all *dugus* follow certain broad guidelines, no two are exactly alike. Families go to great expense to secure fresh seafood, pork and fowl, while cassava bread is carefully prepared. Money is collected from family members to pay drummers and the *buyei*, who can commune with the dead.

"A grandmother's interest in her descendants can continue – just as their concern for her continues – after her physical body has passed away," explains a sociologist, Dr Catherine L Macklin. "The family responds to this concern by giving what may in a limited sense be called a combination of party, feast, and family reunion – attended by family members who are deceased, as well as those who are living."

Where the solemnity and secrecy of the Garifuna religion breeds distrust among outsiders (as recently as the 1960s, some Garifuna were afraid to hold *dugus* in Dangriga for fear of disapproval from local magistrates), this same spiritualism spawns a wealth of creativity among its people in the form of music, dance and art. From clubs and dancehalls throughout Belize blares the energetic rhythm of Punta Rock, a modern musical interpretation of a cultural dance by Dangrigan Pen Cayetano and his turtle shell band. During the Punta dance, the man attempts to seduce the woman. While turning down these advances, the woman makes her own overtures. The seductive movement of pumping hips and the rhythmic drum beat make this one of Belize's most popular dances.

Map on page 242

BELOW: life goes on on Commerce Street, Dangriga.

Dangriga's growing community of artists and artisans take their inspiration from nature.

BELOW: hanging out at Tobacco Caye.

Garifuna arts and crafts

The Garifuna are also skilled artists and craftsmen. Primitivism dominates in their painting, with great elaboration of detail, flat colors, and unreal perspective. The lobby at Pelican Beach Resort displays some of the earlier works of Benjamin Nicholas, one of the better-known painters. Especially impressive is the mural of the 1832 Garifuna landing. Mr. Nicholas' studio (27 Oak St) is open to the public and paintings can be commissioned – but be prepared to wait a half year or more for your artwork. Benjamin's son, Isaac, is also a prolific painter and his gallery is located on Commerce Street.

Pen Cayetano of Punta Rock fame is also an accomplished artist, having displayed at many art exhibitions in the United States and Europe. Pen's work is more realistic than other Garifuna painters, but it still retains the attractive aspects of primitivism. Although he now lives in Germany, Pen returns to Dangriga once a year, usually for the settlement day celebrations when he holds displays of his paintings.

Dangriga teems with crafts. For the past 30 years, Austin Rodriguez (32 Tubroose St) has hollowed out hefty logs of cedar and mahogany – harvested from his own land – to make drums. He cures his own deer and cow hides with lime, salt and sun before working them over the head of drums ranging in size from 6 inches to 2 ft (15–60 cm) in diameter. He claims a well-made drum will last 100 years. Throughout the town, skilled craftsmen abound, creating – stuffed cotton dolls in traditional Garifuna dress, dried coconut-leaf baskets and hats, and maracas made of dried calabash gourds. Mercy Sabal has a selection of handmade dolls on sale at her home, and Luke Palacio runs a little museum on St. Vincent Street that features Garifuna crafts and tools. You can also visit Gem's Photo, a local store on St. Vincent Street that has a wide selection of gift items on sale. And there is a cassava farm located 4 miles (7 km) out of Dangriga, which you can visit to witness the elaborate processing of the root to produce cassava bread.

Dangriga nightlife

Because Dangriga does not consider tourism a priority, you will find yourself immersed in another culture without the trappings of commercialism. If you feel adventurous, spend an evening or two exploring the town's colorful nightlife. Most of the rum shops and dance halls are found along Commerce Street. **Len's Cool Spot**, on the southside in the Sabal's Community, is a popular nightclub for the younger generation, featuring live bands on weekends. The **Y2K** bar on the main street close to the river features a "local box" (cassette player and music system) and also features live bands from time to time. The **Recreation Center** on Front Street near the sea is a popular hangout where the men gather to play dominoes. The **Kennedy Club**, which caters for a more mature clientele, also features a "local box" (a hired cassette player and music system) and has a second-floor outdoor patio overlooking the street. The **Round House**, actually a hexagonal, plain concrete structure on the beach to the north of town, is a rather trendier venue, where both locals and tourists congregate and dance on the sand.

Into the Caribbean

Some 12 miles (20 km) offshore from Dangriga lie a row of tiny coral cayes perched on top of **Tobacco Reef** like gems on a necklace. All are lined with perfect sands and dotted with coconut palms, and can be easily reached in an hour's boat ride from Dangriga. There are some beautiful clusters of coral in the shallow waters off these cayes, offering great snorkeling opportunities. In addition to the usual kaleidoscopic array of tropical fish, there is also a good chance of spotting moray eels, turtles and nurse sharks (generally harmless to humans unless provoked, this species is unusual among sharks for its habit of resting motionless on the seabed.)

Of the three inhabited islands, each has a different character that will appeal to different types of visitors. The smallest is **Carrie Bow Caye ❹**, home to the Smithsonian Institution's Marine Laboratory. Since 1972, scientists from all over the world have come here to study the intricacies of coral reef and mangrove biology. Though much of the work is esoteric – such as measuring flow rates from the openings of sponges or listing obscure animal groups – an invaluable database has been collected.

Since the waters around Carrie Bow Caye are pristine, this database can be used as a measuring device to gauge the health of other sites along the barrier reef. Although drop-in visitors are discouraged, scheduled visits are welcomed (arrangements can be made in Dangriga, through Pelican Beach Resort, which has another resort on neighboring South Water Caye, below.)

Just north of Carrie Bow Caye lies **South Water Caye ❺**, a small and beautifully maintained caye. **International Zoological Expeditions** has a study center and accommodation here, offering courses in marine biology to students

Map on page 242

ABOVE: protecting the wildlife.
BELOW: Smithsonian Institution, Carrie Bow Caye.

from 6th grade (US) up to university graduate level. There is a dormitory sleeping up to 30 students and comfortable wooden cabañas sleeping from 3 to 12. IZE has a classroom, equipped with wet tables for observation of species, a library and other reference material. Diving and snorkeling is also offered, with a range of activities run by PADI certified instructors.

Snorkeling is ideal off the southern point of South Water Caye; pristine coral reef can be reached just by walking off the small, sandy beach, without the need of a boat. Day visitors are welcome here; there are several jetties on the shore side of the caye, and tables and hammocks slung in the shade are ideal for picnicking or unwinding after a rigorous morning's snorkeling. Pelicans bob and dive for fish by the shore, and frigate birds may also be seen wheeling overhead, and will compete with the pelicans when one of the fishermen is cutting up his catch and throwing scraps into the water.

Further north, **Tobacco Caye ❻** has been used for centuries as a trading post and fishing camp. Several rustic but good value guesthouses and cabañas are dotted around the island. These are run by local fishermen and their spouses who supplement their incomes by offering boat tours, modest meals and accommodations. As the only caye advertising camping, Tobacco is a favorite with budget-minded travelers.*

Most of the other cayes in Stann Creek District are mangrove covered, and some are home to pelicans and cormorants. One, **Man-O'-War Caye ❼**, supports one of the largest colonies of nesting frigate birds in the entire Caribbean. Some cayes have temporary fishing camps while most are uninhabited. The reefs surrounding many of these remote cayes are spectacular, making this central portion of the long Belize Barrier Reef one of the best kept secrets in the country.

BELOW:
Garifuna kids,
Hopkins Village.

Beyond Dangriga

While Dangriga is the largest Garifuna settlement in Belize, smaller colonies lie scattered further down the coast. Eight miles (13 km) south of Dangriga lies the village of **Hopkins ❽**. It can be reached by sea from Dangriga across the **Commerce Bight Lagoon**, or from the west along a 4-mile (7-km) road linked to the Southern Highway. The entrance road crosses over a wide, marshy area rich with coastal birds such as tiger herons, cormorants and great egrets.

The seashore at Hopkins is lined by scores of tall coconut trees sprouting from mountains of soft sand. Nets, draped over palmetto poles, lie drying in the sun beside fishing dories pulled up on the beach. Clumps of Maya-style homes – palmetto walls and palm-frond roofs – sit perched on stilts with magnificent views of the azure Caribbean to the east and jungle covered mountains to the west. This sleepy but famously friendly village is less than a generation old, and relies heavily on harvesting seafood from the reef that lies 5 miles (8 km) offshore. Tourism is on the increase thanks to its strategic location, and the village is developing, with a growing number of basic guesthouses, cabañas, bars, and craftshops (King Kasava, by the crossroads at the northern entrance to the village, is an enterprising business, offering gifts, local handicrafts, tourist information and nightly drumming performances). With its rising fortunes, Hopkins is a village in transition, with its traditional thatched and wooden houses being slowly replaced by solid brick buildings painted in warm pastel hues. Hopkins makes a great stop for a swim after a visit to the Cockscomb Wildlife Sanctuary, followed by a nap in a hammock on the secluded beach.

Garifuna cuisine

Most meals in Stann Creek are served with one form or another of the versatile cassava – an integral part of Garifuna heritage (some writers even translate the word Garifuna as "cassava-eating people"). Cassava, or manioc, is a woody shrub or herb which, like potatoes, has tuberous roots. But unlike potatoes, the juice in the fibers of the manioc root is poisonous. The secret of extracting the root, passed down through the Caribbean, involves a two-day process. First, the root is dug out before daybreak. The skin is peeled off, and the root is grated into a mash on stone-studded boards. This mash is placed into a *wala*, a long, narrow, loosely woven tube made of palm fronds. When stretched, the *wala* compresses the mash, squeezing out the poisonous fluid. The resulting dehydrated cassava mash is then sun dried and made into flour, which can be sifted and baked into flat round loaves. The coarse "trash" left from the sifting is baked black and simmered with ginger, sugar and sweet potatoes into a favorite drink called Hiu. Like a fevergrass tea called bachati, and citrus juice, all sweetened with heaps of sugar, Hiu is one of the typical Garifuna drinks.

Local women often take pleasure in discussing their community and culture over a meal of local Garifuna foods, based on coconut milk, garlic, basil

Map on page 242

TIP

Performances of the wanaragua and many other Garifuna dances can be arranged on request in Dangriga. Ask your hotel manager, or contact the various dance groups around town, who will perform for a small fee.

BELOW: roadside store, Hopkins Village.

Marking the site of the Sittee Sugar Mill, near Hopkins.

BELOW:
Garifuna matron.

and black pepper. Banana and plantain (a larger, starchier banana that must be cooked) are grated, mashed, boiled or baked. Fish boiled in coconut milk, called *serre*, served with mashed plantain called *hudut*, is a deliciously rich meal. If you would like to sample some good local cuisine, you're sure to find somewhere in Hopkins.

Ruins of the sugar industry

A coastal road heading south out of Hopkins leads to the village of **Sittee ❾**, perched on the high but eroding banks of the Sittee River. During the 18th century, the river was a major artery for the flow of sugar and timber from the interior. The old **Sittee Sugar Mill**, discovered in 1990 as bulldozers cleared land to make way for citrus plantations, lies one mile east of the Southern Highway on the Sittee road. The original mill was opened in 1863, owned by the Serpon Estate and the Regalia Estate, who imported the mills from England and Scotland, transporting them overland by mules. The mills were powered by locomotive engines, one of which has been identified as being made in Richmond, Virginia.

The site now is all but abandoned, apart from a basic shelter and a mural by the roadside, depicting the sugar processing as it was done here in the 19th century. Vines and trees hide towering smokestacks and huge rusted gears. One of the first steam railway engines in Belize sits in a jungle clearing, a tree growing from its boiler. Parts of an old sawmill lie strewn about the banks of the river, often found by farmers chopping bush from the citrus groves.

Today, instead of the whine of sawmills and the clank of steam engines, toucans and parrots squawk above the river banks, feeding on the wealth of man-

DUGU FESTIVITIES

During Christmas, the popular *wanaragua*, or John Canoe dance, is performed in Dangriga, bringing the town alive with its color and vitality. The dancer wears a mask, which resembles an English face with a pencil-thin moustache, topped by a colorful hand-made hat similar to the English naval hats of the 18th century. The entire body of the dancer is covered with white and black clothing and knee rattles made of shells. The war-like dance was first performed to hone the skills of warrior-slaves.

A carnival atmosphere consumes Dangriga during the celebration of Garifuna Settlement Day on 19 November, which commemorates the landing of Garifuna leader Elijio Beni and his followers at the mouth of the North Stann Creek River. This is the most important local holiday, when the town swells with Garifuna from all over Central America and the United States. Singing and dancing crowds, all in traditional Garifuna costume, follow drummers from house to house until sunrise, when everyone gathers at the riverside for a re-enactment of the Landing. This is followed by a procession to the Sacred Heart Roman Catholic Church, to attend the special Mass performed entirely in Garifuna to the rhythmic beat of the drums. *(See also Holidays and Music, pages 87–90).*

goes, figs and other natural fruit trees that thrive in the rich alluvial soils. Three-ft (1-meter) long iguanas bake in the sun on towering fig trees. Manatee frequent the lower reaches of the river and jaguar have been spotted swimming across the river from bamboo forests on one side to dense mangrove swamps on the other. A boat trip up the river is a perfect introduction to the biological wealth of tropical watersheds, for the Sittee River drains a huge region fringing the north border of the Cockscomb Basin.

North of Dangriga lie the superb wildlife habitats of **Southern Lagoon** ❿ and **Northern Lagoon** ⓫. Surrounded by limestone hills, mangrove forest and savanna marshland, they provide breeding and calving grounds for one of the highest concentrations of manatee in the Caribbean. Two islands in Northern Lagoon support tremendous nesting colonies of white ibis, great egrets and other small herons, while on the coastline opposite Southern Lagoon is found the largest nesting concentration of loggerhead and hawksbill turtles in Belize. The government of Belize has recognized the lagoons' ecological significance by declaring them protected against development as part of a Special Development Area.

A narrow, 2-mile (3-km) long spit of land called **Gales Point** juts into the middle of Southern Lagoon, and is a popular spot for day-trips from Dangriga. A small creole settlement of the same name is another fishing and farming community that has turned to tourism for its future – tourists are especially fascinated by the manatees here. The village has built a hotel, while local figure Raymond Gentle rents rooms and offers basic meals. Mr Gentle is true to his name – he is a friendly, gentle man who can arrange tours to view manatees, the bird islands, or the spectacular **Ben Lomond's Cave** (bring a flashlight). ❑

Map on page 242

TIP

A few miles/km inland from Dangriga, near Melinda Forest Station, is the **Marie Sharp's Factory**, makers of the hot pepper sauces famous throughout Belize. Tours of the small factory are available Mon–Fri, 9am–4pm.

BELOW: manatee at Gales Point.

Garifuna Odyssey

While the Garifuna do not have the ancient historical legacy of the Maya in Belize, they have made their own, distinctive cultural mark. They settled near **Dangriga** only after an epic two-century journey across the Atlantic and around the Caribbean (note: technically, the people are called the Garinagu and the culture and language are Garifuna, but the people are commonly referred to as Garifuna).

They are a unique racial blend of escaped African slaves and indigenous Caribbean islanders. Their story begins on **St Vincent**, where, before the arrival of Europeans, the island was occupied by the **Arawak** people, who had traveled up the Orinoco in South America and settled in the Caribbean in around 1000 AD, living off hunting, farming and fishing. The Arawaks were subsequently followed by the **Carib** people, who also arrived from South America. The Caribs eventually subdued the local Arawaks and absorbed

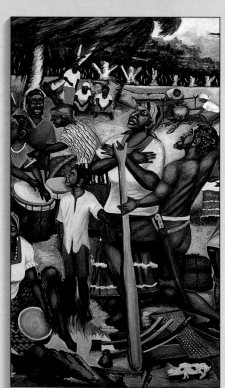

their culture, from which a new people emerged, known as the "Island Carib". Historians often depict the Caribs, a disciplined, war-like people, as ferocious cannibals – a view probably conjured up by people fleeing from their superior armies, and encouraged by Europeans when they arrived to colonize the Caribbean themselves.

The English and French first ventured into the Caribbean in 1625, beginning 35 years of warfare against the Caribs. In 1660, a British peace treaty guaranteed the "perpetual possession" of the islands of St Vincent and Dominica to the Carib people. But eight years later the British broke the treaty and took possession of the islands.

Meanwhile, in 1635, two Spanish ships carrying captured Nigerian slaves were shipwrecked off the St Vincent coast. Some of the African captives managed to swim ashore and found shelter in the Carib settlements. The relationship between the indigenous Caribs and marooned Africans followed a stormy course over the next century and a half, from reluctant acceptance to intermittent warfare and, finally, wholesale fusion of the two cultures.

By 1773, this hybrid people, now known as the **Garifuna**, was the dominant population of St Vincent. Unfortunately, Europeans were now ready to take over the Caribbean entirely. More and more British settlers landed on St Vincent, until there was no question of Britain's design: the colonial forces would never tolerate a free black community at the very heart of their own slave plantations. In 1796, following repeated raids to remove the British settlers, the Black Caribs attempted one all-out attack. It was a bloody defeat. Five thousand Black Caribs were captured and the great Carib chief and statesman **Joseph Chatoyer** (Satuye) was killed in a sword duel with a British soldier.

Less than a year later, fearful of a resurgence of the Black Caribs' power, Britain deported some 2,000 Garifuna to the island of **Roatan**, the largest of what are now known as the Bay Islands, off the northern coast of Honduras. Many died of disease on the journey, and the rest were abandoned with sup-

LEFT: artist's impression of the Garifuna's first landing site in 1832 near Dangriga.

plies for only three months. With minimal supplies and resources, the marooned Garifuna struggled to survive, and the remaining 1700 were soon taken by the Spanish to Trujillo on the mainland of Honduras.

An abortive takeover by royalists against the republican government of Honduras in 1823 found the Garifuna siding with the losing faction and facing continued persecution. Again, it was time for the community to move on, this time to another British colony – **British Honduras** (now Belize).

In 1832, under the leadership of **Elijio Beni**, a large group of Garifuna landed on the coast of Stann Creek, followed by many more. They've been there ever since. November 19, **Garifuna Settlement Day**, is a national holiday in Belize, commemorating the landing of Elijio Beni and his followers and the end of the 200-year exodus *(see Dugu Festivities, page 250)*.

The Garifuna today

While many Garifuna continue in traditional occupations like farming and fishing, since the early 1900s many looked to education as a means for advancement. Garifuna people quickly took on professional training and virtually every school, at every level, has Garifuna teachers and principals. They also entered the public service and medical profession and are increasingly becoming involved in the arts.

A growing number of successful Garifuna musicians include The Ugandani Dance Group, Garifuna drummers and *paranderos* (musicians who perform traditional *paranda*-style music) as well as **Punta Rock** artists such as Andy Palacio, the Original Turtle Shell Band, founded by visual artist Pen Cayetano, and relative newcomers, Lugua and the Larubeya Drummers. These well-known names and others have all popularized Garifuna music, not only locally but also exporting it to the United States and Europe as well.

With the boom in ecotourism in Belize, many Garifuna have capitalized on their cultural heritage, producing handicrafts *(see page 246)*, giving traditional storytelling performances, and running courses in arts and

crafts. The popularity of all these enterprises has produced the double benefit of providing local employment and helping the Garifuna maintain their cultural skills and identity.

Most recently, the son of a Belizean Garifuna family living in Los Angeles, Milton Palacio, made it into the NBA (National Basketball Association), playing for the Vancouver Grizzlies. All these successes have served to enhance the image of the Garifuna in Belize.

Even so, there is a growing realization that the language is in danger of being lost as young people become more comfortable speaking English or creole. There is a move to establish language training in some of the Stann Creek villages and in Belize City where so many families have migrated in search of better work opportunities. The Garifuna Settlement Day activities, such as the Thanksgiving masses and re-enactment ceremonies allow the younger generations to participate in this living culture and share it with other Belizeans and visitors from abroad.

The Garifuna's story is one that is worth telling in any language. ❑

RIGHT: Garifuna drumming is an intrinsic ingredient of Settlement Day celebrations.

COCKSCOMB BASIN

Map on page 242

Its rugged isolation has attracted an impressive wealth of animal species to this sanctuary, in particular the awesome jaguar, whilst Victoria Peak is drawing a growing band of hardy hikers

S een from satellite photographs, the Cockscomb Basin looks like a huge meteor crater blasted from the center of the Maya Mountains. From closer to earth, it is a lush mountain basin, full of pristine tropical forest and riddled through with jungle streams. It has one of Central America's densest concentrations of jaguar, and was the site of the world's first jaguar reserve, the **Cockscomb Basin Wildlife Sanctuary ⑫**.

Although it is the jaguar for which the sanctuary is famous, you will be lucky to glimpse one of the big cats, which mostly hunt at night. The chance to experience nature attracts an increasing number of people to visit since the basin has an intense concentration of other wildlife that makes up the jaguar's prey. Ernesto Saqui, the director of the sanctuary, once said that the healthy jaguar population is direct evidence of the overall quality of the habitat. "Without plenty of peccary, deer and other prey species, we wouldn't have so many jaguars."

PRECEDING PAGES: scorching sunset over Victoria Peak. **LEFT:** tracking wildlife in the basin. **BELOW:** the jaguar – at rest, but alert.

Refuge for the endangered

The Cockscomb Basin, referred to locally as simply "the Cockscomb," is spread over 160 sq miles (415 sq km) of rugged gullies and steep slopes in the middle of Belize, all carpeted by dense rainforest. Hemmed in on all sides by ridges or the Maya Mountains, the Cockscomb actually consists of two smaller basins, each a complete watershed for two of Belize's major rivers. Annual rainfall averages from 100–120 inches (2.5–3 cm), with the wettest months from June to October.

Over the past 50 years, selective logging and hurricanes have created dense secondary forest in much of the basin, with an upper canopy of 45–130 ft (13.5–40 meters). This tangle of vegetation, while inhospitable to humans, allows animal life to flourish.

This rugged sanctuary supports a profusion of endangered wildlife. The bird list for the sanctuary stands near 300 species, including the brilliant scarlet macaw, the great curassow, the colorful keel-billed toucan, the king vulture and the secretive agami heron. The sanctuary is predominantly known to be a safe haven for the largest raptors, such as the solitary and white hawk eagles. Besides the jaguar, four other species of wildcat prowl the basin's forests – the puma, ocelot, margay and small jaguarundi. There is also an abundance of reptiles and amphibians roaming around, including iguanas, various snakes, and the red-eyed tree frog that periodically appears in the ir thousands at the start of the rainy season.

Special recognition should be given to the Belize Audubon Society and the Wildlife Conservation Society, thanks to whom howler monkeys transplanted from northern Belize again roar at dawn.

The locally named "Give and Take" plant, whose sharp spines can give you a nasty scratch, but which also has a sap that acts as an antiseptic.

BELOW:
Cockscomb park wardens in repose.

But the natural state of the Cockscomb has not always been so pristine. Humans have lived here since the time of the ancient Maya, who left a Classic-era ceremonial site called Chucil Baalum, now buried in the forest. In 1888, the Goldsworthy expedition to the Cockscomb Peaks recorded mahogany logging camps hard at work. And from the 1940s, regular logging operations were taking place in the western portion of the basin. Old logging camps with names like "Go To Hell" and "Salsipuedes" (Leave If You Can) are dotted about the basin. In support of the fledgling timber industry, a small Maya community of workers grew around the main logging camp at Quam Bank, site of the present-day headquarters of the Wildlife Sanctuary. The hunting of jaguar and other wildlife flourished. Only the inhospitality of the jungle prevented an all-out onslaught on its natural inhabitants. Meanwhile, Hurricane Hattie wreaked devastation on much of the forest in 1961, knocking down many of the taller, older trees.

Fight to save the jaguar

In 1974, the Belizean government forbade jaguar hunting, but ranchers and hunters in the 1980s began a campaign to overturn the law. Alleged livestock kills were blamed on the increased jaguar population, with one Belizean businessman claiming that the big cat had run him out of the cattle business. Citing the disappearance of calves, he pronounced: "I got tired of raising beef to feed the jaguars." The government requested a study of the cats' distribution, numbers and habitats in Belize.

In October 1982, Dr Alan Rabinowitz, a young wildlife researcher working with the New York Zoological Society, answered the call. He examined forested sites throughout Belize and ranked them according to several criteria, including

jaguar density, prey abundance and development potential. The Cockscomb received extraordinarily high marks on all counts. Since the jaguar had been very little studied, the results prompted Rabinowitz to spend two more years within the Cockscomb. He managed to trap and radio-collar six jaguars. Subsequent tracking of the cats led to some of the first data on the ecology and behavior of the cat in Central America.

Founding the Sanctuary

In the Cockscomb, Rabinowitz found that jaguars consumed at least 17 different kinds of prey, including snakes and fish – but no cattle. Only injured cats (often with shotgun wounds) or those incapable of catching natural prey, such as the old or very young, turned to the livestock. If Belize could set aside enough territory to protect a "viable population," the cats would leave the cattle alone. Armed with Rabinowitz's hard scientific data, conservation groups within Belize successfully lobbied the government to award full protection status to the Cockscomb. In 1984, the Cockscomb Basin became a forest reserve and no-hunting zone, and in 1986, 3,600 acres (1,460 hectares) around Rabinowitz's research camp were set aside as the world's first jaguar reserve. Finally, in 1990, the entire 100,000 acres (40,000 hectares) of the Cockscomb Basin was declared a Wildlife Sanctuary, managed by the Belize Audubon Society and funded entirely by private contributions.

Today, the Cockscomb Basin Wildlife Sanctuary stands as the flagship protected area for Belize and an important refuge for the jaguar. The small Maya village, that once existed within the basin has been relocated to the entrance road to the sanctuary, allowing the jungle to regrow and animals to roam at will.

Map on page 242

Altogether, 55 different mammals make their home in the Cockscomb Basin, 75 percent of the total of mammal species found in the whole of Belize.

BELOW: teaching a group of Belizeans at Cockscomb's visitors' center.

The entire staff of the sanctuary, all Maya indians, come from this new community, called Maya Centre, while other villagers derive indirect income from the sanctuary as naturalist guides or by selling crafts to the ever-increasing number of tourists. A craft center is situated by the roadside at the entrance of the reserve, where local handcrafted souvenirs are sold.

The sanctuary is about an hour's drive south of Dangriga on the Southern Highway, with a rough 6-mile (10-km) track entrance road beginning at Maya Centre leading to the headquarters of the sanctuary. Twelve self-guided hiking trails – all carefully mapped, well maintained and safe – can provide days of rainforest exploration, while a new visitors' center explains the geological, anthropological and natural history (an entrance fee of BZ$10 is charged to enter the sanctuary).

Two families in Maya Centre Village provide cabaña accommodation and camping facilities. Enquire at the local store or contact Julio Saqui (tel: 520 2020) at Julio's Cultural and Jungle Tours.

Bringing in the baboons

The Cockscomb Sanctuary has been so successful that a project is underway to restore one of its former residents, the black howler monkey (known in Belize as the baboon), whose distinctive roar once filled the air. However, in the early 1960s, they were driven to local extinction by the combined effects of hunting, yellow fever and hurricane destruction of the forest canopy. A few individual monkeys had been seen nearby, but none made it into the sanctuary because of the high ridges surrounding the basin.

When the sanctuary was made legally secure in 1990, Dr. Rob Horwich, founder of the Community Baboon Sanctuary in Bermudian Landing *(see page 187)*, formed a team of local and international conservationists to re-establish a viable, self-sustaining population of the baboons in the Cockscomb. In 1992, three complete troops of baboons were relocated without loss, including two pregnant females, with more expected to follow.

BELOW: Dr. Alan Rabinowitz, founder of the sanctuary, and Ignacio Pop, warden, at Maya Center.

Part of the project included training staff to monitor the baboons' progress through radio telemetry. Instead of entering the sanctuary armed with machete and shotgun, warden Hermelindo Saqui, who is in charge of tracking the transplanted monkeys, wears headphones and carries a directional antenna.

"The baboons are all healthy and beginning to roar again," he proudly reports, "as if they had never left."

Hiking and relaxing

Cockscomb's network of well-marked and maintained trails offer the chance of spotting some of the sanctuary's wildlife, whilst taking in its scenic beauties, such as delicate waterfalls spraying the pristine jungle. There are short walks of less than an hour, and long hikes of several days. Self-guiding maps are available at the visitors' center, but for the longer walks it's more suitable to hire a local guide. For the best views of the basin, follow the muscle-building **Ben's Bluff Trail** (a 2½-mile/4-km hike to the top of a forested ridge) to get a wholesome view of the entire Cockscomb Basin.

The truly hardy can even hike to **Victoria Peak**, Belize's second-highest mountain and possibly its most spectacular. This demanding three to four-day

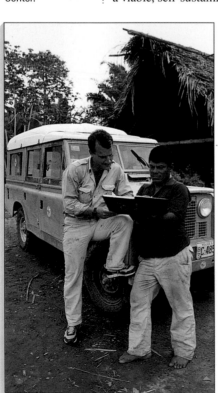

hike is rapidly gaining a reputation as one of the best mountain trails in Belize. But it's not for the faint-hearted; it could be done in three days, but more comfortably you should allow one and a half days to reach the base of the peak and another half a day to get to the top. The terrain is up and down some quite steep hills, through hot and humid jungle, and wading through numerous creeks. The final ascent is a steep climb on all fours, hauling yourself up by clutching onto trees. Your reward at the top – of course – is a great view of the whole sanctuary and the surrounding, undisturbed jungle.

Although the trail is well-marked, you are advised to take a local guide, who will know what to do if you get into trouble (i.e. they know jungle remedies in case of accident, they can make an arm sling from jungle leaves, and can construct temporary overnight shelters with a sleeping platform off the ground). Hikers must register with the Belize Audubon Society. There are now rudimentary camping shelters and pit toilets at two points along the trail. You have to take all your own food for the journey, so the option of hiring a porter from the **Maya Centre** village might appeal; they charge BZ$40–50 per day. Plentiful creek water en route is drinkable, but it's wiser to filter it (using water bottles with built-in filters, which are commercially available from specialist stockists). Suitable footwear and clothing is also very important; lightweight, fast-drying clothes are best as you'll get wet a lot: tight-fitting shorts, like those worn by cyclists, have been recommended, as they also prevent chafing.

The best time of year to climb Victoria Peak is in the dry season, from January to May; as well as avoiding the worst of the insects, which are a real nuisance during the wettest season from July to September, it is also much more colorful then, when the flowering plants, including orchids, are in bloom.

Besides this major adventure, taking a night walk along one of the sanctuary's shorter trails is a perfect way to meet some of its nocturnal animal residents, and admire the incredible variety of plant species of the forest (long pants, sturdy footwear, a torch and insect repellent are recommended). You'll see ferns, and orchids, and trees such as mahogany and ceiba.

Food and accommodations

Overnight accommodations within the sanctuary are grouped around the visitors' center, comprising comfortable dorms, rooms, and some private cabins. There is one cabin, designed for school groups, with its own classroom and kitchen. There is also a campsite nearby, with tents available to rent. If you're traveling independently, you'll need to bring your own food and cook it on a gas stove in the cabin kitchen for BZ$4. A small shop located just beyond the craft center by the entrance sells basic snacks, supplies, and cold drinks. There is a rainwater cistern for drinking, and fresh water is drawn from nearby streams for bathing. Reservations are recommended if you want to stay overnight in the sanctuary (see Travel Tips, Attractions, page 331 for details).

You can also make a day-trip to the sanctuary from the nearby villages of Hopkins, Seine Bight, Placencia or even in Dangriga, where you'll find everything from basic cabañas to luxurious resorts. ❏

TIP

To cool down after a morning hike, try inner-tubing down the South Stann Creek River or swimming in crystal-clear pools beneath refreshing mountain waterfalls. Ask at the Visitors' Center for details.

BELOW: jaguar spotted in the wild.

PLACENCIA

*The best beaches in mainland Belize, plus some of the
loveliest offshore coral cayes combine to make Placencia
one of the country's emerging holiday destinations*

Map
on page
266

I n the seaside bars of Placencia, local patrons have been known to indulge in mild dispute about what their village's name actually means. Some insist it is French for "pleasant point," others say "peaceful point," while still others believe it means "patience." The exact meaning doesn't really matter, as Placencia is both pleasant and peaceful – and a good dose of patience doesn't hurt if you're going to enjoy its indisputable attractions.

But see Placencia as it is, while you can. As a gateway to the longest sand beaches in Belize, the village is poised on the pinnacle of discovery. Less than 20 years ago, it could only be reached by fishing boat; in 10 years' time, you won't recognize it. Although badly hit by Hurricane Iris in 2001, the village has recovered well, and is as attractive as ever.

French heritage

Placencia's name, shared by the village and its peninsula, was given by Huguenots. Members of this strict Protestant sect fled religious persecution in Europe, tried out Nova Scotia in Canada, then immigrated to Belize in 1740. They chose this remote point, which the ancient Maya had once used as a fishing camp (as excavated pottery shards and house mounds indicate).

The Huguenots were eventually beaten by the tropical heat and diseases from the nearby swamps, abandoning the settlement in 1820. But they did have occasional good times: dozens of 17th-century bottles and clay pipes have been dug up at the appropriately named **Rum Point**, a couple of miles (3 km) north of town, where it is thought that Huguenot men came to smoke and drink alcohol out of sight of their womenfolk and away from religious restrictions.

Though little concrete evidence exists, local legend has it that buccaneers often used the excellent protection of the lagoon at the Placencia Peninsula as a harbor. They too probably put Rum Point to good use. Today the site is occupied by the **Rum Point Inn**, a luxurious beachside resort of futuristic design.

Placencia was restarted as a fishing camp in the mid-1800s, and with the wealth of marine life and proximity of the Barrier Reef, prospered. Though many of the fishermen have given up their lines and spearguns for binoculars and dive gear, cashing in on their local knowledge to guide tourists around, the village still celebrates June 29 as Fishermen's Day. A Catholic Mass, boat parade and the blessing of the fishing fleet precedes a town-wide party where visitors are welcomed.

The dirt road running 26 miles (42 km) along the peninsula's spine was only built in 1986, connecting Placencia to the **Southern Highway**. If you're driving

PRECEDING PAGES:
off Placencia's
palm-clad cayes.
LEFT: rasta at rest.
BELOW: rustic
beachfront charm.

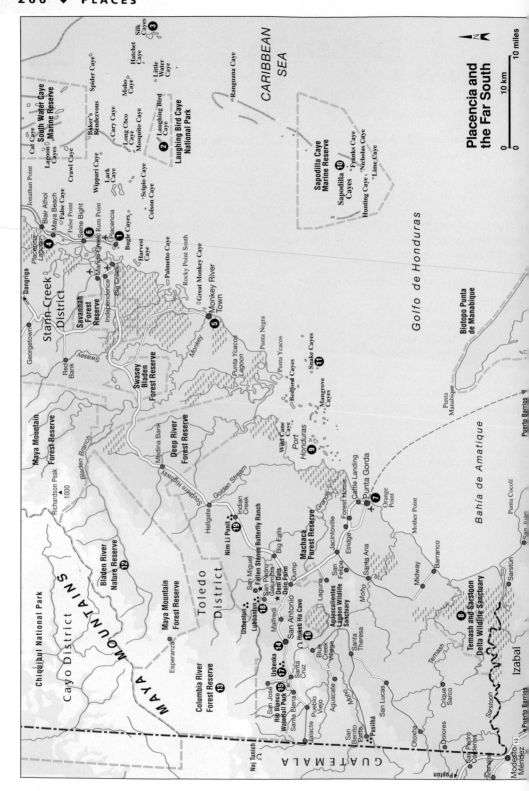

Placencia and
the Far South

here, take special care: during dry spells, clouds of dust can block your vision, and oncoming vehicles materialize out of nowhere; watch out for buses driven at breakneck speeds and narrow wooden bridges.

Dangriga may be only 51 miles (82 km) north, but the monotonously flat, two-hour drive through citrus groves and banana plantations can be exhausting. There is a well-worn airstrip 2 miles/3 km north of town, and, until the long-awaited paving of the Placencia Road actually happens, most people still prefer to fly here. On arrival, it is possible to take a taxi from the airstrip into Placencia village for around BZ$10.

Tropical calm

Placencia ❶ must be one of the most laid-back places in Belize – which is saying a lot. **Main Street** is actually a narrow, raised concrete sidewalk running through the village, first built 30 years ago (and rebuilt after Hurricane Iris struck the peninsula in 2001), as a means of wheelbarrowing fish around without fighting the sand. It still serves as the main artery of life in town, and, as the riding of bicycles or motorcycles on it is prohibited, the leisurely pace of life is maintained. Pastel-colored clapboard houses on stilts are randomly clustered alongside the walkway, with locals hiding beneath shaded porches during the heat of the day. Near sunset, children appear selling hot *panades* (fish- or bean-filled ground-corn patties) and beach volleyball games start on both sides of the walkway.

The north end of the sidewalk starts at the beach designated for campers and tents. To the south, it ribbons its way past numerous local businesses. Along this "busy" 100-ft (30-meter) section, you can browse around several small gift-shops selling hand-painted T-shirts (some bearing slogans such as "Iguana Rock With You"), fine wooden carvings and other local crafts. Beware of buying any black coral on display, however; it is strictly protected under international agreement and you are not allowed to bring it through customs if returning to Europe, the United States or Canada – you may even be landed with a fine if caught in the attempt).

Stroll across the walkway toward the beach and sample local creole dishes or fresh seafood at one of the growing number of beachfront bars and restaurants. Or try some homemade ice-cream and pastries for dessert at a snack stall. Then take in the volleyball next to one of Placencia's oldest structures, the octagonal **Anglican Church**, built in 1943 (thanks to termites, not many of Belize's older wooden buildings last very long, and those that do survive the voracious insects then have to contend with the hurricanes).

Just beyond the church a path to the right leads to the **Purple Space Monkey Internet Café**, one of a growing number of such establishments springing up all over Belize. With its traditional thatched roof, the café also stands as a fine symbol of the old linking with the new.

The walkway ends at the eastern tip of the Placencia Peninsula, near the police station, fishermen's co-operative and what could be termed the heart of town – the J-Byrd bar. Here you can buy a refreshing beer

Map on page 266

Placencia's Purple Space Monkey Internet Café: rustic meets high-technology.

BELOW: Placencia's concrete sidewalk.

TIP

The best way to get around the long, narrow Placencia peninsula is by bicycle; sturdy machines with chunky tires can be hired in town, or are free if you're staying at one of the upscale resorts.

while consulting the locals for advice or any directions that you may need.

A sandy path continues around the peninsula toward the lagoon, with another string of resorts, restaurants, a bank, a rental business, and a gas station. This is also the Placencia Tourism Center, the best place to find out what's going on locally. A wide selection of seafront bars and resort restaurants offer relaxing places for a sunset drink and meal. Just offshore are many foreign yachts tugging at their anchors and local fishing skiffs bringing in their daily catch.

Opposite the post office, along the dusty road leading out of town sits a warehouse called **Wallen's Market & Hardware** – this is the place to buy meat, produce, cold drinks or any other odds and ends. Opposite Wallen's Market is the **ball field**. Here, on some Saturdays and Sundays, games of cricket begin around 10am.

Belize's finest coastline

Placencia is one of the few places in Belize where you can walk for miles along a sandy beach. It is possible to stroll 7 miles (11 km) north to the village of **Seine Bight** without interruption. Despite the many upscale resorts lining this coast, there are still many secluded beaches to call your own for the afternoon. Belizean law actually prohibits construction within 66 ft (20 meters) of the shoreline of beach areas, specifically in order to ensure free access to all, although many resorts have all but taken over their own stretch of sand.

Swimming is best at the points of land where sand builds up. Snorkelers will find meadows of grass beds bordering the coastline, dotted by clusters of small coral patch reefs. Beware of boats while swimming. Tourist and fishing boats continually ply the coastal waters of Belize. In Placencia village, the town council has placed buoys along the shore to mark an idle zone – for all boats – to help protect swimmers.

Belizeans have always known that the diving is also better in the southern half of the country. The problem has always been a lack of infrastructure, pushing up travel costs.* Today there are four major dive operators – Placencia Dive Shop, Rum Point Divers, Seahorse Diving and the Turtle Inn – all offering complete dive packages. Several scuba shops offer equipment rental and instruction, while smaller outfits such as the Paradise Hotel do snorkeling trips to nearby cayes and take visitors to **Gladden Spit** to see whale sharks feed on snapper eggs during the spring at full moon.

What makes the diving so interesting off Placencia is that it marks the change in the Barrier Reef's structure from northern Belize to the south. North of **Columbus Caye**, the area behind the reef is mainly flat, with extensive grass beds and patch reefs. As you move south toward Placencia, the reef structure transforms into a region of sink holes, pinnacles and formations called "faroes" – atoll-like structures that support a vast array of marine habitats (an example is **Laughing Bird Caye National Park ❷**, named after the laughing gulls that used to nest here). South of Columbus Caye, the Barrier Reef drop-off becomes a near-vertical wall beginning in only 35 ft (10 meters) of water.

BELOW:
Placencia character.

Around the cayes

A typical diving excursion might include a morning dive outside the Barrier Reef on the drop-off amongst marine life such as spotted eagle rays, hawksbill or loggerhead turtles. Lunch can be taken on one of the picturesque islands inside the reef, such as the **Silk Cayes ❸**, followed by snorkeling around the rich waters. The final dive for the day could be at any of the hundreds of possible sites inside the inner reef. On the way home, if you pass by **Long Coco Caye**, chances are that a pod of dolphins will chase your boat's bow wake. If you are lucky, you can slip quietly into the water and observe from a distance the graceful underwater ballet of these marine mammals.

Even if you can't dive, snorkeling can offer more than a glimpse of the wonders of the Belize marine waters. Coral gardens abound in 10 to 15 ft (3–5 meters) of water around the **Scipio** and **Colson Cayes**. Frigate birds, brown boobies and brown pelicans nest on a trio of small islands around what is known as **Lark Caye**. The rich birdlife above the water is fueled by an explosion of marine life below, including tremendous schools of small herrings and anchovies. The bottom is alternately carpeted by sea grass, colonial anemones and corals, and sinkholes and drop-offs are accessible even to beginner snorkelers.

Both Laughing Bird Caye and the Silk Caye group (sometimes called the Queen Cayes) offer spectacular underwater scenery, in deep water as well as snorkeling depth.

The rich variety of marine habitats also makes Placencia an excellent place for sport fishing. Grassy shallows around many of the islands are home to schools of bonefish, tarpon and permit. Trolling along drop-offs and channels nearly always lands barracuda and jacks, and occasionally the mighty kingfish.

Map on page 266

Placencia has a good range of dive shops, snorkeling tours and fishing operators.

BELOW: Placencia's pastel shades.

Outside the Barrier Reef, the catch includes grouper and snapper. Kingfisher Sports specializes in fly fishing, while Seahorse Diving is run by the three Young brothers, who know the southern Belize reefs as well as anyone in the country. Even so, new sites are discovered frequently and there is enough sea to keep divers visiting new sites year after year.

TIP

Kayaks and canoes are ideal for getting close to the noise-shy manatee, although local regulations prohibit motor boats from running their engines within 25 yards/meters of sighted manatee.

RIGHT: towering banana container ship at Big Creek.

Placencia Lagoon

The mangrove habitat is one of the most important ecosystems in Belize and the brackish waters of **Placencia Lagoon** ❹ provide the perfect conditions for the taproots of the white mangrove plant, which has formed a tangled fringe all along its shores. Mangrove is a halophytic plant, which has the unique ability to thrive in salty water, by filtering out 80 percent of the salt through its roots.

Kayaking and canoeing around the long thin lagoon is an ideal way of silently viewing the tremendous amount of wildlife living among these ecologically important aquatic plants. Most of the larger resorts dotted along the seashore a short walk across the peninsula road provide access, guides and watercraft for a quiet afternoon's paddling. Even when the sea is choppy on the other side of the peninsula it is usually calm on the lagoon and its numerous side channels provide the ideal opportunity for exploring in a small boat.

Though unpredictable, herbivorous manatee feed in the extensive grass beds and calve in the secluded bays and rivers emptying into the lagoon. White ibis, snowy egrets, boobies and pelicans feed, roost and nest around and on many of the small mangrove islands. Beneath the water level, the mangrove also provides a home to marine species: lobsters protect their young among the underwater roots, whilst other crustaceans and various fish feed and find shelter here.

BANANA BOATS

In the late 19th century, plantation owners began growing bananas in the flat fertile land between Placencia and Dangriga for export to Europe. In the early 1900s, however, most of the crops were ruined by diseases and in the 1940s the banana plants were virtually wiped out by the sigatoka virus.

A slow recovery has been underway since the 1960s, boosted by British importers, and a new deep-water port has been dredged at Big Creek allowing container ships to take bulk loads of the fruit.

Environmentalists aren't so enthusiastic, however. While providing employment and foreign exchange for Belize, the heavy use of fertilizers and pesticides on nearby plantations is affecting the delicate offshore ecosystems, while large expanses of tropical forests are being leveled to plant bananas.

In the past, some importers branched out from fruit, and offered a round-trip in private passenger cabins in one of Fyffes' cargo ships on a 14-day cruise from London to Belize. British readers may be interested to note that HP sauce used to stand proud on the dining table and the purser's store even sold Old Spice aftershave. Sadly, these trips no longer operate.

Map on page 266

Excursions from Placencia

Nestled together across the lagoon from Placencia, the small towns of **Big Creek**, **Independence** and **Mango Creek** owe their existence to the revived banana industry in Belize *(see below)*. Prior to the 1940s blight, bananas were loaded on railroad cars and shipped to the coast at **Monkey River Town** ❺ to be loaded on shallow drafted barges. This creole and Garifuna outpost has never recovered from the industry's crash. The empty shell of the town's former medical center stands as a reminder of its more affluent past. Again, tourism is the *deus ex machina* for keeping the young people at home. Much of the surrounding forest along the Monkey River has been declared a Special Conservation Area and a few small, communal guest houses have appeared. There are a couple of inns and restaurants right by the jetty (where you can order lunch in advance if going up the river in the morning), and the Osprey Gift Shop by the river mouth offers local handicrafts, fishing and wildlife tours, snacks and drinks.

Located 10 miles (16 km) south of Placencia, the town is accessible only by boat. On the way is **Rocky Point South**, a manatee hangout. A slow ride up the jungle-lined river is a chance to view iguana, monkeys, crocodiles and a variety of tropical birds. Most day excursions will also moor on the riverbank and take you into the jungle for an hour or so. Howler monkeys will probably make an appearance here (but beware of standing directly beneath them as they have a habit of urinating when excited!). Mosquitoes are also a hazard, even in the middle of the day in the dry season, so bring plenty of repellent.

About 5 miles (8 km) upstream is a clear swimming hole (don't worry about the crocodiles, they are very shy and non-aggressive) and a sandbar where you can eat a picnic lunch before drifting quietly back down the river.

You might be lucky enough to spot a crocodile sunning itself on the banks of the Monkey River.

BELOW: red mangroves on the Monkey River.

Map on page 266

Seine Bight

The Garifuna people of **Seine Bight** , the neighboring town to the north of Placencia on the peninsula, are some of the friendliest in Belize. It is, or was, home to most of the workers in the resorts up and down the peninsula, so they more than welcome tourists. With 600 inhabitants, it is often referred to as a "grandmother village" because many younger people have left to find jobs, sending money back to the grandparents who take care of the children.

The town is pure Garifuna. Ask for Mr Nick (Nicholas), the self-appointed town tour guide. He can take you through sandy yards below wooden houses on stilts (protection against termites and seasonal floods); introduce you to gray-ing men playing dominos in the shade of a laden breadfruit tree; or let you watch a medicine woman mixing a herbal brew for the common cold. But mainly he likes to visit the few bars in town to take some "bitters". His colorful tour is the perfect way to experience the culture, not just observe it.

Seine Bight is struggling to open up the village to tourism and still protect the Garifuna culture. A few small tourist establishments have sprung up to explore the possibilities. The **Kulcha Shack** serves Garifuna dishes and has four modest rooms with an outside bath. At least once a week, the owner Dewey Nunez puts on a Garifuna cultural night, with turtle shell bands and dancing.

On the north end of town is a more upscale lodging called the **Nautical Inn**. Owner Ben Ruoti from Arizona runs a wildlife project here, in conjunction with Belize Zoo, breeding green iguana in order to return them into the wild. This species has become endangered in recent years, mainly due to loss of habitat. The reptiles are kept in an enclosure in the resort grounds and subsequently released when they are big enough to fend for themselves. ❑

BELOW: time for a siesta in Monkey River Town.

Manatees

We arrive in our skiff at the mangrove embankment known as Manatee Hole and shut off the powerful outboard engines. Our Belizean guide cautions us to silence, picking up his boat-pole and propelling us quietly through the shallow lagoon deep into our destination. A dense carpet of sea grass – essential food for manatees – can be clearly viewed through the shallow clear water surrounding us. Suddenly a shadow looms beneath our boat, and a round, glistening grey protuberance breaches the still water's surface. Two round holes open wide with an audible puff of breath. The first manatee has arrived.

The **West Indian Manatee** (Trichechus manatus), popularly known by some as "sea cow", is an endangered species worldwide. Over 100 countries who have signed CITES (Convention on International Trade of Endangered Species) agree that no part of it should be traded on the international market.

Official protection has been important for these large, gentle creatures, up to 12 ft 6 inches (3.8 meters) in length. Like a cross between a dolphin and a seal in body design, they share this somewhat ungainly appearance with few relatives worldwide, including three manatees and the more widespread dugong – the manatees' counterpart in Australasia. The West Indian Manatee occurs from southern North American coasts and rivers, throughout the Caribbean. The North American manatee population is considered a distinct subspecies from the remainder, which are termed **Antillean Manatees**. Belize is home to the largest population of Antillean Manatee, which may serve as a source population to neighboring countries.

Manatees are slow to reproduce – a trait that renders them vulnerable to extinction. One calf, occasionally twins, is born after an 11–13 month gestation and cared for extensively by the mother for 1–2 years. New calves are born only once every 2–5 years. As the calf matures it is gradually introduced to its plant diet. In the sea this is turtlegrass

and manatee grass; in fresh water it is a variety of aquatic plants. Manatees reach sexual maturity at age 3–4.

While most Belizeans and visitors regard manatees in a positive light, there remain threats; poaching and collisions with boats are two of the main culprits, whilst drowning in fishing nets and poisoning by chemical pollutants are also suspected dangers.

The most important things you can do to protect manatees are:

● Speak only quietly while you are on manatee grounds;
● Keep rubbish inside the boat;
● Refrain from buying items made with manatee bones (ivory), which may be offered for sale by some vendors.

Your best chance of seeing a manatee is on an organized tour, led by a skilled and licensed Belizean guide. A variety of trips are available at various sites up and down the coast: at Sarteneja; Caye Caulker, San Pedro and Belize City (Manatee Hole) as well as Punta Gorda, Monkey River and Placencia *(see Travel Tips, Tours, for details).* ❑

RIGHT: the docile manatee, possibly the source of crazed sailors' visions of mermaids.

THE FAR SOUTH

Map on page 266

The remote south of Belize is the latest area of the country to open up to tourists: with its undeveloped cayes, mountain rainforest scenery and rich Maya culture, it has much to offer

The residents of the remote **Toledo District**, to the far south of Belize, often refer to their home as "the forgotten land." It is the poorest part of the country, with pot-holed dirt roads when you turn off the paved Southern Highway and isolated Maya villages surviving on subsistence farming. In the early 1980s, a paper was even circulated proposing to give the area south of the Monkey River to Guatemala in exchange for relinquishing its 150-year-old claim on Belizean territory. Fortunately for Toledo and all Belizeans, the proposal was met by widespread riots, and was quickly rejected.

But Toledo is rich in Belize's other resources – primary rainforest, monstrous caves and jungle-covered ruins – making it an exciting destination for the adventurous traveler. You can expect low costs and no frills. Outside of Punta Gorda, the only town of any size, menus are usually restricted to tortillas cooked over an open fire, home-grown vegetables, and coffee. Accommodations are most likely a hammock or bunk bed under a thatched roof; or if you want, you can even be hosted by a local Maya family *(see box on page 284)*. Travel arrangements can change from day to day, so it is best to be flexible, open minded and in no rush to get from place to place.

The Toledo District is first and foremost Maya country: over half the population belongs to one of two Maya groups: Mopan or Kekchi. Traveling south along the **Southern Highway**, clusters of thatched huts appear with increasing regularity. Maya women herd their children along the roadsides while balancing washloads on their heads; Maya men return from their *milpas* or working plantations with machetes and shotguns in hand.

The lay of the land

The Toledo District can be divided into two main areas. The uplands, located in the interior, include the southern ramparts of the **Maya Mountains**; these are the rugged remains of a hard, white, limestone shelf, now blanketed by some of the most pristine rainforest in Belize. The coastal lowlands consist of softer sediments, formed from the deposits of silt-laden rivers; here, striking groups of steep, jagged, limestone hills stick up like Maya pyramids.

Six major rivers snake past, draining the torrential rains of the uplands. They often flood at the height of the rainy season, in September and October, creating vast flood plains and seasonal swamps, cutting off side roads (but not the main highway) for days at a time.

This complex terrain has influenced human settlement of the far south. For centuries, Maya cities and ceremonial centers dotted the region. Pacified and converted by the Spanish in the 1600s, thousands of the Maya farmers were driven out by the British in

PRECEDING PAGES: a misty Maya Mountain view. **LEFT:** Toledo's helter skelter roads. **BELOW:** colorful Maya weavings.

The Ack family offer a warm welcome at Parrot's Guesthouse, San Pedro Columbia.

BELOW: the Maya Mountains, the highest – and emptiest – region of Belize.

the 18th and 19th centuries. Many settled in the vast lowland forests of Petén department in northern Guatemala, home of some of the greatest Maya ceremonial centers, in particular, Tikal and El Mirador.

In the mid-1800s, Garifuna settlements were founded at Punta Gorda, Punta Negro and Barranco, followed by Confederate gun runners seeking asylum at the end of the American Civil War. Sugar soon became the dominant cash crop and by 1870, twelve sugar mills were in operation, all owned by the North American immigrants. But the price of sugar began to drop; tired of fighting the rains and insects, most of the North Americans returned to their homeland.

Maya coming home

From the 1880s, two distinct groups of Maya – Mopan and Kekchi – began moving back into the region as laborers. Although related, tradition separates the two cultures, and their languages are as distinct as Italian and Portuguese (with different words for everything from "sun" to "tortilla").

Coming back from the Petén, the Mopan Maya have a long tradition as independent small farmers; they settled in the uplands of Toledo around the village of San Antonio. The Kekchi Maya, on the other hand, came to the lowlands of Toledo, from the high-altitude Alta Verapaz Department of central Guatemala, where they had suffered under exploitative conditions on foreign-owned coffee plantations. Their villages are small and isolated, often requiring long treks over muddied trails to reach, making them the most self-reliant as well as the poorest of the many ethnic groups in Belize. Adding to the melange are mestizos, creole (of Afro-Caribbean origin), Chinese and East Indians who came as loggers and sugar-cane laborers and never left.

Urban hub of the south

Known locally as "PG," **Punta Gorda** is the southernmost town in Belize, and is the capital of the Toledo District. In the past, most travelers only passed through Punta Gorda en route to somewhere else (it is a departure point for the twice-daily skiff service to Puerto Barrios, Guatemala and Puerto Cortés, Honduras). Today, although the town receives fewer visitors than most other parts of the country, more people are venturing south to seek out the genuine atmosphere of a frontier outpost without the hard edge of Belize City. Buses leave the capital six or seven times a day, and the trip takes 6–7 hours on the well-paved Southern Highway, taking in some stunning scenery on the way.

The air is crystal clear here, possibly due to the annual 160 inches (400 cm) of rain continuously washing the dust from the air. Perched on a limestone escarpment, much of Punta Gorda lies only 15–20 ft (4.5–6 meters) above sea level. Concrete walls, some leaning into the water as if under a tremendous weight, appear to hold the town upright.

The long, narrow town only stretches back three or four blocks from the coastline, which slopes to pebbly, dark sand beaches where fishing dories lie pulled up on shore. Further south, the Caribbean ceaselessly nibbles away at the land, dragging old houses and graveyards into the sea.

The pace of life is slow in PG, even by Belizean standards. The town is spectacularly overgrown: nature has gobbled up most remains from the colorful past and now seems to be working on reclaiming the town itself. Huge mango trees tower majestically along the streets, providing welcome midday shade; flowering bushes and potted plants decorate the verandas of lichen-stained clapboard homes; and tall grass flourishes in most yards.

Map on page 266

*Punta Gorda is the base for the **Toledo Cacao Growers' Association**, which administers some 140 organic farms, major producers of cacao beans for export to Europe (see details on page 289).*

BELOW: the shady greenery of Punta Gorda.

*Punta Gorda's
seafront Cyber Café.*

BELOW: Garifuna
elders in a dory,
Barranco.

The people of Punta Gorda still retain the genuine friendliness found only in untrampled places. Taking pictures invariably attracts locals to discuss what you are doing and offering advice on where to get the best view of the town. Only about 6,000 people call Punta Gorda home, but it has the highest number of tourist rooms per capita in the country. All along Main and Front streets, both of which run parallel to the coastline, you will see signs for guest houses and hotels. Most are pretty basic, but many are improving their facilities in response to the rising tourist trade.

There are few tourist attractions in town. Fishermen leave in their dugout canoes at sunrise, returning around noon with fish for the market. Little blue herons, snowy egrets and flocks of sandpipers forage for invertebrates on the beaches north of town, all but ignoring quiet bird-watchers. In the center of town is a stocky clock tower, built by a local politician to commemorate himself and his political party. The plaque at the base speaks for itself. On Wednesdays and Saturdays, Main Street swells with color as Indians from all over the district converge to sell produce, embroidery and plastic wares.

The best places to check for the most recent tourist information are at the Belize Tourist Office on Front Street, Nature's Way Guest House or the **Toledo Visitors' Information Center** on Front Street near the Punta Gorda Wharf. The leading authority on the area's burgeoning ecotourism industry is the **Toledo Institute for Development and Environment** (TIDE), who run a wide range of activities, from organizing training courses in sport fishing for local fishermen to providing information for visitors on recommended specialist nature guides and tours to the cayes and the Maya Mountains. You can contact them on tel: 722-2129, e-mail: tidetours@btl.net, www.tidetours.org.

Moves are underway to create a **Punta Gorda Nature Trail**, which will lead visitors on a 4-mile (6-km) walk around the town's physical and cultural attractions, starting on the coast and continuing through mangrove swamps, stopping off at a small zoo and a traditional Maya home and two farms. Proceeds from the trail are invested in sustainable agriculture projects

Another of Punta Gorda's attractions is the **Garifuna Village Project**, known locally as the Habiabara Garinagu Cerro project. Although nearly half of Punta Gorda's population is Garifuna, they are finding it difficult to keep their culture alive, so a small group of progressive Garifuna are using 40 acres (16 hectares) of ancestral lands to build a "conservation of culture" project with a small museum, restaurant, and arts and craft shop.

Excursions from Punta Gorda

About 4 miles (6.5 km) outside of town is the small but impressive **Church of the Nazareth**. Royal palms line the drive to this spacious chapel and nearby novitiate for the Pallotine Sisters. For an all-encompassing view of Punta Gorda, the Caribbean, and a glimpse of Honduras, follow the New Road west for just over a mile (2 km) to the city's waterpump station, where an old military trail leads up **Cerro Hill**. Though fairly strenuous, the 30-minute hike follows along a well-marked trail with good footing in the dry season.

Joe Taylor Creek snakes along the northern boundary of town. A two- or three-hour ride in a dugout canoe, paddling between limestone outcrops, is a good introduction to the mangrove/riverine habitat in Belize. The lower reaches of the creek are lined by mangroves, which quickly meld into broadleaf forest; orchids and bromeliads add to the river-bank vegetation.

Map on page 266

The Fajina Craft Center, Punta Gorda, is run by a group of local artisans.

LEFT: the Church of the Nazareth.
RIGHT: lumber mill worker.

Conch shells make up for scarce building material on the cayes.

To experience the largest and oldest mangroves in Belize, hire a boat to travel the 13 miles (20 km) south to the **Temash River**. Declared part of the 41,000-acre (16,400-hectare) **Temash and Sarstoon Delta Wildlife Sanctuary ❽** in 1992, the Temash River trip is spectacular if only for the tall red mangrove forest towering over both river banks. Amongst the orchids and huge bromeliads that coat the thick stilt roots of the mangroves, the 6-inch (15-cm) wide, iridescent blue wings of the Blue Morpho butterfly can be spotted.

Many of the tributaries draining into the Temash are black from the tannin of the decaying matter in surrounding swamps. Gibnut, peccary and warrie (a species of peccary), as well as their natural predators the jaguar and crocodile, are abundant here, one of the most remote places in Belize.

The Temash is only one of many rivers along the Toledo coast. The **Sarstoon River**, forming the southern border with Guatemala, nourishes the only comfrey palm forests in Belize at its mouth. Between the Sarstoon and Temash Rivers lies an expanse of sand bars, too shallow even for the use of an outboard motor. Huge schools of minnow and shrimp support a thriving population of sea-birds. The coastline is quickly eroding away here as tall, thin white mangroves topple into the sea like a giant game of pick-up sticks. Manatee are common along many of the river mouths, feeding on the rich grass beds and calving in the quiet lagoons and bays of the rivers.

The cayes of Toledo

Just north of Punta Gorda is **Port Honduras ❾**, a large bay containing over 100 small mangrove islands. Four major rivers drain into this bight, turning the water brown during most of the year. This influx of nutrient-laden sediment

makes it a prime feeding ground for marine fish, manatee and dolphin; fishing is also excellent around the many coral shoals, river mouths and channels. The ancient Maya knew of the wealth of marine resources and established an important ceremonial center on **Wild Cane Caye**, as well as fishing camps on many of the islands. In recent years, all this coastal stretch has been rapidly gaining a reputation as a superb site for fly-fishing, particularly for the highly-rated permit (*see Fishing, page 109–111*). With tightening limitations on net fishing in the protected waters, an increasing number of local fishermen are adapting their skills to become game-fishing guides, and the tourist information offices in Punta Gorda can provide you with details of a number of recommended experts.

The farther south in Belize you travel, the farther the Barrier Reef splits from the mainland. Off Punta Gorda, the reef lies nearly 40 miles (64 km) east and makes a great hook as the Caribbean deepens into the Bay of Honduras. On the shank of the hook lie six gems, the **Sapodilla Cayes ❿**, the southernmost islands in Belize and now a marine reserve, protected by TASTE (the Toledo Association for Sustainable Tourism and Empowerment). The reserve covers an area of about 48 sq miles (125 sq km), and is rich in fish and other marine life, and the crystal clear waters make it ideal for diving and snorkeling. You may well see angelfish and parrotfish as well as larger species such as whale sharks, manta rays and dolphins. A high coral sand beach in the shape of a horseshoe lines the eastern shore of **Hunting Caye**, one of the most beautiful beaches in Belize. Large numbers of turtles come here to nest during the late summer and fall months. You can expect to pay high prices for transportation to the Sapodillas, and it will probably be necessary to camp overnight on the islands because of the distances involved. The best place to stay is on **Frank's Caye**, which has a cluster of mid-price cabañas, well spaced apart, and with their own power generator. Meals are included and they have snorkeling equipment and kayaks for guests' use.

Alternatively you can camp on **Nicholas Caye**, or sling a hammock in one of the half-finished cabañas that cover most of the island, run by a resident caretaker (who will happily cook basic meals, including fish you may catch). Despite its lovely beach, Hunting Caye is the least attractive of the Sapodillas, badly littered by a run-down resort used by day-trippers from Guatemala. It does, however, also have a lighthouse, an immigration post and a Belize Defence Force guard station.

Closer to the shore and less expensive to visit are the **Snake Cayes** ⓫, a group of four islands 17 miles (27 km) northeast of Punta Gorda. Only West Snake Caye has a clean coral sand beach, which makes for fine snorkeling and a picnic. As on all the cayes, be prepared for insects.

Into the interior

The 92,000-acre (37,000-hectare) **Bladen River Nature Reserve** ⓬ lies along the southern slope of the Maya Mountains, encompassing most of the upper watershed of the Bladen Branch of the Monkey River. Protected by the government of Belize in 1990, the Bladen is probably Belize's most pristine

Map on page 266

TIP

If you're paddling in the shallow water around the cayes, drag your feet across the sand rather than step down, as this will alert stingrays, which sometimes lie invisibly under the surface, and which can give you a painful sting.

BELOW: ready-made relaxation on Frank's Caye.

protected rainforest. Largely unexplored, the Bladen River valley contains massive limestone outcrops, sinkholes, caves, waterfalls, and such environmentally endangered animals as the jaguar, Baird's tapir and Southern River otter; there are also over 200 species of bird.

Within one of the remote alluvial valleys lies an uninvestigated Maya ruin called **Quebrada de Oro** (Spanish for Passageway of Gold). Access is via a 5-mile (8-km) dirt road, inaccessible during the rainy season. Since nature reserves receive Belize's highest level of preservation, it is necessary to get permission to enter them. Information concerning permits and access can be found at the Belize Audubon Society in Belize City or BFREE (Belize Foundation for Research and Environmental Education) in Bladen *(see Travel Tips page 329)*.

To the southwest, and adjacent to the Bladen River Nature Reserve lies the 103,000-acre (41,000-hectare) **Columbia River Forest Reserve ⓭**, which a 1993 study found to harbor the most biologically diverse ecosystem in Belize. This is one of the only large, continuous tracts of undisturbed rainforest left in Central America. Rugged limestone hills are pock-marked by caves and sinkholes – one of which, near the village of **Esperanza**, swallows a whole river as if it were a giant drain. This reserve is not a place for weekenders: you must be totally self-sufficient in terms of equipment and food. Guides can be hired at the village of **San José** for strenuous treks into the back country. Again, permits are necessary from the Forestry Department in order to enter any forest reserve.

Maya villages

Lying in the heart of Maya country, among the rolling foothills of the Maya Mountains, **San Antonio ⓮** is at the center of a group of villages in the vicinity,

TIP

Every August, the village of San Antonio holds the Deer Dance, a colorful festival of music and costumed dance, as part of the Festival of San Luis.

BELOW: the spiritual glow inside San Antonio's church.

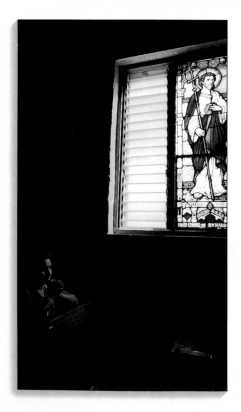

TOLEDO'S ECOTOURISM PROJECTS

One especially rewarding way of visiting Toledo district is through several village projects offering accommodation and guided visits to local attractions. The projects provide villagers with a livelihood, and an alternative to the timber industry that is causing deforestation in the region at an alarming rate.

The **Toledo Guesthouse and Eco-Trail Program** is run by a grassroots organization of Mopan, Q'eqchi' Maya and Garifuna leaders: the Toledo Ecotourism Association, in the Tourist Office on Front Street, Punta Gorda, tel: 722-2096, fax: 722-2198. Guesthouses sleeping eight people in bunk beds or hammocks have been constructed in several villages, where families chosen on a rotating basis host visitors. Nature trails, planned and constructed by the villagers, lead to local sites of interest. These can be found in the communities of **San Miguel** (bat cave and a river walk), **San Pedro Columbia** (river trip), **Santa Elena** (waterfall and ruins), **Laguna** (wetland and caves), **San José** (forest walk), and **Barranco** (Garifuna village and Temash River).

The villagers have a wealth of knowledge in herbal medicine, flora and fauna, and Maya folklore, which they are proud to share with visitors, enabling you to gain a unique experience of this traditional way of life.

where some enterprising grassroots ecotourism organizations *(see box on page 284)* are bringing more money into the community, including helping to finance local schools.

Lying some 20 miles (32 km) northwest of Punta Gorda, San Antonio is the second largest town in Toledo, but is a quiet and simple market outpost. The center of town is dominated by a stone **church** built of limestone salvaged from surrounding ruins. The early morning and late afternoon light pours through the beautiful stained-glass windows, illuminating the well-worn woodwork of the church interior.

A short walk out of San Antonio, along the road below the church, is the tranquil San Antonio waterfall and pool. A few wooden benches make it a perfect place for lunch and a cooling afternoon swim. Watch for multicolored dragonflies feeding among the stream-side vegetation, and hummingbirds, that bathe in the spray coming off the small falls.

Eight miles (13 km) farther on, between the villages of **Santa Cruz** and Santa Elena, you'll come across the **Río Blanco Waterfall Park** ⓯. Declared a protected area in 1992, this 500-acre (200-hectare) preserve has been called an Indigenous Peoples' Park – it is controlled by the nearby villages of Santa Cruz and Santa Elena, for their own use.

Here, the **Río Blanco** flows through wide, shallow pools and gentle cascades formed of smooth slabs of mudstone and sandstone, before pouring over a 12-ft (3.5-meter) ledge into a deep pool. It's an ideal swimming spot and a popular stop-off if you're touring the Maya Mountains. The sign marking the entrance to the park has been knocked down, so ask any of the Maya farmers working the fields nearby for directions.

Map
on page
266

You can get up close to a green iguana on Blue Creek's tree-top canopy walkway.

BELOW:
hand-pumped
water wells supply
villages in the
Maya Mountains.

Blue Creek

One of the most impressive natural sites in Toledo is the **Hokeb Ha Cave** at **Blue Creek** ⑯. The huge cave entrance is carved from the summit of a hill where the Blue Creek gurgles up from underground. After leaving the cave, the creek cascades over limestone boulders, under the towering shadows of the surrounding rainforest. Archeologists have found inside many Late Classic ceramics and an altar, leading them to theorize that the Hokeb Ha cave was used specifically for ceremonial purposes. The cave lies within the Blue Creek Preserve, a private sanctuary, with cabins by the riverside and various facilities, including an excellent canopy walkway strung between the trees, 80 ft (24 meters) above the river. To get there from San Antonio, follow the road to Punta Gorda 2½ miles (4 km) to Malfredi, at the junction with the road to **Aguacate**. Follow this road 5½ miles (9 km) to **Blue Creek Village**. Park before the bridge, walk along the gravel path to a swimming hole, then follow the muddy river path 15 minutes up-stream to the cave.

*Lubaantun was the alleged home of the **Crystal Skull**, found by the daughter of the British explorer, F.A. Mitchell-Hedges in 1924. The true origin and maker of the precisely made artifact remains a mystery to this day.*

BELOW: Santiago Coc, the caretaker at Lubaantun.

Archeological discoveries

Toledo is rich in Maya ruins, but the government of Belize lacks funds to maintain them for tourists. Many are overgrown, with little, if any, information available. For example, **Uxbenka** (Ancient Place) ⑰ is a small ceremonial center built on a hill outside the Maya village of Santa Cruz. Lacking the large-scale architecture of some bigger sites, Uxbenka was briefly open to the public as an example of the Maya practice of terracing hills. While a guide from Santa Cruz can still be hired if you want to tour the site, almost everything is overgrown by tall grass and thorny scrub, and all you'll see now are scattered piles of cut

stones. Eroding stelae lie exposed to wind and rain. There is a rough track off the main road, but it is too narrow for most vehicles to negotiate, so it's much easier to walk the short distance – worth it mostly to admire the hill-top view through the trees.

A much better-maintained site is **Lubaantun** (Place of Fallen Stones) , the largest in Toledo, which lies high on a ridge above a valley cut by the Columbia River, 1½ miles (2 km) from the village of **San Pedro Columbia** (and about 13 miles/21 km west of Punta Gorda). The ruins were first excavated in 1915, and subsequent archeological study suggests that Lubaantun was built completely without the use of mortar; each stone was precisely cut to fit snugly against its neighbor. The slim, square-cut stones are one of the distinctive features of Lubaantun; it is also exceptional among Maya ruins for the complete absence of carved stelae, particularly in contrast with those of nearby Nim Li Punit. The site consists of five main plazas, around which are grouped 14 main structures, including several ball courts. Pottery and other archeological finds discovered at the site are on display in the visitors' center. Those lucky enough to visit Lubaantun will find local caretaker Mr Santiago Coc an enthusiastic tour guide with a wealth of information (he assisted with the 1970 Cambridge excavations of the site).

Uphill from nearby **Indian Creek** village is the ceremonial center of **Nim Li Punit** (Big Hat) , with splendid views and 26 stelae, eight of them carved, and among them the tallest ever found in Belize. The ruins were first discovered in 1976, and archeologists think that the center may have had a reciprocal relationship with Lubaantun: Nim Li Punit being a religious and political center, while Lubaantun concentrated on trade and commerce. The site's name comes from a detail of a figure carved on one of the site's stelae (Stela 14), which is the longest such ancient monument found in Belize. This stela, together with several others, is on display in the attractive visitors' center at the entrance to the site. There is a small, walled ballcourt in the center of the site, as well as a burial site, named the "Plaza of the Royal Tombs."

One example of Belize's positive approach to eco-tourism just ouside of San Pedro Columbia is the 20-acre (8-hectare) **Dem Dats Doin Experimental Farm**, which is trying to replace the Maya's slash-and-burn traditions of milpa farming, which are only sustainable at low population densities, with a more environmentally sound system of agriculture for the 21st century.

Described as an "Integrated, Energy Self-Sufficient, Low Input, Organic Mini-Biosphere," it is run by a couple of transplanted Americans. Between a biogas digester and photovoltaics, they have reached 95 percent energy self-sufficiency. For a small fee (free for schools), the owners will give you a personal tour complete with flow charts and illustrations to help you understand the operation.

The farm's owners can, if asked in advance, also make arrangements for visitors to stay with a local Maya family *(see Travel Tips, Where to Stay, for contact details).* ❏

Map on page 266

TIP

Opening times at Belize's Maya sites are Monday–Friday, 8am–5pm, Saturday and Sunday, 8am–4pm; free entry, or a small fee is charged at some sites

BELOW: naïve-style painting by Marcos Larios, a Garifuna artist from Dangriga.

TRADITIONAL LIFE IN TOLEDO'S FORESTS

The Maya farmers live much as their ancestors did a thousand years ago, and today they are welcoming tourists into their homes

Nestled in the foothills of the Maya Mountains in the interior of Toledo district are a cluster of small villages, inhabited by Kekchi and Mopan Maya farmers, originally from Guatemala, who have settled here over the last two hundred years. Many of the farmers still employ the traditional slash-and-burn land use, but a few use organic methods, producing a wide range of crops, including maize, bananas, citrus fruits, cacao, herbs and vegetables. Each family transports their own produce by local bus to trade at the weekly market in Punta Gorda.

FAMILY LIFE

A number of Maya families in the Maya Mountains are branching out from farming and opening up their communities in response to a growing influx of tourists. Several innovative projects enable visitors to experience life in the Maya villages firsthand, either in simple guesthouses, or in some cases, with the families themselves. In order to fairly share out the workload – and the benefits – from this tourism influx, a rota system is operated.

Your visit is guaranteed to give you an insight into a rare way of life, but don't come expecting a lie-in: breakfast starts at 4.30 am, with tortillas toasting over the fire for father's "pack-lunch," after which the children are dressed in time to walk through the jungle to catch the bus to school.

◁ **TRADITIONAL COSTUME**
Whilst most Maya men have long since taken to jeans and t-shirts, many women still wear hand-embroidered, colorful blouses and skirts.

△ **INFORMATION CENTER**
The Dem Dats Doin Farm, near San Pedro Columbia, has information on sustainable agriculture aimed at replacing traditional, but destructive, Maya milpa farming.

◁ **DOMESTIC DUTIES**
Washing day means a walk to the stream where the clothes are rubbed clean on smooth stones. A machete is always taken along as protection against snakes.

△ **FAMILY WORKFORCE**
Maya children are hardworking students, getting free education up to age 12, after which the boys go to work in the fields and the girls may help their mothers sell handicrafts to tourists.

◁ **HOME COMFORTS**
The Maya homes are simply built of wood, with roofs of thatched palm leaves, floor of beaten earth, adobe stove, and a hammock – the most comfortable item of furniture.

▽ **CULTURAL CENTER**
Punta Gorda's Toledo Maya Cultural Council safeguards the Maya culture and represent Maya concerns to the Government of Belize.

◁ **JIPIJAPA HANDIWORK**
As part of your stay with a Maya family you may be taught how to make baskets from the jipijapa plant, after a process of shredding, washing, bleaching and drying the fibers.

LOCAL EXPORT SUCCESS STORY

One of Belize's most successful agricultural products in recent years has been the humble cacao bean, grown by the Maya since ancient times.

Today, farmers in Toledo District produce a world-leading crop, using strictly organic methods. The harvested and fermented beans are stored by the Toledo Cacao Growers' Association in Punta Gorda, and sold in their entirety to Green and Black's chocolate manufacturers in the UK. The trade is overseen by Fair Trade Agriculture, a system set up to enable developing countries to sell their produce at prices comparable with those in the developed world. In the case of the Belizean cacao farmers, this means earning two to three times what they were being paid before by a well-known US chocolate producer. Green and Blacks have a 5-year contract with the Toledo farmers, which has brought a steady income into the community, helping to fund local schools and health care.

Map on page 298

AN EXCURSION TO TIKAL

*Across the Belizean western border in Guatemala
lie the remains of one of the most magnificent
ancient cities anywhere in Central America*

Certain archeological sites become national symbols, appearing on everything from travel posters to airline ads, guidebook covers, and the local currency. What would Peru be without Machu Picchu, Cambodia without Angkor Wat, Egypt without the Sphinx? The Maya ruins of **Tikal**, one of the wonders of the ancient world, play the same symbolic role for Guatemala.

It's a rare traveler to Central America who hasn't seen a photo of the Temple of the Giant Jaguar (Temple I) at Tikal jutting above the tropical rainforest like a ghostly ship lost in a sea of green. The image is so famous as an emblem of Guatemala that a caption is usually unnecessary. Luckily, this spectacular ancient city is located in the Guatemalan department of Petén, on Belize's western border – making a Tikal pilgrimage an easy option.

Orientation in Guatemala

The Belizean domestic airlines run regular tours from Belize City and San Pedro, landing at the airport at **Santa Elena** outside the town of **Flores**, main jumping-off point for the ruins some 55 miles (90 km) away. Alternatively, visits can be organized by land from San Ignacio, crossing the frontier at Benque Viejo and following the 55-mile (90-km) route to Flores.

Flores is situated on an island in Lake Petén Itzá, connected by a causeway to the mainland. Taking travelers to Tikal is the town's major business: buses, taxis and mini-vans leave for the site throughout the day. There are hotels and pensions catering to both fat and thin wallets in Flores and Santa Elena, as well as three moderately priced hotels at Tikal itself (*See Travel Tips, Where to Stay.*) The ruins are so extensive that at least two days are necessary to see them thoroughly, although you could touch on the highlights in a single day.

The distances involved may be relatively short, but traveling from Belize to Guatemala plunges you into an entirely different world. The change is apparent at the frontier, where Spanish supplants English and Belize creole, quetzales replace dollars and kilometers roll by instead of miles. Volcanic applies not only to the geology of the Guatemalan highlands – where there are at least six volcanoes over 11,000 ft (3,400 meters) – but also to the country's history and politics. The long-suffering citizens have been embroiled in bloody wars and repression since the time of the Preclassic Maya (*see History panel, page 296*).

Unlike sparsely populated Belize, Guatemala has a population of over 10 million people packed into 42,042 sq miles (109,306 sq km). Two thirds of the country is mountainous; the narrow Pacific lowlands are divided among large estates growing sugar, maize, bananas and cotton; coffee is cultivated on the western

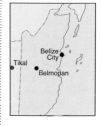

PRECEDING PAGES: woven Guatemalan textiles for sale; temples towering over the treetops. **LEFT:** the Temple of the Jaguar. **BELOW:** a Maya textile weaver.

Tikal's Past

Tikal was one of the great Classic Maya cities mysteriously abandoned around AD 900. But Maya civilization did not disappear – it continued in an altered form in southeastern parts of Mexico and in areas of Guatemala. Today, there are still keepers of the 260-day calendar in highland Guatemalan towns, healers use traditional methods, copal incense is burned to old gods, Maya languages are spoken, and women weave and wear their beautiful trajes.

This culture survived a second shock, the Spanish conquest in the early 1500s. After Hernán Cortés conquered Mexico, the Spanish turned to the south and Pedro de Alvarado's forces invaded Guatemala in 1523. The Itzá Maya, held out in Tayasal (Flores) for almost two centuries, until 1697, when they were finally defeated.

Guatemala was a Spanish colony from 1524 until 1821, during which time the Maya indígenas – at least, those surviving diseases

introduced from Europe – became virtual serfs on large Spanish land-holdings. After independence from Spain, Guatemala briefly became part of Mexico, then joined the short-lived United States of Central America (along with El Salvador, Honduras, Nicaragua and Costa Rica). The Central American federation soon splintered and the Republic of Guatemala was founded in 1839.

The 19th and 20th centuries witnessed a dismal procession of dictators supported by the armed forces, large landowners and, at first, the church. Reform-minded presidents came to power in rare free elections in 1944 and 1950 and were instantly seen as a threat. In 1954, as President Jacobo Arbenz was instituting desperately needed land reform, he was overthrown in a CIA-engineered coup. The country still suffers from the interference.

In 1977, the Guerrilla Army of the Poor was founded in the Guatemalan countryside, opposing the terrible inequities in land distribution and wealth (as well as governmental incompetence and corruption following a disastrous 1976 earthquake). Guatemala erupted in a bloody internal conflict, resulting in the destruction of at least 400 highland villages and the disappearances and deaths of thousands of civilians (mainly *indígenas*) at the hands of the army and right-wing death squads. More than 200,000 Maya indígenas have taken refuge in Mexico; others fled over the border to Belize and El Salvador.

In 1992, a Maya indígena, Rigoberta Menchú, won the Nobel Peace Prize for her efforts on behalf of human rights in Guatemala. In 1996, after a decade of fraught negotiations between the armed forces and the Guatemalan National Revolutionary Unity, peace accords were finally signed. General elections in 1999 brought Alfonso Portillo of the right-wing Republican Front to the presidency. The peace has held since then, but the government still faces the challenge of alleviating widespread poverty and lasting stability for ordinary Guatemalans.

Meanwhile, refugees, archeologists, anthropologists and tourists have returned to Guatemala in increased numbers. And at the center of the country's attractions remains the ruins of Tikal.   ❑

LEFT: carved wooden carnival masks.

slopes of the mountain ranges. Guatemala's Caribbean coast can also be reached via Punta Gorda in Belize's south. Once a prime banana-growing region, it's better known now for its surfing beaches.

In northern Guatemala, around Tikal, the mountains drop off to the low grasslands and dense, hardwood rainforests of the Petén, a sparsely populated region that constitutes one-third of the country's territory. The rainforest around Tikal is rich in the flora and fauna already familiar to visitors to Belize – the classic menagerie of deer, fox, jaguar and howler monkeys.

About 55 percent of Guatemalans are *indígenas*, descendants of those remarkable people, the ancient Maya. The other 45 percent are *ladinos*, which is a cultural rather than racial term. A person becomes *ladino* by adopting Euro-American- style dress rather than wearing *traje* (traditional dress), by speaking Spanish rather than one of the more than 20 different Maya languages and by adopting other non-indigenous cultural traits. Most *indígenas* live in the highlands and in Alta Verapaz, farming ridiculously small *milpas* (fields) of maize and beans.

Tikal at its zenith

Before starting a walk through the site, imagine the city in its original glory, around AD 705. At its height, Tikal was home to 100,000 people, all living within an area of 23 sq miles (60 sq km). The great city's many temples were constructed of limestone rubble; limestone also provided lime for stucco and plaster to cover the temples' surfaces, which gleamed white above the jungle. Flashes of red and touches of other colors glinted off the roof combs. The colors were symbolic: green represented the young maize plant (considered sacred),

Map
on page
298

Archeologist Michael Coe of Yale University called Tikal's Central Acropolis "an incomparable architectural achievement in ancient America."

BELOW: young Maya boy selling cotton candy.

as well as jade and the quetzal feathers worn by royalty, water, fertility, and the ceiba tree at the center of the world.

The living scene

Picture the city alive with activity. Smoke drifts from thousands of cooking fires in outlying residences and from copal incense lit by priests on the temple steps, mingling with low, scudding clouds. Nobles and other upper-class citizens wager on games in the ball court just south of where laborers are working on the construction of Temple I. This pyramid represents a sacred mountain, considered to be the source of maize.

According to Maya cosmology, in the center of the world stands a giant ceiba tree, whose roots extend through the nine layers of the underworld, ruled by the Nine Lords of the Night, and whose branches reach to the top of the thirteen layers of the upper world, also ruled by deities. These gods were all considered manifestations of the creator god, called Hunab Kun or Itzamna. (If this is confusing compare it to the Christian Trinity.) It is no accident that the ruler of Tikal in AD 705, Hasaw Chan K'awil, constructed the pyramid-tomb with nine levels, each slightly smaller than the one below, like the tiers of a wedding cake, since nine is the number of the Lords of the Night. The top of the temple was capped by a roof comb with a large carving of Hasaw Chan K'awil himself.

Nearby, in the East Plaza, the market activity is at its height. Men and women with babies tied on their backs sit behind piles of maize, squash, breadnuts, chili peppers, beans, tomatoes, yucca, sweet potatoes, cacao (these chocolate beans also functioned as currency throughout Mesoamerica), salt, honey, mats, flowers, dyes, tobacco leaves, cotton textiles and pottery. A few women sell

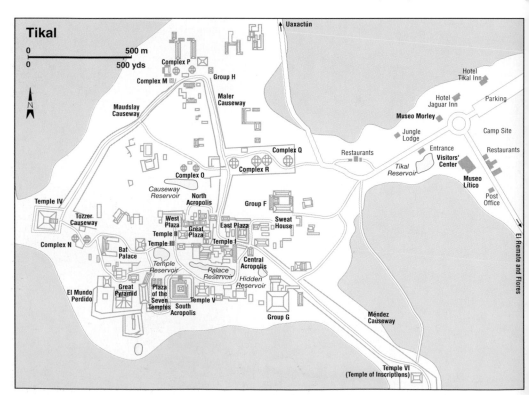

hot tortillas and beans to hungry clients. At one end of the market there might be a boy with a tame parrot or monkey, and a row of vendors with fish, venison and a few tethered rabbits, turkeys, turtles and ducks.

At the other end of the market, specialty trade items might include stingray spines from the Caribbean for ritual self-mutilation; obsidian cores for tools; volcanic rocks from the Guatemalan highlands used for grinding stones; and Spondylus shell beads from Ecuador. Clients pause, bargain and trade, then load their purchases in net bags, slinging their tumplines across their foreheads, and heading home along the paved causeways (*saches*), followed by their children carrying tiny bundles.

The divine ruler of Tikal, Hasaw Chan K'awil, is a striking figure sporting a quetzal feather headdress, jade necklace, ear ornaments, wristlets and pectoral jewelry, a jaguar skin over a kilt and underskirt, belt, cotton loincloth, elaborate loin ornaments, anklets, deerskin sandals and miscellaneous ritual paraphernalia. He reposes on a small hassock in the Great Plaza surrounded by retainers waving away mosquitoes. Like all Maya rulers, he is quite strange-looking by our standards. His forehead slopes back sharply, a mark of beauty to the Maya, who practiced cranial deformation – when Hasaw Chan K'awil was a baby his mother would have tied a board over his forehead to elongate his skull.

Hasaw Chan K'awil interrupts his inspection of the construction of Temple I, which will commemorate his reign and serve as his tomb, to receive a delegation from Kaminaljuyú in the highlands. Their arrival is heralded by six musicians playing trumpets, drums, flutes and rattles. Related by blood to the rulers of Kaminaljuyú, he is involved in secret talks with them concerning an alliance against other Maya city-states. Like the city-states of ancient Greece, the Maya

Map on page 298

The Maya associated certain colors with the four directions: white was linked with north, yellow with south, red with east, and black with west.

BELOW: ancient Maya carving on a Tikal altar.

BELOW: the
long climb down.

polities are a fractious lot and fight among themselves to try to claim power and assert their dominance over aggressive rivals.

Inside Temple II, constructed earlier by Hasaw Chan K'awil, his mother pierces her tongue and pulls a thorn-embedded cord through it. She collects her blood on bark paper, which she will offer to the gods for the success of her son's venture, along with the blood-soaked cord. Both ritual blood-letting and the sacrifice of prisoners of war are carried out at Tikal to propitiate the gods before important ventures and to commemorate such events as the end of a time period and the ascension or death of a ruler. Later on, Hasaw Chan K'awil will use a stingray spine to pierce his cheeks, ears and penis, for the gods demand blood.

Walking tour of the ruins

The best place to start a tour of the ruins is the **Morley Museum** located just outside the ruins in Tikal village, at the western end of the airstrip. Among the displays is a reconstruction of Hasaw Chan K'awil's tomb, including ceramics, incised bone artifacts, and jade jewelry – necklaces, ear ornaments, wristlets and head-dress decorations. (Other artifacts from Tikal are housed at the National Museum of Archeology and Ethnology in Guatemala City.) The museum also sells maps of the ruins and books on archeology and natural history.

The path from the museum to the ruins ends at a three-way junction. The trail to your right leads to **Complexes P**, **Q** and **R** and the **North Zone**; the left fork takes you to the **Temple of the Inscriptions (Temple VI)**; and the branch straight ahead leads to the heart of the site: the **Great Plaza, Temples I** through **V**, the **North**, **Central**, and **South Acropolis**, the **Ball Court**, and other important buildings.

Go straight ahead first to the reconstructed **Great Plaza** area, which is today

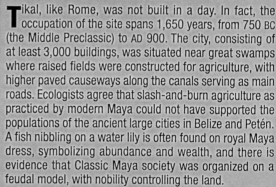

THE ROOTS OF THE RUINS

Tikal, like Rome, was not built in a day. In fact, the occupation of the site spans 1,650 years, from 750 BC (the Middle Preclassic) to AD 900. The city, consisting of at least 3,000 buildings, was situated near great swamps where raised fields were constructed for agriculture, with higher paved causeways along the canals serving as main roads. Ecologists agree that slash-and-burn agriculture as practiced by modern Maya could not have supported the populations of the ancient large cities in Belize and Petén. A fish nibbling on a water lily is often found on royal Maya dress, symbolizing abundance and wealth, and there is evidence that Classic Maya society was organized on a feudal model, with nobility controlling the land.

Much of what we know about Tikal has resulted from recent archeological research. The University of Pennsylvania's Museum conducted extensive excavations between 1956 and 1969, when the Guatemalan Institute of Anthropology and History took over the excavation and restoration work. Other scholars have made considerable progress in deciphering the Maya's written language, providing us with an understanding of the meaning of the glyphs on the stelae and buildings throughout the site *(see The Ancient Maya, pages 21–26)*.

the center of the Tikal ruins (in the Classic era, however, the heart of the city was the East Plaza, where the main market was located). The Maya frequently built new constructions over old; in the Great Plaza, four different plaster floors were laid one on top of the other between 150 BC and AD 700. Seventy stelae and altars, originally painted red, are located in and around the plaza. The stelae, each of which originally had an altar beside it, commemorate the rulers of Tikal. Many of these rulers are carved in bas relief in profile on one side of the stela, although some are shown full face. The other sides contain glyphs giving dates and genealogies (sometimes including a god and the Tikal emblem glyph).

Hasaw Chan K'awil's tomb, **Temple I**, is also called the **Temple of the Giant Jaguar**, because of the jaguars carved on the lintels inside it. The temples represent one of the main architectural styles at Tikal, a squared-off wedding-cake pyramid topped by a temple with a roof comb in a two-thirds to one-third ratio. The pyramid is about 100 ft (30 meters) high, and the roof comb rises another 50 ft (15 meters). The three small rooms at the top were probably the preserve of priests and kings, adorned with beautifully carved zapote wooden beams and lintels. The tomb is embedded deep beneath the temple, and a collection of stately goods buried with him is now on display in the Morley Museum.

What surprises many people is the small interior size of these buildings. The Maya had not developed the true arch in their architecture, but used instead the corbeled vault. Stones on each wall are progressively set inward until they almost meet and are topped by a row of capstones, resulting in long, narrow rooms, usually with carved wooden lintels over the doors. The temples were not designed to hold large numbers of worshippers, however, but to impress the great mass of people standing in the plaza below.

A licensed guide can help you make the most of a visit to Tikal. They speak English, have archeological knowledge and are good at identifying local wildlife. A four-hour tour for upto four people costs $US40.

BELOW: the Central Acropolis.

Opposite Temple I, to the west, is **Temple II**, also called the **Temple of the Masks** after two huge masks, now barely visible, that were carved on each side of the stairway just below the temple door. A giant face once adorned the roof comb. This temple was also built by Ah Cacau and may have been dedicated to his wife or mother; the portrait of a woman is carved on one of its lintels.

Temple III, the **Temple of the Jaguar Priest**, is situated behind Temple II. This building has not been reconstructed and is probably the last pyramid and temple built at Tikal, since the stela in front carries the date AD 810.

Temple IV is located farther to the west. It stands 212 ft (65 meters) high, making it the tallest structure at Tikal and one of the tallest pre-Hispanic buildings still standing. The temple was built during the reign of Hasaw Chan K'awil's son, Yik'in Chon K'awil (Divine Sunset Lord, also known as Ruler B), around AD 741, but there is some debate as to whether he is buried under it. From here there are spectacular views of the other temples rising out of the rainforest.

The best approach to **Temple V** is along the path from the Plaza of the Seven Temples, as you emerge from the forest you see the restored monumental creamy limestone staircase. The structure was thought to be among the last of the great temples to be built, but findings from burials here indicate that it was in fact the earliest, dating from around AD600 and almost certainly constructed by Tikal's governor at the time, Kinich Wayna. The temple was built early in the Mid-Classic hiatus during a period when it was believed no new monuments were erected.

Dismantled pyramids

On the north side of the Great Plaza is the **North Acropolis**, a group of buildings that were begun around 200 BC as monuments to the ancestors of various rulers. Such early classic kings as Jaguar Paw, Stormy Sky and Curl Nose are buried beneath pyramids in this group. Like the Great Plaza floor, the pyramids have been built over several times by later rulers. How do we know what's inside? The University of Pennsylvania dismantled the pyramid and temple called structure 5D-33, revealing successive onion-like layers. This edifice is in the first row (the third from the left as you face the North Acropolis). What you see now are two earlier cores and part of the last pyramid, which was originally more than 100 ft (30 meters) high and which hid the rest of the Acropolis.

To the south is the **Central Acropolis**, also known at the Palace Group. The 42 palace structures span 4 acres (1.6 hectares) and housed rulers, priests and administrators. They represent a second major architectural style at Tikal: elegant, rectangular buildings, one to five stories high, with narrow, windowless, corbel-vaulted rooms, all grouped around a courtyard to form an enclosed area. At the time of their occupation, these palaces were stuccoed and painted inside and out and richly furnished with mats, ceramics, and textiles. Some have built-in platforms that may have served as beds and benches. The buildings were probably used primarily for sleeping and storage, as Tikal's climate allowed most activities, including teaching, to be carried on outside.

Southeast of the Central Acropolis is **Group G**, another palace and administrative complex. Group G is also called the **Palace of Vertical Grooves** because of the unusual vertical stone facings on the exteriors. These structures, too, were built over earlier buildings; the walls of one room covered entirely by the last construction were embellished with graffiti.

Map on page 298

Ancient games

The **Ball Court** is between Temple I and the Central Acropolis. The ball game was a quintessential Maya activity – almost every Maya site has a court. We know something of the game because it was portrayed on ceramics and mentioned in the Maya creation epic, the *Popol Vuh (see pages 21–26)*.

There are also ball courts in the **East Plaza**, and three courts, side by side in the **Plaza of the Seven Temples** – which, situated southwest of the Central Acropolis, received its name from seven unexcavated temples that line the east side of the complex. Preliminary work indicated that the plaza was plastered over a number of times, beginning in the Preclassic era.

Tikal has nine twin pyramid complexes, which were built to mark the end of a katun, a period of 7,200 days or almost 20 years. The twin pyramids were used for one katun, after which another set was constructed.

The third main architectural style found at Tikal is the truncated pyramid (a layered pyramid without a temple on top). A good example of this style is the **Lost World Pyramid**, which is southwest of the Central Acropolis. Originally this structure was 100 ft (30 meters) high, with four stairways flanked by giant masks. Its core may date to as early as 500 BC; it was rebuilt in its final form some time before AD 300.

The pyramid's main function was calendrical or astronomical. Mayanists insist that the word "observatory" should not be used to describe these temples because many were not used to follow the movements of the planets and stars, but were used in such ceremonies as those marking the end of a solar year or the beginning of a 52-year cycle.

BELOW: Temple IV, crowning the jungle tree canopy.

The trail leading southeast past Group G is actually a causeway. It leads to the **Temple of the Inscriptions (Temple VI)**, as does the left fork of the trail at the entrance to the ruins. This pyramid and temple were completed around AD 736 to mark the inauguration of Ruler B. Later the roof comb was added; its glyphs give a different date, AD 766.

The entire east side of the roof comb contains glyphs listing the genealogies of Tikal rulers over a period of nearly 2,000 years. The stela and altar on the west side of the temple commemorate Ruler B, who must have been a bellicose sort: the altar shows a bound, face-down captive, perhaps someone who was sacrificed at Ruler B's accession to the throne or captured by him in warfare and sacrificed on some other occasion.

At the opposite end of the ruins is the **North Zone** and **Complexes P, Q**, and **R**, reached by the right-hand trail at the entrance or by a causeway leading north behind Temple I. **Complexes Q** and **R** both have twin pyramids with stairways on all four sides that face each other on the east and west sides of a plaza. The north side was occupied by a stela and altar marking the *katun* ending, while a single story palace-type building anchored the south. **Complex P** is unexcavated, but also contains twin pyramids and a stela and altar erected by Ruler B. ❑

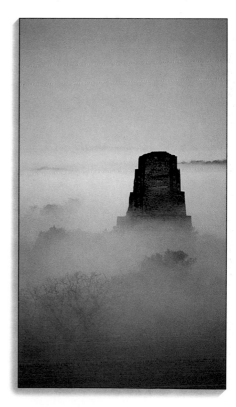

INSIGHT GUIDES
Travel Tips

CONTENTS

Getting Acquainted

The Place

Mention that you are going to Belize and most people will look blank or ask, "Is that in Africa?" But the word is slowly getting out, especially among North American travelers, that Belize is the most accessible and easygoing slice of tropical wilderness in the western hemisphere. Located on the Caribbean coast of Central America, 750 miles (1,200 km) from Miami, Houston and New Orleans, Belize is almost 9,000 sq. miles (23,300 sq. km) in area. Its neighbors are Mexico to the north and Guatemala to the west and south.

Belize is in the Central Time Zone (GMT -6 hrs), and does not observe Daylight Savings.

Topography

Perhaps Belize's most striking natural feature, clearly visible from the air, is the seemingly endless coral reef. At 185 miles (297 km) long, it is second in size only to Australia's Great Barrier Reef. Three of the four atolls in the western hemisphere are located here, including Lighthouse Reef, with its almost perfectly circular and much photographed Blue Hole. The Hole itself is from 180–300 ft (55–90 meters) deep, while the sea bed forms a complicated system of stalactite caves.

Half Moon Caye Natural Monument, a 45-acre (18-hectare) area of Lighthouse Reef was set up to preserve the rare red-footed booby bird as well as members of the lizard family. Loggerhead and hawksbill turtles come ashore to lay their eggs on the sandy beaches.

Inside the reef itself the shallow waters are rich in precious marine life. Hol Chan Marine Reserve off Ambergris Caye provides a concentration of fragile coral and tropical fish (and is the most accessible for divers).

Back on the mainland, the coastal and northern areas of Belize are flat and hot, mostly made up of mangrove swamps and lagoons that provide the spawning environment for marine life. Further inland, rising to around 3,000 ft (915 meters) above sea level, the vast central and southern regions are covered by tropical pine, hardwood and rainforests. These largely uninhabited regions are rich in flora and fauna as well as containing a number of pristine waterfalls. The limestone formation of the country has left it riddled with cave systems rivalling the largest in the world.

Climate

Belize enjoys a subtropical climate, tempered by brisk prevailing tradewinds from the Caribbean Sea. There are two seasons: the rainy season is from June to January, with a brief dry period in August; the dry season is from February to May. It should be stressed that this is a flexible division, and torrential tropical downpours can occur at any time of the year.

While most visitors come to Belize during the winter months of the northern hemisphere, divers prefer the clearer waters during late spring and summer when the on-shore winds die down. December and January are the coolest months, but the temperature rarely falls below 55°F (13°C) at night.

Coastal temperatures usually reach 96°F (36°C); inland can be hotter. The steamiest part of Belize tends to be on the flatlands around the capital, Belmopan, where it is barely possible to walk the streets during the day; the mountainous area around San Ignacio, while hot during the day, can actually be quite cool at night, getting down to around 50°F (12°C) in winter.

Average rainfall in the north of Belize is 50 inches (127 cm) and a much heavier 173 inches (439 cm) in the extreme south.

Weather Check

Regular weather reports are broadcast on LOVE FM 95.1 and other local radio stations, or you can call 225-2480 to hear a recorded message from the Belize Meteorology Department. A fax service is available on 225-2101. Monitoring the weather is especially important during the hurricane season, which officially begins on June 1 and runs through until the end of October. Should you wish to check the weather before you arrive, daily updates are available by email at www.naturalight.com. Also check the Weather Channel's "Tropical Update" broadcast during the hurricane season.

People

Belize's population of around 250,000 people is one of the most diverse on the planet – culturally, ethnically, and linguistically.

Unlike neighboring Guatemala, only a small percentage of Belizeans are direct descendants of the original Amerindians, the Maya (in Belize, the main Maya groups are the Yucatec, the Mopan and the Kekchi).

The largest ethnic group, making up more than 40 percent of the population, is now mestizos (those of mixed Maya and European, mostly Spanish, blood), and the number is rapidly increasing with immigration of farmworkers and refugees from neighboring countries. The second largest group, the creoles, descended from the mix of early British settlers and African slaves brought from Jamaica (although the term creole is now used to include all racial combinations of Europeans and North Americans with members of the local population). While mestizos are concentrated in west-central and northern Belize, the creole population more densely occupies the Belize district and makes up over 50 percent of Belize City.

The Garinagu or Black Carib population (usually called Garifuna which is, strictly speaking, the name for their culture and language) makes up approximately six percent of Belizeans. Concentrated in the Stann Creek district, particularly in the towns of Dangriga and Punta Gorda, the Garifuna are a cultural and racial mix of Carib Indians, African slaves and to a lesser extent Europeans, who arrived in Belize early in the 19th century after an extraordinary migration around the Caribbean.

Additional nationalities making up the Belizean mélange include East Indians, Chinese, Lebanese and Mennonites (a community that numbers around 6,000).

Considering the large number of ethnic groups in Belize, there has been surprisingly little racial conflict. But there is a growing mestizo-creole tension: creoles view the growing number of "Spanish" immigrants as a threat to the true Belize identity, while the incoming Central Americans bring certain anti-black prejudices with them.

Although English is the official language, many mestizos only speak Spanish, while the increasingly used creole language has both an English and a Spanish version. Creole is popularly referred to as Spanglish since it is more a mixture of English and Spanish than a true creole. (You might, for example, hear: *Ella tiene long hair*, meaning: She has long hair.) As a result, both languages are taught in primary and secondary schools. The Garifuna have their own language besides English, as do the Maya communities. Mennonites have kept their unique German-Dutch dialect for the past 400 years.

Religion

About 62 percent of the population is Roman Catholic, but as Belize welcomes more and more nationalities into the population, the number of different religious groups also increases. At present the list

includes Anglican, Methodist, Mennonite, Bah'ai, Hindu, Muslim, Presbyterian and Seventh Day Adventist.

The Garifuna people practice their own unique religion, which is often incorrectly compared by outsiders to Haitian-style voodoo. The central focus is the concept of a continued communication with ancestors, who are held in great reverence. Their spirits are summoned to assist with problems and provide guidance for the living. The Garifuna Mass is a synthesis of Roman Catholicism and African traditions and is now being openly shared with other Belizeans and visitors, especially around Settlement Day in November. The Mass is celebrated in the Garifuna language but written translations are often provided. Garifuna women are very active in their church and young people are being encouraged to participate. The magical practice of *obeah*, whereby rituals, symbols, fetishes and amulets are utilized to direct positive or negative energy to individuals is frowned upon by the average Garifuna.

Economy

Traditionally based on logging, the Belize economy is currently supported by broader-based agricultural exports that account for about 30 percent of the GNP. Timber is still a major export, although most of it is now pine and cedar rather than hardwood such as mahogany, which for centuries went to capitals around the world. Other major crops are sugar cane and citrus fruit, bananas, honey, maize, beans, rice and an increasing array of tropical fruits.

Tourism now provides the second-largest contribution to the economy, nearly 20 percent of the GNP, and there is a growing awareness of its potential among the country's citizens. Tax concessions and other incentives encourage the development of light manufacturing industries, which now account for 12 percent of the GNP. They include clothing and textiles, plywood and veneer manufacturing, matches,

beer, rum, soft drinks, furniture, boat building and battery assembly.

Since World War II, as the economy has diversified and the infrastructure developed, the standard of living for Belizeans has improved. Compared to other Central American countries, Belize is relatively prosperous, with an adequate school system and improving sanitation and health services. However, there is an increasing gap between the rich and the poor, with 30 percent of Belizeans living below the poverty line, earning less than one US dollar per day. The majority of these people live in the Toledo district, the Cayo district and in Belize City. Many hope tourism can help stop this trend. Already about one in four Belizeans are estimated to depend on tourism in some way for their livelihood.

Belize remains, however, heavily dependent on foreign aid and most oil, food, manufactured goods and consumer items are imported, often paid for by loans and grants from foreign governments and private development agencies. These include the government of the UK, the Canadian International Agency (CIDA) the European Development Fund (EDF) and the Caribbean Development Bank (CDB). The United States Agency for International Development (USAID) was formerly active in Belize. During the 1980s, Belize's major exports were marijuana and other illegal drugs – a trade that has been cut back but hardly extinguished.

Finally, much of Belize's foreign exchange is derived from citizens who have migrated to the US (LA, Chicago and New York) and send money home to their families.

Government

In 1964, the British colony of British Honduras (as Belize was then known) was granted an internal, elected self-government. The People's United Party (PUP) remained in power for nearly 20 years, guiding the colony's name change to Belize in 1973 and finally the declaration of independence on September 21, 1981. Britain remained in charge of foreign relations, defense and internal security; a 3,000 strong military presence was maintained to deter the Guatemalans from pressing their 150-year-old claim to Belize.

In 1994, Britain withdrew its military force from Belize, leaving only a very small number of soldiers as a symbolic deterrent to possible Guatemalan invasions.

Belize has inherited the principles of parliamentary democracy after the British system – the prime minister and cabinet make up the executive branch, while a 29-member elected House of Representatives and eight-member appointed Senate make up the legislative branch. Belize is a member of the British Commonwealth, the United Nations, the Non-Aligned Movement and the Organization of American States, as well as the Caribbean Community (CARICOM).

Politics is very much in evidence in Belize, if only because most newspapers are owned by political parties. In 1984, Belizeans voted into power the United Democratic Party (UDP), who adopted more pro-western, business-oriented policies. The PUP won power back with such nationalistic slogans as "Belize for Belizeans" and "Belize is not for sale," only to lose again to the UDP in elections in mid-1993. The government flopped with PUP being re-elected in 1998 – they took an astonishing 26 seats, leaving the UDP only three. In 2003 the PUP won an unprecedented second term.

The government's biggest challenge remains the growth in drug-related violence. Belize has become a major staging-post in the smuggling of cocaine from South America to the United States. Colombian cartels drop packages on remote islands off the coast and Belizeans ship them north. "Drugs have corrupted all levels of our society, from the top of the administration to the poorest people on the street," said Glenn Tillett, former editor of the Belizean newspaper *Amandala*.

Planning the Trip

Entry Regulations

VISAS

Visas are not required for most nationalities, including citizens of the United States, Canada, Australia, New Zealand, as well as members of the European Union and CARICOM. All that are needed for people from these countries are a valid passport and an onward or round-trip ticket.

A visa, plus clearance from the Director of Immigration, is required for nationals of certain countries, including the following: China, Colombia, Cuba, Egypt, India, Libya, Pakistan, Peru, Sri Lanka, Thailand, and Yugoslavia. Check with the local Belizean consulate or contact the Immigration and Nationality

Embassies & Consulates

United States
Belize Embassy
2535 Massachusetts Avenue NW, Washington DC 20008.
Tel: 202-332 9636
Fax: 202-332 6741
Canada
Belize High Commission to Canada
112 Kent Street Suite 2005, Place de Ville, Tower B, Ottawa, Ontario, Canada K1P 5P2.
Tel: 613-232 7389/7453
Fax: 613-232 5804
United Kingdom
Belize High Commission
22 Harcourt House, 19 Cavendish Square, London W1M 9AD.
Tel: 020-7499 9728
Fax: 020-7491 4139

Service, New Administration Building, Belmopan, tel: 822-2611, fax: 822-2662.

All visitors are permitted to stay for up to 30 days. To apply for an extension contact the Immigration Office, Government Administration Building, Mahogany Street, Belize City, tel: 222-4620, fax: 222-4056, or any immigration office. A moderate fee is charged and applicants may be asked to demonstrate sufficient funds (currently US$50 a day) for the remainder of their stay, as well as an ongoing ticket.

If you're crossing into Belize from Mexico by land, visas can be obtained from the Belizean Consulate in Chetumal, just north of the international crossing.

For visiting Tikal in Guatemala from Belize, some nationalities need a visa. Check if you need one, and get it before arriving.

CUSTOMS REGULATIONS

Removal, sale and exportation of the following are prohibited by law in Belize: black or any other kind of coral without a license; archeological artifacts; orchids; shells, fish and crustaceans; turtles and materials from turtles.

HEALTH MATTERS

No vaccinations are required before traveling to Belize as there are no endemic diseases. But you will need a yellow fever certificate if you are arriving within six days from, or via, an infected area. Typhoid, hepatitis A and polio vaccinations are recommended by most doctors. Belize now ranks number one in Central America for Aids cases per capita and is in the top five in the Caribbean. The problem is being blamed partly on foreign visitors – particularly those from elsewhere in Central America and from the United States. Certainly, visitors who decide to have sex with anyone in Belize should use condoms, which are inexpensive and widely available at all pharmacies and even fried chicken stands and grocery stores. Brothels are supposedly illegal, but they are easy to find (even conveniently located) although health officials warn against frequenting them.

There is malaria in some parts of Belize. Most travelers visiting the cayes or San Ignacio don't need to worry too much, but if you are heading for extended stays in jungle areas, it is advisable to begin a course of anti-malaria tablets. Your doctor can prescribe the latest version: most courses start one week prior to arrival and continue for four weeks afterwards. (Of course, no visitor escapes without bites from regular non-malarial mosquitoes – "flies" to Belizeans – but there is no need to panic.)

Those with fair complexions

should be careful in the strong sun. Drink plenty of water on walking trips and, like Belizeans, avoid much activity between 11am and 3pm on hot days. Watch out on boat trips to the cayes and use sunscreen on your back and legs when snorkeling.

Divers and snorkelers should be careful to avoid touching the coral, especially when getting from a boat into shallow water. Disturbances to live coral outcroppings can result in their death, while cuts and abrasions from the reef nearly always become painfully infected and take a long time to heal. Once in the water, the various moray eels, barracuda, stingrays, sharks and so on look menacing but are nothing at all to worry about. Your guide will steer you away from strong currents through cuts in the reef. Those

susceptible to motion sickness and planning a live-aboard dive trip with several days on a boat should consider taking Dramamine tablets or patches with them.

The quality of food and its preparation in Belize is good so there is not as great a risk of stomach problems as in neighboring countries. Tap water is potable in some towns and resort areas but tap water in the cayes or in the south of Belize is not recommended for drinking. Drink bottled water, sold at all gas stations, stores, etc. You will quickly discover a variety of "jungle remedies" on sale at many guesthouses for common traveler's ailments. For more serious conditions, your hotel should be able to recommend a doctor.

Festivals and Sporting Events

The following is a selection of Belize's most colorful annual events. Specific dates may change from year to year; your best bet is to ask at your hotel or a local tour operator on arrival. Also check out www.travelbelize.org.

February
San Pedro Carnival
Groups compete in *comparsas* (special dances) and children throw eggs, flour and paint at each other in remembrance of the Maya God Momo. Night-time street parade.

International Billfish Tournament
Organized by the Belize Game Fish Association. Cash prizes. Contact fishing lodges for entry information.

March
Baron Bliss Day
Harbor regatta, horse and cycle races and a kite contest.

La Ruta Maya River Challenge
Canoe race from Hawksworth Bridge in San Ignacio to Belcan Bridge in Belize City. Any three-person team may enter. Contact Cayo Tropical Juices in San Ignacio.

San José Succotz Fiesta
Local fair in Cayo for the patron saint of the village with marimba

music, rides, games and food.

April
Holy Saturday Cross Country Cycling Classic
International cycle race from Belize City to San Ignacio and back again.

May
Cashew Festival
Crooked Tree, Belize District
Celebration of all things cashew, with music, dance, storytelling, handicraft stalls, food and drink.

Belmopan National Agriculture and Trade Show
Three-day event with local produce, rodeo and livestock competitions.

June
Caye Caulker and **Placencia Lobster Fests**
Fishing villages mark the start of the lobster season with music, dance, and lots of lobster cuisine.

Día de San Pedro
Ambergris Caye
Three-day fiesta to celebrate the patron saint.

July
Benque Fiesta
Celebration of the patron saint of Benque Viejo del Carmen with a procession, a special Mass and fair.

August
La Costa Maya Festival
San Pedro, Ambergris Caye
Week-long event with a beauty pageant and musical performances from the Mundo Maya countries.

September
Battle of St George's Caye (Sept 10) Belize City
Commemorates the defeat of the Spanish by the British and their slaves in St George's Caye, 1798, with a parade and street fair.

Belize City Carnival
Costumed bands, floats and dancers in a Latino-Caribbean style.

Independence Day (Sept 21st)
Belmopan, Belize City
Official ceremonies and a street fair.

October
Pan-American Day
Orange Walk, Corozal
Street fairs and beauty pageants in celebration of Mestizo culture.

November
Garifuna Settlement Day
Dangriga, Punta Gorda, Belize City Early morning canoe re-enactment of arrival of first Garifuna in 1832, thanksgiving Mass and more.

The Disabled Traveler

Belize is not exactly disabled-friendly. Even landing in the country is a challenge since the airlines all use staircases for getting on and off planes. Public transport is not equipped for wheelchairs and few of the hotels and restaurants are either. Call ahead to be on the safe side. Cruise ships dock offshore and use small tenders to ferry passengers ashore – until a terminal is built – and rough waters can make getting on and offshore difficult for travelers needing assistance. The Bank of Nova Scotia in Belize City has an access ramp and the Radisson Fort George Hotel is the only one with an elevator and specially adapted bathrooms. Members of the tourism industry will try to do what they can to make your stay enjoyable. However, it may just take a bit of extra planning so make sure you communicate your needs to your hotel manager or tour operator.

What To Bring

AROUND TOWN

Belize is a very casual place – often astonishingly so – and travelers should pack accordingly. The heat and year-round humidity dictate lightweight clothing of natural fibers; clothes become damp and

Maps

The most detailed map of Belize available is the *Traveler's Reference Map of Belize*, scale 1:350,000, published by ITMB Publishing, widely available in Belize. The Lands Department in Belmopan sells topographic maps of Belize: two sheets at a scale of 1:250,000 cover the entire country. There are also scale 1:50,000 maps of most of Belize.

The Belize Tourism Board sells a good road map for tourists, which is also available at higher prices in hotel gift shops.

crumpled very quickly, so bring plenty of changes. At the cayes, you can get by in shorts, a T-shirt and sandals most of the time, or just bare feet and a swimsuit, even in restaurants. However, most of the larger resorts maintain a trendy profile after dark, so pack a more formal tropical outfit to wear under the thatched roof at dinner. Do not wear bathing suits or skimpy clothing on the streets of Belize City or other towns; it is considered offensive, as are bare feet.

Most of the time, you'll need to dress for the weather rather than for style. Don't underestimate the power of the tropical sun: it can burn in half an hour or less. If you're spending all day in the sun on a fishing charter or day-trip to the cayes, wear a hat and even long sleeves. Bring your swimsuit rather than buying one on arrival (Belize City has a very small and bizarre range, although San Pedro on Ambergris Caye has a better stock). Bring your own fins, mask and snorkel if you don't want to pay the rental price of around BZ$20 a day.

The two absolute essentials that you will use are sunscreen and insect repellent. Bring them with you: outside the resorts a bottle of sunscreen is almost impossible to buy. Bring twice as much as you think you'll need: anyone with a fair complexion should be lathered in suntan lotion from dawn until dusk.

As for insect repellant, mild versions that work well at home are next to useless against the swarms in Belize. Nothing less than a high concentration DEET will do the trick – most readily available in the brand OFF. ("Army strength" insecticide is available from camping stores but, if it leaks, will eat away at almost anything it touches.) Again, bring twice as much as you think you'll need. Resort gift shops will shamelessly charge BZ$20 for the last can of spray, or more if the mosquitoes are bad that day.

Those intending to spend any time in Belize City should consider a money belt for carrying passports and valuables.

Although regular film is available, professional quality film and technical items are difficult to obtain.

The electrical current is the same as in the United States, 110 volts/60 cycles.

IN THE RAINFOREST

In the rainforest, it is probably best to wear shorts and T-shirts and apply plenty of insect repellent. Long-sleeved cotton shirts and trousers are often recommended, but the reality is that this is rather hot and Belizean mosquitoes bite straight through them (although if you are intending to spend a considerable time in the jungle, it might be worth investing in specially made lightweight cotton clothing, available from specialist outfitters, which will also help protect you from other minor scratches and grazes).

The rainforest can become very muddy, especially during the rainy season, so bring suitable footwear: light walking or tennis shoes.

The climate in the mountains around San Ignacio is slightly cooler than along the coast (there are thankfully fewer mosquitoes there, too). Bring a lightweight jacket for the evenings, even during the warmer months. Wet weather gear is very useful at any time of the year.

Currency

The Belize dollar is stabilized at a fixed exchange rate of BZ$2 to US$1, convenient for calculating costs. There is an official network of *Casas de Cambio* where currency can be exchanged both ways.

In tourist resorts, prices are often quoted in both currencies. Most people refer in conversation to the US version as dollars and the Belizean dollar as simply "Belize". In common parlance, then, a price for a mango daiquiri might be "four dollars or eight Belize." If there's any doubt about which currency is being referred to, just ask. As the US currency is not always easy to come by, most locals will readily accept, even prefer, if you pay in US. It is especially popular in the summer months and before Christmas when everyone wants it for vacations abroad. Even though, technically, you are supposed to change foreign currency, even US dollars at a bank, you will lose on the exchange. That doesn't happen on the street or with local businesses where the US dollar is accepted at BZ$2 to US$1.

Prices are surprisingly high in Belize, especially if you're coming from Guatemala. In fact, most things cost more or less the same as they do in the United States. There are few cheap hotels, and a main course in almost any tourist restaurant is over BZ$20.

Changing US currency or travelers' checks is rarely a problem in most hotels and restaurants, which deal with either currency. Banks are open Monday to Thursday 8am–1pm and later on Fridays. They will offer fair exchange rates for most currencies with a 3 percent fee. Almost all the hotels and tour operators will accept the major credit cards, although a five percent tax is often added.

Be aware that many Belizean establishments don't accept travelers' checks – you may have trouble cashing them even in larger supermarkets in Belize City. Try to change them at your hotel or at a restaurant used by tourists. Carry small denominations of cash when shopping: some people have trouble changing 50s, let alone 100-dollar bills. Taxi drivers, especially, never seem to have change. Don't flash large amounts of money in public.

Getting There

BY AIR

There are many flights from the US to Belize, although European visitors still have to change planes at one of the US gateways, or in Mexico or Guatemala.

American Airlines operates a daily non-stop flight from Miami, while Continental Airlines offers a direct service from Houston, Texas, daily.

US Airways also operates a scheduled service from Charlotte, North Carolina and weekly flights from Newark.

Taca International Airlines of El Salvador have a good reputation (for punctuality and in-flight service Taca is regarded by frequent travelers in the region as better than the American airlines). Direct flights leave daily from Miami and Houston; connections from New York and Washington go via Miami; from San Francisco and Los Angeles, via San Salvador. Same-day connections to Europe and other US cities are sometimes possible.

American Airlines
United States
Tel: 800-4337 0330.
Belize City
Tel: 223-2522.
www.aa.com.
Continental Airlines
United States
Tel: 800-231 0856.
Belize City
Tel: 227-8309.
www.continental.com
Taca International
Belize City,
Tel: 227-7363.
US Airways
United States
Tel: 800-622 1015
www.usairways.com

Tour Operators

Capricorn Leisure,
2 Haven Avenue, Port Washington, New York 11050. Tel: 516-944 8383/800-426 6544; fax: 516-944 8458; e-mail: traveler@ix.netcom.com
Close Encounters,
PO Box 1320
Detroit Lakes, Minnesota 56502
Tel: 888-875 1822
www.belizecloseencounters.com
Cox & Kings,
Gordon House, 10 Greencoat Place, London SW1P 1PH.
Tel: 020-7873 5000;
fax: 020-7630 6038;
www.coxandkings.co.uk
Explore Worldwide Ltd,
1 Frederick Street,
Aldershot, Hants, GU11 1LQ.
Tel: 01252 760000;
fax: 01252-760001;

e-mail: info@explore.co.uk.
www.exploreworldwide.com
Island Expeditions,
368-916 W. Broadway,
Vancouver, Canada V5Z 1K7
1-800-667 1630
e-mail: info@islandexpeditons.com
www.islandexpeditions.com
Journey Latin America Ltd,
12–13 Heathfield Terrace,
London W4 4JE.
Tel: 020-8747 8315/3108;
fax: 020-8742 1312;
www.journeylatinamerica.co.uk
Magnum Belize Tours,
808 Washington Avenue,
PO Box 1560, Detroit Lakes,
Minnesota, 56501.
Tel: 218-847 3012/800-447 2931; fax: 218-847 0334;
e-mail: Information@ magnumbelize.com.

South American Experience,
47 Causton Street,
London SW1P 4AT.
Tel: 020-7976 5511;
fax: 020-7976 6908;
e-mail: info@southamerican experience.co.uk
www.southamericanexperience. co.uk
Trips Worldwide Ltd,
9 Byron Place,
Bristol BS8 1JT.
Tel: 0117-929 2199;
fax: 0117-929 2545.
www.tripsworldwide.co.uk
Victor Emanuel Nature Tours,
2525 Wallingwood Drive,
Suite 1003,
Austin, Texas 78746
Tel: 1-800-328 8368;
e-mail: info@ventbird.com
www.ventbird.com

Public Holidays

The following are public holidays in Belize:
New Year's Day
Baron Bliss Day (Mar 9)
Good Friday
Easter Saturday
Easter Sunday
Easter Monday
Labor Day (May 1)
Commonwealth Day (May 24)
St George's Caye Day (Sept 10)
Independence Day (Sept 21)
Pan American Day (Oct 12)
Garifuna Settlement Day (Nov 19)
Christmas Day
Boxing Day.

BY CAR

Few travelers drive all the way from the US to Belize, although it can be done with a valid driver's license, vehicle registration papers and a selection of good maps. Some travelers hire cars in Cancún and drive to Belize, although this is not permitted by hire companies (insurance doesn't extend across the border, and since many Belizean roads are in poor condition, this is extremely risky.)

Upon entering Belize, customs issues a permit waiving customs duty on the car as long as it is not sold in Belize. The permit is valid for up to three months and must be surrendered to the Customs Frontier Station upon departure. Third-party insurance is compulsory and can be bought at the frontier station or in any of the major towns.

If you wish to stay longer than three months, a Belize Driving Permit is obtainable from the Licensing Authority in Belize City in return for a completed medical examination form, two recent photographs and a moderate fee. Website: safari@btl.net

BY BUS

Regular bus services connect all the main towns in Belize. Faster, more comfortable **express services** run between all main towns, including Punta Gorda. These do not stop along the highway but only in the main terminals. Buses depart from the Novelos Terminal, West Collet Canal, Belize City. tel: 207-2025.

BY SEA

No permit is required for arriving in Belize by private boat, but you must immediately report your arrival to immigration officials. You will need to present vessel documents, clearance from your last port of call, and four copies of the crew and passenger list as well as four copies of a list of stores and cargo.

There is a scheduled daily ferry service from Punta Gorda to Puerto Barrios, Guatemala, with other services to Izabal and Río Dulce, in Guatemala, and to Honduras. Contact **Requena's Boat Service**, Punta Gorda, tel: 722-2070; e-mail: watertaxi@btl.net.

Practical Tips

Security and Crime

Crime is a growing concern in Belize, so exercise caution, even in the daytime, both in Belize City and elsewhere. Don't walk the streets at night. Hold-ups and petty theft are regular occurrences after dark, so everyone telephones for a taxi, even to travel short distances (but make sure you confirm the price with the driver before you get in the car to avoid misunderstandings).

Women need to be particularly careful about going out alone at night, even in a taxi. Never leave a bar or your hotel with someone you don't know. If you do decide to look for a little nightlife, tell hotel staff where you are going and when you expect to return. They should be able to steer you towards the more upscale discos and clubs and indicate the places with more questionable reputations.

Belizean women and visitors are being advised to keep an eye on their drinks since the so-called date-rape drugs seem to have made their way onto the local black market. So, enjoy yourself, but keep your wits about you and your senses clear.

The city is quite safe by day, although keep an eye out for pickpockets. Also, loitering around the Swing Bridge are a number of panhandlers, hustlers, dealers and "tour operators" who can be quite persistent. When you cross the Swing Bridge during the day, avoid conversation and don't hang around taking photos with expensive camera equipment.

Most tourists avoid Belize City altogether, which is a pity because it holds a great deal of dilapidated colonial charm and the situation is no worse than most Central or North American cities.

In the event of a assault, robbery, theft, or other crimes, it should be reported immediately to the police. The main benefit of this is to get a copy of the police report in order to claim from your travel insurance company. Travel insurance is essential.

Special **Tourism Police** patrol Belize City and most of the popular resort areas. If you are the victim of a crime they can help you with the formalities of reporting the incident.

Medical Services

Considering the high quality of food and its preparation, as well as the potable tap water in most tourist areas (with the exception of Caye Caulker and outside main towns in the south), it is uncommon for visitors to contract stomach problems. However, should you require the services of a physician, your hotel should always be able to recommend one nearby.

If you require daily medication, bring an ample supply since your brand may be unavailable or extremely expensive in Belize.

Few pharmacies are open late at night or on weekends and, should you need urgent medical attention, be warned: district hospitals are supposed to have doctors on call at night and on weekends, but serious illnesses or injuries are usually referred to the Karl Heusner Memorial Hospital in Belize City. So, if the worst happens and you have the option, your best bet is to go directly there, rather than waste time at the less equipped district centers. Medical Associates, tel: 223-0303, next to the hospital in Belize City provides a more rapid service, although it is more expensive.

Public Hospitals
Karl Heusner Memorial Hospital, Belize City
Tel: 223-1548.
Corozal Hospital
Tel: 422-2076.
Dangriga Hospital

Tel: 522-2078.
Orange Walk Hospital
Tel: 322-2072.
Punta Gorda Hospital
Tel: 722-2026.
San Ignacio Hospital
Tel: 824-2066.

Weights and Measures

The British imperial system of measures is generally used, with speed and road signs in miles, not kilometers. Exceptions are fuel, which is sold by the American gallon (= 0.8 UK gallons; 3.8 liters), and some imported goods, which are weighed using the metric system.

Business Hours

Most stores and offices are open from Monday–Friday 8am–noon and 1–5pm. Some stores are open in the morning only on Wednesday and Saturday, or in the evening from 7–9pm. Banks are open Monday–Thursday 8am–1pm; Friday 8am–1pm and 3–6pm.

Tipping

You will become aware that many in the service industry depend almost entirely on tips, although there are no definite rules about what to do or how much to give. Baggage handlers and hotel porters expect a couple of dollars. Many hotels add 10 percent service to the final bill, to be divided among the unseen employees. If you enjoyed your guided day trip, it is customary to tip the guide a few dollars.

Tipping in restaurants depends slightly more on the tone of the establishment and the customer's satisfaction. Tips are not obligatory, but if you're happy with the service (rather rare in a country where waiters tend to be slow and sullen) you can either round up the total or add 10 percent. It is not necessary to tip the taxi driver since a price should be firmly established before entering the car.

Emergency Numbers

Police Tel: 90 or 911
To report a crime Tel: 227-2210 (Belize City).
Ambulance/Fire Tel: 90 (in Belize City only).

Media

NEWSPAPERS

Apart from the weekly independents, *Amandala*, and *Reporter*, most newspapers are owned by political parties and thus dwell on bad-mouthing the opposition. The main ones are the *Belize Times* (run by the PUP) and the *Guardian* (UDP). The *Reporter* is a fairly independent business-oriented newspaper.

While in San Pedro, try the small *San Pedro Sun* and in Placencia there's the *Placencia Breeze*, both provide tourist information.

RADIO AND TELEVISION

Belizeans prefer the radio to most other forms of media. Strolling around Belize City at lunchtime, you will hear its crackling cadences rise and fall from popular eateries and open doorways. LOVE FM 95.1 has official announcements and continual weather information interspersed with the usual rock and reggae selection.

Other radio stations include KREM 91.1 FM, WAVE Radio 105.9 FM, FM 2000 at 96.1 and Reef Radio in San Pedro. There is also Radio Ritmo and My Refuge Christian Radio in the Cayo District and Estereo Tu Y Yo in Orange Walk.

Broadcasts from stations in Chetumal, Mexico can also be received clearly in the north. The only nationwide Spanish station is Estereo Amor.

Belize has two television channels and US cable TV is available almost everywhere.

Postal Services

Belize City's post office was based in the rambling old colonial Paslow Building on the north side of the Swing Bridge (intersection Queen and North Front streets), which was destroyed by fire. The post office is now located next door. Belizean stamps are among the most beautiful in the world with their depictions of native flora and fauna, and are highly prized by collectors. Allow up to 5 days for mail to arrive in the United States and at least 10 days to Europe, Asia or Australia. The post office is open from 8am–5pm (until 4.30pm on Friday).

Telecommunications

Your hotel will have fixed rates for local and international calls. Check the rate before you make the call. The more expensive hotels also have fax and telex services available.

Telephone, e-mail and telex services are also available at **Belize Telecommunications Ltd** on Church Street, just off Central Park, 8am–6pm weekdays, closed Sat and Sun. Internet access is available also at **Mailboxes Etc.**, 166 North Front Street. International Direct Dialing is available from most of Belize.

Many payphones don't accept change, but phone cards are widely available at most grocery shops, gas stations and some hotels. Email services are available at BTL in Belize City and there are a few cybercafes in Caye Caulker, Placencia, Punta Gorda, San Pedro, and San Ignacio. **Cell phone numbers**, **Email addresses** and **fax numbers** are listed in the pink pages at the front of the telephone directory. **International dialing code for Belize:** 501.
International calls, tel: 115.
Belize Directory Assistance, tel: 113.
Intelco is set to break the BTL monopoly some time in the future, so please note that many of the phone numbers and e-mails listed

Belize Websites

www.belizenet.com
www.belizeit.com
www.belizefirst.com
www.belize.net
www.gobelize.com
www.travelbelize.org
www.scubadivingbelize.com

within these pages are subject to change.

Tourist Offices

Belize Tourism Board
Central Bank Building,
Gabourel Lane, PO Box 325,
Belize City, Belize.
Tel: 223-1913
Fax: 223-1943
US and Canada, tel: 800-624 0686
e-mail: btbb@btl.net
www.travelbelize.org
The office is open from 8am–noon and 1–5pm.

For information on conservation issues and Belize's ecology generally, contact:
Belize Audubon Society
12 Fort St, PO Box 1001
Belize City.
Tel: 223-5004.

Embassies and Consulates in Belize

British High Commission
34/36 Halfmoon Avenue,
Belmopan.
Tel: 822-2146.
Canadian Consulate/Consulat du Canada
83 North Front Street,
Belize City.
Tel: 223-1060.
United States Embassy
29 Gabourel Lane, PO Box 286,
Belize City.
Tel: 227-7161;
Fax: 223-0802.

All current embassy and consulates are listed in the Green Pages of the Belize Telephone Directory.

Getting Around

On Arrival

Most travelers' first vision of Belize is the quaint Phillip Goldson International Airport. Immigration can be cleared quickly, although Belizean customs officials often insist on checking every tourist's luggage and large arrivals can result in long delays (bear this in mind if connecting with an internal flight). There is a tourist information booth past immigration, as well as a currency exchange window near the exit (if this is closed, you can get by on US$ without problems). It is better to have booked a hotel for your first night in Belize before you arrive, rather than trying to arrange accommodation from the airport. You can always move on once you have got your bearings.

Many tour operators put travelers straight on to connecting flights or provide a mini-van service to their hotels and jungle lodges.

Independent travelers will find a taxi rank outside the airport doors. Rates into Belize City are fixed by a cartel and are fairly hefty for the 20–25 minute ride. You should not pay any more than BZ$40 for a taxi from the airport to Belize City. The rate is per trip, not per person. Make sure this is clear before you set out and get the name of the driver so you can complain immediately to the Belize Tourism Board if you are overcharged.

Once in Belize City, taxis should not charge more than BZ$6 to take one passenger to any drop within the city, including the municipal airstrip. They may add an extra dollar for picking you up at your hotel, rather than on the street. Fuel costs may mean these prices change. Check with your hotel what the current rate is. In the city it should be per person, not per trip. The rate to outlying areas will be higher. If you find a taxi driver you like, get his or her card or number so you can use them again, especially at night.

Rates to other parts of Belize can be negotiated. On arrival, although tipping is not mandatory, you could round up the amount or add something if your driver helps with your bags. Belizeans know how to receive tips graciously.

By Bus

Buses run half-hourly between Belize City, Belmopan and San Ignacio, hourly to Orange Walk, Corozal and Chetumal, and less frequently to Dangriga and Punta Gorda.
Novelo's Bus Service, West Collet Canal, Belize City, tel: 207-2025 (for destinations in the north and west); tel 522-2160 (for the south).
James Bus, services to Belmopan and Punta Gorda, tel: 722-2625

By Taxi

Downtown Belize City is small enough to handle on foot and during the cool part of the day this is the

way to get around. At night, you should travel by private car or taxi, even for short distances, because of the prevalence of street crime. Hotels and restaurants are used to calling for taxis, which arrive almost immediately. Always confirm the price with the driver before setting off. In Belize City, the numbers are: 223-2916/0371; 227-2888.

Some resorts will hire taxis to transfer small groups from the airport. In San Pedro, you might use a taxi to get from your hotel into town at night, unless the resort has a shuttle service. (Many resorts have complimentary bicycles for this purpose, or motorized golf carts to hire from the more luxurious establishments.)

Taxis can also be hired to get between towns or to explore the countryside (in San Ignacio, for example, the taxi cartel has fixed rates to jungle lodges and ruins.)

Car Rental

An exhilarating way to start your trip is to pick up a hire car or jeep from the airport and simply drive off. In the interior, your own transport comes in very handy: you are free to visit wildlife reserves and ruins

at your own pace or make trips from your lodge (which is often in the middle of nowhere) to town.

Renting a car in Belize is expensive, however, and a hefty damage deposit is demanded (you pay for the first US$1,000 in any crash). A meticulous inventory of scratches or dents is the car company's way of telling you to take it easy. Fuel is also very expensive.

Rules of the road

Drive on the right-hand side of the road. Speeds and distances are measured in miles; the signposting, isn't great but it's hard to get lost.

The major drawback is the poor condition of some roads and some hire car companies will only hire out 4WD vehicles if you're traveling in the south. The route out to San Ignacio on the Western Highway is now paved all the way, although conditions worsen dramatically as soon as you turn off the highway.

Driving south is not always so smooth. The Hummingbird Highway, from Belmopan to Dangriga is paved the whole way, driving time about one hour. The Southern Highway, from Dangriga to Punta Gorda, is nearly all well paved. Driving time from Dangriga to

Boat Trips

The alternative to flying from Belize City to the cayes is to take one of the many boat services.

In Belize City, the Marine Terminal is next to the Swing Bridge. Members of the Water Taxi Association make scheduled runs to Caye Caulker and San Pedro every day from 9am to 5pm. Life-jackets should be available on all boats. The trip to San Pedro takes around one hour and 15 minutes.

It's easy to take the same services for the 30-minute ride between San Pedro and Caye Caulker, or hop onto any number of other boats plying the route. Keep in mind you can always find a boat that will take you privately for a price. For fishing and snorkeling, there are many independent (and

cheap) boat operators competing with the resorts and large tour operators. The arrangements are flexible: meet them at the docks in town or arrange a pick-up from your resort; you can also choose where you want to snorkel or fish.

More structured activities, such as scuba-diving, sailing or waterskiing can easily be arranged through your hotel or with one of the many operators lining the main street of San Pedro, which is the commercial center of the cayes (see also a listing of recommended activity specialists on page 329).

Transport to and from other cayes by boat is mostly arranged by hotels. Alternatively, book your own boat at the docks.

There are also international

boats from Belize to Guatemala and Honduras: the *Gulf Cruzer* leaves from Placencia at 9am on Fridays BZ$130 or US$65 (van pick-up in Belize City at 6am for Placencia; tel: 223-1235 for details), arriving in Puerto Cortés, Honduras, around 1.30pm. From Dangriga, the *Nesymein* – a fast skiff leaves for Puerto Cortés at 9am on Wednesdays and Saturdays (US$50 one way), arriving about 1.30pm, tel 522-3227.

From Punta Gorda Requena's boat leaves at 9am for Puerto Barrios in Guatemala (US$12.50 one-way). Tel: 722-2070; e-mail: watertaxi@btl.net. There's also a boat service leaving for Puerto Barrios at 4pm.

Placencia is about 2 hours in the dry season, and about 3 hours from Dangriga to Punta Gorda in dry conditions. The Manatee Highway, or Coastal Road, from Belize City to Dangriga, is an unpaved gravel road, used as a short-cut, turning off the Western Highway at La Democracia and joining the Hummingbird Highway about 13 miles (21 km) west of Dangriga. Total driving time from Belize City to Dangriga is about 2½ hours in good conditions. Elsewhere two-wheel drive cars are fine on most roads if it doesn't rain. If you can afford it, 4WD vehicles are best, especially on mountain tracks leading to ruins and in the rainy season – sudden rainstorms can render these dirt roads impassable, so check their condition before setting out.

There is a wide choice of car rental companies in Belize City, with the following the most recognized:
Avis, Radisson Fort George Hotel, Belize City. Tel: 223-4619; e-mail: avisbelize@btl.net.
Budget, 771 Bella Vista, Belize City. Tel: 223-2435
Fax: 223-0237
Web: www.budget-belize.com
Crystal Auto Rental (the "rent-a-wreck" of Belize), 1.5 Miles Northern Road, Belize City.
Tel: 223-1600; 800-777 7777 (toll-free in Belize).
Fax: 223-1900.
Web: www.crystal-belize.com
Hertz, 11A Cork Street, Belize City.
Tel: 223-5395.
Fax: 223-0268
Has the best reputation for price, reliability and condition of cars. Also has office at International Airport:
Tel: 225-3300
e-mail: safaritiz@btl.net

By Plane

In response to the poor state of the roads, many small propeller plane services have been set up to cover most of Belize. This is by far the most common and convenient form of getting around.

Flights leave on time and few take more than half an hour. The most common are from Belize International Airport to San Pedro – 20 minutes, with great views of the coral reef – and south to Placencia, Dangriga and Punta Gorda. If leaving from Belize City, check whether the flight will be departing from the International Airport or the smaller Municipal Airport off Princess Margaret Drive.

With airstrips now on Ambergris and Caulker Cayes, many visitors avoid Belize City altogether and fly direct to their jungle resorts and Maya ruins inland. The domestic airlines run daily tours to Tikal in Guatemala.

Scheduled air services
The following airlines serve Ambergris Caye, Caye Caulker, Caye Chapel, Dangriga, Placencia, Punta Gorda, Flores and Guatemala:
Maya Island Air departs from Belize City's International and Municipal airports.
Tel: 226-2345 or 225-2219; fax: 226-2192. US reservations: tel: 800-225 6732.
www.mayaislandair.com.
Tropic Air Tel: 226-2012 or 225-2302; fax: 226-2338. US reservations: tel: 800-422 3435.
www.tropicair.com.
There are no regular services to western Belize or Cancún.

Charter Services in Belize City
Caribee Air Service
Tel: 224-4253.
Javier's Flying Service
Tel: 224-5332.

On Departure

A departure tax of BZ$40 (US$20) is levied at the International Airport and can be paid in either currency. There is also a BZ$30 departure tax for those leaving Belize by land (which can also be paid in either currency). The departure tax includes a BZ$2.50 (US$1.25) security tax and a Protected Areas Conservation Trust fee of BZ$7.50 (US$3.75). Drivers must pay an exit fee of BZ$5 and surrender their Belize driving permit.

Where to Stay

Choosing a Hotel

Belize can offer tourists a great array of accommodation ranging from comfortable budget hotels to luxurious beach resorts and jungle lodges with vast tracts of pristine wilderness as their grounds.

Alternatives include small private guesthouses, huge, internationally owned hotel chains, diver-oriented resorts on the outer cayes, lodges that cater to the ecotourist with bird-watching lists and evening discussions, and health resorts providing herbal body wraps.

The style or specialty of each hotel or lodge can be radically different, and is often created by the environment. Although staying in urban centers might give a traveler more insight into the local Belizean character and culture, most visitors come to taste nature.

For accommodation in lodges and on some cayes, it is difficult to give price guides as they usually offer deals that include diving or fishing trips, or rainforest treks, etc. They are usually expensive, but very convenient and worthwhile.

There is a 7 percent room tax added to the price, and sometimes an additional 10 percent service charge for upscale accommodations.

Hotel Listings
BELIZE CITY

Belize City has hotels on both sides of Haulover Creek, connected by the Swing Bridge. Although the commercial center is on the south side, most of the better hotels are located on the northern side, which is also a far more attractive neighborhood.

Belize Biltmore Plaza
Mile 3, Northern Highway
Belize City
Tel: 223-2302
Fax: 223-2301
US reservations tel: 800-528
12324
www.belizebiltmore.com
e-mail: sales@belizebiltmore.com
Large, sophisticated hotel 3 miles
(5 km) from downtown Belize City,
on the road to the airport.
Swimming pool, private bathrooms
and tropical garden. The Friday
evening happy hour has live music
and is popular with the business
community. **$$$**

Bellevue Hotel
5 Southern Foreshore
Belize City
Tel: 227-7051
Fax: 227-3253
e-mail: bellevue@btl.net
Located on the southern foreshore,
with lovely views of the harbor, this
old house has some renovated
rooms. There is a pool at the back
and a thatched poolside bar good
for Friday happy hour. **$$$**

Radisson Fort George Hotel
2 Marine Parade, PO Box 321
Belize City
Tel: 223-3333
Fax: 227-3820.
US reservations tel: 800-333 3333
www.radissonbelize.com
The Radisson Group runs the
Holiday Villa Belize Inn and it has
become the Executive Club wing of
the Fort George Hotel. All the
facilities expected of a luxury hotel
with an emphasis on business
travelers – full meeting and
conference facilities, courier,
secretarial services – as well as
pool, cable TV, and travel agent.
Located in the Fort George area
$$$

Bakadeer Inn
74 Cleghorn Street (off Douglas
Jones Street)
Belize City
Tel: 223-0659
e-mail: mcfield@btl.net
For those who prefer US motel-style
accommodation. Comfortable,
clean rooms, all with private bath.
Full American breakfast on request.
$$

Chateau Caribbean
6 Marine Parade,
PO Box 947, Belize City
Tel: 223-0800
Fax: 223-0900
www.chateaucaribbean.com
Old-style mansion and seafood
restaurant facing out to sea with an
atmosphere of Caribbean days gone
by. Some rooms in the original
building are very nice, although
renovation is needed throughout.
$$

Colton House Guest House
9 Cork Street
Belize City
Tel: 203-4666
www.coltonhouse.com
In the safe and historic Fort George
area, this is one of the best guest
houses in the country. Six non-
smoking rooms in this beautifully
restored wooden colonial house, all
with private bathroom, air-
conditioning and balcony. **$$**

Price Guide

The following price categories
indicate the cost of a double
room. Prices increase during high
season (November–March).
$$$: BZ$160–$400
$$: BZ$60–$160
$: under BZS$60

Coningsby Inn
76 Regent Street
Belize City
Tel: 227-1566
Fax: 227-3276
e-mail: info@coningsbyinn.com
Modern rooms in an elegantly
restored colonial building in a quiet
part of the city, just behind the
Southern Foreshore and a block
from the historic House of Culture.
There's a good restaurant and bar
for guests, and the owners can
arrange tours. **$$**

Grant Residence
126 Barrack Road
Belize City
Tel: 223-0926
Fax: 223-0885
www.grantbedandbreakfast.com
Four spacious, comfortable rooms
in a well-maintained guest house on
the sea front just north of the city
centre. Smoking is allowed in the
rooms; fans and sea breezes keep
the place cool. **$$$**

The Great House
13 Cork Street
Belize City
Tel: 223-3400
Fax: 223-3444
www.greathousebelize.com
One of the city's most beautiful old
colonial homes. It was built in 1927
and renovated to offer 12 private
rooms with balconies. There are
shops and a restaurant (Smokey
Mermaid) on the ground floor,
beautiful sea and harbor views;
within walking distance of
downtown. Across the street from
the Radisson Hotel. **$$**

Villa Boscardi
6043 Manatee Drive
Buttonwood Bay
PO Box 1501, Belize City
Tel/fax: 223-1691 or 614-7734
www.villaboscardi.com
A beautiful, comfortable bed &
breakfast in a quiet area north of
the city center, just off the Northern
Highway, which is popular with both
tourists and business visitors. The
air-conditioned rooms have phone
and cable TV, fax and email – a
relative rarity in Belize hotels.
Continental breakfast included and
guests can use the kitchen at other
times. Free airport shuttle; good
4WD vehicle and cell phone are
available for hire. **$$**

Budget

Sea Side Guest House
3 Prince Street
Belize City
Tel: 227-8339
e-mail: seasidebelize@btl.net
The dorm room is popular with
seasoned travelers. Most rooms
share hot and cold showers, a few
have en-suite showers. Big sitting
area and breakfast available. **$$**

Freddie's Guest House
86 Eve Street
Belize City
Tel: 223-3851
Three comfortable rooms, one with
en-suite bath. A good value small
hotel, a real gem. No meals but
tea/coffee maker for guests. **$**

BELIZE DISTRICT

Belize River Lodge
Ladyville
Tel: 225-2002
Fax: 225-2298
e-mail: bzelodge@btl.net
www.belizeriverlodge.com
Sitting on the banks of the Old
Belize River, some 10 miles (16
km) north of Belize City, the Belize
River Lodge is primarily a fishing
lodge, but becoming popular with
birders and ecotourists. You stay in
rustic, mahogany paneled guest
houses and enjoy family-style dining
in the main building. Trips to Altun
Há Maya ruins can be arranged as
well as safari boat trips upriver.
Live-aboard yacht fishing or day
trips are also available, with
experienced guides. **$$$**

**Community Baboon Sanctuary Bed
and Breakfasts**
Bermudian Landing
via Belize Audubon Society.
Tel: 223-5004
e-mail: base@btl.net
Stay with a creole family within the
Baboon Sanctuary to see black
howler monkeys and learn about
the traditional lifestyle of rural
creoles. For room, board and guide
fees contact the Audubon Society,
or the Sanctuary Manager. **$**

El Chiclero Inn
Burrel Boom
Tel: 225-9005
e-mail: soffit@io.com
A small hotel with large and
spacious air-conditioned rooms, run
by retired Americans. Busiest time
of year is March when La Ruta
Maya River Challenge passes by
and team families book the entire
hotel. It has good food, a quiet
location with a pool and river beach,
and there is a local winery nearby.
The Inn can be reached by taking
the Boom turn-off on both the
northern and western highways. **$$**

Manatee Lodge
Gales Point village
Tel/fax: 220-8040
US reservations tel: 877-462 6283
www.manateelodge.com
A wonderful old lodge with modern
amenities that sits on the tip of the
narrow sandy Gales Point

peninsula, surrounded on three
sides by the calm waters of
Southern Lagoon. Spacious (non-
smoking) rooms. It's a perfect base
to explore this little-visited area of
Belize. Call to arrange a pick-up by
boat to make the trip along inland
waterways. Service charge. **$$**

Maruba Resort and Jungle Spa
401/2 mile, Old Northern Highway
Maskall Village
Tel: 322-2199
Fax: 220-1049
US reservations tel: 800-MARUBA-7/
713-799 2031
www.maruba-spa.com
Thirty miles (50 km) north of Belize
International Airport. A unique and
eccentric lodge, with cabins
designed by the owner along
different themes. Luxurious health
and beauty services such as
Japanese spa, massage and herbal
body wraps available, as well as an
excellent Californian-Belize
restaurant. The sculpted jungle
grounds, with various artworks and
waterfall swimming pool, are
designed for peace and tranquility.
Recommended for the visitor who
wants to relax and be pampered.
Tours are conducted to Lamanai
and Altun Há. Meal plans available.
Airport pickup is US$45 extra. **$$$**

Crooked Tree Village

Bird's Eye View Resort
Crooked Tree Village
Tel: 223-2040
Fax: 222-4869
e-mail: birdseye@btl.net
A basic building, but a favorite with
birdwatchers owing to its great
lakeside location. Each room has
an en-suite bathroom and some are
dormitory-style with several beds.
The Belizean food and service are
also highly recommended. **$$**

Paradise Inn
Crooked Tree Village
Tel: 205-7044
www.adventurecamera.com/
paradise
Thatched wooden cabins with
private bathrooms, on the shore of
Crooked Tree Lagoon. The inn is run
by a very friendly family who serve
tasty, home-cooked meals, and your
guides are the sons of the owners,
with their own boats so you can
reach some remote waterways in
the Wildlife Sanctuary. **$**

NORTHERN CAYES

The northern cayes, accessible
from Belize City, are dominated by
Ambergris Caye, the most
developed resort region in all
Belize, but there are also several
more peaceful groups of cayes,
some with superb marine wildlife
reserves, including Lighthouse
Reef, the Turneffe Islands, Caye
Caulker and the Bluefield Range.

Ambergris Caye/San Pedro

San Pedro is the sandy township on
Ambergris Caye where you can find
plenty of inexpensive places to stay,
each with its own relaxed beachy
quality. The larger resorts can be
found along the shoreline at varying
distances out of San Pedro.

Belize Yacht Club Ltd
PO Box 62
San Pedro
Tel: 226-2777
Fax: 226-2768
US reservations tel: 800-688
0402/305-757 0735.
www.belizeyachtclub.com
Luxury suites complete with
kitchens and verandas are
ensconced within a formidable
enclosure a short walk south of San
Pedro. Marina facilities available.
Appropriate for longer stays. **$$$**

Captain Morgan's Retreat
3 miles (5 km) north of San Pedro
Tel: 226-2207
Fax: 226-2616
US reservations tel: 888-653 9090.
e-mail: belizevacation@yahoo.com
Attractive thatched cabañas on
palm-shaded beach. One transfer

each way from the airport is included in the price. The usual fishing, snorkeling and diving can be arranged. **$$$**

Journey's End Resort
4½ miles (7.2 km) north of San Pedro
Box 13, San Pedro Town
Tel: 226-2173
Fax: 226-2028
US reservations tel: 800-460 5665; fax: 713-780 1726
e-mail: info@journeysendresort.com
Large complex of cabins and hotel blocks at the northern end of the caye. All the usual activities are provided from the resort's marina and a large pool is located at the back. The resort has floodlit tennis courts, basketball court, two restaurants and three bars, one with wall-to-wall slot machines and complimentary use of sailboards and canoes. Best suited for large groups or the swinging singles scene. Free scheduled boat transfers into town. Restaurant could be better. Meal plan available. **$$$**

Mata Chica
5 Miles North
San Pedro
Tel: 220-5010
Fax: 220-5012
www.matachica.com
e-mail: matachica@btl.net
On the beach, a boat ride out of town, is one of the most beautiful resorts on the island, perhaps the whole of Belize. Well worth a trip for dinner if you can't stay. Creatively designed by artistic French and Italian owners, each cabaña has a different style. Ask for a larger one in the second row in from the beach but still with sea view, or for a villa. The Mambo restaurant on the property is one of the best on the island and the Jade Spa has some relaxing treatments. **$$$**

Mayan Princess Resort Hotel
Barrier Reef Drive
San Pedro town
Tel: 226-2778
Fax: 226-2784
www.mayanprincesshotel.com
Pleasant hotel in the middle of San Pedro town offering clean, air-conditioned suites with balcony, friendly staff, nearby dive center

and watersports. **$$$**

Ramon's Village Reef Resort
San Pedro Post Office
San Pedro
Tel: 226-2071
Fax: 226-2214
US reservations tel: 601-649 1990; fax: 601-649 1996.
e-mail: ramons@btl.net
Just outside San Pedro on one of the better sections of beach, Ramon's is a well-managed system of furnished cane cabañas, each with fan and private bath. The grounds include a salt-water swimming pool, the famed Purple Parrot Bar and a dining pavilion that serves excellent food. Some suites have kitchenettes. **$$$**

Victoria House
Victoria House Resort
Ambergris Caye
Tel: 226-2067
Fax: 226-2429
US reservations tel: 800-247 5159; from outside US tel: 404-373 0068; fax 404-373 3885
www.victoria-house.com
Extremely comfortable and elegant resort where Harrison Ford stayed during the filming of the *Mosquito Coast*. Choice of spacious suites with air-conditioning and balconies or private cabañas, all with perfect Caribbean Sea views. Watersport activities available from private marina, including open-water dive certification program. To get into town, rent a golf cart, take the scheduled shuttle bus or use the complimentary bicycles. The restaurant is good, and they'll cook your day's fishing catch. **$$$**

Changes in Latitudes
Tel/fax: 226-2986
e-mail: latitudes@btl.net
Wonderful, well-run B&B (serving a full breakfast) south of the town center, next to the Belize Yacht Club, just half a block from the sea. Rooms are on the small side but are very comfortable, with private bathroom, and there's a small garden for relaxing. Great for information and tours. **$$**

Coral Beach Hotel and Dive Club
Box 614, San Pedro.
Tel: 226-2013
Fax: 226-2001

e-mail: foreman@btl.net
On the main street of San Pedro, with no fancy facilities, where the emphasis is on diving. Packages including diving and meals are available. **$$**

Paradise Resort Hotel
Box 888, Belize City
Tel: 226-2083
Fax: 226-2232
e-mail: paradise@btl.net
Another tasteful compound of South Pacific-style bamboo and thatch cabins, with the convenience of being on the northern edge of the township. With its own sandy beach, bar and gift shop, diving, fishing and travel services. **$$**

Royal Palm Villas
PO Box 18, San Pedro
Tel: 226-2244
Fax: 226-2329
www.royalpalminn.com
About 1½ miles (2.5 km) south of San Pedro; spacious rooms with wooden floors and ceiling fans or more expensive apartments. Tranquil atmosphere on a wide beach and with friendly management. Meal plans available. **$$**

San Pedro Holiday Hotel
PO Box 61, San Pedro
Tel: 226-2014
Fax: 226-2295
www.sanpedroholiday.com
The quaint old hotel lobby opens onto the main street of San Pedro, a hive of activity with its tour desk, swimwear boutique and friendly bar. Walk through the lobby and you find yourself suddenly on the beach once again. Rooms and apartments with fans or air-conditioning. **$$**

Sun Breeze Beach Resort
PO Box 14, San Pedro
Tel: 226-2191
Fax: 226-2346
US reservations tel: 800-688 0191
e-mail: sunbreeze@btl.net
www.sunbreeze.net
Yet another hotel compound located on the beachfront only minutes from town, with all rooms air-conditioned (which also blocks the occasional noise from the nearby airstrip). The dive shop can arrange lessons and certification. **$$**

There are also plenty of no-frills hotels in the heart of San Pedro, such as:

Lily's Caribena,
Tel: 226-2059
Fax: 226-2623
e-mail: lilies@btl.net
Small budget hotel in the center of San Pedro, south of the dock. **$**

Ruby's
Tel: 226-2063
Fax: 226-2434
e-mail: rubys@btl.net
Close to the airport in San Pedro, on the seafront. Small, family-run hotel, with clean, comfy rooms. **$**

Caye Caulker

There are only a few luxurious hotels on Caye Caulker and this is part of the attraction for many visitors. There are, however, many relaxing and good value places to stay. Just stroll around and take your pick. Note that, as Caye Caulker is becoming more popular, reservation is recommended for most of the following hotels, especially in high season.

Lazy Iguana
PO Box 59, Caye Caulker
Tel: 226-0350
Fax: 226-0320
e-mail: momiller77@aol.com
www.lazyiguana.net
A beautiful and elegant B&B, located south of the center of the island, set in orchid-filled gardens. Very comfortable air-conditioned rooms with private bath; the thatched rooftop shelter has panoramic views of the island and the sea – best enjoyed from one of the hammocks. **$$**

M&N Hotel and Apartments
Tel: 226-0229
Located on the main thoroughfare near the soccer field. It has golf-cart rentals and an air-strip pickup. **$$**

Seaside Cabanas
Tel: 226-0498
Fax: 226-0125
www.seasidecabanas.com
Spacious wood and thatch cabañas arranged around a pristine sand patio, conveniently located on the beach by the main dock. All have private bathrooms and there are

lots of extras, including phone, fridge, a private deck with hammocks and a small, friendly bar for guests. Kayaks for rent and first-class tour information. **$$**

Shirley's Guest House
South of the village
Tel: 226-0145
e-mail: shirley@btl.net
Near the airstrip and a good choice if you want peace and privacy on an otherwise quite lively island. Comfortable clean *cabañas* in spacious grounds. **$$**

Treetops Hotel
PO Box 29, Caye Caulker
Tel/fax: 226-0240
e-mail: treetopsbelize@yahoo.com
Four immaculately clean rooms, some with private bathroom, and two luxury suites, all with fridge and cooled by powerful ceiling fans. Just south of the center, set back half a block from the sea but with nothing to obstruct the view. **$$**

Trends Hotel
Tel: 226-0094
e-mail: trendsbze@btl.net
Right on the water's edge, with volleyball court, and hammocks on the verandas. Next to Sandbox restaurant and main water-taxi pier. **$$**

St George's Caye

St George's Lodge
Box 625, Belize City
Tel: 209-9121
www.goodliving.com
US reservations tel: 800-678 6871; fax: 941-488 3953
Catering mainly for divers, this is a highly rated resort. With four diving guides and four dive boats, a good choice for certification. Cottages with thatched roofs and sea breezes. Reduction for non-divers and children. **$$$**

Bluefield Range

Ricardo's Beach Huts
Tel: 227-8469
Accommodation in basic "over-water" cabañas on a group of mangrove cayes about 21 miles (34 km) southeast of Belize City. Learn about the lives of the fishermen who manage a commercial fishing/lobster venture within these

small cayes. Room prices include transportation to the caye and all meals. Tents also available, and three-day/two-night packages. **$$**

Turneffe Islands

Blackbird Caye Resort
81 W Canal Street
Belize City
Tel: 223-2772
Fax: 223-2449
US reservations tel: 800-326 1724
www.blackbirdresort.com
An environmentally sensitive eco-tourism resort popular with divers and conservationists due to the beauty of its surroundings. Swim with dolphins in a protected lagoon. Weekly packages available. **$$$**

Turneffe Flats
Tel: 220-4046
US reservations tel: 800-815 1304/605-578 1304
www.tflats.com
Package deals include accommodation at the **Fort George Hotel** in Belize City, boat trip to the island, meals, fishing, and accommodation at the camp. Deep-sea fishing day trips. **$$$**

Turneffe Island Lodge
PO Box 480
Belize City
Tel: 220-4041
US reservations tel: 800-874 0118
www.turneffelodge.com
Situated on Caye Bokel, a private 12-acre (5-hectare) island. Recognized as one of the finest fishing locations for backcountry and flats fishing, particularly bone-fish, permit, and tarpon. Also a favorite with divers because it is close to some of the best dive sites, including the "Elbow." Accommodation is in 12 double rooms on the water's edge, some with air-conditioning. **$$$**

Lighthouse Reef

Lighthouse Reef Resort
Northern Two Caye, PO Box 26
Belize City
Tel: 223-1205
US reservations tel: 800-423 3114/914-439 6600; fax: 863-439 2118
e-mail: lighthousereef@btl.net
Handy base for diving expeditions to

Belize's outer most atoll. Luxury accommodation with air-conditioning, restaurant, bar and shop. Fishing and other sightseeing excursions arranged. **$$$**

ORANGE WALK DISTRICT

Orange Walk Town
D-Victoria House
40 Belize-Corozal Road
Orange Walk Town
Tel: 322-2518
Fax: 322-3472
Not many visitors stay in Orange Walk Town itself, but this is a good hotel if you do. Plain, air-conditioned rooms and private showers. Hotel has pool and enclosed parking. **$$**
Lamanai Outpost Lodge
Tel: 223-3578
Fax: 220-9061
US reservations tel: 888-733 /864
e-mail: outpost@lamanai.com
www.lamanai.com
Large wooden cabañas with private porch and open on three sides with screen windows that help maximize ventilation. Meals are very good, served in an open-sided restaurant lit by lantern. Run by an Australian couple who offer a range of activities from crocodile-spotting trips on the river to night-time nature walks. There is excellent bird-watching, and the hotel is in an unspoilt location on the bank of New River Lagoon and adjacent to the Maya ruins at Lamanai. Air transport (15 minutes) from Belize City can be arranged for an additional fee. It is accessible by road or river, year round. **$$$**
Chan Chich Lodge (**Río Bravo Conservation Area**)
PO Box 37, Belize City
Tel: 223-4419
US reservations tel: 800-343 8009; fax: 508-693 6311.
www.chanchich.com
Currently rated as the best of Belize's jungle resorts, it is located within the plaza of a classic Maya ruin, buried in the farthest west of Orange Walk District, close to the Guatemalan border. Tasteful cabañas, constructed of local

woods, receive rave reviews. Pristine forest surroundings afford glimpses of tropical birds, monkeys, and (possibly) jaguars. Possible to get here by road if you're hardy, but most people prefer to fly. **$$$**

Price Guide

The following price categories indicate the cost of a double room. Prices increase during high season (November–March).
$$$: BZ$160–$400
$$: BZ$60–$160
$: under BZS$60

COROZAL DISTRICT

Hokol Kin Guest House
4th Street South
Corozal
Tel: 422-3329
Fax: 422-3414
e-mail: maya@btl.net
www.corozal.net
Large rooms with private bath, some suites, and some verandas overlooking the sea. Tours to ruins available. Airport pickup and conference facilities. **$$**
International Cozy Corner Guest House
2nd Street North
Corozal
Tel/fax: 422-0150
e-mail: blperse@btl.net
At the north end of Corozal, just off the road to the border this guest house has comfortable rooms and delightful gardens making it an ideal place to stay. The owners will pick up guests from town. **$$**
Tony's Inn & Resort
South End, Corozal Town.
Tel: 422-2055
US reservations tel: 800-447 2931
e-mail: tony@btl.net
www.tonysinn.com
Large, luxurious rooms in the plushest resort in the region, on the coast to the south of town. Great food, well-kept gardens and beach-side bar. Tours are conducted throughout the Corozal district. Friendly, helpful management. **$$$**

BELMOPAN AND SAN IGNACIO

Belmopan
Bull Frog Inn
25 Half Moon Avenue,
PO Box 28, Belmopan
Tel: 822-2111
Fax: 822-3155
e-mail: bullfrog@btl.net
A motel-style place with air-conditioned rooms and cable TV; the restaurant is by far the best place to eat in Belmopan. **$$**

Teakettle
Pooks Hill Jungle Lodge
Teakettle
Tel: 820-2017
Fax: 822-3361
e-mail: pookshill@btl.net
Set in pristine rainforest 5 miles (9 km) from the village of Teakettle on main Western Highway, 5 miles (9 km) to the west of Belmopan. Lovely rustic thatched cabañas with electricity and private bathrooms. Warm and friendly atmosphere with good home cooking. Owners also have developed an iguana-breeding program. Fantastic horseback riding and river-tubing nearby. Best to take the full-board option; its remote location means there is nowhere else to eat anyway. **$$**
Warrie Head Ranch & Lodge
Teakettle
c/o Belize Global Travel Services
41 Albert Street, PO Box 244
Belize City
Tel: 227 0755
Fax: 227-5213
www.warriehead.com
This old logging camp has been converted into a working citrus and vegetable farm, popular with groups of tourists. Comfortable rooms and a café serving tasty home cooking. The protected forest offers sights of howler monkeys, river swimming and walking trails. **$$$**

San Ignacio
Almost everyone who comes to this region stays not in the San Ignacio township but in the lodges that dot the surrounding countryside. Most hotels in San Ignacio itself are budget places, with one exception.

San Ignacio Resort Hotel
18 Buena Vista Road,
PO Box 33, San Ignacio
Tel: 824-2034
Fax: 824-2124
www.sanignaciobelize.com
A basic concrete building but well
situated, with pleasant terraces
facing across the Macal River. The
breezy dining room is popular at
lunchtime, especially with visiting
archeologists, and it seems to have
its own typically Belizean character.
No service charge. **$$$**

Martha's Guest House
10 West Street
PO Box 140, San Ignacio
Tel: 824-3647
Fax: 824-2732
e-mail: marthas@btl.net
www.marthasbelize.com
The best hotel in town, with
beautiful, tiled rooms; most have a
balcony and some have private
bathrooms, and there's a spacious
rooftop suite. Deservedly popular,
it's a really friendly place, with
excellent service. There are two
lounges and e-mail facilities for
guests, and the best restaurant in
San Ignacio is downstairs. Also a
shuttle to airport. **$$–$**

Casa Blanca
10 Burns Avenue
San Ignacio
Tel: 824-2080
e-mail: casablanca@btl.net
Immaculate rooms, with en-suite
shower and TV; some with air-
conditioning. Very friendly. **$**

Jungle Lodges

The following are isolated cottage-
style resorts in the region around
San Ignacio and the Mountain Pine
Ridge:

Blancaneaux Lodge
Central Farm
Cayo District
Tel: 824-3878
US reservations tel: 800-746 3743
www.blancaneaux.com
One of Francis Ford Coppola's
ventures. An incredible lodge in an
exquisite setting, real luxury in the
jungle. Wonderful views from all the
cabañas. A wood-burning pizza oven
and fine wines for Italian-style

dining. Good base to explore the
Cayo District. **$$$**

**Casa Cielo Cabañas and Mountain
Equestrian Trails** (MET)
Mile 8, Chiquibul Road, Georgeville
Cayo District
Tel: 820-4041
US reservations tel: 800-838 3918
www.metbelize.com
The best place for horseback riding.
Guests stay in comfortable
cabañas. Trips throughout Mountain
Pine Ridge and surrounding terrain.
Also nature treks, horse-drawn
wagons, tours to Tikal and
swimming. **$$$**

Caves Branch Jungle Lodge
Hummingbird Highway
Tel: 820-2800
www.cavesbranch.com
Twelve miles (20 km) south of
Belmopan this is one of Belize's
finest adventure lodges. Luxury
cabaña suites and villas, with
private shower, while a jungle
bunkhouse, camping and rustic
wooden thatched cabañas share
clean bathrooms and showers.
Meals are huge and tasty buffets.
Tours include rappelling, caving,
climbing, tubing and mountain
biking. **$–$$$**

duPlooy's Jungle Lodge
Tel: 824-3101
Fax: 824-3301
www.duplooys.com
Large and comfortably furnished
bungalows on the shady bank of the
Macal River. duPlooys is renowned
for birdwatching, with a treetop
boardwalk extending from the bar to
an observation shelter above the
river. This resort is also home to
the Belize Botanic Garden and a
world-famous orchid collection.
Guides make the tours among the
best in the country. **$$$**

Ek' Tun Resort
Benque Viejo
Cayo District
Tel: 820-3002
US reservations tel/fax: 303-442
6150
e-mail: info@ektunbelize.com
Along the Macal River with
rustic/luxurious cottage
accommodation and gourmet
meals. Hiking, canoeing, fishing and
birding. **$$$**

Five Sisters Lodge
Tel: 820-4005
www.fivesisterslodge.com
One of the most romantic spots in
Belize in the heart of the Mountain
Pine Ridge Forest Reserve, and
popular with honeymooners. The
lodge takes full advantage of its
forest setting and nearby waterfalls
(Little Vaqueros and Five Sisters,
the latter providing a splendid view
from the Lodge's dining room
veranda). Outstanding service. **$$$**

Hidden Valley Inn
Mile 4, Cooma Cairn Road
Belmopan
Tel: 822-3320
US reservations tel: 800-334 7942
www.hiddenvalleyinn.com
Luxurious accommodation in
cottages in the Mountain Pine Ridge
area. There is a pool and a hot tub.
Meals are eaten in the wooden
main lodge building, which also
houses a library and telescopes for
bird spotting. Good base for visiting
the Caracol ruins and there's an
extensive trail system for hiking or
mountain bikes. **$$$**

The Lodge at Chaa Creek
San Ignacio
Tel: 824-2037
Fax: 824-2501
www.chaacreek.com
Probably the most comfortable
place in the San Ignacio region, with
spectacular views of the Macal
River valley. Elegant private
bungalows are decorated with Maya
tapestries; there are no locks, all
windows open onto the river, and
the grounds are impressive. About
20 minutes' drive from San Ignacio.
Good meals, pleasant open-air bar;
highly recommended. The resort
has a health spa, offering sauna,
massage and a wide range of
therapeutic treatments. The
Rainforest Medicinal Trail is next
door, and tours are offered to
Mountain Pine Ridge, Xunantunich
ruins, Chumpiate Maya Cave.
Canoeing, rafting and horseback
riding also available. **$$$**

**Maya Mountain Lodge and
Educational Field Station**
San Ignacio
Tel: 824-2164
Fax: 824-2029

US reservations tel: 800-344 MAYA
www.mayamountain.com
Nestled in the rolling hills bordering
the Macal River, about 1 mile (1.5
km) above San Ignacio, this lodge/
classroom/reference library is run
like a tight ship by the environmentally conscious Bart and Suzi
Mickler. Meet them and their young
family for an after-dinner
discussion. The lodge has unspoilt
surroundings and you will be urged
to take one of their trails marked
with botanical points of interest.
Cabins are nicely decorated, some
with hammocks on private porches.
There is a comprehensive list of
local tour options as well as horse-
riding and canoeing. Home-style
dinners. **$$$**
Mount Pleasant Hidden Valley Inn
4 Miles Coona Cairn Road
Mountain Pine Ridge Forest
Reserve
Box 170, Belmopan
Tel: 822-3320
Fax: 822-3334
US reservations tel: 800-334 7942;
fax: 830-222 1992
www.hiddenvalley.com
One of the more luxurious choices
in the Mountain Pine Ridge area,
whose large private reserve
contains the Thousand Foot Falls.
Accommodation in cozy cottages,
warmed at night by a log fire.
Access to waterfalls and river
swimming, mountain trails, etc.
Meals included. **$$$**
Pine Ridge Lodge
17 Miles, Mountain Pine Ridge
Forest Reserve
Tel: 824-3180
www.pineridgelodge.com
More modest establishment of
Belizean-owned cabins near
Thousand Foot Falls (good
restaurant, a popular stop-off for
day-trip visitors). Hiking, swimming
and nature trails, etc. **$$**

STANN CREEK DISTRICT

Dangriga
Pelican Beach Resort
PO Box 2, Dangriga
Tel: 522-2044
Fax: 522-2570

The following price categories
indicate the cost of a double
room. Prices increase during high
season (November–March).
$$$: BZ$160–$400
$$: BZ$60–$160
$: under BZS$60

www.pelicanbeachbelize.com
Very pleasant and efficiently run
hotel just outside Dangriga. Breezy
rooms facing out to sea with private
bath. A great base for visiting the
southern cayes. Tours can be taken
from here to the Cockscomb Basin
Wildlife Sanctuary, Gales Point and
other local points of interest
including the town itself. Visits can
also be arranged to the
Smithsonian Research Center on
Carrie Bow Caye. **$$$**
Chaleanor Hotel
35 Magoon Street
PO Box 164, Dangriga
Tel: 522-2587
Fax: 522-3038
e-mail: chaleanor@btl.net
A fairly large hotel for Dangriga,
featuring good-sized rooms with
private bathrooms in the main
building, and some budget rooms
with shared bathrooms in a wooden
building next door. **$$**

Hopkins
This famously friendly Garifuna
village just down the coast from
Dangriga is just waking up to
tourism and has a few modest,
family-run guesthouses and hotels.
Seagull's Nest Guesthouse (tel:
523-7015). There are a couple of
good seafront bar/restaurants built
on stilts on the shore. The locals'
favorite is the **Lugudi** bar, two
blocks in from the seafront, where
the reggae and Punta Rock
pounding out from giant floor
speakers will give your eardrums a
good blasting.
Jaguar Reef Lodge
One mile south of Hopkins Village
Tel: 520-7040; 800-289 5756 (US
toll free).
e-mail:jaguarreef@starband.net
www.jaguarreef.com

Set on a 7-mile (11-km) white sand
beach, this luxury resort offers
accommodation in 14 immaculately
appointed thatch-roofed cabañas
and two suites, decorated with
Guatemalan weavings and local
handicrafts, all set in beautifully
maintained grounds with a small
pool. Good meals, cozy bar with
nightly wildlife video programs, and
well-stocked souvenir shop. Jaguar
Reef also offers diving trips and
instruction, sea kayaks and bikes.
Tours to the Cockscomb Basin
Wildlife Sanctuary and other local
sites. Fishing and snorkeling. **$$$**
Hopkins Inn
PO Box 121, Dangriga
Tel/fax: 523-7013
www.hopkinsinn.com
Four whitewashed private cabins
with fridge and coffee maker, right
on the beach south of the center.
The owners offer great tours to the
cayes and the room rates include
continental breakfast. **$$**
Mama Noots Resort
Tel/fax: 422-3666
e-mail: mamanoots@lincsat.com
www.mamanoots.bz
A few miles inland from Hopkins the
eco-resort is located in a forest
clearing beneath Bocawina
Mountain. All rooms have en-suite
hot water showers and balconies
with hammocks. The resort is within
walking distance of the Mayflower
ruins and trails lead through the
forest to spectacular waterfalls.
Meals are good and most of the
vegetables arc organically grown in
the garden. **$$$**
Tipple Tree Beya
Tel: 520-7006
e-mail: tipple@btl.net
Comfortable rooms in a neat
wooden building on the beach at
the southern end of the village,
some with en-suite bathroom. The
English owner is helpful and
knowledgeable about tours and has
a house for rent. **$–$$**

Placencia
Diannis Guest House
Tel: 523-3159
Fax: 523-3337
e-mail: diannisbelize@yahoo.com
A two-storey hotel on the beach at

the southern end of the village. Clean rooms with fans, private bath and coffee-making facilities. Friendly service, a breezy veranda with hammocks, internet access and kayaks for rent. Good value. **$$**

Inn at Robert's Grove
Seine Bight
Tel: 523-3565
Fax: 523-3567
Tel: 800-565 9757 (toll free in US)
www.robertsgrove.com
A luxurious, colonial-style hotel right on the shore five minutes' drive north of Placencia's airstrip. Large and beautifully furnished rooms and suites, some with private veranda. Excellent restaurant, bar and pool, with poolside bar. Complete range of resort facilities available: tennis, kayaks, dinghies (boathouse across the road by the lagoon for paddling around the mangroves), and bicycles. Local excursions including day-trips for snorkeling out on the cayes and to Monkey River. They also run the **Ranguana Reef Resort**, three rustic cabañas on Ranguana Caye, 18 miles (29 km) offshore. **$$$**

Kitty's Place
Placencia
Tel: 523-3227
Fax: 523-2320
www.kittysplace.com
Laid-back beachfront units just to the south of the airstrip, popular with ex-pats for long stays (variety of cabañas, large rooms and fully equipped apartments and bungalows). Good food in the upstairs restaurant is accompanied by jazz and blues on the music system. Bicycles available for the short ride into town. Well-stocked gift shop and a wide range of activities organized. **$$–$$$**

Luba Hati
Seine Bight
PO Box 1997, Belize City
Tel: 523-3402
Fax: 523-3403
www.lubahati.com
Extremely tasteful resort about five minutes' drive north of Placencia's airstrip. Mediterranean-style main building and variety of cabañas, each individually decorated with handicrafts from around the world.

Excellent restaurant, roof terrace, hammocks on the pier, massage and sauna in the beach house, and wide range of local activities out to the cayes and into the interior. **$$$**

Maya Breeze Inn
Maya Beach
Placencia
Tel/fax: 523-8012
www.mayabreezeinn.com
A few miles north of Placencia village, it has magnificent beaches and elegant accommodation. The four beautiful, brightly-painted wooden cabins provides a secluded getaway. Each cabin has a small kitchen and private deck. Rates include a continental breakfast and use of kayaks and bikes. **$$$**

Price Guide

The following price categories indicate the cost of a double room. Prices increase during high season (November–March).
$$$: BZ$160–$400
$$: BZ$60–$160
$: under BZS$60

Miller's Landing Resort
Tel: 614-7576
Fax: 523-3011
www.millerslanding.net
Rustic and laid-back small resort just down the beach from the Inn at Robert's Grove. Private cabins and rooms with fan in wooden building, airy bar and great restaurant, pool and hammocks in a shady garden. Offers tours to Cockscomb Basin, Mayflower Maya ruins and birding up the Monkey River. Visitors can also enjoy diving, sailing, and snorkeling trips. **$$**

Pickled Parrot Cabañas
Placencia Village
Tel: 606-7336
e-mail: pickledparrotbz@yahoo.com
Two hardwood cabañas in a tropical garden in the heart of Placencia village. Double rooms with hot shower, fan and fridge. Porch with hammock. The restaurant is the best in the village. **$$**

Ranguana Lodge
Placencia
Tel/fax: 523-3112

www.ranguanabelize.com
Five cabañas on the water's edge at the north end of town, all with fridge and free coffee-making facilities, including three with sea views. **$$$**

Rum Point Inn
Tel: 523-3239
Fax: 523-3240
Tel: 888-235 4031 (US toll free)
www.rumpoint.com
A luxury complex, facing the sea about 2 miles (3.5 km) north of Placencia township, including five uniquely designed cabañas. Individual stained-glass patterns set into the rounded, whitewashed concrete walls allow for delicate light patterns, creating a soothing environment. Very good dining and small library in an attractive communal house facing out towards the sea, swimming pool and gardens. Diving and snorkeling trips and tours of inland attractions. **$$$**

Sea Spray Hotel
Tel/fax: 523-3148
e-mail: seaspray@btl.net
www.seasprayhotel.com
The oldest hotel in Placencia, in the centre of the village. The renovated hotel has a range of beach-front rooms with private bath, and offers internet access in its beach-side restaurant. **$$**

South Water Caye

Blue Marlin Lodge
PO Box 21, Dangriga
Tel: 522-2243
Fax: 522-2296
Tel: (US toll free) 800-798 1558 or 305-351 9688
www.bluemarlinlodge.com
Real diving resort atmosphere on this pristine caye about 10 miles (16 km) southeast of Dangriga. Variety of rooms and cabañas, with all luxury comforts. Certification course available. Also billiards, windsurfing and more. Hot water showers, fans, "over-water" dining. Diving packages available. **$$$**

Pelican Inn; Osprey's Inn; Frangipani House
c/o The Pelican Beach Resort
PO Box 14, Dangriga
Tel: 522-2044
Fax: 522-2570

e-mail: pelicanbeach@btl.net
A choice of basic but comfortable
dormitories, apartments or
separate wooden vacation houses
in an idyllic spot at the southern
end of the caye, all run by the
Pelican Beach Resort in Dangriga.
Visits available to nearby Carrie
Bow Caye for the Smithsonian
Research Center, as well as
snorkeling trips and other reef
excursions. **$$$**

Glover's Reef
Glover's Atoll Resort
PO Box 563
Belize City
Tel: 520-5016
e-mail: glovers@btl.net
www.glovers.com.bz
Bring your own food, or catch it.
Rustic cabins, well-water, outhouse,
gravity shower, etc. Inexpensive
deals including the boat trip to this
private island are available. **$**

Tobacco Caye
Tobacco Caye Lodge
PO Box 213, Belize City
Tel: 520-5033 or 227-6247
www.tclodgebelize.com
The best accommodation on the
caye – comfortable rooms in
modern wooden houses with a
deck. The Lodge goes right across
the caye from the reef to the
lagoon, a perfect place for viewing
sunrise and sunset. Meals included
in room rates and there's a good
beach bar. **$$$**
In addition, there is a range of
modest accommodation, usually
run by the families of local
fishermen, including **Lana's on the
Reef** (tel: 522-2571); **Ocean's Edge**
(tel: 614-9633; US tel: 281-894
4295, toll free: 800-967 8184).

TOLEDO DISTRICT

Punta Gorda
El Pescador
Three miles from Punta Gorda, off
the Southern Highway
Tel: 722-0050
e-mail: info@elpescadorpg.com
www.elpescadorpg.com
Spacious wooden cabins each with

a deck overlooking beautifully
landscaped grounds. The hilltop
location offers breathtaking views
over the Rio Grande Valley, Paynes
Creek National Park and the ridges
of the Maya Mountains. Originally
conceived as a fishing lodge,
guests report record catches of
permit, tarpon, snook and bonefish,
El Pescador is also gaining a
reputation for wildlife tours. The
best resort in Toledo. **$$$**
Nature's Way Guest House
65 Front Street
PO Box 75, Punta Gorda
Tel: 702-2119
Dormitory and private rooms in a
wooden house overlooking the sea
at the southern end of town. An
established favorite, this is the best
place to learn about Toledo's
environment. Great breakfasts (no
other meals) are served in the tiny,
flower-filled garden. **$**
Sea Front Inn
PO Box 20, Punta Gorda
Tel: 722-2300
Fax: 722-2682
e-mail: seafrontinn@btl.net
www.seafrontinn.com
Aptly named three-story modern
hotel to the north end of town, run
by very friendly US expats. The Sea
Front Inn is the best hotel in Punta
Gorda, with comfortably and simply
furnished rooms with TV, fan and air
conditioning. Also has a new annex
with several apartments for long-
stay guests. Wonderful upstairs
dining room/lounge catches the
cool sea breezes. Excellent
breakfasts and self-service
"honesty" bar. Very popular with fly-
fishing groups, land and sea tours
organized through the tour operator
Wild Encounters. Book ahead in
high season. **$$**
St. Charles Inn
23 King Street
Tel/fax: 722-2149
Family-run budget accommodation
with comfortable, well-furnished
rooms in a wooden building. All
rooms have a TV, en-suite bath and
a balcony. Only a block from the
center of town. **$**
Toledo Ecotourism Association
Punta Gorda
Tel/fax: 722-2531

e-mail: btbtol@btl.net
Innovative project designed to open
up village homes and culture to
tourists and help fund the
preservation of traditional Maya life.
Guests stay at the Village Guest
House (**$**), clean and comfortable
and lit by kerosene lamps. They see
local farms, forests, rivers and
waterfalls, and join village families
for meals. Contributions to
conservation, village health and
education programs are welcome.
There is also the chance to watch
or help in the cocoa harvesting.
Tranquility Lodge
Southern Highway/San Felipe Road
Jacintoville
PO Box 118, Punta Gorda
No phone at present
e-mail: mspennyl@yahoo.com
This new hotel, set in spacious,
orchid-filled gardens, is just off the
Southern Highway, 7 miles (11 km)
from the sea at Punta Gorda. It's
convenient for visiting the Maya
villages and ruins of Toledo and the
southern cayes of Belize. The air-
conditioned rooms are on the
ground floor of an elegant thatched
building; above is a restaurant with
all-round screens, allowing
panoramic views. It's very popular
with bird watchers – 200 species of
bird have been seen in the grounds
– and a rock-lined creek serves as
a natural swimming pool. **$$**
The Lodge at Big Falls
Big Falls village, Southern Highway
Tel: 722-2878
email: info@thelodgeatbigfalls.com
www.thelodgeatbigfalls.com
Spacious, very comfortable
thatched cabañas with tiled floors
and a wooden deck with
hammocks. The lodge is set in
beautifully landscaped grounds on a
bend of the Río Grande, just a few
miles/km south of Nim Li Punit
Maya site. Great birdwatching along
riverbank trails and a good
restaurant. **$$$**

Blue Creek
Blue Creek Rainforest Lodge
Blue Creek village
Tel: 722-0013 (in Punta Gorda)
c/o International Zoological
Expeditions

Tel: 800-548-5843 (toll free in US)
www.ize2belize.com
Simple but comfortable wooden
cabins on the bank of Blue Creek,
surrounded by trees in a 200-acre
(80-hectare) private reserve.
Upstream is the impressive Hokeb
Ha Cave. The Lodge is often
occupied by student groups but
other visitors can stay here when
it's not busy. **$$$**

San Pedro Columbia
**Fallen Stones Butterfly Ranch and
Jungle Lodge**
PO Box 23, Punta Gorda
Tel/fax 722-2167
A ranch on a ridge-top overlooking
the Columbia River Forest Reserve,
about 40 minutes by road from
Punta Gorda, beyond the ruins of
Lubaantun. Accommodation is in
comfortable wooden cabins, with
private shower and an observation
deck. The property has abundant
wildlife, particularly birds and a visit
to the butterfly ranch (which ships
pupae of the gorgeous Blue Morpho
to butterfly houses in Europe) is
fascinating. **$$$**

TIKAL NATIONAL PARK (GUATEMALA)

Jungle Lodge
Tel: (00) 502-476 8775 (in
Guatemala City)
Fax: (00) 502-476 0294
Comfortable, spacious bungalows
in well-maintained grounds and a
pool. There are also some very
good budget rooms with shared
bathrooms. **$$-$$$**
Jaguar Inn
Tel: (00) 502-926 0002
Fax: (00) 502-926 2413
www.jaguartikal.com
Nine attractive bungalows with
porches. Also has inexpensive
camping and hammock rental. **$-$$**
Tikal Inn
Tel: (00) 502-926 1917
Fax: (00) 502-926 0065
e-mail: hoteltikalinn@itelgua.com
Thatched bungalows around the
beautiful pool or rooms in the main
buildings. The best-value hotel of
the three in the park. **$$**

Eating Out

What to Eat

Belize's national dish may be rice
and beans, but that doesn't mean
that local cuisine stops there. The
tropical reef fish, lobster and conch,
available in season on the cayes
and transported across Belize, are
luxurious ingredients for a national
cuisine. (Note that lobster is out-of-
season from mid-February to mid-
June and conch should not be
eaten during the out-of-season
months of July, August and
September.) Belize can also offer
an exotic range of tropical fruits,
especially inland. Try a "sour-sap"
milkshake for a start, then ask for
whatever other bizarre produce is
the local favorite.

The latest jungle resorts offer
gourmet dining using local meats
such as brocket deer, usually with a
range of vegetarian dishes (beyond
rice and beans, that is). The
Garifuna Belizeans of the south
coast enjoy their traditional *cassava*
or coconut bread while the creoles
make fry jacks or Johnny cakes.

All Belizeans, however, are loyal to
the national brew – Belikin beer –
with the cheaper domestic version
more highly regarded than the export
label. Remember that tap water
should not be drunk on Caye Caulker
or outside main towns in the south.

Many tourists find themselves
eating regularly at the resorts,

Price Guide

The following price categories
indicate the cost of a meal for
one without drinks:
$$$: BZ$40–100
$$: BZ$20–$40
$: under BZ$20

either out of convenience or
because meals are included in their
package deal. It is also the case
that many of the resort hotels are
located in isolated spots, far from
the nearest town, only a few of
which have developed enough of an
infrastrucure for tourism to support
independent restaurants. Even so,
try to experience some of the
smaller Belizean restaurants
outside of the resort areas, many of
which are simple roadside or
seafront shacks. This is a good way
to meet some Belizeans and begin
to appreciate their friendliness. The
following choices include some to
tempt you away from the hotel
complex.

Where to Eat

BELIZE CITY

Big Daddy's Diner
2nd Floor
Commercial Center
Market Square
Tel: 227-0932
Cafeteria offering standard rice and
beans and other specialties. Great
view of the harbor from the upper
deck. It serves a Belizean breakfast
(fry jacks and beans) as well as
lunch and take-out. Very popular
with lunch time workers, so get
there after the rush. **$**
Chef Bob's Grill
164 Newtown Barrack Road
Tel: 223-6908
Easier to get to by car, since it's a
little out of the way. The Grill is a
fairly pricey establishment popular
with locals for dinner or special
occasions. There is great variety on
the menu. Try the cold shrimp
salad Jamaican-style. **$$$**
Harbour View Restaurant
Fort Street
Tel: 223-6420
One of the finest restaurants in the
city, with sweeping views of the
historic buildings across the
harbour mouth. Carefully prepared,
delicious food in a blend of East
and West – try the five-course
tasting menu on Tuesday. Live
music some evenings. **$$**

Jambel Jerk Pit
2B King Street
Tel: 227-6080
Restaurant serving the same spicy blend of Jamaican and Belizean dishes – including of course jerked chicken and fish — as the long-established Jambel Jerk Pit in San Pedro. Here you can dine either indoors or in a shady outdoor patio adorned with palms. Always a good daily special. **$**

Macy's Cafe
18 Bishop Street
Tel: 227-3419
A lunch time hive for Belizean business people enjoying what may be the best creole cooking in the city. The food is cheap and plentiful – try the fish balls. **$**

Pepper's Pizza
4 St Thomas Street
King's Park
Tel: 223-5001
Jamaican and Belizean-owned, but the pizza holds its own against those of North American chains. It also offers good lunch time specials (try the buffalo wings and twisty bread). Free delivery with any order over BZ$10. **$**

Wet Lizard
On the waterfront, where North Park Street meets the sea. Delicious seafood and pasta served on brightly painted tables in wooden building overlooking the harbour mouth. There's a good-value daily special and great mixed drinks. Closed Sun and Mon **$$**

AMBERGRIS CAYE/ SAN PEDRO

The caye's main hotels all have their own restaurants. Any stroll along the beachfront or sandy streets of San Pedro takes you past an endless string of blackboards advertising the daily specials – the competition is high. New places are opening (and closing) every week, mostly quite decent, but the following are known successes:

Capricorn
On the beach, 3 miles (5 km) north of town
Tel: 226-2809

Some of the very best gourmet dining on the island – and the boat ride up here is part of the enjoyment. A wonderful variety of imaginative dishes from around the world, with an emphasis on tasty appetizers with plenty of garlic and fantastic seafood entrees. Booking advised for dinner. Capricorn also offers accommodation. **$$$**

Celi's Restaurant
adjacent to Holiday Hotel
Tel: 226-2014
Daily fish specials are very good and desserts are excellent. **$$**

Elvi's Kitchen
Pescador Drive
Tel: 226-2176
Large thatched roof enclosure supported by a growing tree, this is a trendy place to hang after sundown. Food ranges from club sandwiches and burgers to fish and lobster. **$$**

Ramón's Village
on the Beach
San Pedro
Tel: 226-2071
Serving international-style dishes, this restaurant can also be recommended to prepare the fish you caught that afternoon. **$$**

CAYE CAULKER

Caye Caulker has an amazing range of good-value, informal restaurants. Your best bet is to ask at your hotel for their favorite places.

Coco Plum Garden
Middle Street (before the airstrip).
Tel: 226-0226
Wonderful café and deli in delightful, shady gardens. Well worth the walk to get here. Breakfast, pizza, sandwiches and cakes. Open at 7am; closed Friday and Saturday.

Jolly Roger
On the main street, south of the center.
The best seafood barbecue on the island. Tasty fish and lobster cooked over hot coals by the very jolly Roger Martinez.

Rasta Pasta
Front Street, (north of the center). Fantastic pasta and seafood, cooked with home-blended herbs and spices, served at tables on the sand. The best restaurant on the island and extremely popular. The chef, Marylin, originally from New York, will cook great kosher meals on request.

COROZAL

Hokol Kin Restaurant
4th Avenue and 3rd Street
Tel: 422-3329
Guest House dining room but welcomes drop-ins. Standard rice and beans dishes, hamburgers and sandwiches.

PLACENCIA

Most Placencia eateries are open from 8am–2pm and 7–11pm.

BJ's Restaurant
on the main road
Tel: 523-3108/3131
A popular place serving local dishes, specializing in seafood (try the conch fritters) and juices. **$$**

The Galley
It's across the playing field (ask anyone for directions). May serve the best sour-sap milkshake in Belize. You might wait up to 45 minutes for it, but the result is pure heaven. Other lovingly made cakes and desserts on display. **$**

Pickled Parrot Bar and Grill
Toward the south end, signed from the road and sidewalk
Tel: 523-3330
A friendly meeting-place, serving the best food in the village under a thatched roof. Renowned for its pizza, there's also great seafood and Belizean and Mexican dishes and delicious blended fruit drinks with or without alcohol. **$$**

The best choices among the resort restaurants are **Kitty's Place**, which does a good price three-course set meal, **Luba Hati**, for excellent Mediterranean dishes, the **Inn at Robert's Grove**, for great steaks and seafood, and **Rum Point Inn,** which has a romantic open-sided dining room, serving elaborate meals (non-residents should book ahead). See the *Where to Stay* section, above, for these resorts' contact details.

BELMOPAN AND SAN IGNACIO

Bull Frog Inn
23 Half Moon Avenue
Belmopan
Tel: 822-2111
Fax: 822-3155
One of the best restaurants in Belmopan. **$$$**
Café Sol
25 West Street, San Ignacio
Good coffee, soup, sandwiches and desserts. Eat inside the café decorated with Guatemalan textiles, or outside in the quiet garden. Closed Mondays. **$**
Eva's Bar and Restaurant
22 Burns Avenue, San Ignacio
Tel: 824-2267
This was the first internet café in Belize; it also doubles as a gift shop and tour desk. Eva's Bar is a great meeting place. **$**

Price Guide

The following price categories indicate the cost of a meal for one without drinks:
$$$: BZ$40–100
$$: BZ$20–$40
$: under BZ$20

Hannah's
5 Burns Avenue
San Ignacio
Tel: 824-3014
A tiny restaurant in a smart wooden cabin but the food is so good that you sometimes have to wait for a table. A delicious range of international dishes from Belizean

to Burmese, using fresh ingredients grown on the owner's farm. Large portions and a good wine list. **$**
Martha's Restaurant
10 West Street, San Ignacio
Tel: 824-3647
Easily the best restaurant in the town center, with service to match. Martha's is famous for pizza but you can enjoy great breakfasts, Belizean specialities, pasta and steaks, and there's always a daily special. The outdoor patio – candlelit at night – is a popular place for dinner. **$$**

TOLEDO DISTRICT

Punta Gorda

Earth Runnin's Cafe and Bukut Bar
Middle Street, near North Street
Tel: 722-2007
Small, friendly restaurant and internet cafe serving good breakfasts with real coffee. Lunch and dinner menus changing daily according to what's available – but there's always good seafood. **$**
El Café
Corner of Main and North streets
Tel: 702-2093
Friendly place serving tasty Belizean dishes at good value prices. Great coffee and organic orange juice to accompany the earliest breakfast in town. Open from 6am. **$**
Grace's Restaurant
19 Main Street
Tel: 702-2414
Popular, clean restaurant serving inexpensive Belizean food. Conveniently located in the center of town; you can change money here and the buses stop right outside. **$**
Titanic Restaurant
Front Street, above the market.
Tel: 722-0169
This open-air restaurant is worth a visit not just to enjoy the views across the sea to the mountains of Guatemala and Honduras, but also because it serves great Belizean and American food. Has the only all-morning happy hour in the country. Open 6am to 11pm.

Attractions

Culture and Festivals

Belizeans are a culturally diverse bunch, but there is not a lot to do in the way of formal musical concerts, performances or the like. The main way of getting to understand creole culture is by meeting people informally in bars, restaurants and on the beach; even such creole celebrations as St. Georges Caye Day every September offers little more to the outsider than a chance to get drunk with everyone else.

Spanish-speaking Belizeans in the north and west have a few more Hispanic rituals and holidays, although they are based around the church and family, as in the rest of Latin America. Mexican-style fiestas are held in Corozal at Carnival time (the period before Lent begins, a shifting date every year), Colombus Day and Christmas, when colorful *posadas* re-enact Mary and Joseph's search for shelter.

The Garifuna population in Southern Belize feel very strongly about their heritage and they come together with great enthusiasm from November 19 to the end of the year in celebration of the anniversary of their ancestors' arrival in Dangriga in 1823. If you are visiting Dangriga at this time you might see masked Joncunu dancers, drumming and impromptu music concerts or hear the conch shells blown on Christmas Eve (although, again, the main activity at these times is drinking).

There are pockets of Mennonite communities in the north Cayo District, each following tradition to varying degrees (some refuse to use machines more developed than horse-drawn buggies, others use full-scale harvesters). While most tourists don't feel inclined to approach the Mennonites, apart from stealing a photograph (which Mennonites object to very strongly), it is interesting to talk to a family and find out how they live. Since it guided tours are inappropriate, you must visit by private transport.

Archeological Sites

For most tourists, the prime cultural attraction in Belize is its wealth of Maya archeological sites (there are an estimated 600 sites in the jungle, the highest concentration in Central America, and four important Maya towns were discovered in 1993 in the Maya Mountains).

For information about Maya archeological sites or permission to visit certain sites, contact: **Belize Department of Archeology**, Belmopan. Tel: 822-2106.

Wildlife Reserves

Belize is justly proud and protective of a variety of mainland ecosystems. Bridging the North and South American continents, Belize has a unique mixture of wildlife, and Central America's best success rate in creating reserves for endangered species. Most popular among tourists are the **Community Baboon Sanctuary** at Bermudian Landing, which protects a healthy population of black howler monkeys, and **Cockscomb Basin Wildlife Reserve**, the world's first devoted to the jaguar. The **Belize Zoo** is home to over 100 species of native Belizean animals, living in natural conditions, including Baird's tapir, Belize's national animal.

Many of the reserves are a bird-watcher's paradise. Most famous are the scarlet macaw, great curassow, keel-billed toucan, collared araçari and king vulture. Entomologists and lepidopterists also flock to Belize, while 4,000 species of plant, including over 250 types of orchid, attract botanists and flora-lovers.

Ecotourism

Belize is a world leader in environmentally conscious tourism strategies. Conservation groups and the government have launched a number of ecotourism projects to help fund conservation initiatives. The **Belize Audubon Society** is a non-governmental environmental organization, set up in 1969 as a branch of the Florida Audubon Society, and independent since 1973. The BAS manages a growing clutch of protected areas around the country, including the **Half Moon Caye Natural Monument**, the **Shipstern Nature Reserve** and the **Crooked Tree Wildlife Sanctuary**. Some of their parks are only accessible to serious researchers, but most are open to the general public and the BAS also operates volunteer work programs and a membership scheme. Contact: Belize Audubon Society, PO Box 1001, 12 Fort St, Belize City. Tel: 223-5004, fax: 223-4985, www.belizeaudubon.org.

The **Programme for Belize** (PFB) was set up in 1988 and runs the **Río Bravo Conservation Area**, a huge spread of former logging land in the remote northwestern corner of Orange Walk District, forming a tri-national park with the Calakmul Biosphere Reserve in Mexico and the Maya Biosphere Reserve in Guatemala (see page 203 for details of Río Bravo's flora and fauna). To visit Río Bravo, contact PFB, 1 Eyre St, PO Box 749, Belize City. Tel: 227-5616; www.pfbelize.org. In the UK: World Land Trust, PO Box 99, Saxmundham, Suffolk, IP17 2BR. Tel 01986-874222. e-mail: worldlandtrust@btinternet.com. In the US: Massachusetts Audubon Society, 208 Great South Road, Lincoln, MA 01773. Tel: 617-259 9500.

Río Bravo Research Station
This venture, run by the PFB (see address above) invites travelers to visit the Río Bravo Conservation Area to increase funding for and provide information about rainforest preservation. Accommodations are in a dormitory or spacious cabaña,

in the heart of the rainforest at La Milpa and Hill Bank field stations. Talks given by experts and demonstrations of jungle conservation and chicle production. Well-organized trails, notably to the famous Maya La Milpa site. Good library and shop, run by friendly hosts. At BZ\$150–200 per person per night, it's not cheap, but the cost includes three meals a day and a couple of excursions or lectures. Day trips to La Milpa, including a visit to the ruins, are available for BZ\$40, but you must arrange your own transportation, as there is no public service.

Conservation Corridors
Tel: 020-8964 5325.
UK-based agency that specialises in finding work placements for people on conservation projects in Belize.

Smithsonian Institute
Arts and Industries Building 1163 Washington DC 20560–0402
Fax: 202-357 2116;
e-mail: education@soe.si.edu.
Operates a marine research station on Carrie Bow Caye, part of Southwater Caye, off Dangriga; primarily a base for scientists, but you can visit by prior arrangement through the Pelican Beach Resort in Dangriga (see page 323).

Siwa-Ban Foundation (SBF)
contact Ellen McRae,
PO Box 47, Caye Caulker
Tel: 226-0178
e-mail: sbf@btl.net.
The foundation lobbied to establish the Caye Caulker Marine Reserve in 1998, covering an area at the northern tip of the caye and part of the nearby reef.

Toledo Ecotourism Association
Punta Gorda
Tel: 722-2096
Fax: 722-2199.
e-mail: ttea@btl.net
Revenue from the association's guesthouse program in the Maya Mountains of Toledo District is directed back into local villages.

Belize Foundation for Research and Environmental Education (BFREE)
Tel: 614-3896
e-mail: bfree@btl.net
A conservation organization, which has a research station in Bladen.

Outdoor Activities

Specialist Operators

Most major hotels and resorts have their own tour desk, which provides day tours to the local attractions. There are numerous tour operators in the United States, Canada and the United Kingdom offering good packages deals to Belize, including sports facilities and instruction. The following operators can organize coastal activities (diving, fishing, sailing), inland activities (horseback riding, trekking, bird-watching, canoeing, mountain biking) as well trips to wildlife reserves and archeological sites.

Diving

Amigos Belize
Tel: 606-6416
www.amigosbelize.com
Reasonably-priced diving and snorkeling packages to Ropewalk Caye, on the windward southeastern side of Turneffe Island Atoll. Snorkeling trips from Belize City, with manatee and dolphin watching on the way out and back.

Amigos Del Mar
San Pedro, Ambergris Caye
Tel: 226-2706
Fax: 226-2648
www.amigosdive.com
Very experienced diver operators, offering full PADI instruction and trips to the reef and outer atolls.

Blue Hole Dive Center
San Pedro, Ambergris Caye
Tel: 226-2982
www.bluedive.com
Highly recommended, offering good-value packages with instruction and trips to the Blue Hole on Lighthouse Reef. Underwater camera and video rental available.

Frenchies Diving Services
Caye Caulker
Tel: 226-0234
e-mail: frenchies@btl.net
This is *the* dive company on Caye Caulker. It offers trips to Hol Chan and the Blue Hole, as well as to locations on the reef around Caye Caulker.

Paradise Down
Front Street, Caye Caulker
Tel: 226-2347
www.paradisedown.com
Full-service dive operation, with fast boats to whisk you to the Blue Hole. Very good, careful and safe instruction.

Sea Horse Dive Shop
Placencia
Tel: 523-3166
www.belizescuba.com
The owner, Brian Young, is a former lobster fisherman who now specializes in trips to see whale sharks and other points of interest in southern Belize. Allow two weeks in advance to book a whale shark trip and allow such a trip to take a full day.

Sea Sports Belize
Princess Marina
Belize City
Tel: 223-5505
www.seasportsbelize.com
This is the only full service dive shop in Belize City. It offers trips to nearby spots as well as charter services to outer cayes and atolls.

Second Nature Divers
PO Box 91, Sittee River Village
Stann Creek
Tel: 523-7038
www.belizediversity.com
Best dive operators in this region, offering full PADI instruction and equipment rental. Arranges trips to the cayes off Dangriga and to Glover's Reef Marine Reserve.

Tobacco Caye Diving
Tobacco Caye
PO Box 161, Dangriga
Tel: 614 6699
www.tobaccocayediving.com
Located on Tobacco Caye, and so right on the reef. Full-service diving and instruction, offering trips to all three of Belize's atolls.

Fishing

Bobby's Operation
12 Main Street
Punta Gorda
Tel: 722-2135
Long-standing, experienced sports fisherman offers recreational fishing trips and boat excursions.

Eloy Cuevas Guiding,
Monkey River village, near Placencia
Tel: 523-2014
Friendly and experienced fly and sport fishing guide, available for private charters.

Tide Tours
Toledo
Tel: 722-2129
e-mail: info@tidetours.org
www.tidetours.org
Catch and release fly fishing.

Turneffe Flats
Blackbird Caye
Turneffe Islands
PO Box 1676, Belize City
Tel/fax: 220-4046
www.tflats.com
Fishing holiday packages based at a remote beach lodge on Turneffe Atoll.

Cruises and Sailing

American Canadian Caribbean Line
PO Box 368, Warren
Rhode Island, RI 02885
Tel: 800-556 7450/401-247 0955
Fax: 401-247 2350
www.accl-smallships.com
Twelve-day trips departing from Radisson Fort George Hotel dock including cayes and Maya ruins.

Heritage Navigation
San Pedro
Tel: 226-2394
The island trading vessel *Winnie Estelle* goes on one-day charters through the cayes.

The Moorings
19345 US Highway 19 North
Clearwater, Florida 33759
Tel: 888-952 8420
www.moorings.com
Crewed or bareboat 7-day catamaran trips in the southern cayes.

Sailing Fantasy
Ramon's Reef Resort,
San Pedro
Tel: 226-2439.
Catamaran trips and rental.

Boat Charters

Caye Caulker Water Taxi Association
Tel: 226-0992
Members of this Association have boats available for charter, as well as scheduled services between Belize City, Caye Caulker and San Pedro.

Chocolate
General Delivery Caye Caulker
Tel: 226-0151
e-mail:chocolate@btl.net
Water taxi to Caye Caulker, San Pedro and charter services to other cayes. One of the best guides for manatee watching and a vocal advocate of the need to protect species and their habitat.

Requena's Boat Service
Punta Gorda
Tel: 722-2070
e-mail: watertaxi@btl.net
Boat charters, as well as services to Puerto Barrios, Guatemala.

Sea Kayaking, River and Caving Trips

Caves Branch Jungle Lodge
PO Box 356, Belmopan
Tel: 822-2800
www.cavesbranch.com
Highly rated experts offering caving expeditions up the Caves Branch River, Blue Hole National Park and St. Herman's Cave; trips on the Sibun River. Superb mountain bikes and private trails to ride them on.

Clarissa Falls Resort
off the Benque road, down a track just before the turning to Chaa Creek, near San Ignacio
Tel: 824-3916
E-mail: clarissafalls@btl.net
Rafting and kayaking on Belize's Mopan River.

Island Expeditions Co.
368–916 W. Broadway Avenue,
Vancouver, BC
Canada V5Z 1K7
Tel: 604-452 3212
Fax: 604-452 3433
Toll-free: 1-800 667 1630
www.islandexpeditions.com
Four to 21-day trips, with good food.

Mayawalk Tours
19 Burns Avenue, San Ignacio
Tel: 824-3070
Tel: (US toll-free) 866-538 6594
www.mayawalk.com
Specialized cave, rappelling and mountain-biking trips in the Cayo jungle. Some of the best adventure in Belize and highly recommended for the astounding Actun Tunichil Muknal Cave tour.

Slickrock Adventures Inc.
PO Box 1400
Moab
Utah 84532
Tel: 800-390 5715
Fax: 435-259 6996
e-mail: slickrock@slickrock.com
www.slickrock.com
Thatched cabins on Glovers Atoll, 35 miles (56 km) offshore. Sea kayak and river adventures.

Horseback Riding

Banana Bank Lodge
47 miles Western Highway, just outside Belmopan
Tel: 820-2020
www.bananabank.com
Now Belize's largest equestrian center, with 60 well-trained horses. Picnic facilities are also available, plus swimming in the river.

Easy Rider
At Arts and Crafts, Burns Avenue
San Ignacio
Tel: 824-3734
e-mail easyrider@btl.net
Great value tours through the Cayo countryside on well cared for horses. Guests are picked up in town and your horse will be selected to match your ability.

Mountain Equestrian Trails
Mile 8
Mountain Pine Ridge Road
Central Farm
Cayo District
Tel: 820-4041
US reservations tel: 800-838 3918
www.metbelize.com
Riding expeditions for the adventurous, tours of up to four days. Also "Turf & Surf" expeditions. Reservations are advisable in high season.

Wildlife/Archeology

Cayo Adventure Tours,
PO Box 88, Santa Elena
Cayo District.
Tel: 824-3246
www.cayoadventure.com
Excellent, expertly led customized tours to Maya ruins, rivers and rainforests.

Far Horizons
PO Box 91900
Albuquerque NM 87199
Tel: 800-552 4575/ 505-343 9400
www.farhorizon.com
Archeologist-run cultural discovery tours and custom itineraries for individuals and groups.

International Expeditions
1 Environs Park, Helena,
Alabama, AL 35080.
Tel: 800-633 4734/205-428 1700
fax: 205-428 1714
e-mail: ietravel.com
Ten-day tours of Maya ruins with optional extensions to Copan in Honduras and the Barrier Reef.

Julio's Cultural and Jungle Tours
Maya Center Village.
Tel: 520-2020
e-mail: lsaqui@btl.net
For the Cockscomb Basin Wildlife Reserve and Victoria Peak, contact Julio Saqui.

Maya Guide Adventures
PO Box 485 Belmopan
Tel: 822-1425 or 600-3116
e-mail: marcos@mayaguide.bz
Superb rock-climbing, jungle treks and caving expeditions for the really adventurous traveler led by Marcos Cucul, a very experienced Kekchi Maya from southern Belize. Also multi-day expeditions crossing the Maya Mountains.

Maya Travel Services
PO Box 532, 42 Cleghorn Street
Belize City
Tel: 223-1623
www.mayatravelservices.com
The best travel planner in Belize.

Toadal Adventure
Placencia Village
Tel: 523-3207
Fax: 523-3334
www.toadaladventure.com
Dave Vernon is an excellent guide for sea-kayaking, mountain biking, natural history and archeology trips.

Nightlife

Bars and Dancing

Belize may not have the discos of Cancún, but this doesn't mean you can't find somewhere to dance or have a drink with friends.

Clubs in the city seem to open and close with alarming frequency. One long-standing exception is the **Bellevue Maya Tavern**, at 5 Southern Foreshore, and **Lindbergh's Landing**, an open-air hut on Newton Barracks Road (next to the grill) is popular with locals and tourists alike, which gets very lively late at night, even on weekdays. Any attempt at a complete list of recommendations here would be futile, however, so your best bet is to ask hotel staff, a restaurant waitress or a taxi driver where they go to party and you'll probably find the current hot spot.

The big hotels have a Friday evening happy hour, often with live music, where local people unwind. The best is at the Biltmore with live jazz at the poolside.

Most clubs play a variety of dance music, with American pop (usually somewhat dated) as popular as Caribbean Dance Hall, Soca and Latino Salsa. You almost always get a hefty serving of Punta Rock somewhere in the middle.

Live entertainment is popular and old 70s numbers seem to be especially common, as well as knock-offs of current Caribbean or Latin hits. If you are lucky, you might find a steel band, a group of Garifuna drummers, Mariachis, a marimba band (most likely in Cayo) or a good local dance band.

San Pedro is packed with bars in every resort (try the **Purple Parrot** at Ramón's) and all around the town – just walk along the dockside and pick one that seems lively. Many have different theme nights providing certain drinks for free, for example you can see the sharks being fed at the **Sharks' Bar**. **Fido's Courtyard** in town and the **Playador Hotel** (on the beach to the south of the town) offer happy hours and live music a couple of times a week. On Wednesday nights **Celi's** has a great beach barbecue, with a local band playing on the beach. Other places to try in San Pedro are **Barefoot Iguana**, (just past the Belize Yacht Club), **Big Daddy's Disco** (by a beach bar next to the park).

In smaller places like **Placencia**, the nightlife scene is unscheduled and irregular, yet something always seems to be happening somewhere. The **Bamboo Room**, at the Serenity Resort just to the north of the airstrip, offers live entertainment weekly, the **Pickled Parrot Bar & Grill**, at the Barracuda and Jaguar Inn, has good music and a lively crowd, while the **Nautical Inn**, up the coast at Seine Bight offers Garifuna drumming, and their own invention: coconut bowling, every Wednesday at 6pm.

In San Ignacio, **Cahal Pech Tavern**, in a giant hut above the town, is a popular place where you can dance to Punta Rock til dawn, and listen to some of the best bands in Belize. The **Blue Angel** Disco has a busy scene on weekend nights. You can drink and rock to Punta till daylight but may be wise to leave a little earlier as the place has a reputation for brawls. Don't even try to find a club in Belmopan – locals go all the way to San Ignacio or Belize City for entertainment. In Dangriga, it's the **Roundhouse** for Punta drumming until dawn, or Dance Hall music with the younger set. Punta Gorda has a few bars, but no club to speak of.

The Midnight Hour

If you're looking for a lively night-time atmosphere, don't go out too early – nothing gets going in some places (especially Belize City) until 11 pm or midnight.

Shopping

Shopping Areas

Unlike Guatemala and Mexico, Belize has not developed a souvenir industry or nurtured indian crafts. However, a couple of small operations around San Ignacio now teach old skills such as Maya pottery and slate carving. Leading the way are the **García sisters**, who run a museum and gift shop in San Antonio. They also sell jewellery made from ziricote (a hardwood) or the occasional mahogany carving.

Carver **David Magaña** runs a tiny shop in San José Succotz by the Guatemalan border. Ask in town for directions to his house. More stalls are being set up by hopeful Maya artists every month in the region around San Ignacio.

Many hotels near San Ignacio stock Guatemalan indian handicrafts, but they are much cheaper in Guatemala, if you are heading on a day trip to Tikal.

In Belize City, the upper level of the central marketplace houses a number of small souvenir shops and the National Handicraft Center is at 2 South Park Street in the Fort George area. It used to be hard to find quality souvenirs in Belize, but things are changing as local companies begin to package their products more attractively and artists get more tourist-market savvy.

Specialty items are always a good bet, with many visitors taking home habanero pepper sauce, cashew nuts, coconut rum, berry or cashew wine or Gallon Jug coffee. Local preserves (chutney and jam) made from mangos, bananas, papayas and other tropical fruits also make nice gifts. Herbal remedies or bush medicines are being sold by individual herbalists.

Woodcarvings of animals and fish or wooden bowls and cutting boards are available from gift shops or street-side artists. The better taxi drivers can take you to woodcarvers' workshops. This gives you the best selection including more abstract, artistic pieces and a chance to talk with the artist. Carvings generally travel well if carefully packed and need only the occasional rub with a little furniture oil if you're taking them to drier climates. If you like the look of several tropical hard and soft woods together, the finest furniture companies in the Cayo district make collapsible chairs and small folding tables that can be flattened to put on a plane, or shipped home. Caeser's gift shop, at Mile 60 Western Highway is best for such items. Garifuna baskets are also widely sold, ranging from huge hampers for linens to picnic baskets to smaller items. Vendors travel around the country at the end of the month selling on the streets, but some shops also stock the baskets.

Look out for the delicate baskets woven from the jipijapa plant fibers by Maya women, who also continue the traditions of their grandmothers making beautiful blouses with Maya animal motifs around the neck and sleeves. Groups of Maya women and their daughters set up stalls at the entrance to the ruins dotted around the archeological sites in the Maya Mountains of Toledo District. You can also find a good selection of decent-quality handicrafts produced by an artisans' cooperative at the **Fajina Craft Center**, opposite the market in Punta Gorda.

More and more painters are starting to make smaller versions of their work for sale to tourists. You can find prints at reasonable prices, or look for greetings cards featuring the work of local photographers and artists. Books on local history and poetry also seem to sell well: those published by Cubola are good. Sister company Stonetree Records produce CDs of Belizean musicians, such as Andy Palacio, Mr Peters and the Larubeya Drummers.

Hammocks made in Guatemala, both the nylon string and cotton cord variety are sold in the better gift shops, but are much more reasonable from street vendors. Be wary of the nylon type – if poorly made, this type readily comes apart.

Mexican jewelry is sold at better shops and look out for cloth dolls in ethnic costumes made by Garifuna women.

Never buy black coral or turtle shell souvenirs: it encourages their depletion, and is illegal.

Places to check out:

Go-Tees
6238 Park Avenue
Buttonwood Bay
Belize City
Sells Belizean-designed T-shirts, wooden bowls, Guatemalan crafts, silver and stone jewelry.

Hop Sing
Albert Street
Belize City
Best prices on T-shirts and hats, some carvings and souvenir items.

Brodies, Save U and **Romacs supermarkets**
Belize City (Brodies is also in Belmopan)
They all stock a good selection of locally made pepper sauce, preserves, coffee and rum. Brodies pharmacy also has some local herbal remedies.

Belize City Handicraft Center
2 South Park Street
Woodcarvings, chairs, posters, Maya slate art, herbal remedies and miscellaneous items.

Hilltop Winery
Burrell Boom
Local fruit wines.

Papagayo Boutique
Biltmore Hotel
Belize City
Silver jewelry from Mexico, Guatemalan cotton clothing, figurines from El Salvador, bathing suits, sarongs, books and prints.

Salty Dog
San Pedro
Good selection of T-shirts and gift items.

Pelican Beach Resort Gift Shop
Dangriga
Better-than-average selection of local crafts, T-shirts and herbal medicines.

Further Reading

Many of the best books written about Belize or by Belizean authors are published in the country and may not be available elsewhere. Cubola Productions is Belize's foremost publisher, subjects include history, politics, the environment, local culture, fiction and poetry.

General

Belize in Focus by Ian Peedle. Latin American Bureau, 1999. One of a respected series of compact guides covering the countries of Central and South America, this book provides a useful overview of Belize's history, economy, culture and environment, with photographs, map and practical tips for visitors.
Belize, Land of the Free by the Carib Sea by Thor Jansen (Bowen and Bowen, Belize, 2000). A coffee-table travelog of contemporary Belize, lavishly illustrated. It makes a wonderful souvenir.
Belize 1798, The Road to Glory by Emory King (Tropical Books, 1991). Bombastic, bodice-ripping account of the Battle of St. George's Caye, and of Belize's burgeoning society, written by one of Belize's larger-than-life American settlers, also the author of **Hey Dad, This is Belize**.
Inside Belize by T. Barry. The Inter-Hemispheric Education Resource Center, 1992. A good rundown of society and politics.
Profile of Belize by Society for the Promotion of Education and Research, Belize City. Cubola Publications/Spear Press. Good for facts and figures.

History

The Baymen of Belize by S. Forbes (compiled by S. Fairweather). The classic account of the Battle of St George's Caye by a participant.

Gives a good idea of life at the end of the 18th century.

The Baymen's Legacy: A Portrait of Belize City by Byron Foster. Cubola Publications, 1987. A vivid, if scattered account of the city.

The Maya Atlas (North Atlantic Books, 1997). An insightful corroboration between academics and villagers, the Atlas documents the history and everyday experiences of the Toledo Maya of Belize.

13 Chapters of a History of Belize by Assad Shoman (Angelus Press, Belize). The only comprehensive history of the country written by a Belizean. Designed primarily as a text for high schools and written from a left-wing perspective. Shoman's impressive credentials – politician, scholar and diplomat – make this a worthwhile read.

Environmental Concerns

Advances in Environmental and Biogeographical Research in Belize by P. Furley. University of Edinburgh, 1989. Heavy-going, but invaluable if you're serious.

A Belize Rainforest: The Community Baboon Sanctuary by Horwich and Lyon. Orang-utan Press. Everything you wanted to know about howler monkeys and much, much more.

The Environment of Belize by Kimo Jolly and Ellen McRae (Cubola Productions, Belize, 1998). A high school textbook, which will also appeal to visitors. Accessible, well-written and informative.

Jagaur, One Man's Struggle to Establish the World's First Jaguar Preserve by Alan Rabinowitz. (Island Press, 2000). The personal story of how wildlife biologist Rabinowitz's 1983 study of jaguars in the Cockscomb Basin of south-central Belize led to the creation of the Jaguar Reserve and the displacement of Maya villagers.

Maya Heritage

The Invisible Maya: Population History and Archeology at Santa Rita Corozal – Precolumbian

Population History in the Maya Lowlands by D.Z. Chase. University of New Mexico Press, 1990. For the serious student.

The Maya by Michael D. Coe Thames & Hudson, 1999. This is the best place to start for a general introduction to the subject. Well illustrated with maps, drawings and photographs and written by one of the century's finest archeologists who also wrote the influential **Breaking the Maya Code**, Thames & Hudson, 1993, which confirmed that Maya gylphs were a written language.

Maya Ruins in Central America in Color: Tikal, Copán and Quiriguá by William M. Ferguson. University of New Mexico Press, Albuquerque, 1984.

The Popol Vuh translated by Dennis Tedlock, Simon & Schuster, 1996. The K'iche "bible," the masterful book of creation that's both one of the most important pre-Columbian texts in the Americas and also an incredibly rich and imaginative read.

The Rise and Fall of the Maya Civilization by J. Eric S. Thompson, University of Oklahoma Press, 1966. Another excellent introduction to the Maya, and, though many of Thompson's more utopian theories have now been overturned, much of the text still reads well. Thompson's **Maya History and Religion**, Norman, 1970, is another useful study.

Tikal, A Handbook of the Ancient Maya Ruins by William R. Coe. University Museum of the University of Pennsylvania, Philadelphia 1967.

Warlords and Maize Men by B. Foster. Cubola Publications, 1989. An easy-to-read introduction to the major Maya sites in Belize.

Archeology at Cerros, Belize, Central America by V. Scarborough. Southern Methodist Press, 1991.

The Blood of Kings by Linda Schele and Mary Ellen Miller, Braziller [UK]; Thames & Hudson [US], 1992. The late Linda Schele was one of the greatest Mayanists of the late twentieth century who proved the Maya did not live a peaceful existence governed by priests and astronomers but were warlike and

obsessed with blood-letting and sacrifice. Read with **A Forest of Kings**, written by Schele and David Freide, Quill/Morrow, 1990.

Chapter 3: Mesoamerica in The Ancient Americas: Art from Sacred Landscapes Edited by Richard F. Townsend. The Art Institute of Chicago, Chicago, 1992.

Time Among the Maya by Ronald Wright. Weidenfeld & Nicholson, 1989. An entertaining and informative account of the author's journeys around Central America, with insights into Maya culture.

Flora & Fauna

Birds of North America National Geographic

Birds of Central America and Mexico by Irby L Davis.

Jungle Walk by Katie Stevens. Listings and illustrations of the birds and animals of Belize. Available in shops and hotels.

Checklist of the Birds of Belize by Wood, Leberman and Weyer. Pittsburgh: Carnegie Museum of Natural History Special Publication. Essential reading for bird-watchers.

The Cockscomb Basin Wildlife Sanctuary by Louise H. Emmons et al. (Orang-Utan Press, USA, 1996). A beautifully written and comprehensive guide to history, geography, culture, flora and fauna of the Jaguar Reserve.

The Ecotravellers' Wildlife Guide: Belize and Northern Guatemala by Les Beletsky. Academic Press, California and London, 1999. An excellent guide for the general reader, with sumptuous color illustrations of the region's wildlife, as well as descriptions of the ecology and the most popular parks and reserves.

Fruits and Vegetables of the Caribbean by M.J. Bourne, G.W. Lennox and S.A. Seddon. Macmillan, 1988.

A Guide to the Birds of Mexico and Northern Central America by Steve N.G. Howell and Sophie Webb. Oxford University Press, 1995. Paperback field guide sumptuously illustrated with color plates and line drawings, covering the 1,070 species found in this region. Often found, well-used and "dog-eared" in Belize's ecotourism lodges – well worth having your own copy.

A Guide to the Frogs and Toads of Belize by Carol Farnetti Foster and John R. Meyer (Kreiger, USA, 1996). Covers 33 species of the frogs and toads (anurans) found in Belize. Illustrated in color, with information on distribution, habitat and breeding.

A Guide to the Reptiles of Belize by Peter J. Stafford and John R. Meyer (Academic Press, London, 1999). A detailed field guide, written by experts, covering the reptiles in Belize. Well-illustrated with diagrams and color photographs.

The Field Guide to Ambergris Caye, Belize by R.L. Woods, S.T. Reid and A.M. Reid. A thorough exploration of the coast and coral.

Orchids of Guatemala and Belize by O. Ames and D.S. Correll. Dover Publications, New York, 1985.

Rainforest Remedies – One hundred healing herbs of Belize by Rosita Arvigo and Michael Balick. Fascinating guide to the endemic plantlife of Belize, illustrated with line drawings. Dr. Arvigo was the founder and director of the acclaimed Ix Chel Tropical Research Station in Cayo District.

Reef Fish Identification – Florida, Caribbean and the Bahamas, by Paul Humann, edited by Ned Deloach. New World Publications, 1994. An excellent handbook, established as the authoritative volume from the diving instructor to the general reader. Beautifully illustrated with useful tips for distinguishing species and details on the ecology of marine life.

Tropical Trees Found in the Caribbean, South America, Central America and Mexico by Dorothy and Bon Hargreaves.

Collins Guide to Tropical Plants by Wilhelm Loetschert and Gerhard Beese. Collins, 1981. A well-illustrated guide to tropical plants.

Language

Creole Proverbs of Belize Cubola Publications, 1987. The often hilarious and poetic everyday sayings of creole Belizeans, gathered by Dr Colville Young.

Other Insight Guides

Other *Insight Guides* that highlight destinations in this fascinating region include: *Bahamas, Barbados, The Caribbean, Costa Rica, Cuba, Guatemala, Belize & Yucatán, Haiti and the Dominican Republic, Jamaica, Mexico, Puerto Rico, and Trinidad and Tobago.* Rainforest enthusiasts will be interested in *Insight Guide: Amazon Wildlife*, which vividly captures in expert text and glorious photography the flora and fauna of the region.

Insight Pocket Guides, contain personal recommendations from a local host, a program of carefully timed itineraries and a fold-out map. They are particularly useful for the short-stay visitor intent on making the best use of every moment. Titles in this region include: *Bahamas, Barbados, Cancún and Yucatán, Cayman Islands, Costa Rica, Jamaica, Mexico City, and Puerto Rico.*

Insight Compact Guides are guidebooks for the independent-minded traveler – in essence travel encyclopedias in miniature: comprehensive yet portable, up-to-date and authoritative. Titles covering this part of the world are: *Antigua and Barbuda, Bahamas, Barbados, Cancún, Costa Rica, Cuba, Dominican Republic,* and *Jamaica.*

Insight Maps are designed to complement our guidebooks. They provide full mapping of major destinations, and their laminated finish gives them ease of use and durability. The range of titles features the following: *Bahamas, Barbados, Costa Rica, Cuba, Dominican Republic, Jamaica, Mexico City, Puerto Rico, and Virgin Islands.*

ART & PHOTO CREDITS

G. I. Bernard/NHPA 1
James Beverage/Naturalight 151, 237, 245, 251, 259, 280
Greg Evans 19, 158/159
Robert Francis/South American Pictures 162T
Andreas M. Gross 76, 77, 94, 155T, 192, 205T, 212, 220T, 237T, 238, 298T
Dominic Hamilton 302, 303
Martin Harvey/NHPA 132
Huw Hennessy 246, 247, 249, 250T, 269, 270, 272, 278, 278T, 280T, 281T, 282T, 283, 285T, 286
Dave G. Houser 167
Darrell Jones front flap top, back flap top & bottom, back cover left, spine top & bottom, 2B, 8/9, 14, 18, 20, 23, 24, 25, 26, 27, 62/63, 70, 71, 72, 78, 80/81, 82, 84/85, 86, 88, 89, 91, 96, 97, 98, 110, 111, 123, 138/139, 146, 150, 152R, 152T, 154, 156, 161, 162, 164/165, 166, 170, 171, 176, 178, 181, 184/185, 187, 192T, 200R, 201, 202, 205, 206, 213, 215, 216, 217, 229, 235, 250, 254/255, 257, 258, 260, 261, 262/263, 264, 265, 267, 268, 277, 285, 290/291, 292/293, 295, 296, 297, 299, 300, 301, 304
Tony Morrison/South American Pictures 5B, 190, 190T, 204
Tony Perrottet front flap bottom, 16/17, 30/31, 32, 33, 34, 35,

50/51, 54, 55, 67, 109, 134/135, 153, 155, 157, 176T, 179, 198, 219, 220, 221L, 224, 225, 230/231
Lesley Player 2/3, 4BR, 56, 58, 59, 169T, 169, 172T, 180, 194/195, 203, 207, 218T, 221R, 226, 227, 234T, 246T, 247T, 258T, 267T, 271T, 279, 287
Tony Rath back cover top right, 10/11, 12/13, 22, 38, 39, 52, 64/65, 66, 87, 90, 92/93, 95, 100/101, 102, 103, 104, 105, 107, 108, 112/113, 114, 115, 116, 117, 118, 120L/R, 121, 122, 126/127, 128, 129, 130, 131L/R, 136/137, 144/145, 149, 152L, 160, 163, 172, 173, 175, 177, 180T, 186, 197, 208T, 209, 210/211, 222, 222T, 228, 232, 239, 241, 243, 244, 256, 271, 274/275, 281L/R, 282, 284, 294
Tony Rath/Courtesy of Pelican Beach Resort 252
Tony Rath/Courtesy of The Angelus Press 40/41, 42, 43, 44, 45, 46, 47, 48, 49
David Sanger back cover center bottom, 4/5, 4BL, 57, 73, 83, 133, 147, 191, 228T, 234, 248, 253, 269T, 300T
Chris Sharp/South American Pictures 193, 198T, 199, 218
Kevin Schafer/NHPA 208
James Strachan back cover center,

6/7, 53, 60/61, 68, 69, 74/75, 79, 99, 119, 174, 196, 200L, 223, 233, 236, 240, 276
Norbert Wu/NHPA 106, 273
Viesti Collection/Trip 142

Picture Spreads

Pages 28/29 *Top row:* all photography by Andreas M. Gross. *Center row:* Andreas M. Gross. *Bottom row:* Darrell Jones
Pages 124/125 *Top row, left to right:* Andreas M. Gross, Darrell Jones, Darrell Jones, Darrell Jones. *Center row:* Jamie Marshall, Darrell Jones, E. Martino. *Bottom row:* Darrell Jones,Tony Rath, E. Martino.
Pages 182/183 *Top row, left to right:* Darrell Jones, Tony Rath, Tony Rath, Tony Rath. *Center row:* Darrell Jones, Tony Rath, Darrell Jones. *Bottom row:* Tony Rath; Tony Rath; Tony Rath.
Pages 288/289 *Top row, left to right:* Lesley Player, Lesley Player, Andreas M. Gross, Green & Blacks. *Center row:* both Lesley Player. *Bottom row:* Andreas M. Gross, Lesley Player, Lesley Player.

Map Production Stephen Ramsay

© 2006 Apa Publications GmbH & Co. Verlag KG (Singapore branch)

INSIGHT GUIDE Belize

Cartographic Editor
Zoë Goodwin
Production **Linton Donaldson**
Art Director **Klaus Geisler**
Picture Research
Hilary Genin, Britta Jaschinski

Index

Numbers in italics refer to photographs

TRULY ADVENTUROUS

TRULY ASIA

In the heart of Asia lies a land of many cultures, wonders and attractions. Especially for the adventure seeker to whom fear is not a factor. There are hundreds of thrills to experience. Mount Kinabalu. Mulu Caves. Taman Negara. These are just a few places where you'll always find that rewarding adrenaline rush. Where is this land, so challenging and exhilarating? It can only be Malaysia, Truly Asia.

Malaysia
Truly Asia